# THE FATHERS
# OF THE CHURCH

A NEW TRANSLATION

VOLUME 89

# THE FATHERS OF THE CHURCH

A NEW TRANSLATION

EDITORIAL BOARD

Thomas P. Halton
*The Catholic University of America*
*Editorial Director*

Elizabeth Clark
*Duke University*

Kathleen McVey
*Princeton Theological Seminary*

Robert B. Eno, S.S
*The Catholic University of America*

Robert D. Sider
*Dickinson College*

Frank A. C. Mantello
*The Catholic University of America*

Michael Slusser
*Duquesne University*

Cynthia Kahn White
*The University of Arizona*

Robin Darling Young
*The Catholic University of America*

David J. McGonagle
*Director*
*The Catholic University of America Press*

FORMER EDITORIAL DIRECTORS

Ludwig Schopp, Roy J. Ferrari, Bernard M. Peebles,
Hermigild Dressler, O.M.F.

Steven R. Cain
Edward Strickland
*Staff Editors*

# ORIGEN
## COMMENTARY ON THE GOSPEL ACCORDING TO JOHN
## BOOKS 13–32

Translated by
RONALD E. HEINE
*Institut zur Erforschung des Urchristentums*
*Tübingen*

THE CATHOLIC UNIVERSITY OF AMERICA PRESS
Washington, D.C.

*Copyright © 1993 by*
THE CATHOLIC UNIVERSITY OF AMERICA PRESS
Printed in the United States of America
*All rights reserved*

The paper used in this publication meets the minimum requirements of the American National Standards for Information Science—Permanence of Paper for Printed Library materials,
ANSI Z39.48-1984
∞

First Paperback Reprint 2006

LIBRARY OF CONGRESS CATALOGING-IN-PUBLICATION DATA
(Revised for vol. 2)

Commentary on the Gospel according to John.
   (The Fathers of the church ; v. 80, 89)
   Translation of: Origenous ton eis to kata Ioannen Euangelion exegetikon.
   Includes bibliographical references and indexes.
   1. Bible.—N.T.—John—Commentaries—Early works to 1800. I. Heine, Ronald E.
BR60.f3069bs2615     270 s [226.5'07]     88-20406
v.1)  ISBN: 0-8132-0080-6; 0-8132-1029-1 (pbk)
     ISBN-13: 978-0-8132-0080-4; 978-08132-1029-2 (pbk)

v.2)  ISBN: 0-8132-0089-X; 0-8132-1465-3 (pbk)
     ISBN-13: 978-0-8132-0089-7; 978-0-8132-1465-8 (pbk)

# CONTENTS

| | |
|---|---|
| Abbreviations | vi |
| Preface | vii |
| Select Bibliography | ix |
| Introduction | 3 |
| Book 13 | 69 |
| Book 19 | 166 |
| Book 20 | 205 |
| Book 28 | 292 |
| Book 32 | 342 |
| Indices | |
|     Index of Proper Names | 421 |
|     Index of Holy Scripture | 427 |

## ABBREVIATIONS

| | |
|---|---|
| ACW | Ancient Christian Writers. New York, New York/Mahwah, New Jersey: Newman Press, 1946– . |
| ANF | Ante-Nicene Fathers. Grand Rapids: Erdmans, 1969 (reprint). |
| FOTC | The Fathers of the Church. New York and Washington, D.C., 1947– . |
| GCS | Die griechischen christlichen Schriftsteller der ersten drei Jahrhunderte. Leipzig, 1897– . |
| LSJ | *A Greek-English Lexicon*. Ed. H. G. Liddell, R. Scott, and H. S. Jones. Oxford: at the Clarendon Press, 1940. |
| LXX | *Septuagint.* Ed. A. Rahlfs. 2 vols. Stuttgart, 1935. |
| NHLE | *The Nag Hammadi Library in English*. Ed. J. M. Robinson. San Fransico: Harper & Row, 1977. |
| OS | P. de Lagarde. *Onomastica Sacra*. Hildesheim: Georg Olms, 1966. |
| PG | Migne. *Patrologiae Cursus Completus: Series Graeca*. Paris, 1857–66. |
| PGL | *A Patristic Greek Lexicon*. Ed. G. W. H. Lampe. Oxford: at the Clarendon Press, 1961. |
| SC | Sources chrétiennes. Paris, 1942– . |
| Vulg. | *Biblia Sacra Iuxta Vulgatam Versionem*. Ed. B. Fischer, I. Gribomont, H. F. D. Sparks, W. Thiele, R. Weber. 2 vols. Stuttgart, 1969. |

Abbreviations of Classical and Patristic texts follow LSJ and PGL. Abbreviations of journal titles follow H. Crouzel, *Bibliographie critique d'Origène*. Instrumenta Patristica VIII. Steenbrugis, 1971.

# PREFACE

It is one of the strange quirks of scholarship that this earliest of all preserved Christian commentaries on a book of the New Testament has never previously been translated into English in its entirety. In the nineteenth century A. Menzies translated what remains of Books 1–10 into English for The Ante-Nicene Fathers series. In the twentieth century to date it has been translated in its entirety only into Italian by E. Corsini, and now into French by C. Blanc. There is a German translation of the larger part of the commentary by R. Gögler, and Book 13 was translated into English by C. M. Moss as part of a dissertation. Three major critical editions of the commentary have appeared since Menzies' translation of the remains of Books 1–10, those of Brooke (1896), Preuschen (1903), and Blanc (1966, 1970, 1975, 1982, 1992).

As in my translation of Books 1–10 (FOTC 80), I have translated from Preuschen's critical edition of the text, with constant consultation of the editions of Brooke and Blanc. The final volume of Blanc's edition and translation (Books 28 and 32) appeared as my work was being prepared for page proofs. I have, therefore, cited this volume only rarely in the present work. I have reviewed Blanc's final volume for JTS (forthcoming), and readers interested in seeing some of the places where we disagree in our understanding of the text in Books 28 and 32 should consult that review. I have again followed the Douay version of the Bible for the spelling of the names of Biblical persons and places.

If my conclusions in the Introduction are correct, the composition of the thirty-two books of this commentary occupied Origen off and on over a period of ten to twelve years, and was interrupted by moves from one place to another and by the composition of several other works in the same period of time. My work on the translation of the nine books of the commentary that have been preserved, including books 1–10 in FOTC 80, has followed a similar pattern. This is not to suggest a comparison between Origen's work and my own, nor of his circumstances and mine, but to indicate the many different places where I have carried out this work and the various library facilities which I have been privileged to use in the course of it. The latter include the library of the University of Illinois, that of Lincoln Christian College and Seminary, various libraries in the Dallas area, the library of the University of Birmingham, England, and finally the marvelous library facilities in the city of Tübingen. The work was begun in Lincoln, Illinois, where a first rough draft of the translation of all nine books was completed, and then worked on with various other projects over several years.

The work on the final stages of this volume represents a large portion of my time as Director of the Institut zur Erforschung des Urchristentums in Tübingen during 1990–1991. I made a thorough revision of the translation of the books contained in this volume, added several annotations, and composed the introduction during that time.

I wish to express my appreciation to my wife Gillian and to Frau Ursula Schneider, secretary of the Institut zur Erforschung des Urchristentums, for their help in proofreading and in preparing the indices. Gillian also helped in putting portions of this volume in the computer, and in many other ways. Finally, I wish to dedicate this volume to Gail, Pamela, and Robert, who lived through the initial stages of this project with me.

RONALD E. HEINE
Tübingen, February 1993

# SELECT BIBLIOGRAPHY

*Texts and Translations*

Blanc, C., ed. and tr. *Origène: commentaire sur saint Jean.* SC 120 (1966), SC 157 (1970), SC 222 (1975), SC 290 (1982), SC 385 (1992).
Brooke, A. E., ed. *The Commentary of Origen on S. John's Gospel.* 2 vols. Cambridge, 1896.
Butler, D. C., ed. *The Lausiac History of Palladius* II. Cambridge, 1904.
Butterworth, G. W., tr. *Origen: On First Principles.* New York: Harper & Row, 1966.
Chadwick, H. *Origen: Contra Celsum.* Cambridge, 1965.
Corsini, E., tr. *Commento al Vangelo di Giovanni di Origene.* Torinese: Unione Tipografico-Editrice, 1968.
Crouzel, H., ed. and tr. *Grégoire le Thaumaturge remerciement à Origène.* SC 148 (1969).
Duchesne, L., ed. *Le liber Pontificalis* I. Paris, 1886.
Freedman, H., and M. Simon, edd. *Midrash Rabbah.* Vol. III. London: Soncino Press, 1939.
Gögler, R., tr. *Origenes: Das Evangelium nach Johannes.* Zürich: Benziger Verlag Einsiedeln, 1959.
Görgemanns, H., and H. Karpp, edd. and trs. *Origenes vier Bücher von den Prinzipien.* Texte zur Forschung 24. Darmstadt: Wissenschaftliche Buchgesellschaft, 1985.
Hartel, W., ed. *S. Cypriani Opera Omnia.* CSEL 3.2. Vienna, 1868.
Heine, R. E., ed. and tr. *The Montanist Oracles and Testimonia.* PMS 14. Macon, GA: Mercer, 1989.
_____, tr. *Origen: Commentary on the Gospel according to John, Books 1–10.* FOTC 80 (1989).
_____, tr. *Origen: Homilies on Genesis and Exodus.* FOTC 71 (1982).
Hennecke, E., and W. Schneemelcher, edd. *New Testament Apocrypha.* 2 vols. Tr. R. McL. Wilson. Philadelphia: Westminster Press, 1963/1965.
Klostermann, E., and E. Benz, edd. *Origenes Werke: Matthäuserklärung* GCS 10–12 (1935, 1976, 1941).
Koetschau, P., ed. *Des Gregorios Thaumaturgos Dankrede an Origenes.* Freiburg, 1894.
_____, ed. *Origenes Werke: Die Schrift vom Martyrium, Gegen Celsus, Die Schrift vom Gebet.* GCS 1–2 (1899).
Lawlor, H. J., and J. E. L. Oulton, trs. *Eusebius* II. London: SPCK, 1928.

# BIBLIOGRAPHY

Lawson, R. P., tr. *Origen: The Song of Songs.* ACW 26. New York: Newman Press, 1956.
Moss, C. M. Diss. Southern Baptist Seminary, 1982. (Book 13)
Oulton, J. E. L., tr. *Eusebius: The Ecclesiastical History* II. London: Heinemann, 1964.
Preuschen, E., ed. *Origenes Werke: Der Johanneskommentar.* GCS Origenis 4 (Leipzig, 1903).
Ramsbotham, A. "The Commentary of Origen on the Epistle to the Romans." JTS 13 (1912): 209–24, 357–68; 14 (1913): 10–22.
Rauer, M., ed. *Origenes Werke: Die Homilien zu Lukas in der Übersetzung des Hieronymus und die griechischen Reste der Homilien und des Lukas-Kommentars.* GCS 9 (1959).
Robinson, J. A. *The Philocalia of Origen.* Cambridge, 1893.
Robinson, J. M., ed. *The Nag Hammadi Library in English.* San Francisco: Harper & Row, 1977.
Staab, P. *Pauluskommentare aus der griechischen Kirche.* Muenster: Aschendorff, 1933.
Whittaker, C. R., tr. *Herodian* II. London: Heinemann, 1970.

## Other Works

Bigg, C. *The Christian Platonists of Alexandria.* New York, 1886.
*Cambridge Ancient History* XII. Cambridge, 1961.
Clark, E. A. *Clement's Use of Aristotle.* New York: The Edwin Mellen Press, 1977.
──────. "New Perspectives on the Origenist Controversy: Human Embodiment and Ascetic Strategies." CH (1990): 145–62.
Cox, P. *Biography in Late Antiquity.* Berkeley: University of California Press, 1983.
Crouzel, H. "L'apocatastase chez Origène." *Origeniana Quarta.* Innsbruck-Wien, 1987, 282–90.
──────. "Le contenu spirituel des dénominations du Christ selon le Livre I du *Commentaire sur Jean* d' Origène." *Origeniana Secunda.* Edizioni dell'Ateneo, 1980, 131–50.
──────. *Origen.* Tr. A. S. Worrall. Edinburgh: T. & T. Clark, 1989.
──────. "Origène s'est-il retiré en Cappadoce pendant la persécution de Maximin le Thrace?" BLE 64 (1963): 195–203.
Daly, R. J. "Origen." *Encyclopedia of Early Christianity.* 667–68.
──────. "Sacrificial Soteriology: Origen's *Commentary on John* 1, 29." *Origeniana Secunda.* Edizioni dell'Ateneo, 1980, 151–63.
Daniélou, J. *Origène.* Paris, 1948.
Dechow, J. F. "The Heresy Charges Against Origen." *Origeniana Quarta.* Innsbruck-Wien, 1987, 112–22.
──────. "Origen and Early Christian Pluralism: The Context of His Eschatology." *Origen of Alexandria: His World and His Legacy.* Edd. C. Kannengiesser and W. L. Petersen. Notre Dame, Ind.: University of Notre Dame Press, 1988, 337–56.

# BIBLIOGRAPHY

Dorival, G. "Origène et la résurrection de la chair." *Origeniana Quarta.* Innsbruck-Wien, 1987, 291–321.
Faye, E. de. "De l'influence du gnosticisme sur Origène." RHR 87 (1923): 181–235.
_____. *Origène: sa vie, son oeuvre, sa pensée* I. Paris, 1923.
Galtier, P. "Les péchés 'incurables' d'Origène." *Greg.* 10 (1929): 177–209.
Görres, F. "Kritische Untersuchungen über die Christenverfolgung des römischen Kaisers Maximinus I. des Thraciers." ZWT 19 (1876): 526–74.
Grant, R. M. *Gods and the One God.* London: SPCK, 1986.
Greer, R. A. *The Captain of Our Salvation.* Tübingen: J. C. B. Mohr, 1973.
Grillmeier, A. *Christ in Christian Tradition* I. Tr. J. Bowden. Atlanta: John Knox Press, 1975.
Gruber, G. *ZΩH: Wesen, Stufen und Mitteilung des wahren Lebens bei Origenes.* München: Max Hueber Verlag, 1962.
Hällström, G. *Charismatic Succession: A Study on Origen's Concept of Prophecy.* Publications of the Finnish Exegetical Society 42. Helsinki, 1985.
Hallman, J. M. "Divine Suffering and Change in Origen and Ad Theopompum." *The Second Century* 7 (1989–90): 85–98.
Hanson, R. P. C. "Did Origen Teach that the Son is *ek tes ousias* of the Father?" *Origeniana Quarta.* Innsbruck-Wien, 1987, 201–2.
Harl, M. *Origène et la fonction révélatrice du verbe incarné.* Paris: Éditions du Seuil, 1958.
Harnack, A. *Geschichte der altchristlichen Literatur bis Eusebius* II.2 Leipzig: J. C. Hinrichs, 1958.
_____. *History of Dogma* III, tr. N. Buchanan. New York: Dover, 1961.
Hartmann, P. "Origène et la théologie du martyre." EThL 34 (1958): 773–824.
Heine, R. E. "A Note on the Text of Origen, *Commentary on John* 19.III.16." JTS n.s. 42 (1991): 596–98.
_____. "Can the Catena Fragments of Origen's Commentary on John be Trusted?" VC 40 (1986): 118–34.
_____. "Stoic Logic as Handmaid to Exegesis and Theology in Origen's Commentary on the Gospel of John." JTS n.s. 44.(1993): 90–117.
_____. "Three Allusions to Book 20 of Origen's Commentary on John in Gregory Thaumaturgus' Panegyric to Origen." Proceedings of the Eleventh International Conference on Patristic Studies. Forthcoming.
Kettler, Fr.-H. "Neue Beobachtungen zur Apokatastasislehre des Origenes." *Origeniana Secunda.* Edizioni dell'Ateneo, 1980, 339–48.
Koch, H. *Pronoia und Paideusis.* Berlin, 1932.
Laeuchli, S. "Origen's Interpretation of Judas Iscariot." CH 22 (1953): 253–68.

Mates, B. *Stoic Logic*. Berkeley: University of California Press, 1961.
Moltmann, J. "Gesichtspunkte der Kreuzestheologie heute." ET 33 (1973): 346–65.
———. *The Trinity and the Kingdom of God*. Tr. M. Kohl. London: SCM, 1981.
Mortimer, R. C. *The Origins of Private Penance in the Western Church*. Oxford, 1939.
Nautin, P. *Origène, sa vie et son oeuvre*. Paris: Beauchesne, 1977.
Neumann, K. J. *Der Römische Staat und die allgemeine Kirche bis auf Diocletian* I. Leipzig, 1890.
Neuschäfer, B. *Origenes als Philologe*. SBA 1–2. Basil: Friedrich Reinhardt, 1987.
Orbe, A. *La Epinoia*. Rome: Pontificia Universitas Gregoriana, 1955.
Outler, A. C. "Origen and the *Regulae Fidei*." *The Second Century* 4 (1984): 133–41.
Pagels, E. *The Johannine Gospel in Gnostic Exegesis: Heracleon's Commentary on John*. New York: Abingdon, 1973.
Patrides, C. A. "The Salvation of Satan." JHI 28 (1967): 467–78.
Prestige, G. L. *Fathers and Heretics*. London, 1948.
———. *God in Patristic Thought*. London: SPCK, 1952.
Rahner, K. "La doctrine d'Origène sur la pénitence." RechSR 37 (1950): 47–97, 252–86, 422–56.
Richardson, C. C. "The Condemnation of Origen." CH 6 (1937): 50–64.
Rudolf, K. *Gnosis*. Tr. R. M. Wilson. San Francisco: Harper & Row, 1983.
Trumbower, J. A. "Origen's Exegesis of John 8:19–53: The Struggle with Heracleon over the Idea of Fixed Natures." VC 43 (1989): 138–54.
Sarot, M. "Patripassianism, Theopaschitism and the Suffering of God. Some Historical and Systematic Considerations." RS (1990): 363–75.
Tabernee, W. "Early Montanism and Voluntary Martyrdom." *Colloquium: The Australian and New Zealand Theological Review*. 17 (1985): 33–43.
Trigg, J. "The Angel of Great Counsel: Christ and the Angelic Hierarchy in Origen's Theology." JTS 42 (1991): 35–51.
Vogt, H. J. "Beobachtungen zum Johannes-Kommentar des Origenes." TQ (1990): 191–208.
———. *Das Kirchenverständnis des Origenes*. Köln: Böhlau Verlag, 1974.
Williams, R. D. "The Son's Knowledge of the Father in Origen." *Origeniana Quarta*. Innsbruck-Wien, 1987, 146–53.

# INTRODUCTION

# INTRODUCTION

This volume contains what remains of Books 13–32 of Origen's *Commentary on John*.[1] The *Commentary on John* is significant not only for studies of Origen, for which it is of central importance, but also for studies of Gnosticism,[2] the history of biblical exegesis,[3] the history of theology,[4] and spirituality.[5]

(2) R. Gögler has pointed out that the *Commentary on John* is the oldest preserved Christian commentary on a writing of the New Testament, and has noted that it is an extensive scholarly and spiritual explanation of the Gospel.[6] G. L. Prestige calls attention to the fact that it was Origen, more than any other single person who established the disciplines of biblical interpretation and biblical theology at the center of the Church's activities.[7] Both disciplines play major roles in

---

1. For my translation of what remains of the previous books, see *Origen: Commentary on the Gospel according to John, Books 1–10*, FOTC 80 (Washington, D.C.: The Catholic University of America Press, 1989). On the size and preservation of the Commentary, including the fragments, see FOTC 80.7–10.

2. See FOTC 80.23–26 on Heracleon, the Gnostic whose interpretation of John and whose theology Origen attempts to refute in several places throughout the Commentary. Passages directly related to Heracleon are set in small type in the translation, and statements that Origen attributes to Heracleon are set in italics.

3. See FOTC 80.10–23 for a brief survey of Origen's exegetical methods in the Commentary, and for a select bibliography of works treating this subject.

4. I shall discuss below some of the more important aspects of Origen's theology that appear in the Commentary.

5. Studies of Origen's spirituality usually focus on his works on the *Song of Songs* and some of his homilies. Passages such as 13.3–42, 19.21–25, and 32.400, and numerous others in the *Commentary on John*, however, show this work to be rich in material related to spirituality.

6. *Origenes: Das Evangelium nach Johannes* (Zürich: Benziger Verlag Einsiedeln, 1959), 15, 35.

7. *Fathers and Heretics* (London, 1948), 54.

this *Commentary*. H. Crouzel, correctly in my opinion, considers the *Commentary on John* to be Origen's masterpiece.[8]

(3) Since I have previously dealt with the general introductory matters related to the *Commentary*,[9] I shall treat here some problems related to the date of composition of the books translated in this volume, and discuss some of the more important aspects of Origen's theology that appear in the *Commentary* as a whole.

## Date of Composition of Books 13–32

(4) Attempting to give precise dates to Origen's treatises is like entering a forest where there are few paths, and even fewer signposts to indicate exactly where the paths lead. Three events do, however, provide signposts of sorts for dating the composition of the *Commentary*. The first is Origen's move from Alexandria to Caesarea in Palestine, the second is the persecution of Maximinus Thrax, and the third is the period of time when Gregory Thaumaturgus was a student under Origen.

### Origen's Move from Alexandria to Caesarea

(5) Origen's move from Alexandria to Caesarea in Palestine, well documented both in the *Commentary*[10] and in Eusebius,[11] provides one important signpost for dating the composition of some of the books. This move occurred sometime between 232–234, and probably, in my opinion, nearer the beginning of this period than the end.[12] Origen states that he had composed the first five books of the *Com-*

---

8. *Origen*, tr. A. S. Worrall (Edinburgh: T. & T. Clark, 1989), 42.
9. See FOTC 80.3–28.   10. 6.1–12, FOTC 80.168–71.
11. *H.E.* 6.24, 26.
12. Cf. my discussion in FOTC 80.4–5. There, following Nautin, I opted for 234 as the date for Origen's move to Caesarea. I now think that date is too late. Eusebius says that Origen left Alexandria for Caesarea in the tenth year of the reign of Alexander Severus. The dates generally accepted for the latter's reign are 222–35, which would place Origen's departure for Caesarea in 232. Alexander was assassinated early in 235, and the persecution initiated by Maximinus, his successor, began soon after he began to reign. Origen wrote four books on Genesis, at least five, and probably eight or more, books of the *Commentary on John*, and his treatise

INTRODUCTION 5

*mentary* before leaving Alexandria,[13] and that he began Book 6 after settling in Caesarea.[14]

### The Persecution of Maximinus

(6) The persecution of Maximinus (235–238) provides a second significant signpost in relation to dating the composition of the *Commentary*. Herodian is our main source of information about the reign of Maximinus. He notes that immediately after Maximinus had seized power he initiated a reign of "savage tyranny," and that one of his first concerns was the systematic elimination "of all the friends accompanying Alexander," his predecessor, from influential positions.[15] Herodian also notes that people of wealth were targeted by Maximinus, and that many lost their property on the basis of trumped-up charges. Once they received a court summons from an informer, they were whisked away to Maximinus' military camp where they appeared before him and were either exiled or executed.[16]

(7) Eusebius says that Maximinus, "through ill-will towards the house of Alexander, since it consisted for the most part of believers, raised a persecution, ordering the leaders of the Church alone to be put to death, as being responsible for the teaching of the Gospel."[17] We may question whether or not the issue inserted by Eusebius about teaching the

---

on prayer after he arrived in Caesarea, but before the persecution of Maximinus. A certain amount of time must be allowed for Origen to get settled in Caesarea and to regain the tranquillity of mind to which he alludes (6.9, FOTC 80.170) after he had separated himself from his problems with Demetrius in Alexandria before he began writing again. He also says that the stenographers who took down his dictations were not with him when he moved to Caesarea (ibid.), and implies that he had to wait for a period of time for them to arrive (6.10, ibid.). All of this seems to me to necessitate that Origen must have left Alexandria either late in 232 or early in 233.

13. 6.8, FOTC 80.170.
14. 6.11–12, FOTC 80.170–71. He had begun Book 6 in Alexandria, but failed to bring this earlier work when he moved, and so he began the book again in Caesarea.
15. *Herodian* II, tr. C. R. Whittaker (London: William Heinemann Ltd., 1970), 7.1.1, 3.
16. Herodian, 7.3.1–4.
17. *Eusebius: The Ecclesiastical History* II, tr. J. E. L. Oulton (London:

Gospel played a part in the persecution, since there seems to have been no religious motive behind it. F. Görres has pointed out that it was not enthusiasm for the old Roman religions that moved Maximinus, since he also plundered heathen temples.[18] The persecution, Görres thinks, arose solely because of Maximinus' hostility towards the house of Alexander, and the fact that Christians had received friendly treatment from that house, especially from Alexander's mother Mamaea.[19] This suggests that Origen especially would have been in danger as "politically suspect" in this persecution, since he had visited Alexander's mother in Antioch at her request.[20] The fact that Ambrose, Origen's friend and patron at whose request he was writing the *Commentary on John*, was wealthy as well as being a Church leader would also have singled him out as a target for the persecution.

(8) We know very little specifically about this persecution, but it seems to have been sporadic. We know that Pontianus and Hippolytus, rival claimants for the episcopal chair in Rome, were both exiled by Maximinus.[21] In Caesarea in Palestine Origen's friend Ambrose, and a presbyter

---

Heinemann, 1964), 6.28. K. J. Neumann, *Der Römische Staat und die allgemeine Kirche bis auf Diocletian*, I (Leipzig, 1890), 210, points out that we are totally dependent on Eusebius for our knowledge of Maximinus' actions against the Christians, for all the other ancient Christian sources which mention the persecution go back, either directly or indirectly, to Eusebius. Neumann thinks, on the basis of certain indirect statements of Origen in his *Exhortation to Martyrdom*, that Eusebius is correct when he asserts that it was only the leaders of the Church who were affected by the persecution (212–13). He also thinks that Eusebius, who is writing 90 years after the persecution, is dependent on the works of Origen to which he refers in *H.E.* 6.28 for his information about the persecution (210).

18. "Kritische Untersuchungen über die Christenverfolgung des römischen Kaisers Maximinus I. des Thraciers," ZWT 19 (1876): 528–31.

19. Ibid. 533. Cf. Herodian 6.9.14; 7.1.7, 8, 10.

20. Eusebius, *H.E.* 6.21.3. See *The Cambridge Ancient History* XII (Cambridge, 1961), 75.

21. L. Duchesne, *Le liber Pontificalis*, I (Paris, 1886), 19 (145). The text says they were exiled in the time of Alexander, but Duchesne notes that this is an interpolation into the text based on a reference to the time of Alexander in the previous sentence. On the banishment of both Pontianus and Hippolytus, Neumann remarks that an attack on the leaders of the Church would naturally affect the leader of the Roman Church first, and if

INTRODUCTION 7

named Protoctetus were imprisoned.[22] This is the extent of our knowledge of the persecution of Church leaders during the time of Maximinus.

(9) Firmilian, a friend of Origen, and Bishop of Caesarea in Cappadocia, refers to a persecution of Christians in Cappadocia during this same period. He indicates, however, (a) that it was a general persecution against all Christians, and not limited to Church leaders, (b) that it was local, for it could be avoided by fleeing to the neighboring provinces, and (c) that it arose because Christians were blamed for a series of earthquakes that had devastated parts of Cappadocia and Pontus. He says that the governor, Serenianus, was "a bitter and awful persecutor."[23] Origen seems to make reference to this same persecution in Cappadocia when he refers to a persecution in which Churches were burned because Christians were blamed for an earthquake.[24]

(10) This persecution in Cappadocia appears not to have been directly related to Maximinus' attack on Church leaders. There may, however, have been an indirect relationship to Maximinus' general policy. Herodian refers to a "severe procurator in the district of Carthage" who exacted savage sentences and confiscations, hoping that Maximinus would take notice of him, "since the emperor used to select men known to be in accord with his own policy."[25] Serenianus, likewise, may have encouraged the popular hostilities against the Christians in the hope that he might gain some kind of recognition and promotion from the emperor.

(11) A question of considerable interest and some impor-

---

two claimed that position, it is understandable that both would be banished(214).

22. They are the addressees of Origen's *Exhortation to Martyrdom* 1, which, as Neumann notes, is the only detailed document to come to us from the time of the persecution (218). It is never said explicitly that they were imprisoned, though it seems a necessary inference from Origen's writing this special treatise for them, and from Eusebius' assertion that "no ordinary distress had befallen them," and his reference to "the confession they made during the period" (*H.E.* 6.28).

23. Ep. 75.10 in *S. Thasci Caecili Cypriani Opera Omnia*.
24. *Comm. ser. in Mt.* 39.     25. 7.4.2.

tance is where Origen was during the persecution of Maximinus. Unfortunately, the evidence does not permit us to answer the question definitively. I shall present the evidence as I see it, but without suggesting that this is the only way it can be taken.[26]

(12) In the fifth century *Lausiac History of Palladius* there is an entry about a virgin Juliana in Caesarea of Cappadocia who is said to have hidden Origen for two years when he was "fleeing from the attack of the Greeks." Palladius ascribes this information to a note he has seen written by Origen himself in a very old book. The note read, "I found this book with Juliana the virgin in Caesarea when I was being hidden by her. She said that she had received it from Symmachus himself, the Jewish interpreter."[27]

(13) Crouzel has correctly observed that if the reference in Palladius is to a persecution of Christians, it must refer to that by Maximinus between 235 and 238.[28] Eusebius provides no information about where Origen was during the

---

26. This question has most recently been treated by H. Crouzel in *Origen* (Edinburgh: T. & T. Clark, 1989), 16–17; and more thoroughly in "Origène s'est-il retiré en Cappadoce pendant la persécution de Maximin le Thrace?" BLE 64 (1963): 195–203. See also P. Hartmann, "Origène et la théologie du martyre," EThL 34 (1958): 776–79. Crouzel and Hartmann think Origen did not take refuge in Cappadocia during the persecution. They follow the suggestion of Koetschau, Preuschen, and Stählin that Palladius confused Caesarea in Cappadocia with Caesarea in Palestine, and think that the reference to flight was not to the time of the persecution of Maximinus when Origen was in Caesarea, but to that of Caracalla when he was in Alexandria (see Hartmann, 778–79). My own position presented in the following paragraphs is closest to that of A. Harnack, *Geschichte der altchristlichen Literatur bis Eusebius* II/2 (Leipzig: J.C. Hinrichs, 1958), 33–34, though I arrived at it independently of Harnack's work.

27. *The Lausiac History of Palladius* II, ed. D. C. Butler (Cambridge, 1904), 64 (160).

28. BLE 64 (1963): 196–97. Crouzel opts for the hypothesis that it does not refer to a persecution of Christians, but refers to Caracalla's attack on the citizens of Alexandria in 215 (ibid., 203; cf. *Origen*, 17). His reasons lie primarily in the difficulty of reconciling a flight of Origen to Cappadocia during the persecution of Maximinus with the absence of any corroborating testimony in Eusebius, and with what he takes to be the time of the arrival of Gregory Thaumaturgus in Caesarea of Palestine. I shall treat the latter problem in my section on Gregory Thaumaturgus, and the former in the following paragraphs here. Crouzel also uses the

# INTRODUCTION

persecution. He does, however, have a reference to Origen receiving books of Symmachus from Juliana which is similar to that of Palladius. He says there were various interpretations of Scripture by Symmachus which "Origen indicates that he had received from a certain Juliana, who, he says, inherited in her turn the books from Symmachus himself."[29]

(14) We must conclude either (a) that Eusebius and Palladius had seen different books by Symmachus in which Origen had written similar, but not identical notes, or (b) that Eusebius had seen the same note that Palladius had seen, but had chosen to omit the reference to Origen being hidden by Juliana, or (c) with Crouzel, that Palladius confused Caesarea in Cappadocia with Caesarea in Palestine, and the reference is not to the persecution by Maximinus, but to Caracalla's attack on the citizens of Alexandria in 215.[30]

(15) The second option, that Eusebius read what Palladius read, but omitted the reference to Origen being hidden, seems most likely to me. P. Cox provides a possible reason for such an omission by Eusebius. She argues that Eusebius' account of Origen does not adequately reflect certain changes in Origen's thinking between his earlier life in Alexandria and his later life in Caesarea, and suggests that Eusebius' difficulties "grew out of his attempt to impress his ideal on the whole of Origen's life." Such an approach, she argues, was inherent in the biographical genre which, from

---

fact that Eusebius (*H.E.* 6.17) cites the note about Symmachus immediately after he refers to Symmachus' translation of the Old Testament being one of the four versions Origen used in his Hexapla, when he is discussing the Alexandrian period of Origen's life, as evidence that Origen's contact with Juliana came in his Alexandrian period (*Origen*, 16). It seems more likely to me that Eusebius has included his discussion of Symmachus and the commentaries of Symmachus which Origen received from Juliana at this particular point solely to identify Symmachus, and that we can conclude nothing about when Origen received the books from Juliana from *H.E.* 6.17.

29. *H.E.* 6.17.

30. See note 28 above. There would have been no reason for Palladius, who had been a student of the Origenist Evagrius Ponticus, and who himself was later accused of Origenism by Jerome and Epiphanius, to have added a potentially discrediting comment about Origen being hidden during a persecution if he had not seen it in his source.

its inception, was "characterized by its single-minded vision of its subjects."[31] I suggest that Eusebius' ideal of Origen's view of martyrdom was shaped by a letter of Origen that he had read in which Origen related the story from his youth about his desire to be martyred along with his father,[32] and by the account of Origen's faithful suffering near the end of his life during the persecution of Decius, of which Eusebius had learned, again, from certain letters of Origen.[33] Such an ideal picture had no room for any reference to its hero being hidden during a persecution, so Eusebius simply suppressed that bit of information in the note he read in the book of Symmachus that Origen had received from Juliana.

(16) It seems easier to me to explain Eusebius' omission of any reference to Origen being hidden during the persecution than to explain why Origen was not arrested if he continued his normal activities in Caesarea in Palestine during the persecution of Maximinus. Since we know that Caesarea was one of the places where arrests of Church leaders were carried out, and since Eusebius and Herodian are in agreement that people who had had friendly relations with the house of Alexander were especially targeted in the persecution, and Origen was a noted Church leader and would have been especially suspect politically because he had been a special guest of Alexander's mother, it seems inexplicable to me that he would not have been arrested had he continued his work in Caesarea during the persecution.[34]

31. *Biography in Late Antiquity* (Berkeley: University of California Press, 1983), 100–101.
32. *H.E.* 6.2.3–6. H. J. Lawlor and J.E.L. Oulton, *Eusebius*, II (London: SPCK, 1928), 192, point out that Photius, 118, says that the story of Origen's mother hiding his clothes to prevent him from offering himself for martyrdom was contained in one of Origen's letters, and that Rufinus, who seems to have read the letter, states that it was contained in the letter Eusebius says Origen wrote to his father (*H.E.* 6.2.6).
33. *H.E.* 6.39.5.
34. It is, of course, a problem that Origen should write an exhortation to martyrdom to his two friends who had been arrested, while he himself was in hiding. E. de Faye, *Origène: sa vie, son oeuvre, sa pensée*, I (Paris, 1923), 196, is certain, for this very reason, that Origen did not take shelter during the persecution. It is perhaps worth noting, however, that Cyprian did something analogous during the later persecution of Decius. In a let-

## INTRODUCTION

(17) Furthermore, Origen himself recommends withdrawal to avoid persecution and martyrdom when that is possible in Book 28 of this *Commentary*.[35] "It is right," he says, "not to shun the confession nor to hesitate to die for the truth if one has been caught in the struggle about confessing Jesus."[36] This would cover the case of Ambrose and Protoctetus, who were "caught in the struggle." People in such circumstances should maintain their confession of Jesus and refuse to deny their faith. Such was his exhortation to his friends. "But on the other hand," he says, "it is no less right also not to provide an opportunity for such a great trial, but to avoid it by every means."[37] He even suggests that one who does not avoid persecution when it is possible for him to do so may be held accountable for his executioner's sin in killing him.[38]

(18) I propose the following scenario for Origen's activities during the persecution of Maximinus. First, he was in Caesarea in Palestine when Maximinus seized power and instituted the persecution. Ambrose and Protoctetus were arrested very early in the persecution. Origen, however, perhaps not yet known to the civil authorities in Caesarea as a leader in the Church because he had arrived rather recently and had probably not immediately assumed a position of leadership in the Church in Caesarea, especially in light of his reasons for leaving Alexandria, was not noticed by the authorities. He, therefore, set about immediately to compose the *Exhortation to Martyrdom* for his two friends.

(19) Eusebius says that Origen composed the treatise *On Martyrdom* at the time of the persecution of Maximinus.[39]

---

ter to the presbyters and deacons at Rome he defends his own withdrawal to a place of hiding during the persecution, and says that he wrote letters of encouragement to the confessors in prison when they were being tortured (*Ep.* 20.1–2). I shall suggest in what follows, however, that Origen probably wrote his *Exhortation to Martyrdom* before he withdrew from Caesarea to Cappadocia.

35. 28.192–201, 209, 244. See my notes on these passages in the Commentary for other places where Origen makes similar recommendations.
36. 28.193.
37. 28.194.
38. 28.195.
39. *H.E.* 6.28.

12                    INTRODUCTION

The treatise can, with a large degree of certainty, be dated in the year 235, and even to the first half of that year. In chapter 41 of the treatise Origen refers to the possibility of his friends and himself being "executed in Germany." K. J. Neumann, argues that the reference to Germany shows that the treatise was written in the year 235 when Maximinus was in Germany. He also points out that Maximinus had left Germany and was in Pannonia by the winter of 235.[40] Origen's reference to the possibility of dying in Germany reflects Maximinus' policy of having political prisoners brought to his military camp where he personally tried and sentenced them.[41] Consequently, this treatise must have been composed at or near the beginning of the persecution. The fact that Origen refers to the possibility that he himself might be executed in Germany suggests, I think, that the treatise was written while he was still in Caesarea where his friends had already been arrested.

(20) Subsequent to the composition of the treatise on martyrdom, perhaps at the urging of friends in the Church at Caesarea who knew that Origen would be a target of the persecution because of his former association with the house of Alexander, and perhaps also at the invitation of Firmilian, Origen withdrew from Palestine to Cappadocia. I would surmise that the earthquakes which set off the general persecution in Cappadocia discussed above[42] had not yet occurred, and that Cappadocia seemed an ideal place for Origen to go, both because there had been no arrests of Church leaders there, and because of his friendship with

---

40. *Die Römische Staat*, 228. A. Harnack, *Geschichte* II/2, 56–57, is too critical when he dismisses the reference as plausible only for Ambrose and Protoctetus, but not for Origen, and suggests that the reference to Germany is a scribal error and that the original reference was to some unknown locality in or near Caesarea, or possibly to a mine in Palestine or Syria. P. Nautin, *Origène, sa vie et son oeuvre* (Paris: Beauchesne, 1977), 76, follows Neumann in this dating.

41. See Herodian 7.3.4. The statement in Herodian is made in reference to prisoners being brought to Maximinus in Pannonia, where he went when he left Germany, but provides a basis, at least, for assuming that this had been his earlier policy as well.

42. See paragraphs 9–10.

Firmilian. Sometime after Origen's arrival in Cappadocia, some earthquakes awakened the latent popular suspicions against Christians, and a fierce general persecution broke out which was encouraged by the governor Serenianus. Since Origen was unknown in Cappadocia except in the immediate Christian circles, it was safer for him there, even in a general persecution, than it would have been in Palestine. It was during this time that Origen was hidden for two years by the virgin Juliana.[43]

(21) If my reconstruction is correct, then we should, perhaps, assume that the persecution of Maximinus marked another interruption in Origen's work on the *Commentary on John*, for he was probably again without his secretarial staff when he was in hiding in Caesarea. Eusebius remarks that Origen "has noted (σεσημείωται) this time of the persecution in the twenty-second of his *Expositions on the Gospel according to John*, and in various letters."[44] Neither the letters referred to nor Book 22 of the *Commentary on John* have been preserved.[45] Nautin thinks, on the basis of the way Eusebius' statement is worded, that he means that the persecution was past when Origen composed Book 22.[46] Regardless of whether one wants to press Eusebius' grammar so far, I shall provide other reasons later for dating the composition of Book 22 sometime after the persecution of Maximinus.

---

43. See paragraph 12 above.
44. *H.E.* 6.28.
45. Preuschen, GCS 4 (Leipzig, 1903), LXXX, argued that Eusebius' reference must be to *Jo.* 32.30–31, where Origen discusses an end to the "wrestling." I agree with Nautin, *Origène*, 79–80, who rejects Preuschen's suggestion and argues that there is no necessary reference to any persecution in Origen's language in Book 32.30–31, and that the reference to Book 22 in Eusebius' text must be correct. The only reference to persecution in the Commentary that I have found is in Book 28.192–201 which I have already discussed. There is a remote possibility that Eusebius made reference to this and originally wrote Book 28 instead of 22. It would have been possible for KB (22) to have been read for KH (28) in the manuscript transmission. Eusebius' remark, however, that Origen "has noted this time of the persecution" suggests that he is referring to something more specific about that particular persecution than can be found in the general comments in 28.192–201.
46. Ibid.

(22) We have seen so far, then, that Origen's work on the *Commentary on John* fell into certain well defined periods which were separated by rather major interruptions. First, he composed the first five books in Alexandria prior to 233. His work was then interrupted by his dispute with Demetrius, Bishop of Alexandria, which resulted in his move to Caesarea. The second phase of his work on the *Commentary* falls in the period between 233 and 235, after his move to Caesarea, but before the outbreak of the persecution of Maximinus, which again interrupted his work. What books of the *Commentary* can we assign to this period between 233 and 235?

(23) We know that Book 6 belongs to this period.[47] We can also, because of some interdependence between the treatise *On Prayer* and Book 10 of the *Commentary*, show that Book 10, and consequently Books 6–10 were composed in this period. The general consensus, with which I agree, is that *On Prayer* was composed after Origen moved to Caesarea, but before the beginning of the persecution of Maximinus, probably in 233 or 234.[48] Koetschau notes that Origen's remarks in *On Prayer* 15.1, "For if, as is shown (δείκνυται) in other places, the Son is different from the Father in essence and substance (κατ' οὐσίαν καὶ ὑποκεί-

---

47. See above, paragraph 5.

48. P. Koetschau, GCS 1 (Leipzig, 1899), LXXV–LXXVII, has the fullest discussion of the evidence for assigning this date to the treatise. He notes two literary allusions in *or.* which help to date it (I pass over his discussion of the allusion to "certain persons" in 28.10, since the specific reference intended is strongly debated). First, in *or.* 23.4 Origen refers to his discussion of Gn 3.8–9 in his commentaries on Genesis. Eusebius, *H.E.* 6.24.2, tells us that Origen wrote 12 volumes on Genesis, and that the first 8 were written in Alexandria. None of this commentary has been preserved, but since he covered only the first four chapters of Genesis in 12 volumes, his comments on Gn 3.8–9 must have been in one of the last four, and therefore, written after his move to Caesarea, which, of course, puts the treatise on prayer also after his move to Caesarea. Koetschau also notes that although there are several opportunities presented by the texts and subjects discussed in *or.* to refer to martyrdom, the subject is never mentioned in the treatise. This, he concludes, demands that the treatise was composed before the persecution by Maximinus had begun. The other literary allusion Koetschau notes is that to *Jo.* 10.246, which I discuss in the text here.

μενον)," are an allusion to Book 10.246 of the *Commentary on John*, where Origen argues against some who think the Father and Son are one "not only in essence, but also in substance (οὐ μόνον οὐσίᾳ ἀλλὰ καὶ ὑποκειμένῳ)." Koetschau argues that the present tense (δείκνυται) in *On Prayer* 15.1 can only refer to a work in which Origen was then involved, and must, therefore, be a reference to 10.246 in the *Commentary on John*. This would put the composition of Book 10 of the *Commentary* slightly before the composition of *On Prayer*, and, consequently, before the beginning of the persecution of Maximinus.

(24) I have found nothing in Book 13 which would suggest a date for its composition. On the basis of 13.1–2 it would appear that Books 12–13 were composed in close succession. My opinion is that Book 13, and perhaps even a few more books of the *Commentary*, were composed before the beginning of the persecution. I will provide an argument in what follows for dating the composition of at least Books 19–32 after the persecution.

### Gregory Thaumaturgus as a Student under Origen

(25) The third signpost for dating the composition of the books of the *Commentary* is the period of time when Gregory Thaumaturgus was a student under Origen.[49] Gregory composed his *Panegyric to Origen* when he departed from his school in Caesarea. Koetschau discovered an allusion in Gregory's speech to a passage in Book 32 of the *Commentary*.[50] This, of course, necessitates that Book 32 was composed before Gregory left Origen's school. I have found

---

49. I use the traditional name when referring to Gregory. It is not significant for our purposes to determine if Eusebius was right or wrong in identifying Theodore with Gregory. See Nautin, *Origène*, 81–86, 161.

50. *Des Gregorios Thaumaturgos Dankrede an Origenes* (Freiburg, 1894), xiii. See also H. Crouzel, BLE 64 (1963): 198. The allusion is Gregory's statement about "venturing with unwashed feet (as the saying goes) to approach ears in which the Divine Word himself . . . dwells" (*Pan. Or.* 2.18), which Koetschau takes to refer to Origen's statement in *Jo.* 32.87, "For me to wash your feet is symbolic of the bases of your souls being purified, . . . since you are to preach the good things, and to approach the souls of men with your feet clean."

three additional allusions in Gregory's *Panegyric* to Book 20 of the *Commentary*.[51] These allusions appear in ch. 17 of the *Panegyric* and involve (a) Gregory's identification of Jesus with the Good Samaritan, (b) his application of the title "the sleepless Guard of all men" to Jesus, and (c) his reference to "those seeds which you have shown us to possess" in conjunction with an exposition of Ps. 125.6 (LXX). The first is an allusion to 20.318 in the *Commentary*, the second to 20.320, and the third to 20.21, 38.[52]

(26) The appearance of these allusions to Books 20 and 32 in Gregory's farewell speech to Origen suggests, it seems to me, that Gregory has heard Origen lecture on at least Books 20–32. Furthermore, since this material appears to have been fresh in Gregory's mind, it may have been in the last year or two of his stay with Origen that he has heard the lectures.[53] Since Books 19 and 20 both deal with chapter 8 of John, I would include Book 19 in this block of material that was produced while Gregory was Origen's student.

(27) Can the period of Gregory's residency with Origen be determined? The question is complicated, and directly related to our previous discussion of Origen's location during the persecution of Maximinus. The position I have taken there, of course, points to the position I will take here, but I must present the evidence, because of the significance of the issue, and because of the way in which the evidence is intertwined.

(28) Crouzel, following Koetschau,[54] takes Gregory's

---

51. See my forthcoming article, "Three Allusions to Book 20 of Origen's Commentary on John in Gregory Thaumaturgus' Panegyric to Origen," in *The Proceedings of the Eleventh International Conference on Patristic Studies*.

52. See the article referred to in the previous note for my argument that Gregory's references must be to these passages in *Jo.*, and not to other works of Origen.

53. It is possible, but less likely, I think, that Gregory knew this material in written form. This would still necessitate its composition before Gregory left Origen as a student. What seems most likely to me is that Origen lectured on this material to his students in Caesarea, and that the secretaries provided by Ambrose sat in the lecture room taking down the lectures which later appeared, perhaps after some revision by Origen, as the books of the Commentary.

54. *Dankrede*, ix.

INTRODUCTION 17

words that Origen's move from Alexandria to Caesarea was "as it were to meet us"⁵⁵ to mean that Gregory arrived in Caesarea shortly after Origen arrived there from Alexandria.⁵⁶ I agree with Harnack, that Gregory's words there are not sufficient to prove that Origen had not already been in Caesarea for a certain period of time when Gregory arrived. He says Origen's move was a "cause célèbre," and the fact that it had occurred a few years earlier would not yet have blurred it.⁵⁷ There is no indication in Gregory's farewell speech to Origen either (a) that he had been with him in any kind of danger, or (b) that he had been forced to be separated from him at any time during his studies. In fact, he laments leaving the life of "peace," "tranquillity, and harmony" that he has enjoyed in his time with Origen to return to the tumult of "marketplaces, lawsuits, and crowds."⁵⁸

(29) Eusebius puts the arrival of Gregory in Caesarea during the reign of Gordian (A.D. 238–244), at which time Origen received a number of students, and says that Gregory spent five years with Origen.⁵⁹ While Eusebius' chronology can never be trusted entirely, it seems to me that placing Gregory's arrival in Caesarea early in the reign of Gordian

55. *Pan. Or.* 5.63.
56. *Origen*, 25; cf. BLE 64 (1963): 198–99; *Grégoire le Thaumaturge remerciement à Origène*, ed. and tr. by H. Crouzel, SC 148 (Paris: Les éditions du Cerf, 1969), 16ff. For a summary of the unconvincing attempts to argue that Gregory arrived in Caesarea shortly after Origen did, but then went to Alexandria to study philosophy during the persecution of Maximinus while Origen was in Cappadocia, and then returned to Origen in Caesarea after the persecution, see Crouzel, BLE 64 (1963): 199–200, and SC 148, 21.
57. *Geschichte* II/2, 94.
58. *Pan. Or.* 16.192.
59. *H.E.* 6.30. He introduces Gordian's succession of Maximinus in 6.29. In *Pan. Or.* 1.3, Gregory says that it has been 8 years since he engaged in any form of rhetorical activity. Some have seen a discrepancy between this and the 5 years Eusebius says Gregory was with Origen (see Crouzel, SC 148, 20–21 for a summary of how various scholars have dealt with this). Gregory does not say, however, that it was 8 years since he had begun to study with Origen, but that it was 8 years since he had ceased to study rhetoric. There was a period of time after Gregory had ceased to study rhetoric that he studied Roman law. It was his interest in this latter subject that he intended to pursue in Beirut, and which he forsook after he encountered Origen. See Lawlor and Oulton, *Eusebius* II, 221–22.

solves the problems we have been discussing. Lawlor and Oulton argue that Gregory's departure from Caesarea must have taken place before Origen's second visit to Athens, which Eusebius also puts in the reign of Gordian.[60] They place this visit in 243 or 244, and, consequently, Gregory's time with Origen in Caesarea from 238-243.[61]

(30) On the basis of Gregory's allusions to Books 20 and 32 of the *Commentary on John* in his farewell speech, and the assumption that he was a student of Origen from 238-243 and had heard Origen lecture on the material included in these books late in his career as a student, I would place the composition of Books 19-32 in 241 or 242.

*Conclusions*

(31) If Origen left Alexandria in late 232 or early 233, at which time he had already begun Book 6 of the *Commentary on John*, we may surmise that he had begun his work on the *Commentary* sometime in 231. If he had finished Book 32 sometime in 241 or 242, then the composition of the *Commentary* covered 10-12 years of his life. He had at least two major interruptions in the course of the work, the first forcing him to leave Alexandria, and the second forcing him to leave Caesarea. We know that he composed *On Prayer*, *Exhortation to Martyrdom*, and at least four books of his commentary on Genesis in this same time period. It is also most likely that nearly all of his homilies were delivered in the latter part of this same period.[62]

(32) There are two traditions concerning Origen's death.[63] One, coming from Pamphilus, would place it in 250-51 and make Origen sixty-six years old when he died.

---

60. *H.E.* 32.2; *Eusebius* II, 222.
61. Ibid., 224, 222. Nautin, *Origène*, 411, agrees in putting Gregory's arrival in Caesarea in 238, but puts his departure in 245. He, too, has Gregory's departure before Origen's second visit to Athens, but puts the latter in 245 during the reign of Philip.
62. See *Origen: Homilies on Genesis and Exodus*, tr. R. E. Heine, FOTC 71 (Washington, D.C.: Catholic University of America Press, 1982), 19-23. He had certainly delivered his homilies on Luke prior to the composition of *Jo.* 32.5, for he refers to those homilies there.
63. See FOTC 71.24-25.

INTRODUCTION 19

The other, coming from Eusebius, places it in 254–55, and makes him sixty-nine years old at his death.

(33) Counting back from either of these dates, Origen was approximately forty-seven years old when he began work on the *Commentary* in Alexandria, and fifty-seven or fifty-eight years old when he finished Book 32 in Caesarea. The *Commentary on John*, therefore, was a work of Origen's maturity as a theologian. This, plus the fact that it has been preserved in Greek, makes it a document of supreme importance.

### Aspects of Origen's Theology in the Commentary on John

(34) A major problem that always faces students of Origen is that of determining accurately what his theological views were. This problem has several roots. One is the extraordinarily large amount of works Origen produced. Jerome lists 786 titles in one of his letters, and other ancient sources estimated the number to have been far greater than that.[64] It could hardly be expected in such a large output of literature that Origen could have been absolutely consistent in everything he wrote. Another root of the problem is the fact that some of Origen's speculations later became dogmas in the hands of some of his devotees, and he in turn was blamed for holding their theological views.[65] These views of later Origenists, often attributed to Origen in ancient sources, must always be carefully distinguished from the views of Origen himself. Still another root of this problem is the relatively small number of Origen's works which have been preserved, and of these, the even smaller number which have been preserved in the Greek language in which he wrote.[66] What is perhaps most regrettable is that Origen's main work of theology, *On First Principles*, has come down to

---

64. See FOTC 71.25.
65. R. J. Daly, "Origen," in *Encyclopedia of Early Christianity* (New York: Garland Publishing, Inc., 1990), 668.
66. See FOTC 71.25–39.

us only in a Latin translation, and the translator, by his own admission, has altered the text in certain ways.[67]

(35) This problem with the preservation of the texts has produced two radically divergent approaches to the attempt to determine Origen's views. One is that associated with E. de Faye, and followed by H. Koch, which concentrates almost exclusively on the texts which have been preserved in Greek, and distrusts all the Latin translations, but especially the Latin translation of *On First Principles*.[68] The other, associated with H. de Lubac, and followed especially by W. Völker and H. Crouzel, is to make massive use of all the Latin translations on a given subject, along with the Greek texts, and the Greek fragments in order to arrive at Origen's true thought.[69]

(36) Both approaches have their merits and their problems. I am not so distrustful of Rufinus as a translator as some, but I recognize that his translations must always be used with caution, especially when he is treating controversial aspects of Origen's doctrine. On the other hand, when one brings together various texts of Origen on a given subject, one must always be mindful of the dating of the various treatises from which the texts come, for it is not impossible that Origen changed his mind on some subjects. To amass texts indiscriminately on a particular subject will obscure if not obliterate that possibility. Furthermore, we are always on safest ground when we have treatises[70] that have been preserved in Greek. What Origen says on a subject in such treatises must always be given priority when texts preserved only in Latin translation differ from them. Origen's teachings in treatises preserved in Greek serve as a kind of touchstone, then, for evaluating his teachings on the same subjects in texts preserved only in Latin.

---

67. *Praef. princ.* 1.3. For my discussion of and evaluation of Rufinus as a translator see FOTC 71.30–39.
68. See my discussion in FOTC 71.30.
69. See FOTC 71.31, and Crouzel, *Origen*, 48–49, 179.
70. I mean in distinction from Greek fragments preserved in catenae. See my article, "Can the Catena Fragments of Origen's Commentary on John be Trusted?" VC 40 (1986): 118–34.

INTRODUCTION                                21

(37) The *Commentary on John*, coming from Origen's maturity, preserved in Greek, and rich in theological discussion, is a significant touchstone for evaluating his thought. I do not suggest that the following analysis contains Origen's complete thought on any of the subjects treated, nor that these are the only theological themes that appear in the *Commentary*. It does, I hope, accurately represent what he says in the *Commentary* on these subjects. I have intentionally refrained, with a few exceptions, from attempting to indicate what he says in other works on these same subjects and thus to make this a "theology of Origen." I have focused on these particular subjects because of their importance in Origen's thought and because certain aspects of his views on each of these subjects has been controversial.

### Doctrine of God

(38) Two quite different concepts of God, held by equally divergent groups of people, form the background to much of what Origen says about God in the *Commentary*. One was that of the Gnostics, who made a distinction between the Creator God of the Old Testament and the Father of Jesus. The former, at best, was an ignorant being far inferior to what they held to be the highest deity. The other view was that which is usually labeled Monarchian, a term first applied to the view by Tertullian.[71] Origen does not use this label in the *Commentary*, but speaks of those who are "afraid they may proclaim two Gods."[72] Those who held this view[73] emphasized that God is one, and that there is no essential difference between Father, Son, and Holy Spirit.

(39) There is a short, creed-like section in Book 32 of the *Commentary*[74] in which Origen sets forth the basic Christian

71. *Adv. Prax.* 3.
72. 2.16, FOTC 80.98.
73. Tertullian, *Adv. Prax.* 9, attributed it to the uneducated. A. Harnack, *History of Dogma* III, tr. N. Buchanan (New York: Dover, 1961), 9, argued that it was also the view of the theologians who refused to give any place to Platonic philosophy in Christian dogmatics.
74. 32.187–193. See A. C. Outler, *The Second Century* 4 (1984): 133–41, esp. 136.

doctrines of God, Christ, and the Holy Spirit. He asserts there, partially in dependence on *The Shepherd* of Hermas, that God is one, that he created all things out of what did not exist,[75] and that the God of the Law and the God of the Gospel is one and the same God.[76] He alludes to the same passages in Hermas again in 1.103 where his emphasis is on God's creation of things "from that which does not exist." In his argument against Heracleon's view that the Word was the cause of creation, and that the Creator was the agent of the Word,[77] Origen asserts to the contrary that all things were made *through* the agency of the Word, but by one greater than the Word, namely the Father.[78] There are, in addition, many references to God as Creator in arguments against the Gnostic doctrine noted above that the Creator and the Father of Jesus are two different beings. Origen stresses repeatedly that the God of the Old Testament and the Father of Jesus are the same, sometimes speaking of the Creator, sometimes of the God of the law and the prophets.[79]

(40) Origen has much to say about the uniqueness of God in the *Commentary*. Most of these assertions are made in contrast to the Son. "God," he asserts, "is altogether one and simple."[80] This is said in contrast to the many things that the Savior becomes on behalf of the needs of the creation. In the same connection, the Father alone is immutable and unchangeable.[81] Of the three hypostases, Father, Son, and Holy Spirit, "only the Father is unbegotten."[82] On the basis of 1 Timothy 6.16 he argues that God "alone has immortality."[83] Consequently, those who seek to kill Jesus seek to kill a

---

75. These first two points are dependent on Hermas, *Shepherd*, Man. 1.1; Vis. 1.1.6.
76. 32.187, 190.
77. See my discussion in FOTC 80.121–22.
78. 2.172, FOTC 80.113.
79. 10.216–20, FOTC 80.302–3; 19.12, 29–32; 20.50, 271–72; 32.190.
80. 1.119, FOTC 80.58.
81. 2.123, FOTC 80.127; 6.193, FOTC 80.222.
82. 2.75, FOTC 80.114.
83. 2.123–25, FOTC 80.127. See G. Gruber, *ZΩH: Wesen, Stufen und Mitteilung des wahren Lebens bei Origenes* (München: Max Hueber Verlag, 1962), 85–89.

man, "since God is not killed."[84] "It is not permitted to say that God dies."[85] Here, however, Origen includes the Word also, and says that the Word, who was in the beginning with God and was God the Word, did not die.[86]

(41) Origen further brings out the uniqueness of the Father in relation to the Son by exploring some of the metaphors of Scripture. One might think, he claims, and here he must have the Monarchians in mind, that since the Savior is referred to as light in John 1.4, and God is said to be light in 1 John 1.5, that this confirms that the Father is not distinct from the Son in essence. Closer examination will reveal, however, that "the light that shines in the darkness and is not overcome by it, and the light in which there is no darkness at all are not the same."[87] In a more obscure manner, he argues for the uniqueness of the Father on the basis of Jesus' words about the fountain of water that springs up into eternal life.[88] "And after eternal life, perhaps it will also leap into the Father who is beyond eternal life. For Christ is life; but he who is greater than Christ is greater than life."[89] Further, Origen uses Jesus' enigmatic statement, "I have meat to eat which you do not know"[90] as a basis for showing the unique self-sufficiency of the Father. Christ, just as men and angels, has need of spiritual food. "He is always replenishing himself from the Father who alone is without need and sufficient in himself."[91]

(42) This emphasis on the uniqueness of God may lie behind Origen's musings on whether God's knowledge and contemplation of himself may not provide him an even greater glorification than that which he receives when he is glorified in the Son. We must say, Origen claims, that God "is gladdened with a certain ineffable satisfaction, gladness, and joy, and that he is pleased with himself and rejoices. Now I use these terms," he continues, "which would not properly be applied to God, because I am at a loss . . . for

---

84. 20.80.
85. 20.85.
86. Ibid. I shall discuss the unity between the Father and Son later.
87. 2.149, FOTC 80.134.
88. Jn 4.14.
89. 13.19.
90. Jn 4.32.
91. 13.219; cf. 2.18, FOTC 80.99.

those unutterable words which he alone, and after him his Only-Begotten, can speak or think in their proper sense about himself."[92] This understanding of God contemplating himself must go back ultimately to Aristotle. The latter asserts that the activity of God which surpasses all others in blessedness is that of contemplation, and that the only proper object for the divine mind to think on is itself.[93] Whether Origen knew this directly from Aristotle or not is difficult to say, for as E. A. Clark has noted, these Aristotelian motifs "had been absorbed into Middle Platonic theology" prior to the time of Clement.[94]

(43) This unique God is surrounded by darkness, so far as human understanding is concerned. He is unknown to all except, perhaps, to Christ and the Holy Spirit.[95] Scripture does not contain "some of the more important and more divine aspects of the mysteries of God."[96] Human knowledge of the Father is possible only through the Son, the Word. One "ascends from knowledge of the Son to knowledge of the Father, and the Father is not seen otherwise than by seeing the Son. . . . It is impossible . . . to behold God apart from the Word."[97] This is, at best, an indirect knowledge mediated by means of a mirror. For the Son "is an image of the goodness and brightness, not of God, but of God's glory and of his eternal light . . . , an unspotted mirror of his activity. It is through this mirror that Paul and Peter and their contemporaries see God, because he says, 'He who has seen me has seen the Father who sent me.'"[98]

(44) This contemplation of God through the mirror of the Son will one day give way to direct knowledge of God, even as the Son now knows him. "There will be a time when one will see the Father and the things with the Father as the Son sees them. Then he will be an eyewitness, as it were, of the Father and of the Father's things in a manner similar to

---

92. 32.350.
93. *Nic. Eth.* 10.8.1178b20–22; *Met.* 12.9.
94. *Clement's Use of Aristotle* (New York: The Edwin Mellen Press, 1977), 79, 85.
95. 2.172, FOTC 80.141.      96. 13.27.
97. 19.35.      98. 13.153.

the Son, and will no longer conceive of the things concerning God, of whom the Son is the image, from the image."[99] Origen is not, however, speaking of any kind of mystical direct vision of God to be expected in this life. It is an eschatological hope. It will come about "whenever that hour comes, which is to begin after the present hour,"[100] or, as he states it in another passage, "this is the goal when the Son delivers the kingdom to God the Father, and when God becomes all in all."[101]

(45) In one passage Origen recognizes a certain correctness in the Gnostic distinction between the God of the Old Testament and the Father made known through Jesus. In discussing Jesus' statement to the Pharisees in John 8.19, "You know neither me nor my Father," he raises the possibility that someone might know God, but not know the Father. "For if there is one aspect of him in accordance with which he is Father, and another in accordance with which he is God, perhaps it is possible for someone to know God, but not to know the Father beyond knowing him as God."[102] On this basis, he asserts, it is possible "to agree with the heterodox view, that Moses and the prophets did not know the Father." This view, for Origen, is based on his understanding that only the Son knows the Father, and that the Father can be known only through the Son.

(46) In contradistinction to the Son, he classes the personalities of the Old Testament as servants who knew God as Lord. He does allow for the possibility that Christ may have sojourned in some of the personalities of the Old Testament spiritually and these, therefore, could have known God as Father through the Son. These, however, spoke and wrote about God as Father in secret, "so that they might not anticipate the grace which is poured out to all the world through Jesus who calls all people to adoption."[103] There is one major

---

99. 20.47; cf. 13.113.  100. 13.113.
101. 20.48. For the significance of 1 Cor 15.22–28 in Origen's eschatology, see below, par. 122, and 135ff.
102. 19.26.
103. 19.28. See M. Harl, *Origène et la fonction révélatrice du verbe incarné* (Paris: éditions du Seuil, 1958), 166–67.

distinction that sets Origen's view apart from that of the Gnostics. He firmly maintained that it was the same God who was known to the personalities of the Old Testament and who was revealed as Father through Jesus.[104] Origen's rapprochement with Gnosticism on this point, therefore, as he is well aware, is on a quite superficial level.

(47) Origen deals with the Monarchian view of God most directly in the following passage. "Many people," he asserts, "who wish to be pious are troubled because they are afraid that they may proclaim two Gods and, for this reason, they fall into false and impious beliefs. They either deny that the individual nature of the Son is other than that of the Father by confessing him to be God whom they refer to as "Son" in name at least, or they deny the divinity of the Son and make his individual nature and essence as an individual to be different from the Father."[105] He answers the problem here by arguing that one should understand a distinction between "*the* God," i.e. God with the definite article, as in John 1.1b, 2a, where it is asserted that "the Word was with *the* God," and God without the definite article, as in John 1,1c, where it is said that "the Word was God." "*The* God" refers to him who is "very God," or "the only true God," whereas "God" without the article refers to "everything besides the very God, which is made God by participation in his divinity." The latter includes the Word, who is God because he is "with *the* God." He would not be God "if he were not with God, and he would not remain God if he did not continue in unceasing contemplation of the depth of the Father."[106] This "true God" is identical with the Father for Origen.[107]

(48) Origen treats another unacceptable view of the relation between the Father and the Son in his later discussion of John 8.42, "I have proceeded from God."[108] He seems to have in mind the same people to whom Tertullian alludes

---

104. 19.27–32.
105. 2.16, FOTC 80.98; cf. 10.246, FOTC 80.309.
106. 2.17–18, FOTC 80.98–99; cf. 13.219.
107. 2.19, FOTC 80.99.
108. 20.152–59.

when he quotes John 8.42 to show the distinction between the Father and the Son against the modalistic Monarchian views of Praxeas. Tertullian immediately adds, to combat a view that made the Father and Son completely separate, "Howbeit they are not separated, though he said he was come forth, *as some seize upon the chance which this saying gives them* [emphasis mine]: for he came forth from the Father like the beam from the sun, like the stream from the spring, like the ground shoot from the seed."[109] Neither Tertullian nor Origen identify those who held this view.

(49) Origen interprets the passage by joining the words from Micah 1.2–4, "The Lord proceeds from his place," with those of John 8.42. On this basis, he asserts that "when the Son is in the Father, being in the form of God before he empties himself, his place, as it were, is God."[110] Even after the Son has proceeded from God, however, the Father continues to be with him, and the Son continues to be in the Father, although "in a different way than he was before he proceeded from God."[111]

(50) At this point in the discussion Origen introduces the view of "others," who take the statement, "I proceeded from God," to mean, "I have been begotten by God." These must hold, he asserts, that the Son was begotten of the Father's essence, analogous to those who are pregnant, and consequently "that God is diminished and lacking, as it were, in the essence which he formerly had, when he has begotten the Son."[112] This view demands also that one think of the Father and Son as corporeal, that the Father is located in a physical place, that the Son exchanged one material place for another, and that the Father has been divided.[113] "These," Origen concludes, "are the doctrines of people who have not even dreamed of an invisible and bodiless nature that is pure essence."[114]

---

109. *Adv. Prax.* 22, tr. E. Evans, *Tertullian's Treatise Against Praxeas* (London: SPCK, 1948), 163. Cf. ibid., 301–2, where Evans also expresses the opinion that these are the same people to whom Origen also refers.
110. 20.153.
111. 20.155–56.
112. 20.157.
113. 20.158–59.
114. 20.158.

(51) Origen has another major discussion of God's essence in the *Commentary* related to the assertion in John 4.24, that "God is spirit."[115] The starting point for this discussion seems to have been Origen's knowledge of the treatments of God in various philosophical schools. He begins by saying that "many have produced lengthy discussions of God and his essence." His summary comments reflect knowledge of the doxographical accounts of God.[116] The discussion focuses on the view that God is corporeal. This was the Stoic view of God, but it was also a view held by some in the Church.[117]

(52) To take the statement, "God is spirit," as a definition of God's essence, Origen argues, demands that one assume that God is a body.[118] This in turn demands that he be subject to change and corruption.[119] Origen considers these conclusions to be blasphemous.[120]

(53) We must, he argues, understand the statement, "God is spirit," in a spiritual manner, in the same way as we understand other statements in Scripture that attribute qualities such as fire or light to God.[121] We must assume that in reality God is "invisible and incorporeal," and can be known only through the Son.[122] Even this knowledge of God is limited, however, for the Savior said, "The Father who sent me is greater than I," and "although the Savior transcends in his essence, rank, power, divinity . . . , and wisdom, beings that are so great and of such antiquity, nevertheless, he is not comparable with the Father in any way."[123]

(54) In another passage Origen suggests that it is on the basis of the unity of the Son's will with the Father's that he

---

115. 13.123–53. See G. L. Prestige, *God in Patristic Thought* (London: SPCK, 1952), 17.
116. 13.123. See H. Chadwick, *Origen: Contra Celsum* (Cambridge, 1965), 21, note 3, and cf. *Cels.* 1.21; 3.75; 4.14.
117. See Prestige, *God in Patristic Thought*, 17, on the Stoics, and paragraph 50 above for this view in the Church.
118. 13.125. Tertullian, *Prax.* 7, takes this position on Jn 4.24, and concludes that God is a body.
119. 13.127–29.
120. 13.130.
121. 13.131–41.
122. 13.137, 146.
123. 13.151, 152.

can say, "I and the Father are one," and "He who sees me sees the one who sent me."[124] This is also the reason he is the image of the Father, for he is the only one "who has comprehended the complete will of God and does it."[125]

(55) The *Commentary* may also throw some light on the question of whether or not Origen thought God suffered in the suffering of the Son. This is an important question in contemporary theology.[126] J. Moltmann asserts that only Origen, of all the Greek and Latin Fathers, "dares to talk theologically about 'God's suffering.'"[127] The few passages in Origen's works that are used to support such assertions are drawn from texts preserved only in Latin translations or in Catena fragments.[128]

(56) J. M. Hallman argues that outside these few passages Origen is quite explicit that it is impossible for God to change or to suffer.[129] He recognizes, however, that in the sixth homily on Ezekiel, Origen states that the Father is not impassible, but that in some way he suffers in the sufferings of the Son, having pity and compassion for human beings, and even endures human sufferings for us.[130] "All authors agree," Hallman says, "on the uniqueness of this text," which "in simple direct assertions, affirms the possibility of the Father."[131] R. M. Grant thinks that Origen has changed his mind about the possibility of God in this text, and that

124. 13.228.
125. 13.231; cf. 13.234.
126. See M. Sarot, "Patripassianism, Theopaschitism and the Suffering of God. Some Historical and Systematic Considerations," RS 26 (1990): 363–75, and the many references to modern works of theology in J. M. Hallman, "Divine Suffering and Change in Origen and *Ad Theopompum*," *The Second Century* 7 (1989–90): 85–86.
127. *The Trinity and the Kingdom of God*, tr. M. Kohl (London: SCM, 1981), 23–4; cf. also Moltmann, "Gesichtspunkte der Kreuzestheologie heute," ET 33 (1973): 354–55.
128. The texts usually cited are *comm. in Rom.* 7.9; *sel. in Ezech.* c. 16; *hom. in Ezech.* 6.6, with the latter considered to be by far the most significant. Hallman (92–3) also cites *hom. in Num.* 23.2 and *hom. in Ex.* 8.5. All of these works would have been composed approximately contemporaneous with or after *Jo.*
129. *The Second Century* 7 (1989–90): 92. He takes no notice of the texts in *Jo.* 32 which we are discussing here.
130. Hallman, *The Second Century* 7 (1989–90): 94.
131. Ibid.

30    INTRODUCTION

the occasion for this change was his discovery of the letters of Ignatius to which he explicitly alludes in his sixth homily on Luke.[132]

(57) It is significant that the passages in question in the *Commentary on John* appear in Book 32, which was clearly composed after the homilies on Luke, for Origen alludes to these homilies in the opening of that Book.[133] This means that Origen has discovered the letters of Ignatius prior to the composition of Book 32, and if these have led him to change his mind on the passibility of God, this change of mind should have occurred prior to the writing of Book 32.

(58) There are two texts in Book 32, both in the exposition of John 13.31, "When, therefore, he [that is, Judas] went out Jesus said, Now is the Son of Man glorified, and God is glorified in him," which suggest that Origen may be thinking that God suffers in some way in the suffering of the Son.[134]

(59) Origen refers to the divine economy (οἰκονομία) three times in these two texts. This term, in Book 32 at least, refers exclusively to the Passion of Christ.[135] He links God with the suffering of the οἰκονομία first, when he asserts that this economy of suffering does not occur "without God," and again, when he says, "It does not say 'the Son of Man is glorified,' alone, for indeed 'God is glorified in him.'" When Origen says the suffering of the Son of Man does not occur "without God," he uses a variant reading of Hebrews 2.9, although he knows the reading "by the grace of God" as well.[136] He usually takes this variant reading to

---

132. *Gods and the One God* (London: SPCK, 1986), 92–93. Grant also cites a Greek text from the late *comm. in Mt.* 10.23, in which Origen states that the impassible Word suffered. H. Crouzel, *Origen*, 183, in accord with his general assumption that Origen does not change his mind in his theology, uses the passage from Ezekiel to show how Origen counterbalances the divine characteristics he has taken over from Middle Platonism with Biblical statements which contradict them. "Everything that is affirmed about God," he says, "must also at the same time be denied."
133. 32.5. See my note below on 32.5.
134. 32.354, 359.
135. See 32.25, 34, 84, 86, 295, 320, 359 (twice), 391.
136. See my note on 32.354.

mean, as R. A. Greer has noted, "'He tasted death for all rational beings except God.'"[137] He obviously does not take it that way here. He has introduced a negative into the phrase which clearly points it away from meaning that God is in some way an exception. Origen must mean by this statement that he understands God to have been involved in some way in "the economy of the suffering of the Son of Man for all men." We must pay careful attention to Origen's precise words in the text to understand what he means here. We discussed above the distinction Origen perceives between the noun "God" with the article and without the article.[138] God with the article means God the Father, and without the article means God the Word. Prior to the statement that Origen makes involving Hebrews 2.9, he has discussed our passage in the light of Hebrews 1.1–3, where the noun "God" appears with the article.[139] "The Son," Origen says, "is the reflection of the total glory of *the* God himself." No one, he asserts, but the Son "can contain the whole reflection of the full glory of *the* God." The sentence we are discussing follows this assertion immediately, and begins with the connectives, "now, therefore," which make it dependent on the preceding statement, that is, because the Son is a reflection "of the full glory of *the* God," the economy of suffering does not occur "without God." The latter phrase, "without God," lacks the article, and must, therefore, mean God the Word, and not God the Father. Nevertheless, it is God the Father who is glorified in the suffering of the Son of Man, for Origen says, "It does not say 'the Son of Man is glorified,' alone, for indeed '*the* God is glorified in him.'"[140]

(60) The other passage referred to above confirms the interpretation we have offered in the words, "But the Son was about to reveal the Father by means of the economy [of suffering], wherefore he said, 'And *the* God is glorified in him.'" This is followed by a quotation that combines John 14.9 and 12.45: "He who has seen me has seen the Father

137. *The Captain of Our Salvation* (Tübingen: J. C. B. Mohr, 1973), 51.
138. See paragraph 47.
139. Heb 1.1; *Jo.* 32.353.       140. *Jo.* 32.354.

who sent me." Origen explains this statement in terms of the Word being the image of the invisible God, but with the addition of the unusual statement for Origen, "and he who beholds the image of the invisible God is able to behold the Father *directly* too, for he is the prototype of the image." We have noted in our discussions above that Origen says in other places in the *Commentary* that Christ is not the image of God himself, but of God's glory. Here he appears to go a step beyond that. It is significant, perhaps, that this additional step is taken in his discussion of the revelation of the Father through the suffering of the Son.

(61) These two passages, preserved in the Greek manuscript tradition of the *Commentary on John*, suggest that Origen did allow for passibility in God the Word, at least, and thereby strengthen the credibility of the Latin translation of the sixth homily on Ezekiel.[141] It is apparent, however, that there is no Patripassianism in Origen's thought.[142] This will become more obvious in our following treatment of Christ and his work.

### The Person and Work of Christ

(62) Origen's treatment of Christ's Person can be divided into two major categories. (1) The Son in relation to the Father, and (2) the Son in relation to the created order. The latter, of course, merges into the work of Christ, which I shall treat specifically in a separate section. What I shall treat in the first two sections are primarily those subjects related to the *being* of the Son in his relation to the Father and to the created order. Certain aspects of the first point have already been discussed in the section on God.

(63) *The Son in Relation to the Father*. Origen notes that

---

141. Whether Origen always held this view, as Crouzel assumes, or changed his mind, as Grant assumes, cannot, of course, be determined from these texts. See note 132 above.

142. On the definition of Patripassianism proposed by Sarot, RE 26 (1990): 370, 375, that it is the refusal "to endorse the Trinitarian distinction between Father and Son," and "therefore holds that in the suffering of Jesus, God *simpliciter*, and not God the Son, was involved," then Origen did not even approach this position.

among the presentations of Christ in the four Gospels John has shown his divinity more fully than the others.[143] The divinity of the Son, indeed, is the underlying assumption of all that Origen says about him. His Christology begins from above.

(64) The Son is eternally with God. Origen has various ways of expressing this, one of which is his concept of the eternal generation of the Son. One cannot speak of a beginning in regard to him.[144] This same idea is expressed in his discussion of Jn 1.1, 2, when he distinguishes between the verbs "coming to be" and "was." The Word "does not *come to be* 'with God' . . . , but because he is always with the Father, it is said, 'And the Word *was* with God.'" "Before all time and eternity 'the Word was in the beginning,' and 'the Word was with God.'"[145] It is the fact that the Son is "by nature a Son from the beginning" that explains why the Spirit is not also called the Son of God. It is also the Son's perpetual presence with God that constitutes his divinity. He would not be God "if he were not with God, and he would not remain God if he did not continue in unceasing contemplation of the depth of the Father."[146]

(65) Although the Son is always with the Father, one must understand that he has his own "substantive existence" (ὑπόστασις),[147] and is distinct from the Father.[148] He is "the image of the invisible God,"[149] and reflects "the total glory of God himself" being the only one who "can contain the whole reflection of the full glory of God."[150]

---

143. 1.22, FOTC 80.37.
144. 1.204, FOTC 80.74; 2.130, FOTC 80.129.
145. 2.8–9, FOTC 80.96–7. See Gruber, *ZΩH*, 278–89, and Harl, *Origène*, 122.
146. 2.18, FOTC 80.99; cf. 13.219–20, and our discussion above in par. 41.
147. 32.193.
148. 10.246, FOTC 80.309; cf. 2.149, FOTC 80.134, our discussion above in par. 41, and R. P. C. Hanson, "Did Origen Teach that the Son is *ek tēs ousias* of the Father?" in *Origeniana Quarta*, ed. L. Lies (Innsbruck-Wien: Tyrolia-Verlag, 1987), 201–2.
149. 1.104, FOTC 80.55.
150. 32.353; cf. our discussion above in paragraphs 43–44.

(66) There is, moreover, a clear subordination of the Son to the Father in the *Commentary*.[151] "The Father exceeds the Savior as much . . . as the Savior himself . . . exceeds the rest."[152] When "the Son of Man is glorified in God," it is a case of "the lesser" being glorified "in the greater."[153] In spite of these subordinationist views, however, Origen rejects the view of those who, "in the delusion of glorifying the Father," declare "that something known by the Father is not known by the Son who refuses to be made equal to the perceptions of the unbegotten God."[154] It is perhaps in this same vein that one should understand Origen's assertion that it is on the basis of the unity of the Son's will with the Father's that he says, "I and the Father are one."[155] Origen is not here expressing the view that Jesus was a man who was given divine status consequent to his perfect willing of what God willed. He makes this assertion in his discussion of the meaning of John 4.34, "My meat is to do the will of the one who sent me." He argues that this does not refer to "performing certain extrinsic deeds," but refers to the complete identity of will between the Father and Son. "The will which is in him is an image of the first will," just as "the divinity which is in him is an image of the true divinity."[156]

(67) Origen criticizes those who, without further examination, assert that Christ is the Word, and think that this sufficiently defines him.[157] The concept of the Word, nevertheless, is central to his own understanding of Christ, and he stands squarely in the tradition of the earlier Word (Logos) theology of the Greek Apologists of the second century, Irenaeus, Clement of Alexandria, and Hippolytus. In

---

151. See Prestige, *God*, 131ff.
152. 13.151–53; cf. 2.32, FOTC 80.102, and H. J. Vogt, "Beobachtungen zum Johannes-Kommentar des Origenes" TQ (1990): 199–202.
153. 32.363–65.
154. 1.187, FOTC 80.71. See R. D. Williams, "The Son's Knowledge of the Father in Origen," in *Origeniana Quarta*, 146–53, on the complexities in Origen's thought on the problems of the Son's knowledge in relation to the Father. See also H. J. Vogt, TQ (1990): 206–7.
155. 13.228.
156. 13.234.
157. 1.125, 266, FOTC 80.59, 88.

INTRODUCTION 35

this line, Origen speaks of the Word as the agent of creation[158] and also as the agent of revelation.[159] In this latter respect, he emphasizes especially the role of the pre-existent Christ as the agent of revelation to the saints of the Old Testament.[160]

(68) It is by means of the concept of the Word that Origen links Christ most closely with God.[161] The Word is one,[162] and, like God, by nature does not die.[163]

(69) It is also the concept of the Word that provides the fundamental link in Christ's mediation between God and the created order of rational beings. Just as one can distinguish between "the God" and all other beings that are divine because they participate in "the God," so one can speak of "the Word" and all other beings that are rational because they participate in "the Word."[164] In a passage where his dependence on Plato is obvious, he asserts that the Word on earth differs from the Word in heaven "inasmuch as he has become flesh and is expressed by means of a shadow and types and images." It is this shadow of the true Word that is known by the multitude of believers, and not the true Word himself.[165]

(70) *The Son in Relation to the Created Order.* This divine Christ assumed human nature for the sake of humanity. While "in his nature, divinity is the beginning, . . . in his relation to us who are not able to begin from the greatness of the truth about him, it is his humanity."[166]

(71) The doctrine of the Incarnation is central to Origen's thought. "Without the man, we would have received

---

158. 1.255; 2.72; 6.188, FOTC 80.85, 113, 221; cf. 2.36, FOTC 80.103-4.
159. 19.35; cf. our discussion above in par. 43. The Word as the agent of salvation will be treated in the section on the work of Christ.
160. 1.37-38; 2.1-3; 6.15-19, 24, 31, FOTC 80.41-42, 95, 172-73, 174, 177; 20.398.
161. 2.18, FOTC 80.99.
162. 2.40, FOTC 80.104-5.
163. 32.322; cf. 20.85; 28.157-59.
164. 2.20, FOTC 80.99-100.
165. 2.49-50, FOTC 80.107.
166. 1.107, FOTC 80.56.

no benefit from the Word, if he had remained God as he was in the beginning with the Father, and not taken up the man."[167] While he certainly thinks that one should advance beyond the vision of the Word become flesh, Origen does not consider the Incarnation to be of minor or passing significance. As he meditates on John's vision of the Word of God mounted on a white horse and clothed in a garment sprinkled with blood,[168] which Origen takes as symbolic of the Word's taking flesh and dying, he remarks that, "perhaps, even if in some way we attain the most sublime and highest contemplation of the Word and of the truth, we shall not forget completely that we were introduced to him by his coming in our body."[169]

(72) Those, such as Marcion, who have annulled his humanity, and the Docetists who denied the reality of his death, have erred, and deprive us of "the most righteous man of all men." "We cannot be saved through that being of theirs."[170] In a creed-like statement Origen asserts that "one must . . . believe in all the truth about him in relation to his divinity and humanity."[171]

(73) The humanity of the Savior was unique in that he was born of a virgin and the Holy Spirit,[172] was sinless,[173] and, in some way, was the first man. On the basis of the statement of John the Baptist, "A man comes before me, who came to be before me, because he was first,"[174] Origen speaks of him as "the first man."[175] He makes a similar statement in reflecting on Romans 5.12–18, when he says that the Christ took up "the man who was first of all men."[176]

(74) It is the assumption of mortality that is central to Origen's thought about the Incarnation. "When he put on man he also put on death."[177] He did not possess the Fa-

---

167. 10.26, FOTC 80.261.  
168. Rv 19.11–13.  
169. 2.61, FOTC 80.110.  
170. 10.24–25, FOTC 80.260–61.  
171. 32.188; cf. 32.192–93.  
172. 20.128, 419; 32.191.  
173. 20.277.  
174. Jn 1.30. I have translated very literally to show the basis of Origen's assertion.  
175. 1.239, FOTC 80.82.  
176. 10.26, FOTC 80.261; cf. 20.87–94.  
177. 6.177, FOTC 80.218.

INTRODUCTION 37

ther's immortality, "for he tasted death for all."[178] "To descend to death for the ungodly not thinking equality with God a thing to be grasped . . . was unique to Jesus' love for man."[179]

(75) Although he continues to be more than man, the fact that he is man means that he is mortal. "It is true to say that he is man and that he is not man. He is man insofar as he is capable of death; not man insofar as he is more divine than man."[180] John 8.40, "But now you seek to kill me, a man who has spoken the truth to you," is an important text for Origen in this respect. He emphasizes, on the basis of this verse, that it is a *man*, and not God or the Word, who will be killed.[181]

(76) Origen perceives a problem in this understanding of the Incarnation, which he solves by making a distinction between the terms flesh and man.[182] Did the Word, he asks, in becoming flesh also become a man? If he did, then it is possible to seek to destroy him. If he did not, then "he has been restored to what he was before he became flesh."[183] Origen does not answer the question here.

(77) He takes up John 8.40 again, however, in his discussion of Caiphas' assertion in John 11.50 that "it is expedient for us that one man should die for the people." "It was expedient even for them," Origen says, "that this one man, insofar as he is man, should die for the people, for Jesus is a man when he dies." He then quotes John 8.40, and comments, "And since he who dies is man, but the truth, and wisdom, and peace, and justice, and him of whom it is written, 'The Word was God,' *were not man*, the Word which was God, and the truth, and wisdom, and justice did not die, for the image of the invisible God, the firstborn of all creation does not admit of death. But this man, the purest of all liv-

178. 2.123, FOTC 80.127.
179. 6.294, FOTC 80.248.
180. 10.23, FOTC 80.260.
181. 20.85.
182. This distinction would later, in the fourth century, characterize Alexandrian in opposition to Antiochian Christology.
183. 20.85–86.

ing creatures, died for the people.'"[184] Origen's answer here is clear. The Word did not *become* man, and did not die with the man Jesus.

(78) John 8.40 appears once more in another major discussion of this problem where the solution receives a slightly different turn. The discussion concerns God's glorification of the Son of Man.[185] Origen notes that the glory resulting from his death for men could not have belonged "to the only-begotten Word, which by nature does not die," but "belonged to the man who was also the Son of Man born of the seed of David according to the flesh." This is why, he asserts, "he said earlier, 'Now you seek to kill me, a man who has spoken the truth to you.'" The exaltation consequent to the death of the Son of Man was not an exaltation of the Word, who "was not capable of being highly exalted." It was an exaltation of the Son of Man and "consisted in the fact that he was no longer different from the Word, but was the same with him." "The humanity of Jesus became one with the Word."[186] This unity is of the nature of that referred to in 1 Corinthians 6.17, where it is said that "'he who is joined to the Lord is one spirit,' so that it is no longer said that 'they are two.'"[187] The exaltation of the humanity of Jesus through his death for mankind is then, in a sense, a reversal of the Incarnation, when the Word emptied himself and assumed the humanity of Jesus.

(79) Origen is obviously wrestling with a very difficult problem, and one closely related to our previous discussion of the involvement of God in the suffering of Jesus.[188] On the one hand, he stresses the unity of the divine and human elements in the incarnate Christ.[189] On the other hand, he cannot think that God the Word, who is eternally with God and is God on the basis of being with God, could die. It is too simple to say that Origen's roots in Greek philosophy caused this problem in his thinking, for Greek philosophy

---

184. 28.157–60. Cf. H. J. Vogt, TQ (1990): 204–5.
185. Jn 13.31–32.   186. 32.322–26.
187. 32.326.
188. See above, paragraphs 55–61.
189. See for example, 1.193–96, FOTC 80.72–73.

INTRODUCTION                                                   39

aside, the thought of God dying raises insurmountable problems for anyone who thinks through even some of its implications. It is instead, a genuine problem for any Christology which begins from above,[190] but wants to avoid Docetic views. Even the so-called Christological settlement at Chalcedon two centuries later was far from a solution to the problem. We can hardly fault Origen, therefore, for failing to be consistent in every respect, or for failing to give a firm and decisive solution to the problem as he wrestled with the various, and often unclear, statements and metaphors about the nature of the incarnate Christ in the Bible.

(80) There is another feature of Origen's Christology that in some respects bridges the two categories under which we have discussed the subject in the first two sections, and leads into the third section on the work of Christ. I refer to his doctrine of the so-called *aspects of Christ* (ἐπίνοιαι Χριστοῦ), some of which the Christ is in his own nature, but most of which, Origen assumes, he became for the sake of the created order.[191] H. Koch sees this doctrine, or, at least, the implicit multiplicity in the Savior which underlies it, as central in Origen's Christology.[192] M. Harl, on the other hand, regards the doctrine as relatively unimportant in Origen's thought, and thinks the doctrine of the two natures of Christ much more important for him.[193] I think the doctrine is important in Origen's thought, but not so important as Koch makes it. On the whole, Harl is nearer to the truth on this subject.

190. See par. 63 above.
191. There is a large amount of literature on this subject. All works that discuss Origen's theology treat it. The following give special attention to the subject. H. Crouzel, "Le contenu spirituel des dénominations du Christ selon le Livre I du *Commentaire sur Jean* d'Origène," in *Origeniana Secunda*, ed. H. Crouzel and A. Quacquareli (Edizioni dell'Ateneo, 1980), 131–50; A. Orbe, *La Epinoia* (Rome: Pontificia Universitas Gregoriana, 1955); G. Gruber, *ZΩH*, 241–326.
192. *Pronoia und Paideusis* (Berlin: Walter de Gruyter & Co., 1932), 65. A. Grillmeier, *Christ in Christian Tradition*, I, tr. J. Bowden (Atlanta: John Knox Press, 1975), 141–44, also treats it as central to Origen's Christology.
193. *Origène*, 229. She attacks Koch for treating it as the central feature of Origen's Christology.

40  INTRODUCTION

(81) The following text is the theological substructure of the doctrine of the aspects of Christ. "God . . . is altogether one and simple. Our Savior, however, because of the many things, since God 'set' him 'forth as a propitiation' and first fruits of all creation, becomes many things, or perhaps even all these things, as the whole creation which can be made free needs him."[194] Origen constructs the doctrine on this basic assumption about the Christ by collecting and examining the various titles applied to Christ in the Bible.[195] These titles, for Origen, fall into two categories. Four belong to the Christ in his nature: Wisdom, Word, Life, and Truth. Christ would have been these even had there been no Fall and no need for redemption.[196]

(82) The other titles, such as Physician, Way, Bread of Life, Light, etc., constitute what Christ is in relation to the various needs of humanity. Origen perceives a certain order in these aspects proceeding from lower to higher, but he never attempts to arrange all the titles of Christ in a progressive order.[197] His most extensive arrangement of the titles in the *Commentary* occurs in the following passage where he compares the aspects of Christ to the steps in the temple. One sets foot first of all on the humanity of Jesus as the lowest step, and proceeds upward until he finally knows God through the Savior. In this context Origen says, "In accordance with his aspects, since a way differs from a door, one must first have gone forth on the way so that later he may thus arrive at the door; and one must experience his rule insofar as he is shepherd, so that he may also enjoy him as King. And we must first profit from him as lamb, so that he may first remove our sin, and later, when we have been

194. 1.119, FOTC 80.58; cf. 6.107, FOTC 80.198; 10.21, FOTC 80.260.
195. 1.123, FOTC 80.59.
196. 1.123, FOTC 80.59; cf. 1.248–51; 2.125–30, FOTC 80.83–84; 127–29; 32.387. Origen sometimes treats some of these, especially Wisdom and Life, as being both for Christ himself and for others.
197. C. Bigg, *The Christian Platonists of Alexandria* (New York, 1886), 168, thinks Origen attempts to arrange the titles of Christ in an ascending scale. He thinks this, plus their correspondence to successive stages of the believer's progress parallels a Valentinian idea.

INTRODUCTION                                    41

cleansed, we may eat of his flesh, the true food. And after
one has carefully examined and received the terms similar
to these, he will hear the words, 'If you know me, you also
know my Father.'"[198]

(83) That these are more metaphors of the process of
spiritual development that people experience in their relationship with Christ than statements about changes in the
nature of Christ himself follows from Origen's cautionary
statement, "Let no one take offense when we distinguish the
aspects in the Savior, thinking that we also do the same with
his essence."[199] He does not see a multiplicity in the *essence* of
the Savior. The aspects of Christ, rather, show what it means
to believe in and follow Christ. They constitute a kind of
road map for a believer's *imitatio Christi*.

He who believes that justice is something would not be unjust, and
he who has believed in wisdom because he has contemplated what
wisdom is, would not say or do anything foolish; furthermore, he
who has believed in the Word that was with God in the beginning
in that he has contemplated him, would do nothing unreasonable.
Furthermore, he who believes that 'he is our peace,' would not
contrive anything warlike and factious. In addition, if Christ is not
only the 'wisdom of God,' but also the 'power of God,' he who believes in him insofar as he is power would not be powerless concerning good things. . . . And if we should [thus] collect the remaining aspects of Christ, we will discover without difficulty from
what has been said how he who does not believe in Christ will die
in his sins. For because he is in opposition to the things that Christ
is in his aspect, he dies in the sins themselves.[200]

The aspects of Christ, then, at the human level at least, are
as much about the differing human perceptions of and ca-

198. 19.38–39.
199. 1.200, FOTC 80.74. This clearly separates Origen's thought from
that of the Gnostics, who made distinctions in the essence of the divine beings. E. de Faye, "De l'influence du gnosticisme sur Origène," RHR 87
(1923): 12, while admitting that Origen did not isolate and hypostatize
the various functions of Christ, thinks, nevertheless, that he dangerously
approached the Gnostic idea. He thinks Origen's discussions of certain
functions, especially of Wisdom, sound as though they exist apart and are
οὐσίαι.
200. 19.155–58.

pacities for receiving the Christ as they are about the Christ himself.

(84) This is not the complete picture, however, for Origen says that as the Savior became a man to men, so has he also become an angel to angels.[201] And, as we shall see in our discussion of the work of Christ, since he considered the Savior's mission to have been to all rational beings, we may assume that the Savior also ministered in whatever way was appropriate to each category of beings. Indeed, in discussing the Biblical statement that the Savior is first and last,[202] he raises the question of whether last refers to man, "or those called the underworld beings, of which the demons also are a part."[203] He stops short, however, of saying that the Savior became one of the beings of the underworld.[204]

(85) *The Work of Christ.* Jesus' statement that he has come "to perfect the work of God,"[205] causes Origen to puzzle over why God's work should need perfecting, and how the work of the greater could be perfected by the lesser.[206] Surely the work, which Origen takes to mean the rational creature, was not created imperfect, "for how would God have placed what was altogether imperfect in paradise to work and guard it?"[207]

(86) He answers that the rational creature was indeed created perfect, but "he became imperfect in some way because of his transgression, and was in need of one to perfect him from his imperfection."[208] This need for perfection refers to all rational beings and not man alone, for all fell

201. 1.217–18, FOTC 80.76–77.
202. Rv 22.13.
203. 1.219, FOTC 80.77.
204. See J. Trigg, "The Angel of Great Counsel: Christ and the Angelic Hierarchy in Origen's Theology," JTS 42 (1991): 35–51. Trigg argues, 45, that Origen's speculation about Christ's suffering for the salvation of angels "would not imply a separate angelic incarnation, because, for Origen, the Son's union with his pre-existent human soul unites him with angels as well as with human beings; 'thrones,' 'dominions,' and so on indicate levels of acquired status among beings who share the same rational nature."
205. Jn 4.34.
206. 13.237.
207. 13.238–40.
208. 13.241.

## INTRODUCTION

and "forsook 'their own habitation' and 'kept not their own beginning.'"[209]

(87) This discussion of John 4.34 brings out what are perhaps the two most significant points of Origen's thought on the work of Christ in the *Commentary*. (1) The work of Christ is central and essential to salvation, and (2) the work of Christ is for all rational beings, and not for man alone. I shall examine how these two points are developed in the *Commentary*.

(88) There is, for Origen, *no* salvation apart from the work of Christ. "Behold the Lamb of God who takes away the sin of the world,"[210] is a key text for Origen in this regard, appearing several times throughout the *Commentary*.[211] The interpretations given to the verse vary, at least in emphasis, from place to place. The term "world," especially receives different interpretations. First, he says it refers to "the world of the Church."[212] He later questions the adequacy of this understanding on the basis of 1 John 2.1–2 and 1 Timothy 4.10, where Christ is said to be the propitiation for the sins "of the *whole* world," and the Savior "of *all* men" respectively,[213] and, asserts that the Lamb of God takes away the sin, "not of a few, but of the whole world."[214]

(89) Still later, by joining 1 Timothy 4.10 and Hebrews 2.9 with John 1.29, he shows that by "the whole world" he means the totality of rational beings. The person capable of understanding the deeper sense of Christ's death for us, he says, "will make use of the words, 'that by the grace of God (or, apart from God) he might taste death for all,' and he will give attention to the words, 'for all,' and to the words, 'apart from God for all.'"[215] He will also use the statement, 'who is the Savior of all men, especially of the faithful.' And

---

209. 13.243–45.
210. Jn 1.29.
211. See R. J. Daly, "Sacrificial Soteriology: Origen's *Commentary on John* 1, 29" in *Origeniana Secunda*, 151–63.
212. 1.21, FOTC 80.37.
213. 6.304–5, FOTC 80.251–52.
214. 6.284, FOTC 80.245.
215. See our discussion of this verse above in par. 59.

because this is 'the Lamb of God who takes away the sin of the world,' he understands in a particular way the words 'to take away the sin of the world,' and not of a part of it."[216]

(90) This comprehensive understanding of the term "world" in relation to Christ's work is in keeping with Origen's understanding of the work of Christ expressed in other passages. He asserts, for example, on the basis of Hebrews 2.9, that Christ's sacrifice was "not for men alone, but also for every spiritual being."[217] "It would be strange," he says, "to declare that he tasted death for human sins, but not further also for any other creature, in addition to man, which happened to be in sins."[218] He questions why one should think that "those who have been clothed in flesh and blood are able, when they change, to take refuge in God through Christ, but all those who experience a purer nature are incapable of experiencing faith in the Savior."[219]

(91) Yet another emphasis that Origen gives to John 1.29 shows how he conceived the work of Christ to affect all beings both before and after the historical work of Christ in the world. He points out that John does not say he who *will* take away the sin of the world "but is not already also taking it away; and he does not say he who took it away but is not also still taking it away. For the 'taking away' affects each one in the world until sin be removed from all the world and the Savior deliver to the Father a prepared kingdom in which there is no sin at all, a kingdom which permits the Father's rule and again admits all things of God in its whole and total self, when the saying is fulfilled: 'That God may be all in all.'"[220]

---

216. 28.154–55.
217. 1.255, FOTC 80.85–6. The Gnostic document entitled "The Tripartite Tractate," which appears to have had some kind of connection with Heracleon or his school (see my discussion in FOTC 80.23–6), has a similar doctrine about the universal need for redemption. "Not only do humans need redemption," it says, "but also the angels, too, need redemption along with the image and the rest of the Pleroma of the aeons and the wondrous powers of illumination" (Tripartite Tractate I,5 124.25–31; translation in *NHLE*, 92).
218. 1.257, FOTC 80.86; cf. 1.217–19, FOTC 80.76–77.
219. 13.413.
220. 1.234–35, FOTC 80.81.

INTRODUCTION 45

(92) What Origen took this perpetual "taking away" of the sins of the world to mean in relation to mankind is best shown in the following passage. On the basis of Hebrews 6.6, which speaks of Christ being crucified again by those who forsake the faith, to which he joins the statement, "Now I am about to be crucified again," from *The Acts of Paul*, he argues that "Now I am about to be crucified" could as well be said "before the sojourn, when the same causes are present. For why," Origen asks, "was he not also crucified previously, as he is about to be crucified 'again'?"[221] "The spiritual economy (οἰκονομία, that is, the Passion of Jesus) related to Jesus has always been present with the saints."[222] Here he has spiritualized and universalized the death of Jesus for the sins of the world. In a later passage, however, he seems to attribute a retrospective power to the Crucifixion of Jesus when he identifies the patriarchs and prophets and "other elect people of God who had previously died" with the "scattered children of God" for whom Jesus was about to die.[223]

(93) The death of Jesus, as we shall see more specifically in the following paragraphs, is always central to Origen's understanding of the taking away of the sin of the world in the *Commentary*. Sometimes he treats it as a symbol, as in the passages discussed above,[224] at other times he speaks of its historical occurrence, as when he refers to the holy and saving visit to the world of the one "who was crucified in the time of Pontius Pilate."[225]

(94) Origen notes that "the ways of that Lamb who takes away the sin of the world, *beginning with his own slaughter*, are many."[226] What he means by the "many" ways of the Lamb, however, are not alternative means of taking away sin in addition to the death of the Lamb, but the various ways in which different people are brought to faith in the Lamb, and, consequently, have their sins removed. Specifically, he means that some people have to experience various kinds of scourging by evil spirits or diseases because of the excessive

---

221 20.91–92.
222 20.94; cf. 2.209, FOTC 80.151; 6.15–24, FOTC 80.172–74; 19.28.
223 28.183–84.      224 20.90–94.
225 32.191.         226 6.298, FOTC 80.249.

extent to which they have given themselves over to sin, whereas others may not need such painful chastisement.[227]

(95) It was solely to take away sin that the Christ came into the world and died. "If . . . the woman had not been deceived and Adam had not fallen into sin, . . . he would have neither descended 'into the dust of death' nor died since there would have been no sin for which he had to die because of his love for men."[228] His death is "distributed like a drug" to all against the adverse influences of sin.[229]

(96) All the major early Christian theories of the atonement are present in the *Commentary*. Jesus' death was a *victory over the devil* and the forces of the demonic realm. Lucifer is "crushed by Jesus" on the battlefield of the earth.[230] The Savior "humbled the denouncer by humbling himself."[231] He "supplanted the activity of the adversary."[232] "The death of Christ has made the powers which war against the human race ineffectual."[233] Jesus "alone has despoiled the principalities and powers and exposed them publicly, and has triumphed over them on the tree, having set the cross as a sign of victory against every opposing power."[234] When Jesus beheld Satan enter Judas at the last supper, "he stripped down for the fight, and in order to prevail against the wicked one for the salvation of men, he said, 'What you do, do quickly.'"[235]

(97) Christ's death is also viewed as a *ransom*, necessitated because we sold ourselves. "In accordance with the Father's love for man," Jesus "submitted to slaughter on behalf of the world, purchasing us with his own blood from him who bought us when we had sold ourselves to sins."[236]

(98) Finally, Christ's death is presented as a *substitution*. Origen alludes to the stories of Greeks and barbarians which tell of such things as plagues or famines being ended

---

227. 6.297–300, FOTC 80.249–50.
228. 1.121, FOTC 80.58–59.
229. 1.233, FOTC 80.80; cf. 1.227, FOTC 80.78–79.
230. 1.78, FOTC 80.49.  231. 6.287, FOTC 80.246.
232. 1.260, FOTC 80.86.  233. 1.233, FOTC 80.80.
234. 20.330; cf. 32.327.
236. 6.274, FOTC 80.242.  235. 32.299.

"because someone gives himself for the common good."[237] But, he says, "never yet has a story been told of one who was able to take responsibility for purification on behalf of the whole universe.... Nor can such a story be told, since Jesus alone has been able to take up into himself on the cross the burden of the sin of all on behalf of the whole universe apart from God, and to bear it in his great strength."[238]

(99) Origen understands this "taking up all the sin of the whole universe into himself,"[239] and his conquest of the demonic forces to have defiled the Christ in some way so that he, in turn, needed to be cleansed after the Crucifixion.[240] He quotes 2 Corinthians 5.21, and then comments that "He made him to be sin who did not know sin, so that he who had sinned in no respect has taken up the sins of all, even if one must dare to say that he ... has become the refuse of the world and the offscouring of all."[241] It is for this same reason, Origen asserts, that it can be said only of the Father, "There is no darkness in him." This cannot be said of the Christ "if 'him who knew no sin he made sin on behalf of us.' ... For if Jesus condemned sin 'in the likeness of sinful flesh' by taking up the likeness of sinful flesh, it will no longer be completely accurate to say of him, 'There is no darkness in him.' And we will add that 'He himself took our infirmities and bore our diseases.' ... Because of these infirmities and diseases, which he removed from us, he confesses

237. 28.162.
238. 28.163; cf. 6.284, FOTC 80.245; 32.354.
239. 28.160.
240. There is a certain similarity here with Gnostic views, though not in the form of the concept of the "redeemed redeemer" put forward by Reitzenstein on the basis of Manichean texts. For a summary of Reitzenstein's views, along with the concept as it appears in various Gnostic texts see K. Rudolf, *Gnosis*, tr. R. M. Wilson (San Francisco: Harper & Row, 1983), 121–31. The latter notes that the basic idea is not foreign to Gnostic traditions, and that many statements in Gnostic texts "only become comprehensible when we start from this [concept]" (ibid., 121–22). The most significant parallel for our purposes noted by Rudolf comes from The Tripartite Tractate (see note 217 above). The text reads, "Even the Son himself ... needed redemption as well—he who had become man—when he gave himself for each thing which we need" (I,5 124.32–125.2; translation in NHLE, 92).
241. 28.161.

that his soul is sorrowful and troubled. It is recorded in Zacharias that he has put on filthy garments which are said to be sins when he is about to remove them."[242]

(100) By a collage of skillfully arranged Biblical texts and images, which reads almost like a liturgy of the Ascension, Origen shows that this cleansing of the Christ takes place in a baptism in the heavenly realm. As he ascends, "bearing victory and trophies, with the body that arose from the dead, . . . certain powers ask, 'Who is this that is coming from Edom, with scarlet garments from Bosra, so beautiful?' And those escorting him say to those stationed at the gates of heaven, 'Lift up your gates, and the king of glory will come in.'" But "when they see his blood-stained right hand and his whole body filled with the works of prowess," they ask, "'Why is your apparel red and your garments like the residue of a full wine-vat which has been trampled down?'" He answers, "'I have crushed them in pieces.'" Then Origen remarks that this is why "he needed to wash 'his robe in wine, and his garment in the blood of the grape.' For after he took our infirmities and bore our diseases, and after he took away the sin of the whole world, . . . perhaps then he received the baptism which is greater than any which could be imagined by men, concerning which I think he said, 'And I have a baptism with which to be baptized, and how distressed I am until it be accomplished.'"[243]

(101) Origen is aware that this interpretation of the baptism referred to in Luke 12.50 differs from the interpretation of the majority. Most, he asserts, take it to refer to Jesus' martyrdom. He thinks this cannot be correct, however, because Jesus forbids Mary to touch him after his Resurrection. This shows that he was still in need of "the cleansing for his manly deeds" which only the Father could give him.[244] Consequently, because "he needed to wash 'his robe in wine, and his garment in the blood of grapes,'" he went up to the Father, the husbandman of the true vine, that, having

242. 2.163–64, FOTC 80.138–39.
243. 6.288–90, FOTC 80.246–47.
244. 6.287, 291, FOTC 80.246–47.

INTRODUCTION 49

washed there after the ascent to the height when he led captivity captive, he might descend bearing various gifts."[245]

(102) Consequent to his assumption that the work of Christ is central and essential to the salvation of all rational beings, Origen held, on the contrary, that "no rational being whatever possesses blessedness by nature as an inseparable attribute."[246] This relates his doctrine of the work of Christ specifically to his argument with Heracleon.[247] The latter held, according to Origen, that there are some "who are of the same nature with the Father,"[248] and "are suitable for salvation . . . because of their constitution and nature."[249] While Origen is certainly concerned to refute Heracleon's view of salvation inherent in the nature of certain spiritual beings, his doctrine of the work of Christ in the *Commentary* exceeds the boundaries of that debate.

### Doctrine of the Holy Spirit

(103) In the creed-like section of Book 32, after the statements of what one must believe about God and Christ, Origen makes the simple statement, "And one must also believe in the Holy Spirit."[250] The shortness of that statement is appropriate to the little amount of attention that is given to the Holy Spirit in the *Commentary* in comparison to what is said about God and Christ. The concentration on the Father and the Son, largely to the exclusion of the Holy Spirit, was not peculiar to Origen, however, but was common to the theological discussions of that period. The Holy Spirit receives hardly more attention even in the later creed of the council of Nicaea.

(104) In his discussion of John 1.3, "All things were made through him," Origen raises the question of whether or not

---

245. 6.292, FOTC 80.247; cf. 1.250, FOTC 80.84.
246. 2.124, FOTC 80.127; cf. 20.290, 292, 296; 28.179–84.
247. See FOTC 80.23–26, and J. A. Trumbower, "Origen's Exegesis of John 8:19–53: The Struggle with Heracleon over the Idea of Fixed Natures," VC 43 (1989): 138–54.
248. 13.148.
249. 13.294; cf. 13.63–64, 92, 341; 20.287.
250. 32.189.

this assertion includes the Holy Spirit. He presents three possible answers to the question. One may say (1) that the Holy Spirit was made through the Word, or (2) that he was not made through the Word but was unbegotten, or (3) that he has "no distinctive essence different from the Father and the Son." Or, if one holds the latter view he may think that the Son differs from the Father, but that "the Spirit is the same with the Father."[251]

(105) Origen rejects the second and third options because he assumes that of the three hypostases only the Father is unbegotten. His own view is "that the Holy Spirit is the most honored of all things made through the Word, and that he is [first] in rank of all the things which have been made by the Father through Christ."[252] On this basis, therefore, Origen also holds the Holy Spirit to be inferior to the Word, although he notes that some texts in the Bible suggest the opposite.[253] The Spirit needs the Son to minister to his hypostasis, not only in order to exist, but to be wise, rational, just, etc.[254] On the basis of John 16.14, "He will receive from me and will announce it to you," Origen asserts that the Holy Spirit is also instructed by the Son. This leads him to ask if this means, then, that the Spirit knows all that the Son knows from contemplating the Father. He does not, however, answer the question.[255]

(106) It is Isaias 48.16, "And now the Lord has sent me, and his Spirit," along with the assertion in Matthew 12.32 that there is no forgiveness for blasphemy against the Holy Spirit, that cause Origen to think that some texts in the Bible suggest that the Spirit is above the Christ. He responds to the latter text by suggesting that it is not because

---

251. 2.73–74, FOTC 80.113.

252. 2.75, FOTC 80.114. Crouzel's attempt to argue that this passage does not show that Origen regarded the Spirit to be a creature on the basis of the pre-Nicene confusion between the verbs γίγνομαι (to make) and γεννάω (to beget) is not convincing (*Origen*, 202). Origen's question is whether the Spirit belongs to the "all things" in Jn 1.3 which are said to have been made through the Word. Origen surely did not think the "all things" had been generated rather than made.

253. 2.86, FOTC 80.116.   254. 2.76, FOTC 80.114.
255. 2.127, FOTC 80.128.

the Spirit is more honored than the Christ that there is no forgiveness for the one who sins against him, but that it is because pardon for all spiritual beings comes through Christ when they turn from their sins. Those, however, who still, in spite of the great help to the good from the Holy Spirit who is in them, fall away and turn from his counsels reasonably receive no pardon.[256] He offers two possible solutions to the problem presented by the text in Isaias, which suggests that the Son was sent into the world by the Holy Spirit as well as by the Father. The text, he suggests, does not mean that the Holy Spirit excels the Christ in nature. It was because of the Incarnation that the Savior was made less than the Spirit for a period of time, for he was made less even than the angels at that time. The other possible solution is that the activity of freeing the creation from its slavery of corruption actually fell to the Holy Spirit, but he was not adequate for the task, and, therefore, sent the Savior as the only one capable of bearing the conflict, but at the same time promising to join the Savior at the appropriate time, which he did at his baptism, when the Spirit descended in the form of a dove and remained with the Christ.[257]

(107) The Spirit is especially connected with prophecy in the *Commentary*. The Old Testament prophets are referred to as "the servants of the prophetic Spirit," and the Spirit can even properly be referred to as "their Spirit," as when it is said, "the Spirit of Elias and the Spirit of Isaias."[258] This association, however, presented a major problem for Origen in relation to the prophecy of Caiphas about the death of Jesus.[259] He devotes a very long discussion to the problem.[260] He poses various questions, but they all have their center

---

256. 2.79–80, FOTC 80.114–15; cf. 28.124–26.
257. 2.81–85, FOTC 80.115–16; cf. 6.220, FOTC 80.228.
258. 6.3, 68, FOTC 80.168, 187; cf. 6.15, FOTC 80.172. For an interesting discussion of Origen's views on prophecy see G. Hällström, *Charismatic Succession: A Study on Origen's Concept of Prophecy*. Publications of the Finnish Exegetical Society 42 (Helsinki, 1985). Hällström takes only slight notice, however, of Origen's discussion of prophecy in *Jo.* 28 (see ibid., 12).
259. Jn 11.51.    260. 28.98–191.

in the assumed connection between the Holy Spirit and prophecy. Does the fact that someone prophesies mean that that person is a prophet?[261] If someone prophesies, does he prophesy by the Holy Spirit?[262] Can the Holy Spirit be in a sinful soul?[263] If it was not the Holy Spirit, then what sort of spirit prophesied in Caiphas?[264]

(108) He answers the first question with a clear "no." The utterance of a prophecy no more makes one a prophet than doing something related to architecture makes one an architect.[265] The second and third questions are treated together because of their interrelatedness.[266] They too receive a negative answer, but the basis on which he says no contains a problem which Origen seems not to have perceived. It was not the Holy Spirit who prophesied in Caiphas, because "'the Spirit was not yet, because Jesus was not yet glorified.' And if indeed the Spirit was not even in the apostles before Jesus was glorified, how much less was he in Caiphas."[267] The problem Origen does not treat, is how, then, the Spirit spoke through the Old Testament prophets prior to the glorification of Jesus. Finally, he answers the last question by asserting that "evil spirits too can bear witness to Jesus and prophesy of him . . . as that spirit which said, 'We know who you are, the holy one of God.'"[268] Origen concludes his discussion by presenting a defense for the view that the Holy Spirit did speak through Caiphas.[269] He denies that this is his own view, however, and leaves it to the reader to draw his own conclusions about Caiphas' prophecy.[270]

(109) "The Spirit was not yet, because Jesus was not yet glorified,"[271] is an important text for Origen in the last two books of the *Commentary*. We have already seen above how he uses this text to answer the problem posed by Caiphas' prophecy.[272] He considered this verse to mark a transition stage in God's dealings with man. In his discussion of Jesus'

261. 28.98.
262. 28.121.
263. 28.123.
264. 28.187.
265. 28.98–105.
266. 28.106–28.
267. 28.127–28.
268. 28.129.
269. 28.188–91.
270. 28.191.
271. Jn 7.39.
272. 28.127–29.

washing of the disciples' feet, he suggests that this act was preparatory to the indwelling of the Holy Spirit.[273] Their feet were being made beautiful, "since they were about to preach the good things."[274] Jesus chose to wash their feet when "the divine plan (οἰκονομία, that is, the Passion of Jesus) was about to take place."[275] The washing would have been inappropriate prior to this for there would have been no one to cleanse their feet in the interval up to the Passion, nor could it have been done at the time of the Passion for there was not another Jesus who could do it.[276] Nor "was it appropriate after the divine plan (οἰκονομία), for by this time *it was the hour of the Holy Spirit*, which visited the disciples who had become clean and had had their feet washed, and by this time had their feet prepared and made beautiful to preach the good things in the Spirit."[277]

(110) Near the end of the *Commentary*, Origen joins John 7.39 with 1 Corinthians 12.3 to explain why the disciples forsook Jesus in the events leading up to the Crucifixion. "Would that they had wanted to follow the Word and confess him, without being scandalized in him. But they could not yet do this, 'for as yet the Spirit was not, because Jesus was not yet glorified,' and 'no one is able to say Jesus is Lord except in the Holy Spirit.'"[278]

(111) In an earlier discussion of baptism in relation to certain texts in Matthew and Acts, Origen makes the giving of the Spirit consequent to baptism.[279] "The history recorded in the Acts of the Apostles bears witness to my word concerning the fact that the Spirit resided so manifestly at that time in those who were baptized, the water having prepared the way for him in advance in those who approached it genuinely."[280] The Spirit, however, "does not appear in everyone after the water."[281] He makes reference here to his earlier statement that "the benefit of baptism depends on the choice of the one who is baptized. It is a benefit for the one

---

273. 32.75.
274. 32.77.
275. 32.84.
276. 32.85.
277. 32.86.
278. 32.399; cf. 32.128–29.
279. 6.165–69, FOTC 80.215–16; cf. 32.75.
280. 6.167, FOTC 80.216.
281. 6.169, FOTC 80.216.

who repents, but it will result in a more grievous judgment for the one who does not approach baptism in this way."[282]

(112) On the basis of 1 Corinthians 12.4–6, Origen asserts that the function of the Spirit in relation to salvation is that he "supplies the material of the gifts from God to those who are called saints thanks to him and because of participation in him. This material of the gifts . . . is made effective from God; it is administered by Christ; but it subsists in accordance with the Holy Spirit."[283]

(113) It is unfortunate that the *Commentary* ends just short of chapters 14–16 of the Gospel, where we might have expected Origen to have had much more to say about the Holy Spirit on the basis of the Paraclete passages in those chapters.

*Resurrection and Eschatology*

(114) Origen's doctrine of the resurrection and his eschatological views were two of the points on which he was later attacked and pronounced heretical.[284] The attack on the former concerned specifically his views on the resurrection of the flesh.[285] There is no extensive treatment of the subject in the *Commentary*. What Origen says on the subject here falls into three categories. (1) The resurrection of Lazarus, (2) Jesus' own Resurrection, and (3) the general resurrection and judgment.

(115) Origen treats the resurrection of Lazarus[286] in

---

282. 6.165, FOTC 80.215.
283. 2.77–78, FOTC 80.114.
284. J. F. Dechow, "The Heresy Charges Against Origen," in *Origeniana Quarta*, 117–20.
285. See Anathema 10 of the Second Council of Constantinople, and Justinian's *Ep. ad Mennam.* (texts in H. Görgemanns and H. Karpp, *Origenes vier Bücher von den Prinzipien*, Texte zur Forschung 24 [Darmstadt: Wissenschaftliche Buchgesellschaft, 1985], 822–31). For an attempt to reconstruct what Origen taught about the resurrection, see the important article by G. Dorival, "Origène et la résurrection de la chair," in *Origeniana Quarta*, 291–321, and J. F. Dechow, "Origen and Early Christian Pluralism: The Context of his Eschatology," in *Origen of Alexandria: His World and His Legacy*, edd. C. Kannengiesser and W. L. Petersen (Notre Dame, Ind.: University of Notre Dame Press, 1988), 340–52.
286. Jn 11.39–44.

INTRODUCTION 55

Book 28.7–71. He begins with the literal meaning of the verses, and discusses first, how Martha's unbelief hindered the removal of the stone from the tomb.[287] After this, he takes up the problems of where Lazarus' soul had been prior to its restoration to his body, and how Jesus knew that it had been restored so that he could thank the Father for having heard his request even before Lazarus came forth from the tomb.[288]

(116) Origen turns to the anagogical sense of the resurrection of Lazarus at 28.49 and takes it to refer to the restoration of those who have sinned after baptism. Jesus wants these people, he says, who have been restored to life by his prayer to come forth from the tomb and to be released from the bonds with which they have been bound.[289] Origen makes no comments on the general resurrection in his discussion of Lazarus.

(117) The *Commentary* ends before reaching the chapters that deal with the Resurrection of Jesus in the Gospel of John. Nevertheless, there are a few passages, such as John 2.18–22, which afford him the opportunity to discuss the Resurrection of Jesus. While other issues are more important to the discussion of this passage, he does assume a literal resurrection of Jesus "which followed from his Passion on the cross."[290] "As far as the literal meaning is concerned," it was "after the Lord was raised from the dead that the disciples understood that the things said about the temple refer to his Passion and Resurrection, and they recalled that the saying, 'In three days I will raise it up' indicated the Resurrection."[291]

(118) In discussing the plot of the Sanhedrin against Jesus Origen asserts, again at the literal level, "No less did they not permit him [to live], but God raised him up and permitted him [to live]."[292] In other passages, it is important to Origen that it is *God* who raised Jesus. He uses this in one instance to refute the Gnostic claim that the creator God

287. 28.14–22.
288. 28.38–48.
289. 28.54–60.
290. 10.229, FOTC 80.306.
291. 10.298, FOTC 80.322.
292. 28.91.

was different from the Father of Jesus. He quotes Acts 5.30, "The God of our fathers raised Jesus, whom you killed by hanging him on a tree," and argues that the apostles knew "that Jesus had been raised from the dead by no other God than the God of the Fathers."[293] A little later he discusses the relationship between God and Jesus in the Resurrection in an argument against the Monarchians. There he asserts that they bring together 1 Corinthians 15.15, which asserts that *God* raised Christ, and John 2.19, where Christ says of the temple, "*I* will raise it up," to prove that the Father and Son do not differ in number, but are the same in essence and substance, and differ only in aspects. Origen asserts that to answer this error he must quote texts which definitely establish that "the Son is other than the Father."[294] He does not, in fact, quote such texts here, but does state "emphatically" that "*the Father* . . . has raised the Christ from the dead."[295]

(119) There is more material on the subject of the general resurrection in the *Commentary*, but no clear and consistent concept emerges. Origen admits, more or less, that he is not clear on this subject in his own mind. "The mystery of the resurrection," he says, "is great, and difficult for many of us to understand."[296] He knows that Jesus taught "many things about resurrection and judgment,"[297] and he thinks that the Resurrection of Christ "contains the mystery of the resurrection of the whole body of Christ."[298] Like Paul, he speaks of the "newness of life" which follows baptism as resurrection, but also, like Paul, he anticipates a future resurrection.[299] "There both has been a resurrection," he says, "and will be a resurrection, if indeed we were buried with Christ and arose with him."[300] Following 1 Corinthians 13.10, he asserts that "we will be given the perfection of faith in the great resurrection from the dead of the whole body of Jesus, his holy Church."[301] Further, in an argument reminiscent of Irenaeus' dictum, that Christ became what

---

293. 10.219, FOTC 80.303.
294. 10.246, FOTC 80.309.
295. 10.247, FOTC 80.310.
296. 10.233, FOTC 80.306.
297. 20.311–12.
298. 10.229, FOTC 80.306.
299. 10.230–32, FOTC 80.306; cf. 1.181, FOTC 80.70.
300. 10.243, FOTC 80.309.
301. 10.304, FOTC 80.323.

we are that he might make us what he is,[302] and in close dependence on Paul's words in 2 Corinthians 4.10, Origen says that Christ "came down to our mortality, that when he died to sin, we, by bearing about in the body the mortification of Jesus, might be able to receive in due order his life forever and ever after our mortality. For those who always bear Jesus' death about in their bodies will also have the life of Jesus manifested in their bodies."[303]

(120) There is little more than a faint echo of the primitive Christian eschatological views in the *Commentary*. Origen alludes to Jesus' teachings about resurrection, judgment, and the age to come,[304] but in a slightly earlier passage, wonders "if indeed there is a present age and another to come."[305] He certainly did not hold the view of two ages as it appears in the primitive eschatology. In reflecting on the sin against the Holy Spirit which "'has forgiveness neither in this age nor in the one to come,'" he concludes that if "there is no forgiveness in the coming age, neither is there any in *the ages which come after it* as well."[306]

(121) In a similar manner, Origen uses the primitive Christian concept of the second coming of Christ, and suggests that "before the second and more divine sojourn of Christ" either "John or Elias will be made manifest" to present testimony concerning life, the Word, and wisdom. We are left to wonder, however, whether he intended anything like what the early Christians meant by this concept, when he goes on immediately to suggest that "we need to investigate if the testimony of John can serve as a forerunner for each of the aspects of the Christ."[307]

(122) It is the doctrine of ἀποκατάστασις, or the restoration of all rational beings to their initial state of contemplating God, however, that lies behind all of Origen's eschato-

302. *Haer.* 5, Praef.
303. 1.227, FOTC 80.79.
304. 20.311–12.
305. 19.87.
306. 19.88.
307. 2.229, FOTC 80.156–57; cf. 2.224, FOTC 80.155.

logical statements.³⁰⁸ His biblical support for this doctrine is 1 Corinthians 15.25–28, where Christ's work is presented as the subordination of all of God's enemies, including death, until God, finally, is all in all. In discussing the meaning of the word "beginning" in relation to a life of justice, Origen asserts that "its stopping point and goal is in the so-called restoration because no one is left as an enemy then.... For at that time those who have come to God because of the Word which is with him will have the contemplation of God as their only activity."³⁰⁹

(123) It is this process of restoration which is implicit in Origen's allusions to not one age, but *many* ages following the present one in the *Commentary*, for he assumed that the restoration would take many ages. This is also the basis for his question concerning the guest at the wedding banquet without the proper wedding garment. When he is bound and cast into outer darkness, will he "continue always to be bound and in outer darkness," since it does not specify "'for the age,' or 'for the ages'" or will he "be released sometime"?³¹⁰ Since the biblical text says nothing about his future release, Origen chooses not to speculate.³¹¹ What he understood the answer to be, however, is apparent in his assertion, based on the language of the Apocalypse, that "at the end of time an angel flying in mid-air with the gospel will proclaim good news to every nation, since the good Father has not completely forsaken those who have fallen away from him."³¹² Or, again, in his statement that "God's help . . . does not give up even the worst men as hopeless."³¹³

(124) Like Francis Thompson's relentless Hound of Heaven, " . . . with unhurrying chase, and unperturbèd pace,"³¹⁴ God's gracious, "excessive love for man," will con-

---

308. See H. Crouzel, "L'apocatastase chez Origène," *Origeniana Quarta*, 282–90; and Fr.-H. Kettler, "Neue Beobachtungen zur Apokatastasislehre des Origenes," *Origeniana Secunda*, 339–48.
309. 1.91–2, FOTC 80.52; cf. 1. 235, FOTC 80.81.
310. 28.63; cf. 19.88. 311. 28.64–65.
312. 1.83, FOTC 80.50. 313. 20.38.
314. Francis Thompson, "The Hound of Heaven," in *The Pocket Book of Verse*, ed. M. E. Speare (Pocket Books Incorporated, 1959), 308.

INTRODUCTION                                59

tinue to pursue each soul down the ages with chastisement, scourging, or whatever is appropriate, for his ways are many, until all are brought back to God.³¹⁵ This, of course, is a form of universalism, which was one of the points on which Origen was attacked. What was most problematical for his contemporary and later detractors was that this doctrine of the restoration of all rational beings to God appears to include the devil also.³¹⁶

*Doctrine of the Devil*

(125) The text of John's Gospel offered Origen many opportunities to address the subject of the devil.³¹⁷ There is, perhaps, more on this subject in the *Commentary* than in any of his other works. I shall not attempt to follow every trail of Origen's teachings about the devil in the *Commentary*, but shall stay on the main road and concentrate on what he says about the essence of the devil, and what he says that may throw some light on the charge that he believed that the devil would be among those finally saved.

(126) The following Old Testament and apocryphal texts were important to Origen's understanding of the devil,³¹⁸ and, as we shall see, references to at least portions of all of them appear in the *Commentary*: Isaias 14.12–20, Job 40.19, Wisdom 1.13–14, and Ezekiel 28.19.

(127) There is only a brief allusion to the Isaias passage in the *Commentary*, when "'Lucifer, who rises early,'" is said to have fallen "'from heaven.'"³¹⁹ This allusion is significant, nonetheless, because it locates the devil originally in heaven among the immaterial rational beings created by God, and also announces his fall from this state of existence. The sig-

315. 6.298–300, FOTC 80.249–50.
316. See C. C. Richardson, "The Condemnation of Origen," CH 6 (1937): 53–54; C. A. Patrides, "The Salvation of Satan," JHI 28 (1967): 467–69; and E. A. Clark, "New Perspectives on the Origenist Controversy: Human Embodiment and Ascetic Strategies," CH 59 (1990): 161–62.
317. In addition to the articles cited in the previous note, see S. Laeuchli, "Origen's Interpretation of Judas Iscariot," CH 22 (1953): 253–68. Laeuchli discusses many of the passages in the *Commentary on John* that deal with Satan.
318. Cf. *Cels*. 6.43–4; *princ*. 1.5.4–5.
319. 1.78, FOTC 80.49.

nificance of his fall from heaven is brought out a little later by the interpretation of the fall and consequent material creation by means of Job 40.19. Origen considers Job 40.19 to express the meaning of the creation more clearly than Genesis 1.1.

I think what is meant is stated more clearly in Job in the statement, "This is the beginning of the Lord's creation, made to be mocked by his angels." For someone might suppose that "heaven and earth" were made "in the beginning" of those things that happened to exist in the genesis of the world. But it is better to say . . . that of those many beings which have come into existence with bodies, the first of those with bodies was that called a dragon, and named also perhaps "the great sea-monster" which the Lord subdued. And we must raise the question if, while the saints continued to live a completely immaterial and bodiless life in blessedness, he who is called a dragon deserved to be bound to matter and a body before all others because he fell from the pure life, so that this is why the Lord should say . . . "This is the beginning of the work of the Lord, made to be mocked by his angels."[320]

What Origen is alluding to here in the words of Isaias 14.12 and Job 40.19 is his view that it was the devil who was the first rational being to turn away from the contemplation of God, and consequently, was the first to be bound to a body because of this fall, and became "the beginning of the work of the Lord," that is, the work of the creation of the material realm.

(128) In a later passage, which plays between the Genesis story of the fall of Adam and Eve and this more abstract view of the origin of the created order and the evil in it, he asserts, in relation to John 8.44, that the devil "will correctly be called a murderer, not because he killed some particular individual, but because he killed the whole race."[321] The Genesis story, especially as interpreted by Paul in 1 Corinthians 15.22, lies behind this statement, but Origen is not thinking of a temptation and fall of man that occurs on the

---

320. 1.95–97, FOTC 80.53; cf. 20.181–82; 32.233–34.
321. 20.224.

physical earth. It is a murder of "the whole race" that occurs prior to the material creation, for he next asks if everything which exists on "the cursed earth" can be attributed to this murder by the devil, and apart from this would not exist.[322] He does not answer that question directly, but it is apparent that this is his view. He then takes the argument a step further and gives the devil a motive for his murder by combining Wisdom 1.14 with Job 40.19. "But he was a murderer from the beginning of the present things, and, I think, after he had become the 'beginning of what the Lord fashioned,' he envied those who were created 'that they might have being.' In this way 'death entered the world by means of envy.'"[323]

(129) Why should the devil have envied those "who were created 'that they might have being'"? Origen hints at an answer in an earlier book of the *Commentary*. In interpreting John 1.3, "without him nothing was made," he notes that some have thought that "the devil is not a creation of God." Origen replies that "insofar as he is the devil, he is not a creation of God, but to the extent that it falls to the devil 'to be,' being made, since there is no creator except our God, he is a creation of God." He illustrates what he means by the example of a murderer whom one would not say is a creation of God insofar as he is a murderer, but insofar as he is a man, was made by God.[324] In a later discussion he states that it was the devil's own free choice that made him evil. In discussing John 8.44, "You are of your father the devil," Origen notes that some take that verse to mean that the devil has a father, that is, they read, "You are of the father of the devil." He rejects this view and asserts, "Some father did not cause evil to subsist in him," that is, he is not evil because he inherited or was made with an evil essence, but "it was the act of turning away from God that engendered it."[325]

(130) After establishing that the devil has his being from God, but not his evil nature, Origen then suggests the possi-

322. 20.234.
323. 20.234–6.
324. 2.97, FOTC 80.119.
325. 20.284.

bility that some may deprive themselves of being. "All . . . who share in 'being'—and the saints share in it—would properly be called 'those who are.' But *those who have turned away from sharing in 'being'* have, by having deprived themselves of 'being,' become 'those who are not.'"[326] "Not being" is the equivalent of evil in Origen's thought. "Now we said before that 'not being' and 'nothing' are synonyms, and for this reason those 'who are not' are 'nothing,' and all evil is 'nothing,' since it too is 'not being.' And evil, which is called 'nothing' has been made without the Word, not being included in the 'all things.'"[327] Origen has here freed God of the responsibility of creating evil and evil beings. He has also provided a reason for the devil to have "envied those who were created 'that they might have being,'" for he was the first who "turned away from sharing in 'being' and, consequently, became the first of "those 'who are not.'"

(131) Origen takes up a similar theme later in discussing the antichrist, who, he says, is the lie, and whose father is the devil.[328] He notes that some may take offense at his assertion that the antichrist *is* a lie, since that would make a lie his substance and relieve him of guilt because he would be capable of nothing other than lying. Origen solves this problem by appealing to Ezekiel 28.19, the fourth of the Scriptures we mentioned above. "If one compares with this what is said in Ezechiel about one who, because of evil, has changed so he has become destruction, 'You have become destruction, and you shall not exist forever,' he will support in the same way the possibility that someone may be of the lie, not by his substance from creation, but having become such and having been endowed with such a nature, if I may use a novel expression, by change and his own choice."[329]

(132) Although this text is about the antichrist, and not about the devil, nevertheless, the recognition that a being's substance can be altered by its own choice of evil shows, again, how Origen must have conceived of the devil's es-

---

326. 2.98, FOTC 80.120.
328. 20.173.

327. 2.99, FOTC 80.120.
329. 20.174.

sence to have undergone a change as a result of his own choice, and consequently, why he would have "envied those who were created 'that they might have being.'"

(133) This objection, which Origen says *someone* might have to his assertion that the antichrist is a lie because this would relieve him of guilt, is very similar to the objection that he himself raises against Heracleon's view of the devil. Heracleon had asserted that the reason Jesus says some could not hear his word was that they were "'of the essence of the devil.'"[330] Origen maintains that it is clear that Heracleon means "that some men are of the same essence as the devil, being of a different essence than those whom they call psychics or pneumatics."[331] This, Origen thinks, necessitates that Heracleon assumes that "the essence of the devil is another essence over and above the essence of other rational creatures."[332] Origen responds with an emphatic denial of this view. "Now we have frequently said that if this impossibility be allowed (I mean that the devil is of a different essence, and is incapable of experiencing better things), we will construct a defense for him that removes him from all responsibility for his wickedness, and will lay the blame on the one who invested him with being and created him, which is the most absurd thing conceivable."[333] God, therefore, in Origen's perception of Heracleon's view, is responsible for the wickedness of the devil, because he made him such, and the devil himself "is unfortunate rather than blameworthy."[334]

(134) Origen will not permit, therefore, the view that the devil is of a different essence from the other rational beings *by creation*, which is what he understood Heracleon to hold. Origen's own view, on the basis of what we have already discussed, is that the devil does indeed have a different essence from that of other rational beings. He was endowed with this different essence, however, not by God in creation, but *by his own choice*. The significance of the distinction for Ori-

330. 20.168.
332. 20.198.
334. 20.254.

331. 20.170; cf. 20.213–19.
333. 20.202.

gen is that on Heracleon's view, God is responsible for the wickedness of the devil, but in his own view the devil himself is responsible.

(135) The question of the restoration of the devil to his original state in the immaterial heavenly realm arises in Origen's discussion of the words in John 13.3, "the Father had given *all things* into his hands." Origen joins the "all" who "will be made alive in Christ" in 1 Corinthians 15.22 with the "all things" given into Christ's hands in John 13.3, and interprets the latter in light of the entirety of 1 Corinthians 15.22–27. This passage, as we noted above,[335] is the biblical basis for Origen's doctrine of the restoration of all things to their original state. He asserts that Jesus' enemies are also a part of the "all things" which are given into his hands.[336]

(136) The fact that Jesus' enemies are included in the "all" who shall be made alive in Christ does not, however, confound "the justice of God . . . nor the fact that each is treated as he deserves."[337] This, Origen thinks, is brought out by the addition of the words, "but each in his own order," in 1 Corinthians 15.23. He thinks these different orders of those "who will be made alive in Christ" are indicated in the words, "'Christ the first fruits, then those who are Christ's in his coming, then the end.'"[338] The end, he asserts on the basis of 1 Corinthians 15.24, will be present after Christ has destroyed "every principality and every authority and power." Origen understands these principalities and powers to be the hostile spiritual powers with which we must wrestle in this life.[339]

(137) After he has established that all hostile powers will be finally subjected to Christ, he turns explicitly to the question of the devil. "But if all things have been subjected, . . . then he too, of whom it is written, 'he exalted himself before the Lord almighty,' will belong to those things subject-

335. See paragraph 122.
336. 32.27.
337. 32.28.
338. 32.29.
339. 13.29.

ed to him, having been conquered, so that he yields to the Word, is subjected to the image of God, and becomes Christ's footstool."[340]

(138) The conclusion that Origen included the devil among those who would be restored is unavoidable on the basis of this text, though Origen would probably not have approved of this way of stating it. Given his argument above[341] concerning the distinction between the devil as a being created by God, and the devil as wicked on the basis of his own choice, he may have argued that insofar as he is the devil, he is destroyed, as are also all the other evil powers, but insofar as he has being, that being, properly changed through ages of disciplinary chastisement in which he is "treated as he deserves,"[342] will finally be restored to its original state.[343]

340. 32.33.
342. 32.28.

341. See paragraph 129.
343. Cf. 32.35–39.

# COMMENTARY ON THE GOSPEL OF JOHN BOOKS 13, 19, 20, 28, AND 32

## BOOK THIRTEEN

PERHAPS IT MIGHT seem to you, most pious and reverent Ambrose, that the account concerning the Samaritan woman ought not to have been broken off so that part of it is in the twelfth volume and the rest in the thirteenth.

(2) But when we saw that the twelfth volume of our explanations had reached a suitable stopping point, we thought it good to stop at the Samaritan woman's account of the well that she mentions—how Jacob gave it, and how he himself and his sons and his livestock drank from it[1]—that we might begin the thirteenth volume with our Lord's answer to her.

> Jesus answered and said to her, Everyone who drinks of this water will thirst again; but whoever drinks of the water that I shall give him, it will become in him a fountain of water springing up into eternal life.
> (John 4.13–14)

### *"Ask and You Shall Receive"*

(3) This is Jesus' second answer to the Samaritan woman. Earlier he said, "If you knew the gift of God and who he is who says to you, Give me a drink, you would have asked him and he would have given you living water."[2] And now, as if to urge her to ask for the living water, he speaks these words.

(4) The Samaritan woman did not respond to his first answer, but raised a question concerning the comparison of the waters. After the Lord's second answer however, when

---

1. Cf. Jn 4.12.
2. Jn 4.10.

she has accepted what he said, she replies, "Give me this water."[3]

(5) It may, perhaps be a dogma of some kind that no one receives a divine gift who does not request it.[4] The Father, indeed, through the Psalm, urges the Savior himself to ask that it may be given to him, as the Son himself teaches us when he says, "The Lord said to me, You are my son, ask from me and I will give you the Gentiles as your inheritance and the ends of the earth as your possession."[5] And the Savior says, "Ask and it will be given to you,"[6] "for everyone who asks receives."[7]

(6) When, however, the Samaritan woman hears about the comparison of the two waters, she is persuaded to ask Jesus for water,[8] being, as we said before, a representation of the opinion of the heterodox who busy themselves concerning the divine Scriptures.

(7) And consider, on the basis of her experiences, how she was not refreshed nor relieved of thirst, although she drank from the well that she supposed to be deep.

*The Meanings of "To Thirst" and "To Hunger"*

(8) Let us see, then, what is meant by the saying, "Everyone who drinks of this water will thirst again." Now it is possible for the words "to thirst" and "to hunger" to have two meanings in the literal sense. One is related to our need for food when we have wasted away and yearn for it because the liquid in us is failing. The other is related to the fact that those who are poor and in need of provisions frequently say that they are hungry or thirsty, although they have eaten to the full.

(9) There is proof of the first meaning in Exodus. When they had been without food, "on the nineteenth day in the second month after they came out of the land of Egypt, all the congregation of the children of Israel murmured against Moses and Aaron. And the children of Israel said to

3. Jn 4.15.
5. Cf. Ps 2.7–8.
7. Mt 7.8.
4. Cf. Mt 7.7.
6. Mt 7.7.
8. Cf. Jn 4.15.

them, Would that we had died, smitten by the Lord in the land of Egypt, when we sat over flesh pots and ate bread to the full, because you brought us out into this desert to destroy this whole congregation by famine. And the Lord said to Moses, Behold I am going to rain bread from heaven for you, and the people shall go out and gather a day's supply daily, that I may test them, whether they will walk in my law or not."[9]

(10) For these are[10] their words when they hunger and lack the necessary food. But also when they lacked water and thirsted, they murmured against Moses, "What are we going to drink?"[11] It was at this time that "Moses cried to the Lord and the Lord showed him a tree, and he threw it into the water and the water was sweetened."[12]

(11) And a little later it is written that when he came into Raphidim, "the people there thirsted for water, and the people there murmured against Moses."[13]

(12) Now, there will appear to be an example of the second meaning in Paul, when he says, "Even to this hour we hunger, thirst and are naked."[14] The first hungering and thirsting, therefore, comes of necessity to sound bodies; but the second befalls those who have suffered.

(13) One must also investigate, therefore, what is meant by "will thirst" in the statement, "Everyone who drinks of this water will thirst again."

First, as in the case of physical thirst or even . . .[15] perhaps what is meant is that even if one be filled for the present, immediately after the drink has been swallowed, the one who drinks will experience the same sensation, that is, he will thirst again having returned to the same condition he was in at the beginning.

(14) Therefore, he adds the statement, "But whoever drinks of the water that I shall give him, it will become in

9. Cf. Ex 16.1–4.
10. Accepting Brooke's emendation.
11. Ex 15.24.   12. Ex 15.25.
13. Cf. Ex 17.3.   14. 1 Cor 4.11.
15. Preuschen thinks some words have been lost here. Brooke deletes "or even" as dittography.

him a fountain of water springing up into eternal life." And who will be able to thirst when he has a fountain in himself?

### The Water That Christ Gives

(15) What is meant in the first place, however, would be something like this: He who partakes, he says, of the [supposed] profundity of doctrines, even if he is satisfied for a little while and accepts the ideas that are drawn out and that he thinks he has discovered to be most profound, will, however, when he has reconsidered them, raise new questions about these ideas with which he was [once] satisfied [since] what he thought was profound cannot provide a clear and distinct apprehension of the things investigated.

(16) Wherefore, even if someone should be convinced by what is said and agree, he will find later, nevertheless, that he has the same deficiency that he had before he learned these things. But I have teaching[16] that is such that it becomes a fountain of living water in the one who has received what I have declared. And he who has received of my water will receive so great a benefit that a fountain capable of discovering everything that is investigated will gush forth within him. The waters will leap upward; his understanding will spring up and fly as swiftly as possible in accordance with this briskly flowing water, the springing and leaping itself carrying him to that higher life which is eternal.

(17) He says that eternal life is the [goal],[17] as it were, of the water that springs up, as indeed Solomon says, when he talks about the bridegroom in the Song of Songs, "Behold he has come leaping upon the mountains, skipping upon the hills."[18]

(18) For, as there, the bridegroom leaps upon souls that are more noble-natured and divine, called mountains, and skips upon the inferior ones called hills, so here the foun-

---

16. λόγος.
17. Accepting the conjecture of Klostermann and Corsini with Blanc. There is a lacuna in the text. Cf. Jn 4.14.
18. Song 2.8. Cf. Origen, *Cant.* 3.11, where he uses Jn 4.14 in one of the interpretations he offers of this verse.

tain that appears in the one who drinks of the water that Jesus gives leaps into eternal life.

(19) And after eternal life, perhaps it will also leap into the Father who is beyond eternal life. For Christ is life;[19] but he who is greater than Christ is greater than life.[20]

(20) When the promise to the one who is blessed because he hungers and thirsts for righteousness is fulfilled, then he who drinks of the water that Jesus will give will have the fountain of water that leaps into eternal life arise within him.

(21) For the Word says, "Blessed are those who hunger and thirst for righteousness because they shall be filled."[21]

(22) And perhaps, since one will need to hunger and thirst for righteousness before he is filled, one must create a hungering and thirsting in order to be filled, that we may say, "As the hart longs for the fountains of water, so my soul longs for you, O God. My soul has thirsted for the strong, living God. When shall I come and appear before the face of God?"[22]

(23) In order that we may thirst, then, it is good to drink first of the fountain of Jacob, not calling it a well like the Samaritan woman. The Savior, at least, does not even now say that the water is from a well as he replies to her statement, but says simply, "Everyone who drinks of this water will thirst again."

(24) But if indeed there were not something useful that resulted from drinking from the fountain, Jesus would not have sat upon the fountain, nor would he have said to the Samaritan woman, "Give me a drink."[23]

(25) One must observe, therefore, that the water was promised to the Samaritan woman when she asked, as if Jesus would supply it from no other source than the fountain, since he says to her, "Go, call your husband and come here."[24]

---

19. Cf. Jn 11.25; 14.6.
21. Mt 5.6.
23. Jn 4.7.

20. Cf. Jn 14.28.
22. Cf. Ps 41.2–3.
24. Jn 4.16.

## The Difference between the Water of the Scriptures and the Water That Jesus Gives

(26) But we shall take note, furthermore, of whether it is possible that the difference between the benefit to those who would associate with and be with the truth itself, and the benefit we are thought to derive from the Scriptures, even if they be accurately understood, is revealed by the fact that the one who drinks from the fountain of Jacob thirsts again, but the one who drinks of the water that Jesus gives possesses a fountain of water within himself which leaps into eternal life.

(27) For indeed, Scripture has not contained some of the more lordly and more divine aspects of the mysteries of God, nor indeed has the human voice and the human tongue contained some, as far as the common understandings of the meanings are concerned. "For there are also many other things that Jesus did, which if they were each written, I suppose not even the world itself would contain the books that would be written."[25]

(28) John is forbidden to write when he is about to record all that the seven thunders said.[26] Paul, too, says that he has heard words that cannot be spoken.[27] These were not words that were not permitted to be spoken by anyone, for angels were permitted to speak them, but not men, "for all things are permitted, but not all things are beneficial."[28]

(29) And he says that "it is not permitted to man to speak" those things that he had heard, "words that cannot be spoken."[29]

(30) Now I think that all of the Scriptures, even when perceived very accurately, are only very elementary rudiments of and very brief introductions to all knowledge.

(31) Consider, therefore, if the fountain of Jacob, from which Jacob once drank but now no longer drinks, and from which his sons also drank but now have a better drink

---

25. Cf. Jn 21.25.
26. Cf. Rv 10.4.
27. Cf. 2 Cor 12.4.
28. Cf. 1 Cor 6.12.
29. Cf. 2 Cor 12.4.

COMMENTARY ON JOHN, BOOK 13

than that, and from which their livestock too have drunk, can mean all Scripture. The water of Jesus, however, is that which is "beyond that which is written."[30]

(32) Now all are not permitted to examine the things that are "beyond that which is written."[31] Unless one has become like them, he may be reproved and hear the word, "Seek not the things that are too high for you, and search not into things beyond your ability."[32]

(33) But if we say that some know that which is beyond what is written, we do not mean that these things can be known to the majority. They are known to John who hears what kind of words were those of the thunders but is not permitted to write them.[33] He understands things but does not write them in order to spare the world, because he thought that not even the world itself could contain the books that could be written.[34]

(34) The "words that cannot be spoken"[35] which Paul has learned are also "beyond that which is written,"[36] if indeed men have spoken the things that have been written. And the things "that eye has not seen" are beyond the things that are written, and the things "that ear has not heard" cannot be written.[37]

(35) The things, too, that have not entered the heart of man are greater than the fountain of Jacob.[38] These things are made manifest from the fountain of water leaping into eternal life to those who no longer have the heart of man, but who are able to say, "But we have the mind of Christ,"[39] "that we may know the things that are given to us by God, which things also we speak, not in the learned words of human wisdom, but in words learned of the Spirit."[40]

(36) And consider if one can call human wisdom not false teachings, but the elementary aspects of the truth, and

30. 1 Cor 4.6.
31. 1 Cor 4.6.
32. Cf. Sir 3.21.
33. Cf. Rv 10.4.
34. Cf. Jn 21.25.
35. 2 Cor 12.4.
36. 1 Cor 4.6.
37. Cf. 1 Cor 2.9.
38. Cf. 1 Cor 2.9.
39. 1 Cor 2.16.
40. 1 Cor 2.12–13.

the things that apply to those who are still men. The things that are learned of the Spirit, on the other hand, are perhaps the fountain of water that leaps into eternal life.

(37) The Scriptures, therefore, are introductions, called the fountain of Jacob. Once they have now been accurately understood, one must go up from them to Jesus, that he may freely give us the fountain of water that leaps into eternal life.

(38) But everyone does not draw water from Jacob's fountain in the same way. For if Jacob and his sons and his livestock drank from it,[41] and the Samaritan woman too comes to it and draws water when she thirsts, perhaps indeed Jacob, with his sons, drank in one way with full knowledge, and his cattle drank in another, both more simply and more beast-like, and the Samaritan woman drank in yet another way than Jacob, his sons and his livestock.

(39) For some who are wise in the Scriptures drink as Jacob and his sons. But others who are simpler and more innocent, the so-called "sheep of Christ,"[42] drink as Jacob's livestock, and others, misunderstanding the Scriptures and maintaining certain irreverent things on the pretext that they have apprehended the Scriptures, drink as the Samaritan woman drank before she believed in Jesus.

The woman says to him, Lord, give me this water that I may not thirst nor come here to draw. (John 4.15)

### The Samaritan Woman Receives the Living Water

(40) This is now the second time the Samaritan woman calls the Savior "Lord." The first time is when she says, "Lord, you have nothing with which to draw and the well is deep,"[43] when she also inquires whence he has the living water, and if he might be greater than Jacob, whom she supposes to be her father. And now she also calls him "Lord"

41. Cf. Jn 4.12.  42. Cf. Jn 10.26.
43. Jn 4.11.

when she asks for some of the water that becomes a spring of water leaping into eternal life in the one who drinks it.[44]

(41) And indeed it is clear that the statement, "You would ask him and he would give you living water,"[45] is true, because when she said, "Give me this water," she received the living water, that she might no longer be at a loss when she thirsted, nor come to the fountain of Jacob to draw water. She could now, apart from Jacob's water, contemplate the truth in a manner that is angelic and beyond man. For the angels have no need of Jacob's fountain that they may drink. Each angel has in himself a fountain of water leaping into eternal life,[46] which has come into existence and been revealed by the Word himself and by Wisdom herself.

(42) It is not possible, however, for one who has not been engaged very diligently in coming to Jacob's fountain and drawing water from it because of his thirst to receive the water that the Word gives, which is different from the water from Jacob's fountain.[47] Consequently, in this respect, most people have a great deficiency in exercising themselves, as it were, for a long time in drawing from the fountain of Jacob.

He says to her, Go, call your husband and come here.
The woman answered and said, I have no husband.
(John 4.16–17)

### The Husbands of the Samaritan Woman

(43) We also said above that the law that rules the soul, to which each one has subjected himself, is the husband.

---

44. Cf. Jn 4.14.  45. Jn 4.10.
46. Jn 4.14.
47. This statement may reflect a Platonic influence. In *Cels.* 6.3, Celsus says that "Plato the son of Ariston points out the truth about the highest good in one of his epistles [Ep. 7.341C] when he says that the highest good cannot at all be expressed in words, but *comes to us by long familiarity* [emphasis mine] and suddenly like a light in the soul kindled by a leaping spark." Origen responds: "When we hear this, we also agree that this is well said" (trans. Chadwick, 317). Cf. Origen, *hom. in Ex.* 7.8 (FOTC 71.313), and H. Koch, 85, 87–88.

But now we shall also cite as evidence for this the Apostle's testimony from the Epistle to the Romans when he says, "Do you not know, brothers (for I speak to those who know the law), that the law has dominion over a man as long as he lives?"[48] Who, in fact, lives?

(44) The law, if we take the use of the term "law" in this clause in common with its use in the following clause.[49] Accordingly, he immediately says, "For the married woman is bound to the law, her husband, while he lives,"[50] as if "her husband while he lives" meant, "Whoever is a husband is law."

(45) Then he says again, "But if her husband die, she is released from the law, the husband,"[51] as if the wife has been released from law when he dies, and she no longer performs the duties of a wife as to a husband.

(46) Then he says, "Therefore, she will be called an adulteress if she be with another man while her husband lives; but if her husband should die, she is free from the law, so that she is not an adulteress if she be with another man."[52]

(47) Now, the law according to the letter has died, and the soul is not an adulteress when it is with another husband, that is, with the law according to the Spirit. But when the husband has died to the wife, perhaps the wife might also be said to have died to the husband, as we consequently understand the statement, "In the same way, my brothers, you also were put to death to the law through the body of Christ, that you might belong to another, who was raised from the dead that we might bring forth fruit to God."[53]

---

48. Rom 7.1. There is no expressed subject for the verb "lives" in the Greek text of Rom 7.1. This allows Origen to treat it as though "the law" were the subject of "lives" as well as the subject of "has dominion over."

49. For this technical meaning of the phrase ἀπὸ κοινοῦ λαμβάνειν, see LSJ, VI.4 under κοινός. Origen is comparing Rom 7.1b and 7.2a. Diodore of Tarsus asks the same question of Rom 7.1 and gives the same answer: "Who lives? The law." K. Staab, *Pauluskommentare aus der griechischen Kirche* (Aschendorff Muenster, 1933), 86.

50. Rom 7.2. Origen's comments show that he read νόμῳ, law, as if it were in apposition to ἀνδρί, husband.

51. Rom 7.2. Here again, Origen appears to read νόμου, law, and ἀνδρός, husband, as if they were in apposition.

52. Rom 7.3.  53. Rom 7.4.

(48) If, then, the husband is to be identified as the law, and the Samaritan woman has a husband because she has subordinated herself to some law on the basis of a misunderstanding of the sound teachings, a law by which each of the heterodox wishes to live, herein the divine Word wishes the heterodox soul to be exposed when she introduces the law that rules her, that, having despised herself as not belonging to a legitimate husband, she might seek another husband. He wants her to belong to another, to the Word who will be raised from the dead, who is not overthrown, nor will he perish, but he remains forever[54] and rules and subordinates all his enemies,[55] for "Christ, having been raised from the dead, dies no more, death no longer has dominion over him. For in that he died, he died to sin once; but in that he lives, he lives to God,"[56] being at his right hand[57] until all his enemies have been made his footstool.[58]

(49) And what more fitting place for the supposed husband of the Samaritan woman to be exposed by Jesus as not her husband than at the fountain of Jacob, if the woman had not on her own denied her husband? For this reason Jesus says to her, "Go, call your husband and come here."

(50) And because she already had, as it were, something of the water that leaps into eternal life[59] since she had said, "Give me this water,"[60] and he does not lie who had promised previously, "You would ask him and he would give you living water,"[61] the woman answered, "I have no husband," having condemned herself on the basis of her association with such a husband.

---

54. Cf. Is 40.8; 1 Pt 1.25.
55. Cf. Ps 8.7; Eph 1.22.
56. Rom 6.9–10.
57. Cf. Heb 10.12.
58. Cf. Ps 109.1.
59. Cf. Jn 4.14.
60. Jn 4.15.
61. Jn 4.10.

> Jesus says to her, Well did you say, I have no husband,
> for you have had five husbands, and he whom you
> now have is not your husband; this you have said truly.
> (John 4.17–18)

(51) I think that every soul that is introduced to the Christian religion through the Scriptures and begins with sense-perceptible things called bodily things,[62] has five husbands. There is a husband related to each of the senses. But after the soul has consorted with the matters perceived by the senses and later wishes to rise above them, urged on to things perceived by the spirit, she may then encounter unsound teaching based on allegorical and spiritual meanings. She then approaches another husband after the five husbands, having given a bill of divorce to the former five, as it were, and having decided to live with this sixth.

### Jesus' Reproof

(52) And we will stay with that husband until Jesus comes and makes us aware of the character of such a husband. But after the Word of the Lord has come and conversed with us, we deny that husband and say, "I have no husband."[63] At this time the Lord also commends us and says, "Well did you say, I have no husband."

(53) But the statement, "This you have said truly," is a reproof, as it were, as though her former statements were not true. Perhaps the statement, "Jews have no dealings with Samaritans,"[64] was not true.

(54) Jesus himself, at least, as we have said previously, has dealings with Samaritans so that he may benefit them also.

(55) And neither is this statement true: "You have nothing with which to draw and the well is deep."[65]

(56) And perhaps this statement is not true, either: "Jacob and his sons and his livestock drank from the well."[66]

---

62. σωματικῶν. This is the term Origen uses of the literal sense of Scripture.
63. Jn 4.17.
64. Jn 4.9.
65. Jn 4.11.
66. Cf. Jn 4.12.

For if Jacob and his sons and his livestock did not drink in like manner with the Samaritan woman, but the Samaritan thinks that she has drunk something that is the equivalent in every way to what Jacob and his sons and livestock drank, it is clear she is lying.[67]

### Heracleon's Interpretation

(57) Let us also see what Heracleon says on these passages. He says that *the [fountain and][68] the life and glory pertaining to it was insipid, temporary, and deficient, for it was physical*. And he thinks he produces proof that it was physical from the fact that *Jacob's cattle drank from it*.[69]

(58) Now we would not object, if he took the knowledge that is in part[70] to be *insipid, temporary, and deficient*, or that which is from the Scriptures in comparison with the words that cannot be spoken, that "it is not permitted to man to speak,"[71] [or] all the present knowledge that is "through a mirror and a riddle"[72] and is set aside when that which is perfect comes. But he would be culpable if he does this to slander the ancient words.

(59) He is not wrong, however, when he says that *the water that the Savior gives is of his spirit and power*.

(60) And he has explained the statement, "But he shall not thirst forever,"[73] as follows with these very words: *For the life he gives is eternal and never perishes, as, indeed, does the first life which comes from the well; the life he gives remains. For the grace and the gift of our Savior is*

---

67. Cf. above, 13.38–39.
68. My addition. Origen's text is obscure here. He uses only the feminine demonstrative pronoun (ἐκείνην), which could conceivably be construed with "life." C. Blanc (SC 222.63) so construes it, rendering it "cette vie." E. Pagels (*Johannine Gospel*, 86) takes it to refer to the Samaritan woman and renders it "her life." Origen uses only the feminine personal pronoun when he says "Jacob's cattle drank from *it*." Here it seems clear that he means the fountain (πηγή) of Jacob. It seems to me that all the feminine pronouns in the words he takes from Heracleon here have reference to the same thing, and the last one seems to me to refer rather clearly to the fountain of Jacob. Origen has earlier identified the fountain of Jacob with the Scriptures (13.30–31) and interprets Heracleon's words as if he too understood the fountain of Jacob in that way. If Pagel's interpretation is correct, it means that Origen has misunderstood Heracleon.
69. Cf. Jn 4.12.
70. Cf. 1 Cor 13.9.
71. 2 Cor 12.4.
72. Cf. 1 Cor 13.12.
73. Cf. Jn 4.14.

not to be taken away, nor is it consumed, nor does it perish, when one partakes of it.

(61) He would be correct when he grants that *the first life perishes* if he meant that life which is according to the letter, when it seeks and discovers the life according to the Spirit by the removal of the veil. But, if he is accusing the ancient words of passing out of existence all together, it is clear that he does this because he does not perceive that those good words contain the shadow of future things.

(62) Now his interpretation of the "leaping water"[74] is not unconvincing. He takes it to refer *to those who partake of that which is richly supplied to them from above and who themselves cause what is supplied to them to gush out for the eternal life of others.*

(63) But he also praises the Samaritan woman *because she demonstrated a faith that was unhesitating and appropriate to her nature, when she had no doubt about what he said to her.*[75]

(64) We too would agree, then, if he were admitting that she had free choice and not hinting that her nature was more excellent. But if he is referring the cause of her consent to her natural state, as something not present in all people, his argument must be refuted.

(65) And I do not know how Heracleon, by taking note of what has not been written, says on the statement, "Give me this water,"[76] that, therefore, *when the Samaritan woman had been pricked a little by his word, she hated henceforth even the place of the so-called living water.*

(66) And furthermore, on the saying, "Give me this water that I may not thirst nor come here to draw,"[77] he says that *the woman says this to show that the water is burdensome, hard to procure, and lacks nourishment.* From what source can he demonstrate that Jacob's water lacks nourishment?

(67) And further, in reference to the clause, "He says to her,"[78] Heracleon says that *it is clear that he is saying something like this: If you wish to receive this water, go call your husband.* Now he thinks that *the one the Savior calls the Samaritan woman's husband is her pleroma, and that by coming to the Savior with him she might be able to acquire power, unity, and union with her pleroma from him.* For Heracleon says that *he did not ask her to summon a physical husband, since indeed he would not have been ignorant of the fact that she did not have a lawful husband.*

---

74. Cf. Jn 4.14.
76. Jn 4.15.
78. Cf. Jn 4.16.
75. See FOTC 80.25–26.
77. Jn 4.15.

## COMMENTARY ON JOHN, BOOK 13

(68) But here he clearly distorts the text when he says that *the Savior said to her, "Call your husband and come here,"*[79] *meaning her consort from the pleroma.* For if this were so, he would have to explain[80] in what manner she must summon her husband that she might come to the Savior with him.

(69) *But since,* as Heracleon says, *she was ignorant of her own husband at the spiritual level, and at the literal level she was ashamed to say that she had an adulterer, and not a husband, will he not issue a vain command who says, "Go, call your husband and come here"?*[81]

(70) Then, on the statement, "You have said truly that you do not have a husband," Heracleon says that *these words were spoken because the Samaritan woman did not have a husband in the world, for her husband was in the aeon.*

(71) We have read: "You have had five husbands," but in Heracleon we have found: *You have had six husbands.*

(72) And he takes the six husbands to mean *all material evil. These were the husbands with whom the Samaritan woman was united and with whom she associated contrary to reason, committing fornication, being insulted, rejected, and forsaken by them.*

(73) But we must reply that if the spiritual [nature] committed fornication, the spiritual [nature] sinned. And if the spiritual [nature] sinned, the spiritual [nature] was not a good tree. For according to the Gospel, "A good tree cannot bear evil fruit."[82]

(74) It is clear that the making of fables is their undoing. But if it is impossible for a good tree to bear evil fruit, and the Samaritan woman was a good tree because she happened to be spiritual, it is fitting to say to him that either her fornication was not sin or she did not commit fornication.

> The woman says to him, Lord, I see that you are a prophet. Our fathers worshipped on this mountain, and you say in Jerusalem is the place to worship.
> (John 4.19-20)

(75) A third time now the Samaritan woman calls our Savior "Lord" when it is related that she made this last statement to him. She does not yet think, however, that he is

---

79. Cf. Jn 4.16.
80. Brooke's reading. Preuschen marks a lacuna.
81. Jn 4.16.
82. Cf. Mt 7.18.

greater than the prophets, or that he is the one of whom the prophets spoke; but only that he is a prophet.

(76) For once her five former husbands were exposed, along with the one who appeared to be her husband after she had forsaken the five, the heterodox view of those continually busy about the Scriptures but incapable of perceiving what the reproving Word from the beginning is, says that he is a prophet, as if he were someone divine and in possession of something higher than what is common to man, but not so great as he was. For this reason she says, "I see that you are a prophet," as though she had opened her eyes and thought it occurred in her vision.

### The Samaritans and the Jews

(77) On the statement, "Our fathers" and what follows,[83] one must understand the disagreement between the Samaritans and the Jews over the place they considered holy. For the Samaritans worship God on the mountain called Garizim, because they consider it to be holy. Moses refers to this mountain in Deuteronomy when he says, "And Moses commanded the people in that day saying, These shall stand on Mount Garizim to bless the people, when you have crossed the Jordan: Simeon, Levi, Juda, Issachar, Joseph, and Benjamin: and these shall stand on mount Hebel to curse: Ruben, Gad, and Aser, Zabulon, Dan, and Nephtali."[84]

(78) Because they think Zion is divine and God's dwelling place, the Jews, on the other hand, think it has been chosen by the Father of all. For this reason they say Solomon built the temple on Zion, and all the Levitical and priestly service is performed there.

(79) As a consequence of these assumptions, each nation has considered its fathers to have worshipped God, but one on this mountain and one on the other.

(80) Even to the present day, if Samaritans and Jews agree to a discussion with one another, each will then object, and the Samaritan will make the speech to the Jew that

---

83. Cf. Jn 4.20.  84. Dt 27.11–13.

is recorded of the woman here, "Our fathers worshipped on this mountain," pointing to Garizim, "but you say in Jerusalem is the place to worship."

(81) But, since the Jews represent those who think sound thoughts (for salvation is from them),[85] but the Samaritans represent the heterodox, consequently the Samaritans deify Garizim, which means "separation" or "division."[86] This separation and division of the ten tribes which were severed from the remaining two occurred in the time of Jeroboam according to the historical account. Jeroboam's name means "judgment of the people."[87] The Jews, on the other hand, deify Zion which means "watchtower."[88] But someone is likely to ask why the blessings in Moses occur on Garizim.

(82) But one must also say on this subject that since the word Garizim means "separation" or "division," one must take "separation" to refer to the time when the people were divided by Jeroboam and the king dwelt in Samaria. And we must take "division" to refer to the blessing, since the wise apply division in an orderly manner to each argument, a procedure necessary to understand the truth.

(83) In as much, then, as the hour mentioned by the Lord has not yet come when they worship the Father neither on this mountain nor in Jerusalem,[89] one must flee the mountain of the Samaritans and worship God on Zion where Jerusalem lies. Christ calls this Jerusalem the city of the great king.[90]

(84) And what else would the city of the great king, the true Jerusalem, be than the Church that is built of living stones? This is the place of the holy priesthood, the place where spiritual sacrifices are offered to God by people who are spiritual and who have understood the spiritual law.[91]

(85) But when the fullness of time is imminent,[92] when one is no longer in the flesh but is in the Spirit, and everyone is no longer still in the type but is in truth, then one

---

85. Cf. Jn 4.22.
86. Cf. Lagarde *OS* 18.24.
87. Cf. Lagarde *OS* 192.19; 169.64.
88. Cf. Lagarde *OS* 198.3.
89. Cf. Jn 4.21.
90. Cf. Mt 5.35.
91. Cf. 1 Pt 2.5; Rom 7.14.
92. Cf. Gal 4.4.

must no longer bring true worship and perfect piety to Jerusalem to be offered. Such a person has been prepared so that he is like those whom God seeks to worship him.

### "The Hour Is Coming"

(86) Twice it is written, "The hour is coming."[93] The first time "and now is" is not added, but the second time the Evangelist says, "But the hour is coming and now is."[94]

(87) And I, at least, think the first means the incorporeal worship that will begin at the time of perfection. The second, however, means, I think, the worship of those being perfected in this life so far as it is possible for human nature to progress.

(88) It is possible, therefore, to worship the Father in spirit and in truth not only when "the hour comes" but also "now is,"[95] even if we are considered to be in Jerusalem because of those who have only reached this point.

(89) When, therefore, "the hour is coming and now is"[96] is written, it is no longer said, "neither in this mountain nor in Jerusalem will you worship the Father,"[97] as it is said where "the hour is coming" has been written without the words "now is."

(90) Still, however, when the Samaritan speaks these words, she holds a false opinion similar to the one expressed about the esteemed well. For in that case she asks, "Are you greater than our father Jacob, who gave us the well and drank from it himself, along with his children and his livestock?"[98] And here she says, "Our fathers worshipped on this mountain."

### Heracleon: The Cause of the Samaritan Woman's Fornication

(91) Now Heracleon comments on these words, that *the Samaritan woman responded properly to what Jesus said to her. For*, he says, *only a prophet knows everything.* This is false in either case, for indeed the angels are able to know such things, and the prophet does not

---

93. Cf. Jn 4.21 and 23.
94. Jn 4.23.
95. Cf. Jn 4.23.
96. Jn 4.23.
97. Jn 4.21.
98. Cf. Jn 4.12.

know everything, "for we know in part and we prophesy in part,"[99] whether we prophesy or know.

(92) And next Heracleon praises the Samaritan woman because *she acted in a manner appropriate to her nature, and neither denied nor explicitly acknowledged her shame.* He says that *after she was persuaded that Jesus was a prophet she questioned him, at the same time revealing the cause of her fornication. She had been ignorant of God and had neglected the service of God and everything essential for her related to life.* In addition, he says, *she had a lowly position*[100] *in life, for otherwise she would not have come to the well that was outside the city.*

(93) I do not know how he thought the cause of her fornication was revealed, or how her ignorance [of God] was the cause of her transgressions and neglect of service to God. He seems to have invented these things at random without any plausible argument.

(94) In addition he says that *because she wants to learn how, by worshipping God in a pleasing manner, she might be delivered from her fornication, she says, "Our fathers worshipped on this mountain," etc.* What he says is very easy to refute. For what is the source of his knowledge that she wishes to learn in what way, having become pleasing to God, she might be delivered from her fornication?

**Jesus says to her, Believe me, woman, the hour is coming when neither on this mountain nor in Jerusalem will you worship the Father. (John 4.21)**

### Heracleon's Understanding of the Mountain

(95) Once Heracleon has seemed to have made a very plausible observation on these words, that is, that *in the case of her former words she was not given the command, "Believe me, woman," but now is,* he then makes his plausible observation turbid by saying that *the mountain means the devil or his world since,* he says, *the devil was one part of the whole material order. The world, however, is the whole mountain of evil, a deserted dwelling of beasts, which the Gentiles and all who preceded the law used to worship. Jerusalem,* he thinks, *is the creation or the creator, which the Jews used to worship.*

(96) But he also gave "mountain" a second meaning. He took it

---

99. 1 Cor 13.9.
100. Accepting Wendland's suggestion to read ταπεινήν in place of ἀεὶ τήν, which Preuschen marks as corrupt.

to be *the creation which the Gentiles used to worship*,[101] and Jerusalem to be *the creator whom the Jews served.*

(97) *You, therefore,* he says, as if addressing the spiritual, *will worship neither the creation nor the creator, but the Father of truth. And he includes the Samaritan woman with these,* Heracleon says, *because he thinks she is already faithful and numbered with those who worship according to truth.*[102]

### The Worship of the Perfect

(98) We, on the other hand, understand the phrase, "neither on this mountain," to mean the piety expressed by the heterodox in their fantasy of Gnostic and supposedly lofty doctrines. And we take the words, "Nor will you worship the Father in Jerusalem," to refer to the Church's rule of faith[103] so far as most people are concerned. The one who is perfect and holy will go beyond even this as he worships the Father in a way that is more contemplative, clearer, and more divine.

(99) For just as the angels (as even the Jews would agree) do not worship the Father in Jerusalem because they worship the Father in a better way than those in Jerusalem, so those who can already be like the angels[104] in their attitude will not worship the Father in Jerusalem but in a better way than those in Jerusalem, even if, because of those in Jerusalem, they accommodate themselves to those in Jerusalem by becoming Jews to the Jews that they may gain Jews.[105] But let me understand Jerusalem as we explained previously and likewise also the Jews.

(100) When, however, someone worships neither on this mountain nor in Jerusalem, once the hour has come he worships the Father boldly because he has become a son. Therefore it is not said, "neither in Jerusalem will you worship God," but "neither in Jerusalem will you worship the Father."

101. Cf. Rom 1.25.
102. Cf. Jn 4.23.
103. κανόνα.
104. Cf. Lk 20.36.
105. Cf. 1 Cor 9.20.

You worship what you do not know; but we
worship what we know, because salvation is from
the Jews. (John 4.22)

*The Meaning of "You"*

(101) The "you," taken literally, means the Samaritans, but in the anagogical sense it means those who are heterodox concerning the Scriptures. And the "we," according to the letter means the Jews, but taken allegorically means I, the Word, and those formed in accordance with me, who have salvation from Jewish words. For the mystery now revealed has been revealed both through the prophetic Scriptures and the appearance of our Lord Jesus Christ.[106]

(102) But see if Heracleon did not take the word "you" in a way that is peculiar and contrary to the natural sequence of the words, and interpret the *"you" to mean "the Jews [and the] Gentiles."*

(103) Now, can it be said to the Samaritan woman, "You Jews," or to a Samaritan woman, "You Gentiles"? The heterodox, however, do not know what they worship because it is something they have made up, and not truth; it is a myth and [not] a mystery. But he who worships the Creator, especially in accordance with the inward Jew[107] and the spiritual Jewish words, worships what he knows.

(104) It is too much now to quote the words of Heracleon that are taken from the book entitled "The Preaching of Peter," and to take a stand about those words. We would also have to examine that little book to see if it is genuine at all, or spurious, or a mixture. Consequently, we intentionally put this off, noting only that Heracleon cites the following words as though they were Peter's teaching: *We must not worship as the Gentiles do, for they accept material things and serve wood and stones, nor must we worship God as the Jews do, since they too, although they think that they alone know God, are ignorant of him, and serve angels, the month, and the moon.*

(105) We must ask, however, in our concern for the truth, how this bodily form of worship arose among the Jews, for it is clear that it was ordained that they offer sacrifices to the Creator of the universe.

---

106. Cf. 2 Tm 1.10.   107. Cf. Rom 2.29.

(106) On the other hand, it is worth noting what has been written in the Acts of the Apostles: "But God turned away and gave them up to serve the host of heaven."[108] And since the Savior declares in a straightforward manner that "salvation is from the Jews," I do not understand how the heterodox deny the God of Abraham, Isaac, and Jacob, the fathers of the Jews.

(107) In addition, if the Savior fulfills the law,[109] and certain things occur in the Lord's sojourn so that what was written in the prophets might be fulfilled, is it not clear how "salvation" comes "from the Jews"?

(108) For Jews and Gentiles have the same God "since it is one God who justifies the circumcision by faith and the uncircumcision through faith."[110] For we do not abolish the law through faith. To the contrary, we establish it through faith.

> But the hour is coming and now is when the true worshippers will worship the Father in spirit and truth.
> (John 4.23)

### The True Worshippers of God

(109) Those who do not profess to worship the Father at all must not be counted among the worshippers of God. But [if], of the total number who profess to worship the Creator, there are some who are no longer in flesh but in spirit, because they walk in the spirit and do not fulfill the desire of the flesh,[111] and there are others who are not in spirit but in flesh and wage war according to the flesh,[112] then one must say that those who worship the Father in spirit and not in flesh, in truth and not in types, are the true worshippers, and that those who do not so worship are not true worshippers.

(110) Now the person who is enslaved to the letter that kills[113] and has not partaken of the spirit that makes alive,

---

108. Acts 7.42.
110. Cf. Rom 3.30.
112. Cf. 2 Cor 10.3.
109. Cf. Mt 5.17.
111. Cf. Gal 5.16.
113. 2 Cor 3.6.

COMMENTARY ON JOHN, BOOK 13        91

and who does not follow the spiritual meanings of the law would be the one who is not a true worshipper and does not worship the Father in spirit. Whenever this same person thinks he has completely attained his goal, because he belongs totally to the typological and literal level of understanding, he then worships God in type and not in truth. For this reason he cannot be called a true worshipper.

(111) [But] perhaps it has been recorded at some time or other with good reason that even the true worshipper who worships in spirit and truth performs certain symbolic acts so that, by acting in a most accommodating manner, he might free those who are enslaved to the symbol and bring them to the truth that the symbols represent. Paul appears to have done this in the case of Timothy, and perhaps also in Cenchria and Jerusalem, as it is written in the Acts of the Apostles.[114]

(112) One must also observe that the true worshippers worship the Father in spirit and truth not only in the coming hour but also in the present. But those who worship in spirit, since they worship as they have received, worship at present in the pledge of the Spirit.[115] But[116] when they shall receive the Spirit in his fullness, they will worship the Father in spirit.

(113) Now, if the one who sees through a mirror[117] does not see the truth, as those skillful with mirrors demonstrate with their reflected images, and Paul and his companions now see through a mirror, it is clear that [if] he worships God as he sees, then he also worships God through a mirror. But whenever the hour that is to begin after the present hour comes, then worship will be in truth which is contemplated "face to face" and no longer through a mirror.[118]

(114) Heracleon thinks, however, that *the expression "we worship"*[119] *means the one who is in the aeon and those who have come with him, for these,* he says, *have known whom they worship, because they worship in truth.*

114. Cf. Acts 16.3; 18.18–22.   115. Cf. 2 Cor 5.5.
116. Accepting Brooke's text.     117. Cf. 1 Cor 13.12.
118. Cf. 1 Cor 13.12.             119. Jn 4.22.

(115) He also asserts that *the statement, "Because salvation is of the Jews,"*[120] *(but not among them, for he did not find pleasure in all of them) was made because he was born in Judea and because salvation and the Word proceeded from that nation into the world.* Furthermore, at the spiritual level of understanding, he explains that *salvation has come about from the Jews since he considers them to be images of those in the Pleroma.*

(116) But he, and those who agree with him, must show how each member of the cult is an image of those in the Pleroma, if indeed this is what they truly think and not merely what they say.

(117) In addition, when Heracleon explains the saying that "God is worshipped in spirit and in truth," he says that *the former worshippers, worshipping in a fleshly and erroneous manner, worshipped him who was not the Father.* Consequently, in his opinion, *all who have worshipped the Creator have erred.*

(118) And Heracleon adds that *they were serving the creature and not the true Creator, who is Christ, since indeed, "all things were made through him, and without him nothing was made."*[121]

## For the Father also seeks such to worship him.
## (John 4.23)

(119) If the Father seeks those whom he prepares to be true worshippers by purifying them and instructing them in the word and in sound teachings, he seeks them through the Son who came to seek and save the lost.[122]

(120) Heracleon says, however, that *that which belongs to the Father has been lost in deep erroneous matter and is being sought so that the Father may be worshipped by his own.*

(121) If he were referring to the story about the lost sheep and the son who fell away from his father's ways, we too would accept his explanation.

---

120. Jn 4.22.
121. Cf. Jn 1.3. Cf. Origen's citation of Heracleon's understanding of Jn 1.3 in *Jo.* 2.100–104, and my note 135 there (FOTC 80.120–122). "Who is Christ" must be Origen's comment. Heracleon, in the passage referred to in Book 2, identifies the true Creator to be the Logos, who used the Creator of the OT, considered to be an inferior being, as his agent in the creation.
122. Cf. Lk 19.10; Ez 34.16.

(122) But since those who share his view fashion myths and present nothing I can make out with clarity about the lost spiritual nature, and teach us nothing clear about the times and aeons before its loss (for they are not even able to explain their own story), we will intentionally disregard them, since we have raised so great a problem.

> God is spirit and those who worship him must worship in spirit and in truth. (John 4.24)

### God's Essence

(123) Many have produced lengthy discussions of God and his essence. Some have even said that he has a bodily nature which is composed of fine particles and is like ether. Others have said that he is incorporeal and is of a different essence which transcends bodies in dignity and power. For this reason it is worthwhile for us to see if we have resources from the divine Scriptures to say something about God's essence.

(124) In this passage it is stated as if his essence were spirit, for it says, "God is spirit."[123] But in the law, it is stated as if his essence were fire, for it is written, "Our God is a consuming fire."[124] In John, however, it is stated as if he were light, for John says, "God is light, and there is no darkness in him."[125]

(125) If, then, we should listen to these words literally, making no inquiry beyond the letter, we would have to say

---

123. In paragraphs 123–30 Origen is polemicizing generally against the Stoics, and those in the Church, such as Tertullian (*Prax.* 7) who held a Stoic view of God. This is quite explicit in his similar arguments in *Cels.* 6.70–71 and 1.21. Cf. also *princ.* 1.1.1–9. The Stoics spoke of God as ether (Cicero, *N.D.* I.14–15), and also as fire (Eusebius, *p.e.* 15.16, quoting Porphyry). They had taken the concept of ether from Aristotle, his fifth element which was the divine element, and used it for the celestial fire (See A. A. Long and D. N. Sedley, *The Hellenistic Philosophers* I [Cambridge: University Press, 1987], 286–87).

124. Heb 12.29; cf. Dt 4.24.

125. 1 Jn 1.5. Cf. the discussion in *princ.* 1.1.1–4 where these same Scriptures are cited.

that God is a body. Now, most people are incapable of knowing what absurd things we encounter when we say this, for few have had an understanding concerning the nature of bodies, and especially of bodies fitted out by reason and providence. And yet they assert as a general definition that the body that provides has the same essence as those that have been provided. The body that provides is perfect, but nevertheless it resembles that which has been provided. Those who wish God to be a body accept the absurd conclusions that present themselves to their argument because they are incapable of opposing those arguments that reason clearly presents.

(126) But I make the following remarks as a refutation of those who say there is a fifth nature of bodies in addition to the [four] elements.[126]

(127) If every material body has a nature that is without quality[127] in its characteristic disposition, and is mutable and subject to variation and change in general, and contains whatever qualities the Creator may wish to bestow on it, God too, if he is material, must be mutable and subject to variation and change.

(128) Those who hold this view are not ashamed to say that since God is a body he is also subject to corruption, but they say his body is spiritual and like ether, especially in the reasoning capacity of his soul. Furthermore, they say that although God is subject to corruption he is not corrupted, because no one exists who might corrupt him.

(129) But because we do not see the consequences if we attribute a body to God when we say, even on the basis of Scripture, that he is some such body as spirit, or consuming fire, or light,[128] unless we accept the conclusions that neces-

---

126. Cf. Origen, *princ.* 3.6.6; *Cels.* 4.60; Cicero, *Academica* 1.7.26. The reference is to the doctrine, probably found in Aristotle's lost work *On Philosophy*, that there was a fifth element, namely ether, from which the νοῦς (mind) was composed in common with the stars, etc., which were also considered to be divine. See Prestige, *God*, 17.

127. It was a rather common doctrine in Greek philosophy that matter was without quality. See Clement, *str.* 5.14.89.5–6; Albinus, *Epitome* 8.2; Plotinus, *Enneads* 2.4.8.

128. Cf. Heb 12.9; 1 Jn 1.5.

sarily follow these assertions, we will disgrace ourselves as foolish and contradicting the obvious. For every fire is subject to extinction because it needs fuel, and every spirit, even if we take the spirit to be simple, because it is a body, admits of change to what is coarser in its own nature.

(130) In these matters, then, we must either accept so many absurd and blasphemous things about God in preserving the literal meanings, or, as we also do in many other cases, examine and inquire what can be meant when it is said that God is spirit, or fire, or light.[129]

(131) First we must say that just as when we find it written that God has eyes, eyelids, ears, hands, arms, feet, and even wings,[130] we change what is written into an allegory, despising those who bestow on God a form resembling men, and we do this with good reason, so also must we act consistently with our practice in the case of the names mentioned above. Now, this is clear indeed from the following assertion that seems more drastic to us. "For God is light,"[131] according to John, "and there is no darkness in him."

### How God Is Light

(132) Let us consider, as intelligently as we are able, how we should consider God to be light. The term light is used with two meanings, one literal and the other spiritual. The latter is apprehended by the intellect and is invisible, as the Scriptures would say. The Greeks would refer to it as incorporeal.

(133) The statement, "There was light for all the children of Israel wherever they dwelt,"[132] is an acknowledged example of the literal meaning for those who accept the historical narrative. There is an example of the intellectual and spiritual meaning in one of the twelve prophets. "Sow for

---

129. Cf. Heb 12.9; 1 Jn 1.5.
130. Eyes: cf. Ps 5.6, 31.8, 34.16; ears: cf. Jas 5.4, Ps 115.2; hands: cf. Ex 15.6, Dt 33.3, Ps 37.3; arms: cf. Dt 11.2, 3 Kgs 8.42 (Vulg.); Ps 70.18; feet: cf. Mt 5.35, Acts 7.49; wings: cf. Ps 15.8, 25.8, 90.4. Cf. Origen *sel. in Gen.* 25; PG 12.93A-B.
131. Cf. 1 Jn 1.5.          132. Ex 10.23.

yourselves in justice, gather in the fruit of life, enlighten yourselves with the light of knowledge."[133]

(134) Now the expression "darkness" too will likewise be used to refer to two corresponding concepts. The statement, "And God called the light day, and the darkness he called night,"[134] is an example of the more common meaning. An example of the spiritual meaning occurs in the statement, "The people who sat in darkness . . . and in the shadow of death, light has dawned on them."[135]

(135) Since these things are so, it is worthwhile to investigate what we should think about God who is said to be light in which there is no darkness.[136] For is God a light to enlighten the eyes of the body, or the eyes of the intellect? The prophet says of the latter, "Enlighten my eyes lest I sleep in death."[137]

(136) I think it is clear to everyone that we would not say that God performs the work of the sun and assigns to another the task of enlightening the eyes of those who will not sleep in death. God, therefore, enlightens the mind of those whom he judges to be worthy of personal enlightenment.

(137) But if God illuminates the mind according to the statement, "The Lord is my light,"[138] then we must assume that he is apprehended by the intellect, and is invisible and incorporeal, because he is the light of the mind. Perhaps[139] also [when God is said to be] a consuming fire, the author does not suppose that he consumes bodily [material] such as wood, grass, and straw.[140]

### How God Is Fire

(138) If, however, [there is spiritual] wood, grass, and straw, perhaps when our God is said to be a consuming fire,

---

133. Hos 10.12.
134. Gn 1.5.
135. Mt 4.16; cf. Is 9.2. (Vulg.); 9.1 (LXX).
136. Cf. 1 Jn 1.5.
137. Ps 12.4.
138. Ps 26.1.
139. The text of this sentence is corrupt. I have followed Brooke's reconstruction.
140. Cf. 1 Cor 3.12.

it refers to the fire that consumes such matter.[141] It is fitting indeed for the Lord to destroy such things and to obliterate inferior materials. When this happens I think there is suffering and distress, but not from any physical punishment, in the ruling parts of the soul, for it is there that the building worthy of being destroyed exists.

(139) God, therefore, is referred to as light, transferred from literal light into invisible and incorporeal light. He is referred to as light because of his power to enlighten spiritual eyes. Furthermore, he is designated a devouring fire, being understood spiritually, from the fire which is literal and is destructive of such material.

### How God Is Spirit

(140) It seems to me that something similar to this is also meant by the statement "God is spirit." For since we are made alive by the spirit,[142] so far as ordinary life, and what we usually mean by the term life, is concerned, when the spirit that is in us draws what is called, in the literal sense, the breath of life,[143] I suppose it has been understood from this that God, who brings us to the true life, is called spirit. In the Scriptures, the spirit is said to make alive.[144] It is clear that this "making alive" refers not to ordinary life, but to that which is more divine. For the letter also kills[145] and produces death, but it is not death in the sense of the separation of the soul from the body, but death in the sense of the separation of the soul from God, and from the Lord himself, and from the Holy Spirit.

(141) And perhaps [if] we assume that the person who is deprived of the divine Spirit becomes earthly,[146] but when he has made himself fit to receive the divine Spirit and has received it, he will be recreated, and [when he has been renewed] he will be saved, we will also understand the spirit better in this way in the following statements. "You will take

---

141. Cf. Heb 12.29.
143. Cf. Gn 2.7.
145. Cf. 2 Cor 3.6.
142. Cf. Gn 2.7; 2 Cor 3.6.
144. Cf. 2 Cor 3.6.
146. Cf. 1 Cor 15.47–49.

away their spirit and they will fail,"¹⁴⁷ and, "You will send forth your Spirit and they will be created, and you will renew the face of the earth."¹⁴⁸

(142) Now, it would be the same also if we take the statement, "He breathed into his face the breath of life and man became a living soul,"¹⁴⁹ in this way, so that we understand the infusion, and the breath of life, and the life of the soul in a spiritual sense.

(143) And we must suppose that the statement, "I will dwell in them and walk in them, and I will be their God, and they shall be my people,"¹⁵⁰ has been written because the previously mentioned power entrusts itself to the abode in the soul, if I may put it this way, once it has found the soul of the saint to be a fit dwelling place, as it were.

(144) We need more training, however, that, having been perfected and [having] our senses exercised [in accordance with] what the Apostle says, we might become capable of discerning things good and evil,¹⁵¹ and true and false, and capable of perceiving things that belong to the spiritual order, that we may be able more attentively and in a way more worthy of God to understand how God is light and fire and spirit, so far as this is humanly possible.

(145) In the Third Book of Kings, the Spirit of the Lord, who came to Elias, makes the following suggestions concerning God: "For he said, You shall go out tomorrow and stand before the Lord on the mountain: behold, the Lord will pass by and a great and strong wind¹⁵² destroying mountains and crushing rocks before the Lord. The Lord is not in the wind (but in others we find: "in the spirit of the Lord"). After the wind, an earthquake; the Lord is not in the earthquake. And after the earthquake, a fire; the Lord is not in the fire, and after the fire, the sound of a gentle breeze."¹⁵³ Perhaps, indeed, these words reveal how many must experi-

---

147. Ps 103.29.   148. Ps 103.30.
149. Gn 2.7.
150. Cf. 2 Cor 6.16; Lv 26.12; Ez 37.27.
151. Cf. Heb 5.14.
152. πνεῦμα, which means wind, as well as spirit.
153. Cf. 3 Kgs 19.11–12.

ence the fire of the direct apprehension of the Lord. This would not be the right time to explain these matters.

(146) But who could more properly speak to us about who God is than the Son? "For no one has known the Father except the Son."[154] We too aspire to know how God is spirit as the Son reveals it, and to worship God in the spirit that gives life and not in the letter that kills.[155] We want to honor God in truth and no longer in types, shadows, and examples,[156] even as the angels do not serve God in examples and the shadow of heavenly realities, but in realities that belong to the spiritual and heavenly order, having a high priest of the order of Melchisedech[157] as leader of the saving worship for those who need both the mystical and secret contemplation.

(147) On the statement, "God is spirit," Heracleon comments *"For his divine nature is undefiled, and pure, and invisible."*

(148) I doubt, however, that these words come from Heracleon since he says in addition how God is spirit when he intends to explain the statement, "those who worship must worship in spirit and in truth." His words are: *"[This statement is] worthy of one who is worshipped in a spiritual manner, and not in a fleshly manner. For those who are of the same nature with the Father are themselves also spirit, and worship in truth and not in error, as also the Apostle teaches when he says that such worship is rational service."*[158]

(149) But let us consider if it is not exceedingly impious to say that those who worship God in spirit are of the same substance with his unbegotten and all-blessed nature. Heracleon himself said previously that *those natures had fallen away when he said the Samaritan woman, who is of a spiritual nature, had committed fornication.*

(150) Now they do not see that everything [which is of the same substance is][159] also capable of the same things. And if the spiritual nature, which is of the same substance [with the divine nature],[160] was capable of committing fornication, it is dangerous

154. Cf. Mt 11.27.
156. Cf. Heb 8.5.
158. Cf. Rom 12.1.

155. Cf. 2 Cor 3.6.
157. Cf. Heb 5.6; Ps 109.4.

159. Following Preuschen's reconstruction. There is a lacuna in the text, and part of the text that is present seems to be corrupt.
160. Preuschen's suggestion for the lacuna.

even to imagine [how many][161] unholy, godless, and impious things follow for the doctrine of God so far as they are concerned.

### The Pre-eminence of the Father

(151) But we are obedient to the Savior who says, "The Father who sent me is greater than I,"[162] and who, for this reason, did not permit himself to accept the title "good"[163] when it was offered to him, although it was perfectly legitimate and true. Instead, he graciously offered it up to the Father, and rebuked the one who wished to praise the Son excessively. This is why we say the Savior and the Holy Spirit transcend all created beings, not by comparison, but by their exceeding pre-eminence. The Father exceeds the Savior as much (or even more) as the Savior himself and the Holy Spirit exceed the rest. And by "the rest" I do not mean ordinary beings, for how great is the praise ascribed to him who transcends thrones, dominions, principalities, powers, and every name that is named not only in this world but also in that which is to come?[164] And in addition to these [what must we] say also of holy angels, spirits, and just souls?

(152) But although the Savior transcends in his essence, rank, power, divinity (for the Word is living), and wisdom, beings that are so great and of such antiquity, nevertheless, he is not comparable with the Father in any way.

(153) For he is an image of the goodness and brightness, not of God, but of God's glory and of his eternal light; and he is a vapor, not of the Father, but of his power; and he is a pure emanation of God's almighty glory, and an unspotted mirror of his activity.[165] It is through this mirror that Paul and Peter and their contemporaries see God, because he says, "He who has seen me has seen the Father who sent me."[166]

---

161. This is part of the lacuna mentioned in the preceding note.
162. Cf. Jn 14.28.
163. Cf. Mk 10.18.
164. Cf. Eph 1.21.
165. Cf. Wis 7.25–26; Heb 1.3.
166. Cf. Jn 14.9; 12.45.

COMMENTARY ON JOHN, BOOK 13          101

> The woman says to him: I know that the Messiah is coming, who is called the Christ. Whenever he comes, he will tell us all things. (John 4.25)

*Jesus Reveals Himself to the Samaritan Woman*

(154) It is worthwhile to see how the Samaritan woman who accepts only the Pentateuch of Moses expects the coming of Christ as announced only by the law. The Samaritans too probably expected the visitation on the basis of Jacob's blessing on Juda, when he said, "Juda, may your brothers praise you; may your hands be upon the back of your enemies; the sons of your father will worship you."[167] And after a few words he continues, "A ruler shall not fail from Juda, and a leader from his thighs, until what is stored up for him come, and he shall be the expectation of nations."[168]

(155) And it is likely also that they have the same hope based on Balaam's prophecies, when he prophecies, "A man will come forth of his seed and will rule many nations, and the kingdom of Gog will be exalted, and his kingdom will be increased.

(156) "God led him out of Egypt as the glory of a unicorn for himself; nations of his enemies will be devoured, and he will deprive them of their strength, and with his missiles he will strike down the enemy; and he lay down and rested as a lion and as a cub. Who will awaken him? Those who bless you are blessed, those who curse you are cursed."[169]

(157) In the following words Balaam himself says again, "I will make [him] known to them,[170] but not now; I bless and he does not approach. A star will appear out of Jacob

---

167. Gn 49.8.
168. Gn 49.10.
169. Cf. Nm 24.7–9.
170. The Hebrew text and the Vulgate both have verbs meaning "I will see," followed by a direct object. The LXX has δείξω ("I will show" etc.) followed by the third personal singular pronoun in the dative. Origen follows the LXX, except that the dative pronoun is plural. δείκνυμι usually is followed by an object in the accusative, and an indirect object in the dative.

and a man will arise out of Israel, and he will shatter the leaders of Moab, and he will plunder all the sons of Seth. And Edom will be his inheritance, and the inheritance of Esau will be his enemy, and Israel acted in strength. And he will arise out of Jacob and will destroy the one who is preserved of the city."[171]

(158) You will observe in addition if the Samaritans think Moses' blessing on Juda should also be referred to Christ, "Hear, O Lord, the voice of Juda, and may you come to his people; both his hands will judge for him, and you will be a helper from his enemies."[172]

(159) And when the Samaritans boast of the patriarch Joseph, I wonder whether some of them take both the blessing of Jacob on Joseph and that of Moses to have reference to the coming of Christ. Anyone who wishes can take these words from Scripture itself.

(160) The Savior himself also, because he knew that Moses had recorded many words of prophecy about the Christ, says to the Jews, "If you believed Moses, you would believe me, for he wrote of me."[173]

(161) One can find, therefore, that most of the things recorded in the law refer typically and enigmatically to the Christ. I do not at present, however, see any other examples that are plainer and clearer than these we have cited. He is called "Messias" in Hebrew, however, which the Seventy translated as "Christ." Aquila translated it as "Elimmen."

(162) We must also consider the statement, "When he comes, he will tell us all things." Did the Samaritan woman say this from tradition or from the law? We must not fail to remark, however, that just as Jesus arose from among the Jews, not only saying that he was Christ but also demonstrating it, so also a certain Dositheos arose from among the Samaritans and declared that he himself was the Christ who had been prophesied.[174] To this day there are Dosithians derived from him, who bring forward books of Dositheos and

---

171. Cf. Nm 24.17–19.   172. Cf. Dt 33.7.
173. Jn 5.46.
174. Cf. Origen *Cels.* 1.57; 6.11; *hom. in Lc.* 25; *princ.* 4.3.2.

certain stories about him, describing how he did not taste death, but is alive somewhere. But this is enough on the literal sense.

(163) But also the heterodox opinion[175] present at Jacob's fountain, which she supposed to be a well,[176] refers to this word, which she assumes to be more perfect, as Christ, and says, "When he comes, he will tell us all things." And the one she awaits and expects, being present with her, says, "I who speak to you am he."[177]

(164) But consider also Heracleon's assertion. He says that *the Church received the Christ and was persuaded concerning him that he alone understands all things.*

> Jesus says to her, I who speak to you am he. And at this time his disciples came, and they were amazed that he was speaking with a woman. Yet no one said, What are you seeking? or, Why are you speaking with her? (John 4.26–27)

(165) We must investigate whether he proclaimed himself as Christ anywhere, and compare the statements with one another. We must compare such statements as, "I am the one who testifies of myself, and the Father who sent me testifies of me,"[178] with the saying, "If you believed Moses, you would believe me, for he wrote of me,"[179] and with any similar sayings in any of the Gospels.

### "I Am Meek and Lowly in Heart"

(166) But let us learn from him on the basis of the literal meaning. At this level we learn that he is meek and lowly in heart,[180] and does not disdain to speak of such great matters with a woman carrying water who goes out of the city because of her great poverty and labors to draw water for herself.

---

175. Cf. above 13.6.
176. Cf. above 13.7; 4.23.
177. Jn 4.26.
178. Jn 8.18.
179. Jn 5.46.
180. Cf. Mt 11.29.

(167) When the disciples arrive they are amazed, for they have previously beheld the greatness of the divinity in him, and they marvel that so great a man was speaking with a woman. We, however, carried away by pride and arrogance, despise those below us, and forget that the words, "Let us make man according to our image and according to our likeness,"[181] apply to each person.

(168) And when we fail to remember the one who formed man in the womb,[182] and formed all men's hearts individually, and understands all their works,[183] we do not perceive that God is a helper of those who are lowly and inferior, a protector of the weak, a shelterer of those who have been given up in despair, and Savior of those who have been given up as hopeless.[184]

(169) He also uses this woman as an apostle, as it were, to those in the city. His words inflamed the woman to such an extent that she left her water jar and went into the city and said to the men, "Come, see a man who has told me everything that I have done. Could this not be the Christ?"[185] When "they went out of the city and came to him,"[186] he did not fail[187] even such a woman, [but] at that time the Word revealed himself most clearly, so that the disciples came and were amazed that she, too, a mere woman and easily deceived,[188] was considered worthy of engaging in a conversation with the Word.

(170) But because the disciples believe that the Word does all things well, they do not rebuke him nor do they question his discussion and conversation with the Samaritan woman.

(171) It may be, too, that it is because they were struck with amazement at the great goodness of the Word, who condescended to a soul that despised Zion and trusted in the mountain of Samaria, that it is written, "They were amazed that he was speaking with a woman."

181. Cf. Gn 1.26.
182. Cf. Jer 1.5.
183. Cf. Ps 32.15.
184. Cf. Jdt 9.11.
185. Cf. Jn 4.29.
186. Jn 4.30.
187. Accepting Brooke's emendation of ὕστερόν to ὑστερῶν.
188. Cf. 1 Tm 2.14; 2 Cor 11.3; Gn 3.13.

(172) But Heracleon says of the statement, "I who speak to you am he," that *it was because the Samaritan woman was convinced that when the Christ came he would announce all things to her that he says, "Know that I who speak to you am he whom you expect." And when he acknowledged that he, the expected one, had come,* Heracleon says, *"The disciples,"* on whose account he had gone into Samaria *"came to him."*[189] But how had he gone into Samaria because of the disciples who also were with him earlier?

> Therefore the woman left her water jar and went into the city and said to the men, Come, see a man who has told me everything that I have done. Could this not be the Christ? (John 4.28-29)

### The Zeal of the Samaritan Women

(173) I think it was not to no purpose that the Evangelist recorded that the woman left her water jar and went into the city. At the literal level, then, this shows the tremendous eagerness of the Samaritan woman who forsakes her water jar and is more concerned for how she may benefit the multitude than for her more humble duty related to material things. For she was very benevolently moved and wished to announce the Christ to her fellow-citizens by bearing witness to the one who had told her "everything that she had done."

(174) And she invites them to behold a man whose speech is greater than man, for his appearance to the eye was human. So must we, too, therefore, forgetting things that are more material in nature and leaving them behind, be eager to impart to others that benefit of which we have been partakers. For, by recording the woman's commendation for those capable of reading with understanding, the Evangelist challenges us to this goal.

(175) We must, however, give attention to the anagogical sense. What is the water jar that the Samaritan woman leaves behind when she has accepted Jesus' words in some way?

189. Cf. Jn 4.27.

Perhaps she lays aside the vessel of the water that was honored for its depth, that is, the teaching, because she disparages those opinions which she formerly held, and has received, in a better vessel than the water jar, some of the water that is now already in her as a beginning of that water which springs up into eternal life.[190]

(176) For if she had not partaken of this water, how would she have benevolently preached Christ to her fellow-citizens, amazed at him who told her "everything she had done"? [How could she have done this] if she had not partaken of the saving water through [what] she heard?

(177) Rebecca herself too, however, a maiden beautiful to behold, went out with a water jar on her shoulders before Abraham's servant finished speaking within himself.[191] Since she was not drawing water like the Samaritan woman, she went down to the fountain and filled her water jar, and, when she came up, Abraham's servant ran to meet her and said, "Give me a little water to drink from your water jar."[192]

(178) Because he was Abraham's servant he was content to receive even a little water from Rebecca's water jar. "And Rebecca quickly let down the water jar upon her arm, and gave him a drink, until he stopped drinking."[193] Because, then, Rebecca's water jar was worthy of praise, she did not leave it behind, but because that of the Samaritan woman was [not], it was left at the sixth hour.

(179) Here, then, a woman proclaims Christ to the Samaritans, and at the end of the Gospels also the woman who saw him before all the others tells the apostles of the Resurrection of the Savior.[194]

(180) But neither is this woman thanked by the Samaritans because she has proclaimed the good news of the perfection of their faith (they say, "No longer do we believe because of your saying, for we ourselves have heard, and we know that this is truly the Savior of the world"[195]), nor is that woman entrusted with the first-fruit of the touch of Christ,

---

190. Jn 4.14.
192. Gn 24.17.
194. Cf. Jn 20.18.
191. Cf. Gn 24.12–16.
193. Cf. Gn 24.18–19.
195. Cf. Jn 4.42.

for he says to her, "Do not touch me."[196] For it was Thomas who was to hear, "Put your finger here, and see my hands; and bring your hand and put it into my side."[197]

(181) The Samaritan woman's relationship with five husbands, and after them her association with a sixth who was not her legitimate husband, was everything that she had done.[198] She disowned the latter man, left her water jar, and reverently rested [on] the Sabbath.[199] She obtained benefit also for those who, on the basis of her former beliefs, dwelt in the same city with herself, that is, in the structure of unsound doctrines. She was also the reason that they came out of the city and came to Jesus.

*Jesus Remains with Them for Two Days*

(182) And in the following words the Samaritans ask Jesus very deliberately, not that he might remain in the city, but "with them,"[200] that is, that he might be in their intellect.[201] For perhaps he could not remain in their city, since they, too, acting properly, came out of the city and came to him.

(183) But we must determine from these words, as the Evangelist gives us opportunity, that certain details such as these are set forth very precisely for their anagogical meanings.

(184) Earlier it was written, "They went out of the city and came to him."[202] And after a few words, "And many of the Samaritans of that city believed in him because of the word of the woman who testified, He told me everything that I have done. When, then, the Samaritans came to him, they asked him to remain with them."[203]

196. Jn 20.17.
197. Jn 20.27.
198. Cf. Jn 4.29; 4.16–18.
199. This seems to be the best way to translate this clause. There is no reference to the Sabbath, or to any other specific time in John's account of the Samaritan woman. Origen may have taken the fact that the woman left her water jar to be an indication that it was the Sabbath, and that she was now concerned to obey the Sabbath laws about work.
200. Jn 4.40.
201. ἡγεμονικός.
202. Jn 4.30.
203. Jn 4.39–40.

(185) First, then, they came to him from the city, and second, the Samaritans came to him while he was still beside Jacob's fountain (for he does not seem to have moved from there), and "they asked him to remain with them."[204] Now it is not recorded after this that he entered the city, but that "he remained there two days."[205]

(186) Furthermore, in what follows, it is not said, "And after two days he departed from the city," but, "And he departed from there."[206] For, so far as the spiritual meaning is concerned, the whole dispensation of benefit to the Samaritans occurred beside Jacob's fountain.

### Heracleon's Understanding of the Water Jar

(187) But Heracleon supposes that *the water jar is the disposition capable of receiving life, and the thought*[207] *of the power that is from the Savior. She left it with him,* he says, *that is, she has such a vessel with the Savior, with which she had come to receive the living water, and she returned to the world to announce the coming of Christ to the elect, for the soul is brought to the Savior through the Spirit and by the Spirit.*

(188) But consider if this water jar, which is completely abandoned, can be praised. For John says, "The woman left her water jar." It is not added that *she left it with the Savior.*

(189) And is it not also unlikely that when she had left *the disposition capable of receiving life and the thought of the power that is from the Savior,* even the vessel *with which she had come to receive the living water,* she went off *into the world* without these *to announce the coming of Christ to the elect?*

(190) And how also, after so many arguments, has the spiritual nature not been clearly convinced concerning the Christ but says, "Could this not be the Christ?"

(191) Heracleon also interpreted the statement, *"And they went out of the city,"*[208] *as the departure from their former way of life which was physical.* And, *"they came,"* he says, *"to the Savior through faith."*

(192) But we must ask him, How does he remain with them for two days? For Heracleon has not observed what we stated beforehand, that it has [not] been recorded that he remained two days in the city.

---

204. Jn 4.40.
205. Jn 4.40.
206. Jn 4.43.
207. ἔννοια, one of the Valentinian aeons.
208. Cf. Jn 4.30.

Meanwhile the disciples asked him saying,
Rabbi, eat. (John 4.31)

*The Disciples Wish To Nourish the Word*

(193) It was fitting also that the matters concerning food were recorded after the explanation concerning the drink and the teaching about the difference of the waters.

(194) The Samaritan woman, therefore, requesting a drink through her perplexities, as it were, . . .[209] but because of him who asked. For she was not able to give Jesus a drink worthy of himself, although he, when she desired a drink after she was asked, wished by this means to benefit her who had given him a drink.

(195) It was fitting now . . . from the Samaritan woman. And the disciples . . . when they had gone off into the city to buy food,[210] either having found suitable food, that is, certain suitable teachings, among the heterodox, . . . to him, "Eat." They thought that the time between the woman's departure into the city and the Samaritans' coming to him was a suitable time for him to eat. For they did not offer him food in the presence of a stranger. Perhaps the Samaritan woman would have been annoyed had she seen the disciples wanting to offer the teacher food, whether real or assumed, from her city.

(196) But neither would they have suitably said, "Rabbi, eat," in the presence of the Samaritans, since they themselves needed to leave the city. For this reason it is properly added, "Meanwhile the disciples asked him saying, 'Rabbi, eat.'"

(197) But it is worthwhile to see why "they asked him," and [did] not [say to him],[211] for it would have been [simpler] to write "Meanwhile the disciples said to him, 'Rabbi, eat.'"

(198) But perhaps also asking, beseeching, and implor-

209. The text is defective.
210. Cf. Jn 4.8.
211. Lacuna in the text, but the words can be supplied from the following statement.

ing [him] to eat indicates something prior to investigation and sometimes also something after investigation. And see whether they take care not . . . the Word . . .²¹² or being made strong by foods, [and] they ask him to eat what they have found.²¹³ For in those in whom the disciples find the Word, they always wish to nurture the Word that, being made strong and vigorous and mighty, he might remain at greater length with those who nurture him, nurturing in return those who offer him food.

(199) For this reason Scripture says he stands at the door and knocks, that if anyone should open the door he may go in to him and dine with him,²¹⁴ so that later the one who entertained may be able to be entertained in return by the Word who dined with man.

(200) But Heracleon says that *they wished to share with him some of the food that they had acquired by purchase from the Samaritans.* And he says these things that . . . the five foolish virgins . . . from the bridegroom.²¹⁵

(201) But how I think . . . to have the same things . . . they are said . . . with the foolish virgins who were locked out it is worthwhile to see, since he includes *with the foolish virgins an accusation of the disciples who fall asleep*²¹⁶ *in the same circumstances.*

(202) But further there is also the dissimilarity of light with food and of olive oil with meat . . . to censure the interpretation. Or, since indeed he was able to clarify the word²¹⁷ in some respect, he ought to support it more fully when he constructs his own interpretation.²¹⁸

---

212. The words τοῖς οἰκεῖ occur after ὁ λόγος before the lacuna.
213. Accepting Wendland's suggestion to read the participle as neuter plural with an article rather than the masculine accusative plural participle without an article.
214. Cf. Rv 3.20.
215. Cf. Mt 25.1–13.
216. Cf. Mt 26.40–44; Lk 22.45; Mk 14.37–41.
217. λόγος. Perhaps it means "argument" here.
218. The translation offered here for chapter XXXII (193–202) is very tenuous because of the many lacunae in the chapter.

> But he said to them, I have meat to eat which you
> do not know. (John 4.32)

*Spiritual Food*

(203) That which is without need has no need of food, and that which has need of food cannot be without need. And it is clear that he who eats does not eat when he does not need food, but when he needs and requires it.

(204) Physical bodies, on the one hand, inasmuch as they are fluctuating in nature, are nurtured by the food that replaces what perishes, but the spiritual parts that are higher than the physical body are nurtured by incorporeal thoughts, words, and sound actions. These higher spiritual parts will not be dissolved into non-being if they should not be nurtured, for not even physical bodies are dissolved into non-being when they are not nurtured, but when the parts of that nature which exceeds physical bodies are not nourished by the kind of foods mentioned above, they lose their distinctive character.

(205) And just as the physical bodies that need food are not nourished by foods that lack qualities, nor does the same quantity of food suffice for all, so must we also assume this to be the case for those spiritual parts that are higher than physical bodies. For in the same way, some of these spiritual parts need more food than others, since they cannot all contain equal amounts.

(206) But not even the same quality of nourishing words and contemplative thoughts [and] the actions appropriate to these words and thoughts are suited to all souls.

(207) For indeed vegetables and solid food[219] do not nourish those in need of improvement from them at the same time.

(208) For as Peter says, let new-born infants desire the rational, pure milk.[220] The same applies if anyone is childish

---

219. Cf. Rom 14.2; Heb 5.12.
220. Cf. 1 Pt 2.2.

like the Corinthians, to whom Paul says, "I gave you milk to drink, not meat."[221]

(209) And let the weak man eat vegetables because he does not believe.[222] Paul also teaches this when he says, "One man believes that he may eat all things, but the weak man eats vegetables."[223]

(210) And there is indeed a time when "the hospitality of vegetables with friendship and grace is better than grain-fed calves with hatred."[224] "But solid food is for the perfect, who by habit have their senses exercised to the discerning of good and evil."[225] But there is also a certain noxious food which we learn of from the Fourth Book of Kings, when certain men say to Eliseus, "Death is in the pot, O man of God."[226]

(211) On the one hand, there is a certain grassy spiritual food for the more unreasonable souls, and another of fodder or straw. These are suggested in the words, "The Lord will be my shepherd, and I shall want nothing.

(212) "In a place of green grass there he has made me dwell; he has brought me up on the water of refreshment."[227] And Isaias also says, "A lion will eat straw like an ox."[228] But they offered straw to the beasts of Abraham's servant in the house of Rebecca.

(213) On the other hand, if someone is more rational and for this reason is also a spiritual[229] man, he eats spiritual bread, as it is written in the Psalms, "Bread strengthens man's heart."[230] And no being other than man is cheered by spiritual wine, "for wine cheers the heart of man."[231]

(214) But we must ascend by reason from irrational and human beings to the angels who are also nurtured, for they are not totally without need. "Therefore, man ate the bread of angels,"[232] when the blessed Abraham was able to offer un-

---

221. 1 Cor 3.2.
222. Cf. Rom 14.2.
223. Rom 14.2.
224. Cf. Prv 15.17.
225. Heb 5.14.
226. 4 Kgs 4.40.
227. Cf. Ps 22.1–3.
228. Cf. Is 11.7.
229. νοητός.
230. Cf. Ps 103.15.
231. Cf. Ps 103.15.
232. Cf. Ps 77.25.

leavened loaves baked in the coals to the three who appeared to him.[233]

(215) But we must now proceed to the statement before us about Christ's food, which the disciples did not then know, for Jesus is telling the truth when he says, "I have meat to eat which you do not know."

(216) For the disciples did not know what Jesus was doing when he was doing the will of the one who sent him [and] perfecting his work.[234]

(217) But that the saying, "I have meat to eat which you do not know," may be understood more clearly, let Paul also say to the Corinthians who need milk and not solid food,[235] and are given milk to drink, and not meat because they cannot yet partake of meat,[236] "I have meat to eat which you do not know."

### The Meat Jesus Has

(218) Furthermore, one who is superior will always say to those who are inferior and who cannot contemplate the same things as those who are on a higher level, "I have meat to eat which you do not know."

(219) And it is not out of place to say that not only do men and angels need spiritual foods, but so too does the Christ of God. For, if I may put it this way, he is always replenishing himself from the Father who alone is without need and sufficient in himself.

(220) Now the common person who is being taught receives his foods from the disciples of Jesus who are commanded to distribute food to the crowds,[237] and Jesus' disciples receive their food from Jesus himself, though occasionally they also receive it from the holy angels.[238] The Son of God, however, receives his foods from the Father alone, without the intervention of any other being.

(221) It is also not out of place to say that the Holy Spirit

---

233. Cf. Gn 18.6.
235. Cf. Heb 5.12.
237. Cf. Lk 9.16.
234. Cf. Jn 4.34.
236. Cf. 1 Cor 3.2.
238. Cf. 3 Kgs 19.5–8.

is nurtured, but we must seek a text of Scripture that suggests this.

Now the food in the great supper is related to the whole mystery of the calling and election. For Jesus says, "A man made a great supper and at the hour of the supper he sent to call those who had been invited."[239]

(222) One needs to collect the parables about suppers recorded in the Gospels. But there are also the promises of eating and drinking in Isaias, who says, "Behold my servants shall eat, but you shall be hungry; behold my servants shall drink, but you shall be thirsty."[240]

(223) Furthermore, in Genesis God places man in the garden of luxury and gives laws about eating some things and not eating others.[241] And man would have remained immortal if he had eaten from every tree in the garden for food and had not eaten from the tree of knowing good and evil.[242]

(224) Consider also what is said in the twenty-first Psalm about those who worship because they have eaten, for it says, "All the fat ones of the earth ate and worshiped."[243] Wherefore, "the Lord will not afflict a just soul with famine,"[244] but whenever we become unjust, he will send forth "a famine upon the earth, not a famine of bread nor a thirsting of water, but a famine of hearing the word of the Lord."[245]

(225) To the extent that we progress, therefore, shall we eat better food and more, until perhaps we reach the point that we eat the same food that the Son of God eats, which the disciples did not know at that time. Heracleon had nothing to say on this text.

---

239. Cf. Lk 14.16–17.
240. Is 65.13.
241. Cf. Gn 2.8.
242. Cf. Gn 2.16–17.
243. Ps 21.30.
244. Cf. Prv 10.3.
245. Am 8.11.

> The disciples, therefore, said to one another, Has someone brought him something to eat? (John 4.33)

(226) Although Heracleon supposes that *these words were spoken in a fleshly manner by the disciples, because they were thinking on a lower level and imitating the Samaritan woman who said, "You have nothing with which to draw, and the well is deep,"*[246] it is worthwhile for us to consider if it is because they see something more divine that the disciples say to one another, "Has someone brought him something to eat?"

(227) For perhaps they thought that some angelic power had brought him something to eat. It is likely that this is why they were taught that the food that he had to eat was greater, which was to do "the will of the one who sent" him "and to perfect his work."[247]

> Jesus said to them, My meat is to do the will of the one who sent me and to perfect his work. (John 4.34)

### *The Will of the Son Is One with the Will of the Father*

(228) It is proper food for the Son of God when he becomes a doer of the Father's will, that is, when he wills in himself what was also the Father's will, so that the will of God is in the will of the Son, and the will of the Son has become indistinguishable from the will of the Father, and there are no longer two wills but one. It was because of this one will that the Son said, "I and the Father are one."[248] And because of this will, he who has seen him has seen the Son, and has seen also the one who sent him.[249]

(229) Now it is certainly more appropriate that we think it is in this way that the Son does the Father's will, on account of whose will even things extraneous to the one who wills turn out well, than that, without having investigated

---

246. Jn 4.11.
248. Jn 10.30.
247. Cf. Jn 4.34.
249. Cf. Jn 12.45.

the matters concerning the will, we suppose that doing the will of the one who sent [him][250] refers to performing certain extrinsic deeds.

(230) For that is not the Father's will in its entirety—I mean that which occurs extraneous to the one who wills, apart from the previously mentioned will. The complete will of the Father is done by the Son when the willing of God that occurs in the Son does that which the will of God wishes.

(231) But it is only the Son who has comprehended the complete will of God and does it, for which reason he is also his image.[251] We must also take the Holy Spirit into consideration. The remaining holy beings, however, will do nothing contrary to the will of God; indeed everything that they do will be done in accordance with God's will. This does not suffice, however, in order to be formed according to the complete will.

(232) One holy being will differ from another in comprehending something greater from the Father's will, or something more of his will, or something more distinct in comparison with another. And again one being comprehends God's will in a different degree than another. But he who said, "[My] meat is to do the will of God who sent me," will do the complete will of God in its entirety.

(233) After this, therefore, he says of God in a thankful manner, "The Son cannot do anything of himself, except what he sees the Father doing; for whatever the Father does, these things the Son also does likewise. The Father loves the Son and shows him all things that he himself does."[252]

(234) Perhaps this is why he is the image of the invisible God. For indeed the will that is in him is an image of the first will, and the divinity that is in him is an image of the true divinity. But even though he is an image of the Father's goodness,[253] he says, "Why do you call me good?"[254] And in-

---

250. My suggestion. Preuschen marks a short lacuna.
251. Cf. 2 Cor 4.4.  252. Cf. Jn 5.19–20.
253. Cf. Wis 7.26.  254. Mk 10.18; Lk 18.19.

deed it is this will that is the distinctive food of the Son himself, on account of which he is what he is.

### Christ Perfects the Work of the Father

(235) Now the subjoined phrase shows that the will concerns the disposition, when it adds after the reference to doing the will, "to perfect the work of God."

(236) But we must carry this investigation further so that we may also know what the statement means, "That I may perfect his work." Someone, then, will say rather simple-mindedly that it refers to the work that had been commanded, which is the work of him who commands, . . . as if, for example, we were to say that builders or farmers declare that they have perfected the work of the one who employed them for the work when they do that for which they were employed. But someone else will say that if God's work is perfected by Christ, it is obvious that this work was imperfect before it was perfected.

(237) In what way, then, was God's work imperfect? And how can God's work be perfected by him who said, "The Father who sent me is greater than me"?[255] The perfection of the work was the perfection of the rational creature. For the Word that became flesh[256] came to perfect this being, which was imperfect.

(238) Does this mean that the work was created imperfectly, and that the Savior was sent to perfect the imperfect? And is it not strange that the Father has become a creator of what is imperfect, and the Savior has perfected the imperfect, because it was imperfectly created?

(239) I think indeed some deeper mystery is stored up in these passages. For perhaps the rational creature was not altogether imperfect at the time he was placed in paradise.

(240) For how would God have placed what was altogether imperfect in paradise to work and guard it?[257] For he who

---

255. Cf. Jn 14.28.
256. Cf. Jn 1.14.
257. Cf. Gn 2.15.

is capable of tending "the tree of life" and everything that God planted and caused to spring up afterwards,[258] would not reasonably be called imperfect.

(241) Perhaps, then, although he was perfect, he became imperfect in some way because of his transgression, and was in need of one to perfect him from his imperfection. And perhaps the Savior was sent for the following reasons. First, that he might do the will of the one who sent him, having become his worker here, too, and second, that he might perfect the work of God, so that each one who has been perfected might be made fit for solid food and be present with wisdom. "But solid food is for the perfect who by custom have their senses exercised to the discerning of good and evil."[259] And he who speaks wisdom says, "But we speak wisdom among the perfect."[260]

(242) And when each of us, a work of God, has been perfected by Jesus, he will say, "I have fought a good fight, I have finished[261] my course, I have kept the faith. As for the rest, there is laid up for me a crown of justice."[262]

(243) But not only did man fall from perfection to imperfection, but so too did "the sons of God," "when they saw that the daughters of men were fair, and took for themselves whomever they chose."[263] And, in general, all those fell who forsook "their own habitation" and "kept not their own beginning [ἀρχή]."[264]

(244) Now, I do not take ἀρχή[265] here to have that meaning that is synonymous with authority, but I take it in that sense which is opposite to "end" and closely connected with "first," so that just as man had a beginning of being in par-

---

258. Cf. Gn 2.9.  259. Heb 5.14.
260. 1 Cor 2.6.
261. τετέλεκα. Words from this same root have been translated "perfect" throughout this chapter.
262. Cf. 2 Tm 4.7–8.
263. Cf. Gn 6.2.
264. Cf. Jude 6. "Beginning" renders ἀρχή, which also can mean "principality." Origen shows in the comments that follow that he takes it in the sense of "beginning."
265. See note 264 above.

adise, [but] an end because of his transgression, so also perhaps in Hades below, or in some such region, some suitable beginning has been given to each of those beings which fell away.

(245) Jesus, however, in perfecting the work of God, and I take this to mean every rational being and not man alone, perfects it in the same way. For because the more blessed beings are persuaded by reason and have no need of labor, they are perfected by reason alone. Other beings, however, unpersuaded by reason, need labors, that after the labors, they may, at some later time when they have been led by reasons be perfected by these.

(246) But both these activities are the one distinctive food of Jesus, namely to do the will of the one who sent him and to perfect his work.

(247) Heracleon says that *by the statement, "My meat is to do the will of the one who sent me," the Savior explains to the disciples that this was what he was discussing with the woman, saying that the will of the Father was his own meat, for this was his food, his rest, and his power.*

(248) *And he said the will of the Father is that men know the Father and be saved. This was the work for which the Savior was sent into Samaria, that is, into the world.* This is how Heracleon understood Jesus' meat and his conversation with the Samaritan woman. I think everyone can clearly see that this is an abject and forced interpretation.

(249) And he has not shown clearly how the Father's will is the Savior's food, or how the Father's will is his rest. For the Lord says elsewhere, as though the Father's will were not at all his rest, "Father, if it be possible, let the cup pass from me; but not what I will but what you will."[266] And from what source also did he learn that *the will of God is the Savior's power?*

---

266. Cf. Mt 26.39; Mk 14.36.

> Do you not say that there are yet four months
> and the harvest comes? Behold, I say to you, Lift up
> your eyes and see the fields, for they are already
> white for harvest. (John 4.35)

### Jesus Poses This Question Spiritually

(250) We must raise these further questions with those who suppose the question, "Do you not say that there are four months and the harvest comes?"[267] was asked in a rather simple, literal way, so that they may be convinced that the Savior has frequently said things that are spiritual[268] and lack meanings that are literal and factual.

(251) For if indeed the season when Jesus spoke these words was four months before harvest, it is obvious that it was winter. Harvest, therefore, begins in Judea around the month the Hebrews call Nisan when the Pasch is celebrated, so that sometimes they make the unleavened loaves from new grain.

(252) But grant that the harvest is not in that month, but in the next one, which they call Iar. Consequently, the season four months before that month is the peak of winter. Whenever, then, we explain that when Jesus spoke these words it was about harvest time, the season being either at its prime or perhaps near its end, the foregoing will be brought to our attention.

(253) And we must observe that after the dispensation about the water that was changed to wine in Cana of Galilee,[269] the Lord is said to have gone down "to Capharnaum, he and his mother, and brothers, and disciples."[270] There "he remained not many days. And the Pasch of the Jews was near, and Jesus went up to Jerusalem."[271] This was when "he found in the temple those selling cattle, sheep, and doves,"[272] and the other things which have been record-

---

267. "Yet" is also omitted in P75, a third century papyrus text of the Gospel of John from Egypt.
268. νοητά.
269. Cf. Jn 2.1–11.
270. Jn 2.12.
271. Cf. Jn 2.12–13.
272. Jn 2.14.

ed, and "he made a whip from cords and drove them all out of the temple."²⁷³

(254) And when he had conversed with Nicodemus,²⁷⁴ "afterwards he and his disciples came into the land of Judea, and there he abode with them and baptized."²⁷⁵ For how long a time shall we assume he stayed in Judea baptizing after the Pasch? For it has not been clearly recorded.

(255) It appears that because the Pharisees knew "that Jesus makes and baptizes more disciples [than] John,"²⁷⁶ he left "Judea" and departed "into Galilee,"²⁷⁷ at which time "he had to pass through Samaria."²⁷⁸ And when he was at the fountain of Jacob, he says, "Do you not say that there are yet four months and the harvest comes?"

(256) But if someone should suppose that Jesus spent more months after the Pasch in Judea baptizing with his disciples so that already the season four months before the harvest was at hand, one must remind him that after he had remained there two days with the Samaritans, he departed to Galilee, and it is recorded (inasmuch as the Pasch and the things that he had done in Jerusalem have just now taken place) that "When he came into Galilee, the Galileans welcomed him, having seen all the things he had done at Jerusalem at the feast, for they also went to the feast."²⁷⁹

(257) But someone will probably object that nothing prevents him, after he spent more time in Judea, from going to Jacob's fountain when he departed for Galilee and said, "There are yet four months to harvest." And this same person will say it is not strange that the Galileans welcomed him because of what he did eight months earlier in Jerusalem.

(258) But we must reply that when he came into Galilee, "he came into Cana of Galilee where" earlier he had made "the water wine."²⁸⁰ There also he healed the sick son of the ruler in Capharnaum²⁸¹ when he said to his father, "Your son

---

273. Jn 2.15.
275. Cf. Jn 3.22.
277. Cf. Jn 4.3.
279. Cf. Jn 4.45.
281. Cf. Jn 4.46–50.

274. Cf. Jn 3.1–21.
276. Jn 4.1.
278. Cf. Jn 4.4.
280. Cf. Jn 4.46.

lives."²⁸² And "after these things there was a feast of the Jews, and Jesus went up to Jerusalem,"²⁸³ at which time he healed the paralytic who had been sick for thirty-eight years.²⁸⁴

(259) But if this feast were that of the Pasch (for its name is not added), the sequence of the account is cramped, and this is especially the case since a little later it is added that "the Jews' Feast of the Tabernacles was at hand."²⁸⁵

*Why the Disciples Say There Are Yet Four Months until the Harvest*

(260) When these matters are examined further there is a deeper pursuit for the one who looks into the meaning of the Scriptures to seek what Jesus intended when he said to his disciples, "Do you not say that there are [yet] four months, and the harvest comes? Behold I say to you, Lift up your eyes and see the fields, for they are already white for harvest." Now, as we said in the case of the matters pertaining to the Samaritan woman when we were examining the words about the waters, so also let us do here.

(261) For who would not agree that the statement "Lift up your eyes and see the fields, for they are already white for harvest" is spiritual and, being spiritual, lacks literal meanings? It would follow from this too that the disciples mean that after four months there will be the harvest comparable, so far as their estimation is concerned, to the harvest indicated by Jesus.

(262) We think, then, that there are some such meanings as follows in the disciples' saying that "there are [yet] four months and the harvest comes." Because most disciples of the Word think it difficult for human nature to grasp the truth when they have discussed a life beyond the present life, and failed, for the present time, to reach the goal of their discussion, they suppose that once they have transcended their relationship with the four elements, they will grasp the truth about these matters.

(263) According to the saying of the Lord, therefore, the disciples say that the harvest, which is the consummation of

282. Jn 4.50.    283. Jn 5.1.
284. Cf. Jn 5.5–9.    285. Jn 7.2.

the works of truth that are gathered in, occurs after the fourth month that is imminent.

(264) Now the term "months" has been taken in the sense appropriate to a literal statement about the harvest. For it would not have been fitting to say, "Do you not say that there are yet four days and the harvest comes?" or, "Yet four years and the harvest comes?"

(265) Especially since the Word wants to elude the majority who understand things more literally, he hides the mystical meaning, but reveals a simpler meaning so that the words the Savior proclaims might be thought to be clear.

(266) Or perhaps the disciples mean something like this when they say, "There are yet four months and the harvest comes": there are four spheres of the four elements which lie below the ethereal nature. The middle and lower sphere is that of earth, and around it [the sphere] of water, and third, that of air, and fourth, that of fire, after which there is the sphere of the moon, etc.

(267) And let us consider whether the disciples assume that those who have been prepared by being in the presence of a purer essence grasp the truth, seeing that one can also [transcend] the sphere of fire, if he is uncorrupted by sin which is the material of everything in the regions that lie before the [way] [into the] ethereal places.

(268) But, to reprove this assumption as unsound, the Word who became flesh[286] says to those who hold these opinions, "Do you not say that there are [yet] four months and the harvest comes? Behold I say to you, Lift up your eyes and see the fields, for they are already white for harvest."

(269) For it also appears unintelligible to us that in this entire discussion he does not discuss a single harvest, although[287] according to those who take the simpler sense as true, he will rebuke the disciples who suppose, in their opinion, that the harvest comes after four months. We have shown in our previous discussion that there was no way the harvest could be present after four months.

286. Cf. Jn 1.14.
287. For ἐπεί in the sense of "although" see H. W. Smyth, *Greek Grammar* (Cambridge, 1963), 2380.

(270) Above all he says, as though correcting the opinion of the disciples, "Do you not say this, but I say this." In addition, is it not strange to give a distinctly allegorical explanation in every detail to the command, "Lift up your eyes," and not to take allegorically also the command, "See the fields, for they are already white for harvest," and this [immediately pre]ceeding[288] question, "Do you not say that there are yet four months and the harvest comes?"

### Heracleon Does Not See the Anagogical Sense

(271) Heracleon too, however, took this text in the same way as the majority and did not consider it to be interpreted anagogically. He says, therefore, that *he means the harvest of crops, as this had yet a four month interval, but the harvest of which he was speaking was already present.* I also do not know how he took the harvest to refer to the soul of believers, for he says that *they are already ripe and ready for harvest, and fit to be gathered into a granary,*[289] that is, into rest through faith, that is, as many as are ready, for all are not. For some souls were already ready, he says, *others were about to be, others will be in the future, while there are others who are still being sown.*[290] These, then, were his words.

(272) But I do not know if it is possible to show how the disciples, when they lift up their eyes, can see *the souls that are already ready,* as he thinks, *to be gathered into a granary.* And further, in what way is it true in reference to souls that, "One sows and another reaps,"[291] and, "I have sent you to reap that in which you did not labor"?[292] And how can the following statement be taken to refer to the soul, "Others have labored, and you have entered into their labor"?[293]

(273) We, therefore, take the harvest when the fruit is gathered into eternal life to have reference to the perfec-

---

288. Accepting Wendland's suggestion for the lacuna.
289. Cf. Mt 13.30, cf. below paragraph 294.
290. ἐπισπείρονται ἤδη. This could also be translated: "are already being sown again/as a second crop." This would imply that the harvest had already been reaped, and the field was being planted for a second crop, which would make this last group the most advanced of all. The progression in the sentence, however, has been from the more prepared to the less prepared.
291. Cf. Jn 4.37.   292. Jn 4.38.
293. Jn 4.38.

tion of the rational principle,[294] which is generative of our mental activity, when it has been perfected by more cultivation. We will discuss how it is sown by one and reaped by another in what follows.[295]

Behold, I say to you, Lift up your eyes and see the fields, for they are already white for harvest. (John 4.35)

### "Lift Up Your Eyes"

(274) "Lift up your eyes" occurs in many places in Scripture when the divine Word admonishes us to exalt and lift up our thoughts, and to elevate the insight that lies below in a rather sickly condition, and is stooped and completely incapable of looking up,[296] as is written for instance in Isaias, "Lift up your eyes on high and see. Who has made all these things known?"[297]

(275) The Savior, too, when he is about to deliver the beatitudes, lifts up his eyes to the disciples and says, "Blessed" are such and such.[298] For no genuine disciple of Jesus is below, nor is anyone who rests in Abraham's bosom.

(276) The rich man who is in torment lifts up his eyes and sees Abraham, and Lazarus in his bosom.[299]

(277) Furthermore, after Jesus restored "the woman" to health "who was stooped and completely incapable of looking up,"[300] she laid aside her stooped condition and her inability to look upwards, that she might lift up her eyes.

(278) On the other hand, no one who experiences passions, and who has clung to the flesh, and been concerned with material things, has observed the command that says,

---

294. λόγος. λόγος σπερματικός was the "generative principle" in organisms in Stoic philosophy. Origen, however, has used the adverb σπερματικῶς, rather than the adjective.
295. See below, sections 301 ff.
296. Cf. Lk 13.11.
297. Cf. Is 40.26.
298. Cf. Lk 6.20.
299. Cf. Lk 16.23.
300. Lk 13.11.

"Lift up your eyes." Consequently such a person will not see the fields, even if they be "already white for harvest." Furthermore, no one has lifted up his eyes if he continues to perform the works of the flesh.

### "The Fields Are White for Harvest"

(279) But "the fields are already white for harvest" when the Word of God is present clarifying and illuminating all the fields of Scripture that are being fulfilled by his sojourn.

(280) But perhaps, too, the white fields that are ready for harvest to those who lift up their eyes are all the beings that are perceptible to the senses, including heaven itself and the beings in it. This would be true because the purpose[301] of being is clear to those who, by being "transformed into the same image from glory to glory,"[302] have assumed a likeness of those eyes that have seen how each of the things that have been made was good. For the declaration concerning each of the created things, "God saw that it was good,"[303] means this: God perceived good in the purposes of each thing, and saw how each of the created things is good in relation to the purposes for which it had come to be.[304]

(281) Now if anyone does not take the statement, "God saw that it was good,"[305] in this way, let him explain how the statement, "God saw that it was good," holds true in the verse, "Let the waters bring forth the creeping creatures having life, and birds flying above the earth under the firmament of heaven,"[306] and even more to the point, "God made the great sea-monsters."[307]

(282) But the purpose of each of these, which God saw, is "good." We must say the same things also about the words, "Let the earth bring forth the living creature according to its kind, four-footed creatures, and creeping creatures, and

---

301. λόγος.
302. Cf. 2 Cor 3.18.
303. Gn 1.10.
304. Cf. Origen *hom. in Gen.* 1.10 (FOTC 71.59–60).
305. Gn 1.10.  306. Gn 1.20.
307. Gn 1.21.

beasts of the earth according to their kind,"[308] to which also is added, "God saw that it was good."[309]

(283) For how are beasts and creeping creatures good, unless the purpose concerning them is good?

(284) Now we say these things because of the command, "Lift up your eyes and see the fields, for they are already white for harvest." The Word which is present with the disciples urges his hearers to lift up their eyes both to the fields of Scripture and to the fields of the purpose in each of the things that exist, that one may behold the whiteness and brightness of the omnipresent light of truth. For, according to Solomon, "All things are manifest[310] to those who have understanding, and correct to those who are willing to share in sense-perception."[311]

> He who reaps receives a reward and gathers fruit
> for eternal life, that he who sows and he who reaps
> may rejoice together. (John 4.36)

### The Different Senses of the Word "Harvest"

(285) I think it is necessary to cite how many different senses the term "harvest" has in Scripture and in how many ways it is applied, so that once we have observed the meaning so far as possible, we may be able to see from the data how the expression is used in the majority of cases.

(286) Let us begin by observing the Lord's teaching about this term in the Gospel according to Matthew when "the disciples came to the Lord" with the request, "Expound to us the parable of the tares of the field."[312] Following some other words, he teaches, "But the harvest is the end of the world. And the reapers are angels."[313]

(287) Yet in another passage our Savior says, concerning the multitude of believers who are at a loss for teaching that

---

308. Gn 1.24.
310. ἐνώπιον. Literally: face to face.
312. Cf. Mt 13.36.
309. Cf. Gn 1.25.
311. Cf. Prv 8.9.
313. Mt 13.39.

would explain to them what they believe, "The harvest is great, but the laborers are few. Pray, therefore, the Lord of the harvest, that he send forth laborers into his harvest."[314]

(288) In addition to these uses, the Apostle refers to the good deeds of men in this life, or their sin, as "sowing." And he refers to the things stored up for each one as he deserves for his right actions or sins in this world as a "harvest." His words are, "For whatever a man may sow, this also shall he reap. For he who sows in the flesh, of the flesh shall reap corruption. But he who sows in the spirit, of the spirit will reap eternal life."[315]

(289) I think the prophet also has used it with a similar meaning in the Psalms where he says, "Those who sow in tears shall reap in joy. When they went, they went and wept, bearing their seeds, but when they come, they shall come joyfully, bearing their sheaves."[316]

(290) The word also occurs in many places with its normal meaning, as for example in the book of Ruth, "And they came to Bethlehem at the beginning of the barley harvest."[317]

Now that we have, for the present, set forth five meanings, it is obvious that the normal meaning is not the meaning here. Nor is it used in that sense which refers to the end. For it is clear that the reasonable exhortation to reap in this passage, "He who reaps receives a reward, and gathers fruit for eternal life," does not have reference to what is meant by the normal usage, nor does it refer to that which concerns the reaping angels.

(291) But neither is it possible here to understand the statement "He who reaps receives a reward, and gathers fruit for eternal life" to have reference to the same things as the statement, "He who sows in the flesh, of the flesh shall reap corruption, and he who sows in the spirit, of the spirit will reap eternal life."[318]

(292) For according to the Apostle's words, it is the same person who sows and reaps, whether in the flesh or in the

314. Mt 9.37–38.
316. Ps 125.5–6.
318. Cf. Gal 6.8.
315. Cf. Gal 6.7–8.
317. Ru 1.22.

COMMENTARY ON JOHN, BOOK 13         129

spirit, and on this basis reaps either corruption or eternal life. But according to the present words, it is one who sows and another who reaps.[319]

(293) It is the same person likewise who sows and reaps in the saying that we quoted in the Psalms. It differs from the apostolic saying in being more mystical and ineffable. For the apostolic saying is simpler, since it does not teach the source of the different natures of the seeds. The saying from the Psalms, however, seems to me to reveal the descent of the more noble souls that come into this life with the saving seeds. They come indeed with groaning as though involuntarily, but they ascend again in joy because they have cultivated well, and have increased and multiplied the seeds with which they came. But in the text before us, "one man sows and another reaps."[320]

(294) And indeed Heracleon will say, and perhaps even some churchman will agree with him so far as this interpretation is concerned, that *these words were spoken with the same meaning as the statement, "The harvest is great, but the laborers are few."*[321] *It refers to those who are ready for harvest and are suitable to be gathered into the granary now through faith,*[322] that is, to be in rest through faith, and are suitable for salvation and the reception of the Word. So far as Heracleon is concerned, *this is so because of their constitution and nature,* but so far as the churchman is concerned it is due to some preparation of the ruling principle of the soul that is ready for perfection, that it also might be reaped.

(295) We must ask those who have understood the saying in this way, therefore, if they are willing to accept that there may have been a harvest that occurred before the sojourn of our Savior similar to that one thus expected to follow the times of the proclamation of the gospel. For if the statement that the harvest is great means that many have believed although the laborers, who are apostles, are few in relation to the multitude of those who have accepted the Word, because of the statement, "See the fields, for they are already white for harvest,"[323] we must draw one of two possible con-

319. Cf. Jn 4.37.
320. Jn 4.37.
321. Cf. Mt 9.37.
322. Cf. Mt 13.30.
323. Jn 4.35.

clusions. Either no one believed before the bodily sojourn of our Savior, but then neither did any believer become a laborer, which is a very strange assertion, for this would mean that Abraham and Moses and the prophets were neither laborers nor among those who reaped, or, if in fact there have also been workers and an earlier harvest, the Savior will appear to make no new announcement to those who lift up their eyes that they may see the fields "for they are already white for harvest."

It can, perhaps, be clear on the basis of these observations that the harvest here refers to none of the things that we have previously mentioned. This is true also of the Apostle's meaning in another passage where he says, "He who sows sparingly will also reap sparingly, and he who sows bountifully will also reap bountifully."[324]

(296) Let us search, therefore, for a seventh meaning which is appropriate to what we have previously set forth on the saying, "Do you not say there are yet four months and the harvest comes?" and on the other saying, "Behold I say to you, Lift up your eyes and see the fields, for they are already white for harvest."[325]

(297) Now we have said that the harvest refers to the Word who clarifies the interpretation of the Scriptures, or that it refers to the way in which everything that God made can be said to be very good.[326] In relation to this, the reaper has two fruits from his reaping: one, when he receives a reward, and the other, when he gathers fruit to eternal life.

### "He Who Reaps Receives a Reward"

(298) I think the words, "he receives a reward," were spoken because of the promises that will follow, as it has been written, "Behold the Lord [comes] and his reward is in his hand to repay each one according to his work."[327] On the other hand, I think it was because of the benefit that occurs from the contemplation itself, which obviously is in the mind by its very nature and is distinctive to the rational soul,

324. 2 Cor 9.6.
326. See above, sections 279–84.
325. Cf. Jn 4.35.
327. Cf. Rv 22.12.

and which is distinguished from the other promises in addition to it, that it was written, "He gathers fruit to eternal life." This reveals a certain spiritual well-being of the ruling principle of the soul. We presented this view also in the third book of the *Stromateis* when we explained the statement, "Your Father who sees in secret will repay you."[328]

(299) Heracleon, however, thinks *the statement, "He who reaps receives a reward," was made because,* as he says, *the Savior calls himself a reaper.* And he supposes *the reward of our Lord to be the salvation and restoration of those who are harvested that results from his resting upon them.* And he says *the statement, "He gathers fruit to eternal life" has been made either because what is gathered is the fruit of eternal life, or even the act itself is eternal life.*

(300) But I obviously think his interpretation is forced when he says *the Savior receives a reward,* and when he confounds the reward and the gathering of the fruit into one act when Scripture openly presents two acts, as we explained previously.[329]

### Who Reaps, Who Sows?

(301) If then we have attained the lifting up of the apostolic eyes and the view of the fields that are already white for harvest, we must now examine, consequent to these attainments, the meaning of the clause, "That he who sows and he who reaps may rejoice together."

(302) It is my opinion that in the case of every art and science of the more important subjects of investigation, he who discovers the first principles sows. Others, receiving and elaborating these principles, by handing on their discoveries to others, become the causes, as a result of what they have discovered, for those of later times who would not be able both to discover the first principles and to conjoin the things that follow, and to apply the goal of the arts and sciences, namely to take up, as if in their harvest, the full fruit of such arts and sciences that have reached maturity.

(303) But if this is true in the case of certain arts and sciences, how much more is it evident in the case of the art of

328. Mt 6.4.
329. See above, sections 297–98.

arts and the science of sciences? For those who come later, by having elaborated the discoveries of former persons, have handed on the resources for one body of truth to be gathered with wisdom to those who next approach these discoveries with diligent inquiry.

(304) So, when every task of the art of arts has been completed, and God who repays gathers all people to one end, "he who sows and he who reaps rejoice together."

(305) And consider if those who "sow" are Moses and the prophets, since they wrote the things "for our admonition, on whom the ends of the world have come,"[330] and proclaimed the sojourn of Christ. And see if [those who] "reaped" were the apostles who received the Christ and beheld his glory,[331] which agreed with the intellectual seeds of the prophets about him, which were reaped by the elaboration and grasping of "the mystery that has been hidden from the ages, but manifested in the last times,"[332] and "in other generations was not known to the sons of men, as it is now revealed to his holy apostles and prophets."[333]

(306) Now, the complete plan[334] related to the revelation of the mystery that has been kept silent for eternal times and has now been made manifest through the prophetic Scriptures and the appearance of our Lord Jesus Christ, at which time the true light made the fields white already for harvest by shining upon them, was a seed.

(307) According to this explanation[335] then, the fields in which the seeds had been sown are the writings of the law and the prophets that were not white to those who had not received the presence of the Word. They become such, however, to those who become disciples to the Son of God and obey him who says, "Lift up your eyes and see the fields, for they are already white for harvest."[336]

(308) As genuine disciples of Jesus, therefore, let us also lift up our eyes and see the fields that have been sown by

---

330. Cf. 1 Cor 10.11.
332. Cf. Eph 3.9; 1 Pt 1.20.
334. λόγος.
336. Jn 4.35.

331. Cf. Jn 1.14.
333. Eph 3.5.
335. λόγος.

Moses and the prophets, that we may see their whiteness and how it is possible already to reap their fruit and gather fruit to eternal life, with the hope also of a reward from the Lord of the fields and the provider of the seeds.[337]

(309) Everyone, whoever he is, who has read "that many will come from the east and the west, and recline with Abraham and Isaac and Jacob in the kingdom of heaven,"[338] will agree that the sower and the reaper rejoice together when "sorrow, grief, and mourning have fled"[339] in the age to come.

(310) But if someone hesitates to accept that even now everyone who sows rejoices with everyone who reaps, let him consider the possibility that the transfiguration of Jesus was a kind of harvest when he appeared in glory not only to the reapers, Peter, James, and John, who went up the mountain with him, but also to the sowers, Moses and Elias.[340] For they rejoice together with them when they see the glory of the Son of God, which Moses and Elias had not previously seen, illuminated to such an extent by the Father and so illuminating those who beheld it. Consequently, Moses and Elias now see together with the holy apostles.

(311) And we take the statement, "He who reaps receives a reward, and gathers fruit to eternal life, that he who sows and he who reaps may rejoice together,"[341] as likewise capable of a general interpretation, because in the words that follow there are said to be more reapers and more laborers, the latter clearly referring to the sowing.

(312) For he says, as though addressing many reapers, "I sent you to reap that in which you have not labored," and, as though many have labored in the sowing, he adds, "Others have labored, and you have entered into their labors."[342] But it is equally possible to take the statement,

(313) "He who reaps receives a reward," in a general way,

---

337. Cf. 2 Cor 9.10.
338. Mt 8.11.
339. Is 35.10.
340. Cf. Mt 17.1–3.
341. Jn 4.36.
342. Jn 4.38.

and the next in the same way, "Everyone who reaps receives a reward and gathers fruit to eternal life, that everyone who sows and everyone who reaps may rejoice together."

### *How Moses and the Prophets Sowed*

(314) Some will accept these interpretations readily and have no hesitations about the conclusion that things hidden to former generations, including even Moses and the prophets, have been revealed to the holy apostles during the sojourn of Christ, who enlightened them with the light of the knowledge[343] of all Scripture. Others, however, will hesitate to assent to this, not daring to assert that so great a man as Moses and the prophets did not, during their earthly life, anticipate the things that have been understood by the apostles, and that this could have happened, although these things have been sown in the divine Scriptures which they themselves served.

(315) Now the former will use the saying, "Many prophets and just men desired to see the things that you see, and did not see them, and to hear the things that you hear, and did not hear them."[344] And they will use, "Behold a greater than Solomon is here,"[345] and, "In other generations it was not known to the sons of men, as it is now revealed to his holy apostles and prophets, that the Gentiles are fellow heirs, and of the same body, and co-partners of his promise in Christ."[346] They will also use what has been written in the Book of Daniel following a vision, "I arose, and there was no one who comprehended it,"[347] along with the statement in Isaias, "The words of this book are as a book of man that has been sealed, which, if they give it to a man who is not educated, saying, Read it, he will say, I am not educated; and they will give it to the educated man, and he will say, I cannot read it for it has been sealed."[348]

(316) The second group, however, will dismiss all these

---

343. Cf. Hos 10.12 (LXX).
345. Mt 12.42.
347. Cf. Dn 8.27.
344. Cf. Mt 13.17.
346. Cf. Eph 3.5–6.
348. Cf. Is 29.11–12.

arguments with the statement, "A wise man will understand the words from his own mouth, and upon his lips he bears knowledge."[349] They will say that Moses and each of the prophets understood the mysteries supplied by them so that they did not pass them on to others without pondering them. Since, however, they will assert, the apostles lived in the time of revelation, they would have said, "Stand fast, and hold the traditions that you were taught,"[350] and, "The things that you have heard from me through many witnesses, the same commit to faithful men who will be able to teach others also."[351] Moreover, this second group will argue that if many prophets and just men desired to see what the apostles saw, and [hear] what they heard when the Savior spoke,[352] they had no desire at all to hear the words of the writings of the law and the prophets, but wanted to hear words greater than these, which are announced to the apostles by the Savior in the spiritual meanings of the law and the unutterable mysteries of the prophets. It was to such mysteries that the saying refers, "I heard secret words, which it is not granted to man to utter,"[353] and words similar to those spoken by the Paraclete.

(317) But in addition to these matters let us also examine what it is that the Evangelist declares to be the reason the reaper receives a reward and gathers fruit to eternal life when he says, "That he who sows and he who reaps may rejoice together."

(318) Now if "[the reaper] receives a reward and gathers fruit to eternal life, that he who sows and he who reaps may rejoice together," perhaps the sower, by sharing in the reward of the reaper and in the gathering of the fruit that is gathered to eternal life, will rejoice together with the reaper.

(319) But someone else will say that Moses and the prophets have accurately understood the spiritual meaning of all the books of the law and the prophets, but that the

---

349. Cf. Prv 16.23.
351. 2 Tm 2.2.
353. Cf. 2 Cor 12.4.

350. 2 Thes 2.15.
352. Cf. Mt 13.17.

things they sowed had to be written in words that were veiled and obscure.[354] And because, "If a prudent man hear a wise word, he will praise it and add to it,"[355] it is clear that the apostles, by using the seeds of mysteries that are even more unutterable and deeper, seeds understood by Moses and the prophets, have gone beyond them to attain visions of the truth that are far greater, when Jesus lifts up their eyes[356] and enlightens their understandings. These visions which were far greater were the harvest of many fields. It was not as though the prophets and Moses were inferior from the beginning and [did not see] as many things as the apostles did at the times of Jesus' sojourn. It was rather a matter of waiting for the fullness of time[357] when it was fitting, in keeping with the special character of the sojourn of Jesus Christ, that special things also, beyond anything that had ever been spoken or written in the world, be revealed by the one who did not consider "being equal to God" robbery, but who emptied himself and took the "form of a servant."[358]

> For in this is the saying true, that it is one who sows and another who reaps. (John 4.37)

(320) If we interpret the words in this passage on the model of what we said about the arts and sciences,[359] it is clear how the saying is true that one sows and another reaps. Or, if we take them to refer to the fact that Moses and the prophets have sown,[360] but those who have lifted up their eyes, as our Savior Jesus instructed, that they might see how the fields were already white for harvest[361] have understood their hidden meaning when the fields had become white, it is also obvious in this way how one sows and another reaps.

(321) But consider if it is possible to understand the use

354. Origen says this himself in *Jo.* 6.22–23. For his discussion of these same issues there, see *Jo.* 6.15–31 (FOTC 80.172–77).
355. Sir 21.15. 356. Cf. Jn 4.35.
357. Cf. Gal 4.4. 358. Cf. Phil 2.6–7.
359. Cf. above, sections 302–4. 360. Cf. above, sections 305–6.
361. Cf. Jn 4.35.

of "one" and "another" to have reference to the fact that the former are justified on the basis of one way of life, and the latter on the basis of a different way, so that we can say that one belongs to the law and the other to the gospel. Nevertheless they rejoice together[362] because there is one goal from one God through one Jesus Christ stored up for both in one Holy Spirit.

(322) But Heracleon explained the saying, "That he who sows and he who reaps may rejoice together,"[363] in this way. *For the sower rejoices*, he says, *because he sows. And because some of his seeds are already being gathered, he has the same hope also for the rest. The reaper, on the other hand, rejoices likewise because he also reaps. But the sower began first, [and] the reaper later.*

(323) *For both could not begin at the same time. Sowing had to come first, then later reaping. When the sower has ceased sowing, however, the reaper will yet reap. For the present, however, both rejoice together as they carry on their individual work because they consider the perfection of the seeds a common joy.*

(324) He also has the following to say on the statement, "In this is the saying true, that it is one who sows and another who reaps": *The Son of Man above the Place sows, and the Savior, who is also himself Son of Man, reaps and sends the angels as reapers, each for his own soul. The disciples represent the angels.* He has not at all set forth clearly who the two Sons of Man are, one who sows and the other who reaps.

> I have sent you to reap that in which you have not labored; others have labored, and you have entered into their labor. (John 4.38)

(325) It is not difficult, on the basis of our previous discussion, to see how Jesus sent the disciples to reap that in which they themselves had not labored, but those before them had labored. For after Moses and the prophets labored that they might be able to advance to an understanding of the mysteries whose traces they left for us in their own

362. Cf. Jn 4.36.
363. Jn 4.36.

writings, the apostles entered into the labor of Moses and the prophets, reaping and gathering into the granaries of their own soul[364] the spiritual sense in those writings as Jesus unfolded their meaning.

(326) Now, the Word always makes the labors of the former men clearer to those who are genuinely disciples, so that they do not have to experience the same labor with those who have sown.

### The Labors of the Angels

But we must consider everything that concerns those [who are sown] by some [and] reaped [by others]. In particular we must consider whether, since the angels have been assigned to the sowing of men, the apostles, who are their co-laborers in the perfection of those who have been sown, perhaps enter into the labor of others by reaping and discovering fruits in those benefitted, which Jesus' sojourn has made ripe for harvest even prior to the anticipated four month period.[365]

(327) And if these things are so, it is worthwhile to see if the service of the angels in sowing souls in bodies is labored because they bring together two somewhat opposing natures into one composition and, at the appointed time, begin to make the constitution concerning each one while they also advance that which was formed earlier to perfection.

(328) But someone will object that on the contrary God himself is said to form men in the statement, "Your hands have made me and formed me,"[366] and in addition, "Before I formed you in the womb, I knew you, and before you came forth out of the womb, I sanctified you."[367]

(329) One must reply to this that just as the law was ordained by angels,[368] [and "the"] word spoken [by angels] became steadfast,"[369] although it is obvious that it was spoken by God, so it is also possible to say that God forms man in

---

364. Cf. Mt 13.30.
366. Ps 118.73.
368. Cf. Gal 3.19.
365. Cf. Jn 4.35.
367. Jer 1.5.
369. Heb 2.2.

COMMENTARY ON JOHN, BOOK 13    139

the womb by the angels who have been appointed over creation.

(330) Now, I do not know if it is applicable also to say something like this to one who is in doubt. Job and David, who said, "Your hands have made me and formed me,"[370] were formed by God because they were God's portion.[371] Jeremias too, who hears the words, "Before I formed you in the womb I knew you,"[372] has been formed by him, since he will be God's portion. But those who are the portion of others are formed by those who have obtained them as their portion.

(331) This explanation will take the command, "Let us make man according to our image and our likeness,"[373] in a more ingenious manner. God says this of all men and initiates the work which is later [performed][374] by others to whom the command comes in relation to the appointed portion. It is to these that God says, "Let us make man."[375] It is to these also that he says in the confounding of the dialects, "Come and let us go down and confound there their tongue."[376]

(332) Now we do not offer this as our opinion, for matters of such magnitude need to be thoroughly examined to see if they are so or not. On the other hand, such an interpretation must not be dismissed contemptuously. Each person is the portion of someone according to the statement, "When the Most High divided the nations, and when he scattered the sons of Adam, he appointed the bounds of the nations according to the number of the angels of God; and Jacob became the Lord's portion, his people; Israel the allotment of his inheritance."[377]

(333) Now if each person is without a doubt someone's portion because God has scattered the sons of Adam, then each of the angels labors on behalf of his own portion, ad-

---

370. Ps 118.73; cf. Jb 12.10.     371. Cf. Ps 118.57.
372. Jer 1.5.     373. Cf. Gn 1.26.
374. My addition. There is no verb in the clause.
375. Gn 1.26.     376. Gn 11.7.
377. Cf. Dt 32.8–9.

ministering what pertains to it. In the sojourn of the Savior, however, when they are brought into captivity to the obedience of Christ,[378] Christ receives them from the portion of all the angels through the servants of the gospel, the apostles, evangelists, and teachers.[379] The Gentiles also approach to become the inheritance of Christ.[380]

(334) Perhaps, then, for this reason it can be said to the apostles, who will be told a little later, "Go, teach all nations,"[381] "Others have labored, and you have entered into their labor."

(335) And if it is the holy angels who have received the remaining portions in addition to the chosen portion and who have been appointed over the dispersion of souls, it is not strange that the one who sows and the one who reaps rejoice together after the harvest.[382]

(336) Heracleon says that *these seeds were sown neither through them nor by them* (and he means the apostles), *but that those who have labored are the angels of the dispensation, through whom, as mediators,*[383] *they were sown and brought up.* And on the statement, "You have entered into their labor," he set forth his view as follows. *Sowing and reaping are not the same kind of labor. For those who sow sow in the cold after wearily digging the earth, and care for it throughout the winter by hoeing and pulling the weeds.*[384] *The others, however, in summer, enter into fruit which has been prepared and reap with rejoicing.*

(337) Now it is possible for the reader, by comparing what we have said and what Heracleon has said, to see what sort of things can be gained from these explanations.

> Now many Samaritans of that city believed because of the word of the woman who testified that, He told me all the things which I have done. (John 4.39)

(338) After the Samaritan woman left her water jar and went into the city to announce the things concerning the

---

378. Cf. 2 Cor 10.5.
380. Cf. Ps 2.8.
382. Cf. Jn 4.36.
384. τὰς ὕλας.

379. Cf. Eph 4.11.
381. Cf. Mt 28.19.
383. Cf. Gal 3.19.

Savior,[385] and while those who believe the word of the woman are coming to the Lord, the Savior meanwhile, addressing the disciples, has spoken the previously mentioned words when the disciples requested that he eat.[386]

(339) And after the words addressed to the disciples that we have examined to the best of our ability, the Scripture takes up again the matters concerning those who have come to the Savior from the city and who have believed because of the testimony of the woman who said, "He told me everything which I have done."[387]

(340) Now if we grasp what was said above about Samaria, the Samaritan woman, and the fountain of Jacob, it is not difficult to see how those who have been frustrated with false teachings leave the city of opinions, as it were, when they happen upon sound teaching. And when they have left it, they soundly believe the saving teaching because of one woman who had earlier received the saving teaching at the fountain of Jacob and who left her previously mentioned water jar in order to summon others that they too might be benefitted in the same way.[388]

(341) *Heracleon has taken the phrase, "out of the city," to stand for "out of the world," and the phrase, "because of the word of the woman," to mean "through the spiritual church." The word "many" signifies that there are many natural men.*[389] *And he says the one woman is the incorruptible nature of the Elect which is simple and single.* We have opposed these interpretations, as we best were able, in our words above.

---

385. Cf. Jn 4.28–29.
386. Cf. Jn 4.31.
387. Jn 4.29; cf. 4.39.
388. Cf. Jn 4.28.
389. ψυχικοί. This was the middle category in the Gnostic classification of humanity as ὑλικοί (material), ψυχικοί (natural), and πνευματικοί (spiritual).

Therefore when the Samaritans came to him, they asked him to remain with them. And he remained there two days. And many more believed because of his word. (John 4.40–41)

*Jesus Remains with the Samaritans*

(342) Someone will plausibly contrast these words with the words, "Go not into the way of the Gentiles, and do not enter the city of the Samaritans."[390] For when the Savior who said, "Do not enter the city of the Samaritans," was asked to remain with the Samaritans, "he remained there two days."[391] It is clear, therefore, that his disciples had also entered with him.

(343) But we must say to this that to go into the way of the Gentiles[392] is to adopt some Gentile teaching which is foreign to the "Israel of God"[393] and to walk according to it. And to enter a city of the Samaritans[394] is to be engaged in some knowledge falsely so-called[395] of those who claim to devote themselves to the words of the law or the prophets or the Gospels or the apostles.

(344) But it is possible that when the Samaritans left their own city and came to Jesus beside Jacob's fountain,[396] Jesus welcomed the decision of those who believed and remained with those who asked.

(345) I think that John deliberately has not written that the Samaritans "asked him" to enter Samaria, or to enter the city, but "to remain with them." For "to remain with the believer" and "to enter his city" are not the same. Moreover, in what follows he does not say, 'And he remained in that city two days,' or, 'He remained in Samaria,' but, "He remained there," that is, with those who asked.

(346) For Jesus remains with those who ask, and especially when those who ask him come out of their city and come to Jesus, as if in imitation of Abraham when he obeyed God

---

390. Mt 10.5.
392. Cf. Mt 10.5.
394. Cf. Mt 10.5.
396. Cf. Jn 4.30.
391. Jn 4.40.
393. Cf. Gal 6.16.
395. Cf. 1 Tm 6.20.

who said, "Go forth out of your country and from your kindred, and out of your father's house."[397]

(347) And Jesus remains two days with those who asked him, for they did not yet comprehend also his third day, since they were not able to comprehend anything miraculous, such as those who dined with Jesus on the third day at the wedding in Cana of Galilee.[398]

(348) The beginning, therefore, of the many who believed from Samaria was the word of the woman who testified, "He told me everything that I have done."[399] But the growth and multiplication of "the many more" who believed was no longer because of the woman's word, but because of the Word himself. For the Word is not perceived in the same way when he himself bears testimony of himself as he enlightens the one receiving him, and when he is testified to by being spoken of by another.

(349) Heracleon has this to say on these passages: *He remained "with them" and not "in them." And the two days means either the present age and the age to come in marriage,[400] or the time before his passion and that after the passion, which he spent with them and converted many more to faith by his own word, after which he was separated from them.*

(350) But we must remark, in relation to his observation, which seems correct, that *"with them" and not "in them" has been written*, that the following statement uses the phrase "with them" in the same way. "Behold I am with you all the days."[401]

(351) For he did not say, "I am in you." And further, when he says *the two days are either this age and the one to come, or the time before the Passion and after the Passion*, he has not understood the ages to come after the coming age, concerning which the Apostle says, "That he might show in the ages to come."[402] Nor does he perceive that it is not only before and after his Passion that Jesus is with those who come to him, after which he is separated from them, for Jesus is always with his disciples, never leaving them, so that they also say, "And I no longer live, but Christ lives in me."[403]

---

397. Gn 12.1.  
398. Cf. Jn 2.1.  
399. Jn 4.39.  
400. Cf. Clement, *exc. Thdot.* 64. The Valentinians spoke of marriages in the pleroma related to the syzygies of the aeons.  
401. Mt 28.20.  
402. Eph 2.7.  
403. Gal 2.20.

> And they said to the woman: No longer do we
> believe because of your saying, for we ourselves have
> heard, and we know that this is truly the Savior
> of the world. (John 4.42)

*It Is Better To Walk by Sight Than by Faith*

(352) They renounce their faith that was based on the speech of the woman when they discover that to have heard the Savior himself is better than that faith, so that they, too, know "that this is truly the Savior of the world." It is better indeed to become an eyewitness of the Word and to hear him, without the use of physical organs and the intervention of teachers, teaching and bringing images before the intellect, which discovers the representations of the truth most clearly, than to hear the message about him through ministers who have seen him when one neither sees him nor is illuminated by his power.

(353) For it is impossible for one who is taught by someone who has seen him and who describes him, to have the same experience that occurred, in respect of the intellect, to the one who has seen him. It is better indeed to walk by sight than by faith.[404]

(354) For this reason, those who walk by sight, as it were, would be said to be engaged in those gifts which come first,[405] "the word of wisdom" given by the Spirit of God, and the "word of knowledge according to the same Spirit."[406] Those who walk by faith, on the other hand, are inferior to the former in rank, although faith is a gift according to the saying, "And to another, faith in the same Spirit."[407]

(355) But we must examine when and how Paul says, "For we walk by faith, not by sight."[408] For how, as the majority understand it, does he who most solemnly speaks the following words walk by faith and not by sight? "Am I not free?

---

404. Cf. 2 Cor 5.7.
405. I.e., in Paul's list of gifts in 1 Cor 12. Because they come first Origen appears to take them to be also of a higher rank.
406. Cf. 1 Cor 12.8.   407. Cf. 1 Cor 12.9.
408. 2 Cor 5.7.

Am I not an apostle? Have I not seen Jesus our Lord? Are you not my work in the Lord?"[409]

(356) Let us see then how we must take the saying, "For we walk by faith, not by sight,"[410] when we understand it in the context of the words that precede it, "Now he who makes us for this very thing is God, who has given us the pledge of the Spirit.

(357) "Therefore always being confident and knowing that while we are in the body we are absent from the Lord; for we walk by faith, not by sight"[411] (and it is clear that we are in the body when we are absent from the Lord), being confident, "we choose rather to be absent from the body and to be present with the Lord."[412]

(358) Since these matters are expressed in this way, in order to understand what it means to be present in the body and to be absent from the Lord, and what it means to be absent from the body and to be present with the Lord, let us ask ourselves what we will say about the Apostle. Was it that being present in the body he was absent from the Lord, or that being absent from the body he was present with the Lord?

(359) But clearly, since "those who are in the flesh cannot please God,"[413] and the saints are not in the flesh, "but in the spirit, if the spirit of God dwells in them,"[414] Paul was neither in the flesh nor in the body, for he speaks the truth when he says, "And I think that I too have the spirit of God."[415] He was not indeed present in the flesh and in the body, since the one who is present in the body walks by faith, not by sight.

(360) And consider if the precise meaning of the Apostle can be that "being in the flesh" and "being present in the body" do not mean the same thing.[416] "For those who are in the flesh cannot please God."[417] Those, however, who are

---

409. 1 Cor 9.1.
410. 2 Cor 5.7.
411. 2 Cor 5.5–7.
412. Cf. 2 Cor 5.8.
413. Cf. Rom 8.8.
414. Cf. Rom 8.9.
415. 1 Cor 7.40
416. Cf. Rom 8.8; 2 Cor 5.6.
417. Cf. Rom 8.8.

present in the body "are absent from the Lord," but they walk by faith, though they are not yet able to walk by sight.[418]

(361) I think that those who walk according to the flesh are in the flesh.[419] Those, however, who do not understand the spiritual meanings of Scripture, but nevertheless are wholly devoted to it and to its bodily meaning, are present in the body and absent from the Lord. For if "the Lord is spirit,"[420] how is he who does not yet contain the Spirit who gives life[421] and the spiritual meaning of Scripture not absent from the Lord? But such a man walks by faith. The one, however, who compares spiritual things with spiritual,[422] and who becomes spiritual, the man who judges all things but is himself judged by no one,[423] is absent from the body and present with the Lord.[424]

(362) Now it seems good to us that we have made these comments, although it has involved a digression into the apostolic sayings. At any rate these comments are most urgent in regard to the distinction in the account of the Samaritans who no longer believe because of the saying of the woman, but who have heard and know that "this is the Savior of the world." There is nothing astonishing, however, in the fact that some are said to walk by faith and not by sight, and others to walk by sight, which is greater than walking by faith.

(363) Heracleon takes the statement, "No longer do we believe because of your saying," in a rather simple way. He says *it lacks the word "alone."* For further, on the statement, "For we ourselves have heard and know that this is the Savior of the world," he says, *For men believe in the Savior first by being led by men, but whenever they read his words, they no longer believe because of human testimony alone, but because of the truth itself.*

418. Cf. 2 Cor 5.6–7.
419. Cf. 2 Cor 10.3.
420. 2 Cor 3.17.
421. Cf. 2 Cor 3.6.
422. Cf. 1 Cor 2.13.
423. Cf. 1 Cor 2.15.
424. Cf. 2 Cor 5.8.

> Now after two days he departed from there into Galilee. For Jesus himself testified that a prophet has no honor in his own country. (John 4.43-44)

### *A Paradoxical Statement*

(364) This text appears very inconsistent. What does the statement, "Jesus himself testified that a prophet has no honor in his own country," have in common with the fact that he has departed from the Samaritans after he had remained with them two days and is going into Galilee?

(365) For if Samaria were his country and he had been dishonored there, and this were his reason for departing after spending no more than two days, it would have been consistent to say, "For Jesus himself testified that a prophet has no honor in his own country."

(366) Or even if it had been written, And after two days he departed into Galilee, but he was not in his own country, "for Jesus himself testified that a prophet has no honor in his own country," the statement would be appropriate.

(367) Perhaps this is the intention of the saying, but John has expressed what he meant obscurely because he was unskilled in the language. For he has not said where in Galilee they welcomed him, "because they had seen all the things that he did in Jerusalem at the feast."[425] But also after this he has recorded that Jesus came "into Cana of Galilee."[426] Now, the Evangelist is clear in his own mind and has no doubt about what is proposed.

(368) Having mentioned previously, therefore, how the Lord leaves Judea and goes into Galilee, and having described what was said near the field that Jacob gave to Joseph beside Jacob's fountain (since "he had to go through Samaria"[427]), and how he remained two days with the Samaritans, he gives an account of his arrival in Galilee, although not a few things indeed were said in the interval.

(369) And since we have said previously that Judea,

---

425. Cf. Jn 4.45.      426. Jn 4.46.
427. Cf. Jn 4.4.

which lies somewhere above, is a symbol of something better,[428] and Galilee of something inferior, in accordance with this, God, who is benevolent, does not disdain to visit those who are needy and inferior. For this reason also he quickly left the Samaritans in order to appear to the Galileans who would eagerly receive him, and to heal the ruler's son.[429]

(370) And after he has done these things in Galilee, he goes up to Jerusalem when the feast of the Jews is at hand and makes the feast better and more joyful by his own visitation.[430]

### "A Prophet Has No Honor in His Own Country"

(371) Now let us see also what the saying means, "For Jesus himself testified that a prophet has no honor in his own country," and let us seek a meaning of the saying worthy of Jesus who gives the testimony.

(372) The country of the prophets, of course, was in Judea, and it is clear that they had had no honor among the Jews, since they were stoned, sawn in two, tried, and put to death by the sword. Because they were dishonored, they went about in sheepskins and goat skins, being in need, afflicted, and ill-treated.[431]

(373) The Jews are reproached, indeed, by the one who addressed them with the words, "Which of the prophets have not your fathers persecuted? And they have slain those who foretold the coming of the Just One."[432] Finally, when they had also dishonored the prophet par excellence because of whom the prophets had become prophets, they said, "Away with him, away with him, crucify him."[433]

(374) But all the prophets have been honored in my country. This includes the one who arose from God in accordance with what Moses said of him, "The Lord your God will raise up for you a prophet like me from your brothers. You shall hear him."[434] For his country was not among the

---

428. Cf. Book 10.131–41 (FOTC 80.285–88).
429. Cf. Jn 4.45–50.   430. Cf. Jn 5.1.
431. Cf. Heb 11.37.   432. Acts 7.52.
433. Cf. Jn 19.15.    434. Acts 3.22; cf. Dt 18.15.

COMMENTARY ON JOHN, BOOK 13        149

Gentiles, who have received salvation by the transgression of Israel.[435]

(375) Now it is also written in other places, "No prophet is acceptable in his country and in his house."[436] And it is useful indeed, once we have brought together the related saying from the Gospels with this one, to see when and on what occasion the Savior said this.

(376) The truth of the Savior's statement is amazing. It is applicable not only to the holy prophets who were dishonored by their fellow countrymen, and to our Lord himself, but also to those who have busied themselves in any field of learning and have been despised by their fellow citizens with the result that some of them, too, have been executed.

(377) One can, however, pick these things up for oneself from Greek stories about philosophers and astronomers or those who were preeminent in any field of learning whatever. And these too are the words of those who dishonor them, "Is not this the carpenter's son? Is not his mother called Mary? And are not his brothers with us? Whence, then, has he all these things?"[437]

(378) What has happened in the case of the prophets is most paradoxical indeed. While alive their fellow citizens dishonored them, but dead they respect them by building and adorning their tombs.[438]

(379) Now when someone abandons the Spirit that gives life, which is present in the intentions of the prophetic writings, and respects and adorns the letter that kills,[439] thinking that the beauty of prophecy is in the bare interpretation of the letter, he builds and adorns the very tombs of the prophets.

(380) This is the work of the scribes and Pharisees who are attacked by the Lord.[440] The scribes, on the one hand, get their name from the bare letter.[441] The Pharisees, on the other hand, are those who have separated themselves and

---

435. Cf. Rom 11.11.
436. Cf. Lk 4.24; Mt 13.57.
437. Cf. Mt 13.55–56.
438. Cf. Mt 23.29.
439. Cf. 2 Cor 3.6.
440. Cf. Mt 23.29.
441. "Scribe" in Greek, is γραμματεύς, and "letter" is γράμμα.

destroyed the divine unity, for "Pharisees" means, "those who have separated themselves."[442]

> When, then, he came into Galilee, the Galileans received him, having seen all the things he had done at Jerusalem at the feast, for they also went to the feast. (John 4.45)

(381) It is worthwhile to see the reason for the reception that the Galileans gave the Savior when he came into Galilee, since it was of such magnitude that it caused them to be amazed and astonished at the Savior with the result that they received him. Furthermore, to what numerous deeds, as it were, performed by Jesus in Jerusalem does the clause refer, "Having seen all the things he had done at Jerusalem at the feast"?

*Jesus' Deeds at Jerusalem*

(382) We find nothing mentioned earlier except that, "He found in the temple those selling cattle and sheep and doves and the money-changers sitting. And when he had made a scourge of cords he drove them all out of the temple, both the sheep and the cattle, and he poured out the coins of the exchangers and overturned their tables. And he said to those selling doves: 'Take these things out of here; do not make my Father's house a house of merchandise.'"[443]

(383) What, then, is so extraordinary in these deeds, that the Galileans were moved on the basis of them to receive the Lord? For it is testified that they received him because they had gone to the feast in Jerusalem and had seen all the things that Jesus did there.

(384) If we recall our remarks on this passage, which show that the Savior's power is seen no less in these acts than in his power to cause the blind to see, the deaf to hear, and the lame to walk,[444] we must say that perhaps the

---

442. Cf. Lagarde *OS* 61.20; 132.2.
443. Cf. Jn 2.14–16.
444. See Book 10.145–49 (FOTC 80.289–90).

## COMMENTARY ON JOHN, BOOK 13

Galileans were [not] misled when they reflected and were astounded at the divinity of Jesus and received him when he came into Galilee, "having seen all the things he had done in Jerusalem."

(385) Now "all things" included driving the sheep and cattle out of the temple with a scourge of cords, pouring out the coins of the exchangers and overturning their tables, and saying authoritatively to those selling doves, "Take these things out of here; do not make my Father's house a house of merchandise."[445]

(386) But I think these were not the only things he did then, but that he also performed other signs. For this statement is added to those words, "Now when he was at Jerusalem at the Pasch on the festival day, many believed in his name, seeing the signs that he did."[446] And furthermore, Nicodemus says, "Rabbi, we know that you have come from God as a teacher, for no one can do these signs which you do, unless God be with him."[447]

(387) It is possible, however, that a Galilean happened to be in Jerusalem, where the temple of God is located, to celebrate the festival, and saw everything that Jesus did there, and especially how he cast out all those selling cattle, sheep, and doves, along with the sheep, the cattle, and the rest, with the scourge he made from cords.[448]

(388) For the feast in Jerusalem marks the beginning of the Galileans' reception of the Son of God when he came to them. For if they had not seen his deeds at the feast, they would not have received him. Nor would he himself have visited them so eagerly, having left those who asked him "to remain with them,"[449] if the Galileans had not been previously prepared to receive him.

(389) Those, however, who have received Jesus have also received the one who sent him, for he says, "He who receives me receives him who sent me."[450] First, then, we must see, that is, understand, all the works of Jesus in Jerusalem.

445. Jn 2.16.
447. Cf. Jn 3.2.
449. Jn 4.40.
446. Cf. Jn 2.23.
448. Cf. Jn 2.15.
450. Cf. Lk 9.48.

152                        ORIGEN

This means we must see how he cleanses the temple, having restored it to be "the Father's house" and no longer a "house of merchandise,"[451] so that, once we have seen these works, we may receive the Word who effects them.

(390) And I think that he who has not seen all the works of Jesus in Jerusalem will not receive Jesus, or that Jesus will not make this visit, of which the visit to Galilee is a symbol,[452] to those who have not formerly gone up to the feast and seen all the things that he did in Jerusalem.

He came again, therefore, into Cana of Galilee where he had made the water wine. (John 4.46)

*The Two Sojourns of the Savior*

(391) We said as much as we were able to say about Cana in our remarks above.[453] But two sojourns in Cana are not in vain for Jesus, for perhaps they indicate the two sojourns of the Savior in the world.[454] The former occurred that he might gladden those who feasted with him, and the second, that he might restore the son who was near death, [not] the son of a king, but of some royal official.[455]

(392) Perhaps the royal official was Abraham or Jacob, whose son (being the people) he will save at the end after the fullness of the Gentiles enter.[456] There can also be two visits of the Word in the soul. The first provides the wine made from water for the gladness of those feasting together, and the second removes every lingering illness and the threat of death.

(393) And since the majority of God's works are veiled, it is not strange if Jesus, while performing many works for the salvation of people everywhere, of which the other places

---

451. Cf. Jn 2.16.
452. Preuschen indicates a textual corruption in this clause. Origen seems to be speaking of Jesus' visit to Galilee as a symbol of his visit to the soul.
453. Presumably in Book 9, which is lost. Book 10 treats Jn 2.12–25. Fragments 28–30 are on Jn 2.1,7,11.
454. Cf. Jn 2.1–2; 4.46.
455. Cf. Jn 4.46–47.
456. Cf. Rom 11.25.

that are recorded are types, visits this Cana twice to confirm for himself the possession of those from this earth who believe in the Father through him.

> And there was a royal official whose son was sick at Capharnaum. [When he heard that Jesus had come from Judea into Galilee, he went to him and asked him to come down and heal his son, for he was at the point of death. Jesus therefore said to him, Unless you see signs and wonders, you do not believe. The official said to him, Lord, come down before my son dies. Jesus said to him, Go, your son lives. The man believed the word that Jesus spoke and departed. As he was going down, however, his servants met him and said that his son lived. Therefore he asked of them the hour at which he had got better. And they said to him that the fever left him at the seventh hour. Therefore the father knew that that was the hour at which Jesus had said to him, Your son lives,][457] and he and his whole house believed. (John 4.46–53)

(394) We do not find the royal official's name used at all by the Jews. For this reason we pay no attention even in the literal sense to who this royal official was and what king he was named after.

(395) A simpleminded man will think that this royal official was one of king Herod's men, and another of similar understanding will say that he was of Caesar's house,[458] performing some duty concerning Judea at the time. He is clearly not found to be a Jew, since it does not follow that because his son was sick in Capharnaum that he was a kinsman of those in those regions.

(396) His dignity appears also from the fact that his servants have already come to meet him while he is going down, to tell him that his child lives, for "servants" are men-

---

457. The bracketed words are not in the lemma. After "Capharnaum" the text has ἕως ("up to") followed by the final words of the lemma.
458. Cf. Phil 4.22.

tioned in the plural. Therefore, let what once happened in the literal sense be as described, and let the son of the royal official have gotten better at the seventh hour, having been freed from his fever by the word of the Savior, and let his whole house have believed.

### The Royal Official and His Son as Symbols

(397) But come, let us inquire, as best we are able, of whom this royal official and his son can be a symbol. We have known of no other great king at least, whose city is the true Jerusalem,[459] and who is king of kings,[460] who has gone into a far country to receive a kingdom for himself and to return,[461] and has ascended as king, than the one who said, "But I have been appointed king by him over Zion, his holy mountain, preaching the commandment of the Lord."[462]

(398) Those who see his day and rejoice are all royal officials,[463] and those who believe in the Father through him are named after his kingdom. We are investigating a particular one of these royal officials and his sick son, and the other events connected with the story.

(399) Now, we said above[464] that all the people are sons of Abraham, as even they themselves boastfully say, "We are the seed of Abraham, and we have never been slaves to anyone,"[465] and, "Are you greater than our father Abraham, who is dead?"[466]

(400) For, as the people boast on the basis of Abraham more than on the rest of the fathers who also come after him, the Savior also says, "Do not begin to say, We have Abraham for our father," or, "Think not to say, We have Abraham for our father. God is able of these stones to raise up children to Abraham."[467]

(401) Moreover, Isaias says to the people, "Look to Abraham your father, and to Sara who bore you."[468]

---

459. Cf. Mt 5.35.
460. Cf. Rv 19.16.
461. Cf. Lk 19.12.
462. Ps 2.6–7.
463. Cf. Jn 8.56.
464. See section 392.
465. Jn 8.33.
466. Jn 8.53.
467. Cf. Lk 3.8; Mt 3.9. The words are spoken by John the Baptist in the Gospels, not by Jesus.
468. Is 51.2.

## COMMENTARY ON JOHN, BOOK 13

(402) Why must we prolong the discourse with examples, when it is clear that Abraham is called father of the people first, for which reason he also receives the name "father" exclusively? We think, therefore, that the royal official is Abraham, and his son who is sick in Capharnaum and about to die is the Israelite race.[469] This race is sick as a result of its piety and observance of the divine laws, and is at the point of dying to God, inflamed by the fiery missiles of the enemy[470] and consequently is said to be feverish.

(403) Now it appears that those saints who have previously departed this life are concerned about the people, as it is written in the Machabees so many years after the assumption of Jeremias, "This is Jeremias, the prophet of God, who prays much concerning the people."[471]

(404) Consider, therefore, if we can take it that Abraham, being some royal official, thought it worthwhile, when his son was sick and about to die, that our Savior help his suffering son, and went to him and asked that he descend and heal his son, for he was about to die.

(405) The reply given him, "Unless you see signs and wonders," refers to the multitude of his sons, and perhaps even to himself.[472] For just as John, although he expected the sojourn of Christ, required the sign that was given, that thereby he might recognize the one who was prophesied (and the sign was: "Upon whomever you see the Spirit descending and remaining upon him, this is the Son of God"[473]), so also the saints who have already died, because they too expect the sojourn of the Christ in the body, observe his character from his signs and wonders, and believe in the one awaited through these signs and wonders.

(406) Earlier, however, the royal official beseeches the Lord to come down to his sick child, fearing that death might come first and prevail over the one who was sick. Christ drives away his fever with a word, and gives the father

---

469. Cf. Jn 4.46.  
470. Cf. Eph 6.16.  
471. Cf. 2 Mc 15.14.  
472. Origen's comment is probably based on the fact that the verb is second person *plural.*  
473. Cf. Jn 1.33–34.

the news concerning the life of his endangered son in the words, "Go, your son lives."

(407) But this royal official has not only a son, but also servants, a humbler and subordinate class of believers, of whom Abraham's servants who were born at home and those who were purchased were a symbol.[474]

(408) These servants who attend the sick child perceive his salvation and go to meet the father to report the good news about the life of his son who was healed by the words, "Your child lives." They were happy[475] because they did not think earlier that their master's child would live. Nor is it to no purpose that the fever leaves him in the seventh hour, for the number seven stands for rest.[476]

(409) The son, however, is in Capharnaum. He who is sick and is healed, who is in the "field of exhortation,"[477] represents those who have become weary, but who are not completely devoid of fruits. And the father's faith reaches its highest perfection when he, along with all his household, believes in Christ after he has come to know of his son's salvation.

(410) In the next words in the text we shall explore, as best we are able, how Jesus performed this second sign after he came down from Judea to Galilee.[478]

(411) We must also consider if this royal official is an image of some power of the rulers of this world,[479] and if his son is an image of those people with him who are under his authority in differing degrees, and, if I may put it this way, is an image, as it were, of the elect who are with him. And we must see if his sickness is his bad attitude contrary to the will of the ruler, and if Capharnaum is the image of the region of the abode of those under him.

(412) For I think that some of the rulers have also been astounded by his power and divinity, and have fled to him

---

474. Cf. Gn 14.14; 17.12.
475. Accepting Wendland's suggestion to read the passive rather than the active participle.
476. Because God rested on the seventh day. See Gn 2.2–3.
477. See Book 10.37 (FOTC 80.264).
478. Cf. Jn 4.54.    479. Cf. 1 Cor 2.8.

for refuge, and have prayed for those they governed. For why are men granted repentance and the opportunity to change from unbelief to faith, yet we are hesitant to say the same thing in the case of the powers?

(413) Or, let someone tell us why it is that those who have been clothed in flesh and blood are able, when they change, to take refuge in God through Christ, but all those who experience a purer nature are incapable of experiencing faith in the Savior and amazement at the marvelous miracles he performed. I think, however, that something happened also concerning the rulers so that they changed for the better in the sojourn of Christ, and consequently whole cities or even nations have been more friendly towards matters related to the Christ than many others.

(414) And according to this interpretation it will not be strange that it is said to the royal official, "Unless you see signs and wonders, you will not believe."

(415) And when the royal official has come to him, he can earnestly request that the power of God come down to the place of the child's sickness and heal the one who is sick. There is absolutely no need, however, that he go down to the royal official's feverish son, for the statement that is made, "Your son lives," is sufficient for the salvation of the child, since the word is active and creative of the things that the speaker wishes.

### Heracleon's Understanding of the Royal Official

(416) Heracleon, however, seems to say that *the royal official is the Demiurge, since he also ruled those under him. And because his kingdom is small and temporal,* he says *he was called a royal official, as if he were some petty king appointed over a small kingdom by the universal king.* And he interprets his son in Capharnaum as *the one in the lower part of the middle region, which is near the sea, that is, which has been combined with matter,* and he says that *his own man was sick, that is, was not in his natural condition, and was in ignorance and sins.*

(417) Then the words, "from Judea to Galilee,"[480] are taken to mean *"from the Judea above."* . . . But I do not know how, moved by the statement, "He was about to die," he thinks *the teachings of those*

---

480. Jn 4.54.

*who suppose that the soul is immortal are overthrown*, assuming that the statement that both the soul and the body perish in Gehenna[481] contributes to the same view.

(418) Heracleon does not think that the soul is immortal, but that it is capable of salvation. He says that *the soul is the corruptible that is clothed with incorruption and the mortal with immortality when its "death is swallowed up in victory."*[482]

(419) In addition to these comments, he also says *the statement, "Unless you see signs and wonders, you will not believe," is properly made to a person such as this whose nature is determined by works and who is persuaded by sense perception, and does not believe the word.*

(420) And he thinks t*he plea, "Come down before my child dies," is made because death is the goal of the law that destroys through sins.*[483] Therefore, he says, *the father needs the only Savior to help the son, that is, such a nature, before he is permanently put to death through sins.*

(421) Furthermore, he has taken the statement, *"Your son lives,"* to have been said humbly by the Savior, since he did not say, "Let him live," nor did he indicate that it was he who had granted him life. But he says that *after he had gone down to the sick boy and healed him of his illness, that is, of his sins, and had given him life through forgiveness, he said, "Your son lives."*

(422) And he says in connection with the statement, the man "believed," that *even the Demiurge is willing to believe that the Savior can heal even when he is not present.*

(423) And he has taken *the servants of the royal official to be the angels of the Demiurge who report in the statement, "Your child lives," that he is behaving properly and fittingly, and is no longer acting inconsistently.* And because he thinks *the angels first see the actions of men in the world, whether they are living rightly and purely since the Savior's sojourn,* he thinks *the servants report the news about the son's salvation to the royal official.*

(424) Further, he says of the seventh hour, that *the nature of the one healed is characterized by the hour.* In addition, he explained the statement, *"He and his whole household believed," to have reference to the order of angels and men who are more akin to the Demiurge.*

(425) He says that *there is a question as to whether certain angels who descended to the daughters of men will be saved.*[484] And he thinks *the destruction of the men of the Demiurge is revealed in the statement, "The sons of the kingdom will go out into outer darkness."*[485]

---

481. Cf. Mt 10.28.
482. Cf. 1 Cor 15.53-54.
483. Cf. Rom 7.13.
484. Cf. Gn 6.2
485. Cf. Mt 8.12.

(426) Isaias also prophesied of these as follows, "I have begotten sons, and exalted them, but they have rejected me."[486] He calls them *alien sons, wicked and lawless seed,*[487] and *a vineyard that produced thorns.*[488]

### Objection's to Heracleon's Interpretation

(427) These are Heracleon's words, which were spoken rather presumptuously and impiously. A lengthy argument would be needed to demonstrate their truth.

I do not know how he doubts even the immortality of the soul, although he has not understood how many things are indicated by the word "death."

(428) For one who perceives the meaning must see, by precise investigation, if the things referred to are mortal in all respects.

(429) For on the one hand, because the soul is capable of sin, and the soul that sins shall die,[489] we also will say that the soul is mortal. But if he supposes that death means the total dissolution and destruction of the soul, we will not agree, because we cannot conceive, so far as the concept goes, of a mortal essence changing into an immortal one, and a corruptible nature changing to incorruption.[490] For this is like saying that something changes from a corporeal into an incorporeal nature, as though something common underlies the nature of corporeal and incorporeal beings, and that this continues constant, as those who are clever about these things say that the material remains although the qualities change into incorruption. But it is not the same for the corruptible nature "to put on incorruption" and for the corruptible nature to change into incorruption.[491]

(430) And we must say the same things also concerning the mortal nature, which does not change into immortality, but puts it on.[492]

(431) Further, since it was seen that the physical nature is

---

486. Is 1.2.
487. Cf. Is 1.4.
488. Cf. Is 5.2.
489. Cf. Ez 18.4.
490. Cf. 1 Cor 15.53.
491. Cf. 1 Cor 15.53.
492. Cf. 1 Cor 15.53.

persuaded by works and sense perception, and not by words,[493] we will ask him what kind of nature Paul's was. For if he were of a spiritual nature, how is it that he believed because of a miraculous manifestation?[494] And if he could not believe in any other way than by means of miraculous manifestation, it follows, from their way of thinking, that Paul too belongs to the physical nature.

(432) And how is it not impious to say that the angels of the Demiurge see the rightness and purity of the life of those who are improved by the Savior's power before the Demiurge sees it? Is it not contrary to the clarity of the teaching about the Demiurge? And is it not also contrary to the Scripture that says, "Will a man be hidden in secret places and I not see him?"[495] And, "The Lord who searches kidneys and hearts,"[496] and, "The Lord knows the thoughts of men, even if they are vain"?[497]

(433) And how will he also maintain the saying, "He who knows all things before they happen"?[498] And why does he think the nature of the one healed is designated by the number of the hour, rather than the nature of the healing that takes place being designated by the appropriate number for rest? But that there are corruptions of physical natures is recorded at the end of his remarks which we set out, when he uses an equivocal term and introduces another nature as a fourth, which he does not wish.

> And this is again the second sign Jesus did when he had come out of Judea into Galilee. (John 4.54)

(434) The saying is ambiguous. On the one hand it means something like this: In coming from Judea into Galilee Jesus has performed two signs, of which the second is the one concerning the royal official's son. On the other hand it means something like this: While there are two signs which Jesus performed in Galilee, he has done the second after he came from Judea into Galilee.

---

493. See above, section 419.
494. Cf. Acts 9.3–18.
495. Jer 23.24.
496. Cf. Ps 7.10.
497. Cf. Ps 93.11.
498. Sus 35a.

(435) The latter is the meaning to be accepted as correct. For Jesus has not performed the first sign since he came from Judea into Galilee (the first sign is the changing of the water into wine[499]), which occurred the day after Andrew, Simon Peter's brother, asked where Jesus was staying, and remained with the Lord about the tenth hour of the day.[500] For it is written, "On the following day he wished to depart into Galilee, and he found Philip."[501]

*The Significance of the Second Sign*

(436) But consider if we can take what the Evangelist indicates about this being the second sign after the Lord came down from Judea into Galilee to refer to the economy of salvation.

(437) Now we said in our discussions above that the two sojourns of our Savior in Cana can be taken as a symbol of his two sojourns on the earth.[502] Cana was so named because it had become the "possession"[503] of him who had received all authority in heaven and upon earth.[504]

(438) On his first sojourn, therefore, after our baptism, he makes us who dwell with him glad, and gives us some of the wine of his power to drink. This was water when it was first drawn, but became wine when Jesus changed it. For the Scripture was truly water before the time of Jesus, but since the time of Jesus it has become wine for us.

(439) On his second visit, however, when he has been entrusted with judgment by God, he releases us from the fever at the time of judgment. He releases the royal official's son from fever and heals him completely, whether he be understood to be the son of Abraham or of some ruler who is called a royal official.

(440) These remarks are related to an interpretation which keeps close to the previous interpretations. But since we must take thought of ourselves, we must say that it is pos-

---

499. Cf. Jn 2.1–11.  500. Cf. Jn 1.38–40.
501. Jn 1.43.
502. See above, sections 391–93.
503. κτῆμα. Cf. Lagarde *OS* 193.25; 203.5.
504. Cf. Mt 28.18; 6.10.

sible for all his creation to apprehend this twofold sojourn.

(441) Now you shall consider in relation to this, if we must say that the first sojourn is of chief importance and the second results from it, so that those who received him on his primary sojourn are made glad, but those who were unwilling previously to drink of his wine are released from every sickness and the fiery darts of the enemy[505] on his second sojourn.

### The Healing in Capharnaum

(442) And the constituents of the first miracle are undivided, for he who makes the water wine and those who drink it are in Cana,[506] but those of the second have a kind of division, as it were, for the sick son of the royal official was not where Jesus was, for he was not in Cana but in Capharnaum.[507]

(443) And the word of power proceeds from Cana, for the statement, "Your son lives,"[508] is made in Cana. The work of that word, however, takes place in Capharnaum, for there the royal official's sick son was healed by Jesus' word during the seventh hour.[509]

(444) Now, we find that this son was healed by a word from Jesus when he was not thought to be present with him, and also that the healing of the servant of the centurion took place in the same way.[510] For we learn also from the centurion that the Lord does not go into his house, because he said, "Lord, I am not worthy that you should enter under my roof, but only speak the word, and he will be healed."[511] Wherefore Jesus says to him, "Go, and let it be done to you as you have believed."[512]

(445) Now we have observed also that both the servant of the centurion and the son of the royal official were sick in Capharnaum. Peter's mother-in-law, too, was lying sick with fever in Capharnaum, and Jesus touched her hand and

---

505. Cf. Eph 6.16.
506. Cf. Jn 2.1–11.
507. Cf. Jn 4.46.
508. Jn 4.50.
509. Cf. Jn 4.52.
510. Cf. Mt 8.5–13.
511. Mt 8.8.
512. Cf. Mt 8.13.

healed her while she was lying ill. Consequently, she got up and served him.[513]

(446) The following people were all healed in Capharnaum during the day: the royal official's son, who was healed during the seventh hour, and the centurion's servant and Peter's mother-in-law, who were healed before it was evening. "And when evening came (in Capharnaum, according to Matthew), they brought many who were possessed with demons to him, and he cast out the spirits with a word, and he healed all who were sick."[514] Some, therefore, are healed later by Jesus, and others earlier. For those healed during the evening are later, meaning that they are inferior to those healed during the day, for they are demon-possessed and sick.

(447) We must earnestly endeavor to assemble the places where those in need of healing were found, and we must note in what sort of places other signs occurred besides those which concern the sick. For example, it was a sign when Jesus said in Samaria, "You have had five husbands, and he whom you now have is not your husband."[515] The woman was amazed at this and said, "I see that you are a prophet."[516] She said to her fellow-citizens, "Come, see a man who has told me everything that I have done. Is not this the Christ?"[517]

(448) We must also observe where, why, and in relation to what deeds Jesus' words are spoken, for only by such observations and examinations will one find, piece by piece, the touchstones,[518] the fruits of one's labors, the blessing in the Psalms, which says, "You shall eat the fruits of your labors."[519]

### Signs and Wonders

(449) Further, we must also say in relation to the statement, "And this is again the second sign Jesus did,"[520] that

513. Cf. Mt 8.14–15.
514. Mt 8.16.
515. Jn 4.18.
516. Jn 4.19.
517. Jn 4.29.
518. Preuschen thinks there is a textual problem here.
519. Cf. Ps 127.2.
520. Jn 4.54.

nowhere are wonders mentioned alone. For if wonders are mentioned anywhere, they are recorded along with signs, as in the statement, "Unless you see signs and wonders, you will not believe."[521] Signs, however, may be seen everywhere without wonders, as even now.

(450) We must investigate if there is some kind of distinction between wonders and signs. Now, I think that the miraculous and marvelous mighty works are called "wonders," because what happens is miraculous and transcends the ordinary, being both marvelous and superhuman. On the other hand, things indicative of certain other things over and above what occurs are said to be "signs." For this reason we find the term "sign" also used to refer to things which are not miraculous.

(451) At least God speaks of a sign in these words, "You shall circumcise every male who belongs to you. And you shall circumcise the flesh of your foreskin, and it shall be for a sign of the covenant between me and you."[522]

(452) Nowhere, however, are wonders mentioned alone, because nothing miraculous happens in Scripture that is not also a sign and symbol of something else beyond the literal occurrence. Consequently, if anything wondrous had been done that was not symbolic of something else, it would have been written that Jesus had performed the wonder itself, or, let us say, Moses, or one of the saints.

(453) Since, therefore, Scripture teaches us that we must seek that of which the event is a sign, it is said, "And this is again the second sign Jesus did." When, however, the royal official is reproached because he will not believe unless he sees miracles, it is no longer said, "Unless you see signs you will not believe,"[523] for the signs that occur are not offered to produce faith, in so far as they are signs, unless the sign happens also to be a wonder. He is told instead, "Unless you see signs and wonders, you will not believe."[524] You, on the one hand, believe because of the miraculous. We, however, in

---

521. Jn 4.48.
523. Cf. Jn 4.48.
522. Gn 17.10–11.
524. Jn 4.48.

addition to this, and because of that of which the miraculous is a sign, bring it to its intended goal.

(454) But you will ask regarding the words in the seventy-seventh Psalm, "How he worked his signs in Egypt, and his wonders in the field of Tanis,"[525] whether "signs and wonders" differ in substance or are the same. On the one hand, in so far as they are signs, they occurred in Egypt, and Egypt itself carries certain spiritual meanings in the anagogical sense. On the other hand, in so far as they are wonders, they occurred "in the field of Tanis." Neither the wonders *qua* wonders, nor the field of Tanis *qua* field of Tanis are given an allegorical interpretation. But both the wonders, in so far as they are signs, and the field of Tanis, in so far as it is Egypt, require an anagogical meaning.

(455) But let us stop the thirteenth book at this point, which embraces an explanation of Jesus' activities from their beginning up to his seventh visit.[526] First he was baptized at Bethabara beside the Jordan;[527] second, he made the water wine when he visited Cana of Galilee;[528] third, he went down to Capharnaum,[529] and it was fitting that there were sick people where he went down; fourth, he went up to Jerusalem;[530] fifth, he spent time with his disciples in the land of Judea;[531] sixth, he taught in Samaria beside Jacob's fountain,[532] which we examined as best we were able; and seventh, he came a second time to Cana of Galilee.[533] In the next book, if God grants, we will discuss what Jesus did and said at the feast of the Jews in Jerusalem.

---

525. Ps 77.43.
526. From what follows, Origen seems to mean the first thirteen books rather than just book thirteen.
527. Cf. Jn 1.28.
528. Cf. Jn 2.1–11.
529. Cf. Jn 2.12.
530. Cf. Jn 2.13.
531. Cf. Jn 3.22.
532. Cf. Jn 4.4–42.
533. Cf. Jn 4.46.

## BOOK NINETEEN[1]

Jesus answered, you know neither me nor my Father; if you knew me you would know my Father also.
(John 8.19)

### The Jews Both Know and Do Not Know Jesus

IF THE STATEMENT that says, "And you know me, whence I am,"[2] and the one that declares, "You know neither me nor my Father," were addressed to the same people, they would obviously appear to be contradictory. But, as it is, the one statement, "And you know me," is addressed to certain people of Jerusalem who had said, "Have the rulers known truly that this is the Christ? But we know this man, whence he is; but when the Christ comes, no one knows whence he is."[3] The other statement, "You do not know me," etc., is addressed to Pharisees who said to him, "You testify of yourself; your testimony is not true."[4]

(2) But his words, "You do not know the Father," are addressed both to the people of Jerusalem, through the words we examined earlier, and to the Pharisees through the words now being examined. He addresses the people of Jerusalem with the words, "I have not come from myself, but he that sent me is true, whom you do not know. I know him because I am from him, and he sent me."[5] To the Pharisees, however, he says, "You know neither me nor my Father; if you knew me, you would know my Father also."

(3) Someone might ask with good reason how the people

---

1. Both the beginning and the end of this book are missing.
2. Cf. Jn 7.28.
3. Jn 7.26–27.
4. Cf. Jn 8.13.
5. Jn 7.28–29.

of Jerusalem to whom he says, "And you know me,"[6] do not know the Father, if the statement is true, "If you knew me you would know my Father also." And John intensifies the difficulty in this passage also when he says, in his catholic epistle, "The one who denies the Father also denies the Son; everyone who denies the Son does not have the Father."[7]

(4) For if "the one who denies the Father also denies the Son,"[8] and "he who confesses the Son has the Father also,"[9] it is clear that the people of Jerusalem, so far as the literal sense is concerned, deny the Son too, when they deny the Father by not knowing the Father.

(5) But if they deny the Son, how is it true to say, "And you know me"? Again, if the same people know the Son on the basis of the statement, "And you know me," they confess the Father, since "he who confesses the Son has the Father also."[10] But if they confess the Father, how is the statement true, "But he who sent me is true, whom you do not know"?[11]

*Christ Speaks of Himself Sometimes As a Man, Sometimes As God*

(6) Now, we must say in respect to these problems that at one time the Savior is speaking of himself as of a man, but at another time he speaks of himself as of a nature that is divine and united with the uncreated nature of the Father. For whenever he says, "But now you seek to kill me, a man who has told you the truth,"[12] he says this knowing that what they are attempting to destroy is not God but man. But if he says, "I and the Father are one,"[13] or, "I am the truth and the life,"[14] or, "I am the resurrection,"[15] and other similar statements, he is not teaching about the man whom they are attempting to destroy.

6. Jn 7.28.   7. 1 Jn 2.22–23.
8. 1 Jn 2.22. Origen has quoted only part of the sentence in Jn, and seems to take it in the sense: He who denies the Father also denies the Son.
9. 1 Jn 2.23.   10. 1 Jn 2.23.
11. Jn 7.28.   12. Jn 8.40.
13. Jn 10.30.   14. Cf. Jn 14.6.
15. Jn 11.25.

(7) In this manner, therefore, we must also learn from the context in our present investigations. The statement, "You know me and you know whence I am,"[16] is made of the man himself, but the statement, "You know neither me nor my Father," is made of his divinity. For the statement, "You know me and you know whence I am,"[17] is preceded by the words, "Some, therefore, of Jerusalem said, Is not this he whom they seek to kill? And behold, he speaks openly, and they say nothing to him. Have the rulers known truly that this is the Christ? But we know whence this man is; but when the Christ comes, no one knows whence he is."[18]

(8) And the statement, "You know neither me nor my Father" is preceded by the words, "The Pharisees therefore said to him, You testify of yourself; your testimony is not true. Jesus answered and said to them: Although I testify of myself, my testimony is true, for I know whence I came and where I go.

(9) ... You judge according to the flesh; I judge no one. And even if I do judge, my judgment is true, because I am not alone, but there is myself and the Father who sent me."[19]

(10) It is clear, then, from these words that the people of Jerusalem said, "We know this man, whence he is,"[20] referring to the fact that he had been born in Bethlehem,[21] and that they understood that he was the one whose mother was called Mary, and his brothers were James, John, Simon, [and] Judas.[22] For this reason, he also testifies to those who said, "We know whence he is,"[23] with his statement, "You know me and you know whence I am."[24] But when he said to the Pharisees, "Although I testify of myself, my testimony is true, because I know whence I came and where I go,"[25] he was speaking about his divine nature and, as one might say, on the basis of which he was the firstborn of all creation.[26]

16. Jn 7.28.  
17. Jn 7.28.  
18. Jn 7.25–27.  
19. Cf. Jn 8.13–16. Preuschen thinks the words at the end of v. 14 were lost by a scribal error.  
20. Jn 7.27.  
21. Cf. Mt 2.1.  
22. Cf. Mt 13.55.  
23. Jn 7.27.  
24. Jn 7.28.  
25. Jn 8.14.  
26. Cf. Col 1.15.

(11) Wherefore, he answers (being a different person, so to speak, than the one who says, "And you know me") those who have asked him about these matters and have said, "Where is your father?"[27] and says, "You know neither me nor my Father." But it was because of the baseness of the Pharisees that they either did not understand that he was speaking of the God of the universe when he said, "The Father who sent me testifies of me,"[28] or, if they did understand that he was speaking about God, they imagined God to be in a place and, therefore, responded, "Where is your father?"[29]

### The Wicked Do Not Know God

(12) We must recognize, however, that the heterodox think that this text proves clearly that the God whom the Jews worshipped was not the Father of Christ. For, they say, that if the Savior said to the Pharisees who worship the Creator, "You know neither me nor my Father," it is clear that the Pharisees did not know the Father of Jesus because he was different from the Creator. Neither did the people of Jerusalem know him, to whom he said previously, "But he who sent me is true, whom you do not know."[30] They say these things, however, because they have not read the divine Scriptures, nor observed the usage of language in them.

(13) For, although one may be able to give a full account of matters concerning God, having learned from the fathers that he alone is to be worshipped, if one does not live rightly, the Scriptures[31] say that this person does not possess knowledge of God. If, indeed, anyone knew the matters concerning the Creator and his priestly service, it is clear that the sons of Heli the priest did, since they had been reared at the place of worship. Nevertheless, because they sinned, these words are written of them in the First Book of Kings, "And the sons of Heli, pestilent sons, did not know the Lord."[32]

(14) So we shall ask the heterodox if the statement, "They did not know the Lord," has not been written of the

27. Jn 8.19.
28. Jn 8.18.
29. Jn 8.19.
30. Jn 7.28.
31. Lit.: "they say."
32. Cf. 1 Kgs (1 Sm) 2.12.

Creator. And, when they answer that these words are about the Creator, we shall ask why it is said of the sons of Heli, "They did not know the Lord." Was it because the words are about God the Creator, or was it because of their wickedness? Now it is clear that it is said that they did not know the Lord because of their wickedness.

(15) And it is possible to find this same thing not only concerning Heli's sons but also concerning other sinful rulers in Israel and Juda. So, therefore, the Pharisees too did not know the Father, since they were not living in accordance with the Creator's will.

*Knowing the Father and Believing in the Father Are Not the Same Thing*

(16) But knowing God can also indicate something else—knowing God being something other than simply believing in God[33]—as is clear from the statement, "As many things as the law says it says to those in the law,"[34] [since] it is clear that [the word "law" also includes][35] the prophets, whose words are said to be law, as we have demonstrated in other places.[36] Therefore it is said in the Psalms, "Be still and know that I am God."[37]

(17) But who would not agree that these words have been written to people who believe in the Creator? It is not possible to know him if one has not become still and purified one's mind, since those who perceive God and see him with

---

33. Preuschen thinks there is a corruption in the text here, for, in his opinion, the words that follow in the remainder of the sentence have no connection with what precedes.
34. Cf. Rom 3.19.
35. The bracketed words are Brooke's suggested emendations.
36. Cf. Origen, *comm. in Rom.*, in *The Philocalia of Origen*, ed. J. A. Robinson (Cambridge, 1893), 55.19ff. The whole of section IX in the *Philocalia* contains a discussion of different meanings given to the same word in Scripture. The discussion focuses on the word "law," being a discussion of Romans 7.7. This may be the reason Origen introduces a verse about the law at this point, i.e. his intention is to remind his readers that the same word can mean different things as he has shown in his discussion of the word "law" in other places. See R. E. Heine, "A Note on the Text of Origen, *Commentary on John* 19.III.16," JTS 42 (1991): 596–98.
37. Ps 45.11.

eyes that are more divine have been thought worthy of this grace because they have made their heart pure, as the Savior testifies saying, "Blessed are the pure in heart, for they shall see God."[38] But at the same time we will also say, in reference to the statement, "No one has known the Father, except the Son,"[39] that to know the Father and to believe in him are not the same thing.

(18) Therefore, the statement, "No one has known the Father except the Son,"[40] is not opposed to the statement, "And Abraham believed in God and it was reckoned to him for justice."[41] But if anyone thinks we are distorting things when we say that believing is not the same as knowing, and that it is possible for one to believe and not to have knowledge of the one believed in by him, let him hear Jesus when he says to those Jews who had believed in him, "If you continue in my word, you will know the truth, and the truth will make you free."[42]

(19) For observe carefully that before the statement, "If you continue in my word, you will know the truth," it has been written, "Therefore, Jesus said to those Jews who believed in him." And what he said was, "If you continue in my word, you will know the truth."[43]

(20) Now there is a great difference between knowing with respect to believing and only believing. "For to one, by the Spirit, is given the word of wisdom, and to another, the word of knowledge, according to the same Spirit, to another, faith in the same Spirit."[44]

*Knowledge of God Leads to Union with God*

(21) I have said these things to show that there is a difference between knowing God and believing in him. Now in the interest of accuracy let us add this too, by way of completing what we have said, that, in respect to the Pharisees to whom he says, "You know neither me nor my Father," one

38. Mt 5.8.
39. Cf. Mt 11.27.
40. Cf. Mt 11.27.
41. Rom 4.3; cf. Gn 15.6.
42. Cf. Jn 8.31–32.
43. Cf. Jn 8.31–32.
44. 1 Cor 12.8–9.

might reasonably have said, "But you do not even believe in my Father," for they did not believe in the one sent by the Father,[45] and he who denies the Son in no way has the Father.[46] By "in no way" I mean neither by means of faith nor knowledge.

(22) But see if Scripture does not also say elsewhere that those who have been made one with and united with something know that with which they have been made one and have been involved. And before such unity and participation, even if they understand the explanations given about a thing, they do not know it.

(23) When, for example, Adam says of Eve, "This is now bone of my bones and flesh of my flesh,"[47] he did not know his wife, for it is when he was joined with her that it is said, "And Adam knew Eve, his wife."[48] And if someone should take offence because we have used the statement, "And Adam knew Eve, his wife,"[49] as an example for the knowledge of God, let him first consider the statement, "This is a great mystery,"[50] and then let him compare what the Apostle says about male and female. He uses the same language of man and the Lord. "He who is joined to a prostitute is one body, and he who is joined to the Lord is one spirit."[51]

(24) Therefore, let him who is joined to a prostitute have known the prostitute, and let the one joined to his wife have known his wife, but more than this, also let him who is joined to the Lord have known the Lord in a holy manner. Now, if this is so, the Pharisees had known neither the Father nor the Son, and he who said, "You know neither me nor my Father," was correct. But if we should not take "to know" in this way, that is, to mean "to be made one with and united with" in accordance with our last interpretation, let someone explain the words, "But now having known God, but rather having been known by God,"[52] and the words, "The Lord has known those who are his."[53]

---

45. Cf. Jn 5.38.
47. Gn 2.23.
49. Cf. Gn 4.1.
51. Cf. 1 Cor 6.16–17.
53. 2 Tm 2.19; cf. Nm 16.5.

46. Cf. 1 Jn 2.23.
48. Cf. Gn 4.1.
50. Eph 5.32.
52. Gal 4.9.

(25) For, in our view, the Lord has known those who are his because he has been made one with them and has given them a share of his own divinity and has taken them up, as the language of the Gospel says, into his own hand, since those who have believed in the Savior are in the Father's hand. For this reason also, unless they fall from his hand, thereby removing themselves from the hand of God, they will not be snatched away, for no one snatches anyone from the Father's hand.

*Can One Know God without Knowing the Father?*

(26) After these matters, you will seek, in relation to the same statement—I mean the statement, "You know neither me nor my Father"—if it is possible for someone who knows God not to know the Father. For if there is one aspect of him in accordance with which he is Father, and another in accordance with which he is God, perhaps it is possible for someone to know God, but not to know the Father beyond knowing him as God, and not to know the Father.[54]

(27) After the Resurrection, therefore, the Savior says to Mary, "Go to my brothers and say to them, I am going to my Father and to your Father, to my God and your God."[55] It is indeed possible to agree with the heterodox view, that Moses and the prophets did not know the Father. This is, perhaps, correct,[56] since assuredly the one who has not known the Father has not known the Son. For, on the one hand, the Son has known the Father, but the servant has known the Lord. And just as we would not be impious if we were to say that the Son has not known the Lord (for since he is the Son, he has not experienced the Father as master), so, while retaining the same God, we will admit nothing outrageous if we say that it was fitting for the Son to know the Father, but for the servant to know the Lord, and neither has the servant known the Father, nor the Son the Lord.

---

54. V omits this last clause.
55. Cf. Jn 20.17.
56. Omitting the negative with Blanc. The discussion that follows shows that Origen is assuming the possibility that God was not known as Father to the writers of the OT.

(28) In fact, although there are countless prayers recorded in the Psalms and the prophets, indeed in the law as well, we have not found a single person who has prayed and addressed God as "Father." Perhaps it is because they did not know the Father. They pray to him as God and Lord, awaiting the one who pours out the spirit of adoption[57] on them no less than on those who believe in God through him after his coming,[58] unless perhaps Christ had sojourned in them spiritually, and they had the spirit of adoption because they had been perfected at some time. But they spoke or wrote about God as Father in secret and not in a manner intelligible to all, so that they might not anticipate the grace that is poured out to all the world through Jesus who calls all people to adoption[59] so that he may declare the name of God to his brothers and praise the Father in the midst of the assembly in accordance with what has been written, "I will declare your name to my brothers, in the midst of the assembly I will praise you."[60]

*The God of the Prophets and the Creator of the World Is the Father of Christ*

(29) The fact, however, that the same God is God of the prophets and Creator of the world can be seen from many places, but for the present it is sufficient to consider Stephen's sermon to the people in the Acts, when he speaks as follows. "Men, brothers and fathers, hear.

(30) "The God of glory appeared to our father Abraham when he was in Mesopotamia, before he dwelt in Charan. And he said to him: Go forth out of your country and from your kindred," etc.[61] Throughout the whole speech one can learn incontrovertibly that the God of the prophets is the Father of Christ Jesus.

(31) We learn the same thing also from the Apostle's words in the Epistle to the Romans. "Paul, a servant of Christ Jesus, called to be an apostle, separated unto the

---

57. Cf. Rom 8.15.
58. Cf. 1 Pt 1.21.
59. Cf. Eph 1.5.
60. Ps 21.23; cf. Heb 2.12.
61. Acts 7.2–3.

gospel of God, which he promised before by his prophets in the Holy Scriptures, concerning his Son, who was born of the seed of David according to the flesh, who was ordained Son of God in power according to the Spirit of sanctification by the Resurrection of our Lord Jesus Christ from the dead, through whom we have received grace and apostleship for obedience to the faith in all the nations for his name, among whom you also are the called of Jesus Christ, to all God's beloved who are at Rome, called to be saints. Grace to you and peace from God our Father and the Lord Jesus Christ."[62]

(32) We have learned clearly from these words that the Creator and the God of the prophets is also Father of Christ, and he is our God and Father.

(33) Not only, then, did the Pharisees not know the one who had given the law, the Father of Christ, either as Father or as God, they also, admittedly, did not believe in him in so far as he was Father of Jesus and his God, and perhaps [not even] in so far as he was the God who created all things.

*The Ascent from the Son to the Father*

(34) But they were also ignorant of the Christ. The Savior rebukes them appropriately when he says, "You know neither me nor my Father." I am investigating whether or not the statement, "If you knew my Father, you would know me," can be equivalent to the statement, "If you knew me, you would also know my Father."

(35) I think these statements cannot be equivalent to one another. The one who knows the Father ascends from knowledge of the Son to knowledge of the Father, and the Father is not seen otherwise than by seeing the Son. "For," he says, "he who has seen me has seen the one who sent me."[63] But he would not have said, "He who has seen the Father has seen me," since he who has beheld the Word of God beholds God, by ascending from the Word to God. It is impossible, however, to behold God apart from the Word.

62. Rom 1.1–7.
63. Cf. Jn 14.9; 12.44.

(36) And he who beholds Wisdom, which God created before the ages for his works,[64] ascends from knowing Wisdom to Wisdom's Father. It is impossible, however, for the God of Wisdom to be apprehended apart from the leading of Wisdom.

(37) And you will say the same thing also about the truth. For one does not apprehend God or contemplate him, and afterwards apprehend the truth. First one apprehends the truth, so that in this way he may come to behold the essence, or the power and nature of God beyond the essence.

(38) And perhaps, just as in the temple there were certain steps by which one might enter the Holy of Holies, so the Only-Begotten of God is the whole of our steps. And, just as the first step is the lowest, and the next higher, and so on in order up to the highest, so our Savior is the whole of the steps. His humanity is the first lower step, as it were. When we set foot on it we proceed the whole way on the steps in accordance with those aspects that follow after his humanity, so that we go up by means of him who is at the same time angel and the other powers.

(39) And, in accordance with his aspects, since a way differs from a door, one must first have gone forth on the way so that later he may thus arrive at the door;[65] and one must experience his rule insofar as he is shepherd,[66] so that he may also enjoy him as king. And we must first profit from him as lamb,[67] so that he may first remove our sin, and later, when we have been cleansed, we may eat of his flesh, the true food.[68] And after one has carefully examined and received the terms similar to these, he will hear the words, "If you know me, you also know my Father,"[69] and, "Since you know me, you also know my Father."

---

64. Cf. Prv 8.22 (LXX).
65. Cf. Jn 10.7,9; 14.6.
66. Cf. Jn 10.11.
67. Cf. Jn 1.29.
68. Cf. Jn 6.55.
69. Cf. Jn 8.19.

> He spoke these words in the treasury while teaching
> in the temple; and no one arrested him because his
> hour had not yet come. (John 8.20)

### The Treasury and Its Offerings

(40) If it were not to learn something useful from the fact that the previously mentioned words related by the Savior were spoken in the treasury, the Evangelist would not have added to what Jesus had said the words, "He spoke these words in the treasury while teaching in the temple."[70] If you pay attention, indeed, wherever the words are added, "These are the words that[71] he spoke" in such and such a place, you will discover the reason for the addition.

(41) Therefore, in order to understand the significance attached to the fact that Jesus spoke these words in the treasury, we will compare what we have learned from Luke and Mark, who also mention the treasury. Luke has the following words. "And he looked up at the rich casting their gifts into the treasury, and saw a certain poor widow casting in two mites. And he said, Truly I say to you that this poor widow has cast in more than all of them, for all these have cast into the gifts of God of their abundance, but she, of her want, has cast in all the living [that] she had."[72]

(42) The following words are from the Gospel according to Mark. "And Jesus stood opposite the treasury and watched, and everyone was casting money into the treasury. And many who were rich were casting in much. But one poor widow came and cast in two mites, which make a farthing. And he summoned his disciples and said to them, Truly I say to you that this poor widow has cast in more than all those who cast into the treasury. For they all cast in of their abundance, but she, of her want, cast in all she had, her whole living."[73]

(43) But now let us state what the comparison of the texts signifies for me when I observe that the treasury was in the

---

70. Jn 8.20.
71. Preuschen thinks the "that" may be the result of dittography.
72. Cf. Lk 21.1–4.  73. Cf. Mk 12.41–44.

temple, in order to understand the passage of John that is before us. If we refer the temple of God and [the things] related to the temple anagogically to the spiritual explanation,[74] let us consequently also understand the treasury in the temple in this way. It is a place of coins contributed for the honor of God and a dispensation of rest for the poor.

(44) Now what else would these coins be than the divine words that have the image of the great King[75] imprinted on them, which are examined by trustworthy money-changers who know how to separate those coins which are counterfeit from the genuine ones, along with those which appear legitimate, and who keep the commandment of Jesus that says, "Be trustworthy money-changers,"[76] and the teaching of Paul who declares, "Prove all things, hold fast that which is good; abstain from every form of evil."[77] Now let each one join in paying into the upbuilding of the Church, bringing to the spiritual treasury what he can for the honor of God and the common good.

### It Is the Motivation, Not the Quantity of the Offering That Matters

(45) But since the community can be benefitted in two ways, that is, by both the words and the deeds that the just man performs, deeds are also fittingly presented to the spiritual treasury. But since the ability of all is not equal nor alike in this life, if, indeed, the householder gave five talents to one, two to another, and one to another, to each according to his own ability,[78] on this basis the living Word accepts what he accepts by observing the ability of those casting into

---

74. Cf. Origen, *Jo.* 10. 265–97 (FOTC 80.314–21) where he interprets the temple and its construction in relation to the Church. Cf. also Homilies 9 and 13 on Exodus (FOTC 71.334–45; 375–87) where the tabernacle and the gifts offered for its construction are interpreted spiritually.

75. Cf. Ps 47.3.

76. Cf. Origen, *comm. ser. in Mt.* 33 (GCS XI, 60), and E. Hennecke, *New Testament Apocrypha* I, ed. W. Schneemelcher, trans. R. McL. Wilson (Philadelphia: The Westminster/John Knox Press, 1991), 88.

77. Cf. 1 Thes 5.21–22.

78. Cf. Mt 25.15.

what we described as a treasury, not by observing the quantity alone of what is contributed.

(46) For this reason, if someone capable of greater things does lesser things in relation to the ability that he has, but greater things in comparison with others capable of lesser things, [the Word rejects him][79] and receives those who have done the lesser things with all their ability rather than those who have contributed more out of an ability capable of providing many times more, [just as] has been written in the words that we quoted from both Luke and Mark.

(47) At the same time, these words teach the one who understands them spiritually that those who are considered to excel should never exalt themselves against those who are inferior so far as the judgment of men is concerned. For let no one who is assumed to perform more and better deeds compare himself with those who do the most insignificant things, so far as human judgment is concerned, and believe that he has done everything of which he has been capable, or that the other person has not given everything that could be demanded by the Word.

(48) Therefore, Jesus looked up at the rich casting their gifts into the treasury, and when he saw the poor widow quickly cast two mites[80] into the cognitive place or the practical, although she understood divine things rather simply and lived in accordance with her understanding, he said, "Truly I say to you that this poor widow has cast in more than all of them."[81]

(49) He said this as he observed how those who were rich in ability and were capable of contributing much more to the common good, from their abundance cast the smallest portion of what they were capable of contributing into the gifts of God.

(50) And observe also the widow's needs and the fact that she constrained herself and brought her whole living

---

79. Preuschen's suggestion. There is a lacuna in the text.
80. Cf. Lk 21.1–2.
81. Cf. Lk 21.3.

into the treasury in the temple, offering her total ability to God.[82]

(51) According to Luke, therefore, when Jesus looks up at the rich casting their gifts into the treasury, he always sees the poor widow also casting in two mites.[83] But according to Mark, he stands opposite the treasury and sees how all the people cast their spiritual money into the treasury in accordance with their ability.[84] And inasmuch as he alone can see the rich, he sees if ever a poor and needy soul contributes with her total ability, and for this reason is justified rather than the many who are rich.

(52) He does not say these things to just anyone, but, as Mark says, to his disciples.[85] For at this time he also summons his disciples and says to them, to teach them to see not as man will see, but as God will see ("For man will look on the countenance, but God will look on the heart"[86]), "Truly I say to you that this poor widow has cast in more than all of those casting into the treasury," etc.[87]

### The Words of Jesus in the Temple Are His Offerings

(53) What is the meaning of all this present discussion for me in explaining the statement, "These are the words that he spoke in the treasury, while teaching in the temple"? It is to show that if all contribute the things to support the needy into the treasury of the temple on behalf of the common good, Jesus, more than all others, should have brought things that were beneficial. These were the words of eternal life[88] and his teaching about God and himself.

(54) His statement, "I am the light of the world,"[89] which was spoken in the treasury, was more valuable than any coin, and likewise his statement, "If you knew me, you would also know my Father,"[90] and all his other teachings in that place.

(55) And all the gold of the others who brought what

---

82. Cf. Lk 21.4.
84. Cf. Mk 12.41.
86. Cf. 1 Kgs (1 Sm) 16.7.
88. Cf. Jn 6.68.
90. Jn 8.19.

83. Cf. Lk 21.1–2.
85. Cf. Mk 12.43.
87. Cf. Mk 12.43.
89. Jn 8.12.

they had into the treasury was like a bit of sand in comparison to the words of Jesus, for every word of his was wisdom. "And all gold in the presence of wisdom is like a bit of sand, and silver will be counted as clay in her presence."[91]

(56) These matters will be understood clearly by those who have learned to listen to the wisdom spoken to the perfect, a wisdom which has been hidden in mystery, "which God ordained before the ages for the glory" of his just ones.[92] They will be understood by those who are able to look at the pre-eminence of God's wisdom beyond the "wisdom of this age" or "of the rulers of this age who are perishing,"[93] who consult their own prophets, as it were, and prefer other words, whatever they might be, rather than the truth. For the remaining wisdoms that are thought to be gold are as a bit of sand in the presence of the wisdom[94] that God created as a beginning of his ways for his works,[95] and the bright and persuasive reason that is thought to be silver, shall be counted as clay [in the presence of][96] the pure oracles of the Lord, which have been tested in fire, purified seven times,[97] and are tried and true, inasmuch as they have come forth from the Word which was with God in the beginning.[98]

### Our Offerings Should Be Genuine

(57) We quoted the words from the book entitled Wisdom simply to see the meaning of the statement, "These are the words that he spoke in the treasury, while teaching in the temple." Let the story about the rich people and the poor widow be observed in the way it has been explained, and if anyone is an imitator of Christ, let him come to the spiritual temple of God which is not in a place, traveling in

91. Cf. Wis 7.9.
92. Cf. 1 Cor 2.6.
93. Cf. 1 Cor 2.6.
94. Cf. Wis 7.9.
95. Cf. Prv 8.22.
96. Cf. Wis 7.9.
97. Cf. Ps 11.7.
98. Cf. Jn 1.1.

his mind, and following the Spirit which is able to lead him to it. And let him bring coins that are genuine, that is, words of eternal life,[99] to the treasury, and works in conformity with such words.

(58) But would that someone among us might be neither poor, nor a widow who is able to bring nothing more than two mites, nor a rich man who brings only out of his abundance,[100] but one who dedicates all his wealth to God.

### The Strength of Jesus' Words

(59) Now, Jesus did not speak all the words that he possessed while he was teaching in the treasury, but as many as the treasury could contain. For I do not think the world itself could contain the whole Word of God.[101]

(60) Nevertheless, although he spoke so many words in the treasury and taught in the temple, Jesus was not yet arrested by anyone, for even his words were stronger than those wishing to arrest him. And as long as he speaks, none of those plotting against him will arrest him, but if he is silent then he is seized.

(61) This is why he is silent when he is examined by Pilate and beaten,[102] since he willed to suffer on behalf of the world. For, if he had spoken, he could no longer have been crucified from weakness,[103] since there is no weakness in the words that the Word speaks.

(62) But the hour of his arrest was not yet present while he was in the treasury, nor even while he was in the temple. The place where Jesus wished to be arrested, and where it was possible, needed to be a certain wadi.[104]

(63) The time of his arrest, too, could not be during the day, "for Judas, having received a band of soldiers and servants from the chief priests and the Pharisees, comes there with lanterns and torches and weapons."[105] Now concerning the statement, "His hour had not yet come," we have dis-

---

99. Cf. Jn 6.68.
100. Cf. Lk 21.1–2.
101. Cf. Jn 21.25.
102. Cf. Jn 19.9.
103. Cf. 2 Cor 13.4.
104. Cf. Jn 18.1.
105. Cf. Jn 18.3.

cussed it more fully in our discussions above.¹⁰⁶ You shall use those discussions also for the present words.

> Again therefore he said to them, I go, and you will seek me, and you will die in your sin. Where I go, you cannot come. (John 8.21)

*Many Believed in Him*

(64) He adds to the previous words not only these in the treasury in the temple, but more, up to the statement, "Truly I say to you, before Abraham was, I am."¹⁰⁷ And after this statement, when they took up stones to stone him, Jesus was hidden and departed from the temple.¹⁰⁸ It was then that he passed by and saw the man blind from birth.¹⁰⁹ We will learn about this, if God grants, when we come to the passage.

(65) Now, he speaks these words so that what is subjoined might occur. "For, when he spoke these words, they believed in him,"¹¹⁰ since the poor, as it were, come to the treasury to receive from there whatever they can and whatever may be distributed to them.

(66) Many, therefore, believed in him, but not many knew him, since of those who have believed in him, those who remain in his word, who truly become his disciples, will know the truth.¹¹¹ But the majority of those who have believed in him do not remain in his word, nor do the majority truly become his disciples.

(67) Wherefore not many will know the truth, and if truth makes free,¹¹² they do not become free; for very few advance to freedom.

(68) But who are those who will know him, or who will

---

106. Origen is probably referring to his discussions of Jn 2.4 or 7.30. The books containing his discussions of both of these passages have perished. The first was probably in book nine, and the second in book eighteen.
107. Jn 8.58
108. Cf. Jn 8.59.
109. Cf. Jn 9.1.
110. Cf. Jn 8.30.
111. Cf. Jn 8.31–32.
112. Cf. Jn 8.32.

lift him up? As he himself teaches, when he says, "When you shall have lifted up the Son of Man, then you will know that I am he."[113] Now, no one who is given milk to drink lifts him up, as he prepares himself for the reception of solid food.[114] For this reason one says to such a person, "I determined to know nothing among you except Jesus Christ and him crucified."[115] The servant of the word is also with such a person in weakness, as Paul says to such people, "And I was with you in weakness, and in fear, and in much trembling."[116]

(69) The Word of God says, therefore, as he begins a second series of lessons in the treasury in the temple, "I go, and you will seek me, and you will die in your sin."

(70) Because of the statement, "When he spoke these things, many believed in him,"[117] I ask whether he says, "I go, and you will seek me, and you will die in your sin," not to all those present, but to those whom he knew would not believe, and, therefore, would die in their sin and would be unable to follow after him. Now, they are unable because they are unwilling, for if they were unable, although they were willing, it could not reasonably be said to them, "You will die in your sin."

### Some Seek Jesus Perversely

(71) But someone will reply, If he spoke these words to those who continue in unbelief, how does he say to such people, "You will seek me"? For it is good to seek Jesus in many ways, since it is the same as seeking the Word, the Truth, and Wisdom.

(72) But you will respond that "seeking" is also sometimes used of those plotting against him, as in the statement, "They were seeking to arrest him, and no one laid hands on him, because[118] his hour had not yet come,"[119] and

---

113. Jn 8.28.
114. Cf. 1 Cor 3.2; Heb 5.12.
115. Cf. 1 Cor 2.2.  116. 1 Cor 2.3.
117. Jn 8.30.
118. Preuschen has ὅτε (when) instead of ὅτι (because). Brooke has ὅτι, as does the text of Jn 7.30. I take Preuschen's ὅτε to be a printing error.
119. Cf. Jn 7.30.

in the statement, "I know that you are Abraham's seed, but you are seeking to kill me because my word has no place in you,"[120] and in the statement, "But now you seek to kill me, a man who has spoken the truth to you which I have heard from the Father."[121]

(73) Wherefore also the statement, "And you will seek me," is made to those who seek incorrectly, and not in opposition to the statement, "Everyone who seeks finds."[122] Now, there are also always differences between those seeking Jesus. Not all seek him legitimately on behalf of their own salvation and to be benefitted by him.

(74) For people seek Jesus with countless motives that fall short of the good. For this reason only those who have sought him correctly have found peace. These might also legitimately be said to seek the Word himself in the beginning, the Word with God,[123] and to seek him that he might lead them to the Father. But whenever the Word is not received when he is present and manifests himself, then he threatens to go and says, "I go." And if we seek him once he has departed, we will not find him, but we will die in our sin.

(75) But he knows from whom he goes and with whom he remains although he is not as yet found, so that when he is sought at the right time he may be found.

(76) And to those indeed who have him in this way although they have not beheld him, it is said, "Say not in your heart, Who will ascend into heaven? that is, to bring Christ down; or who will descend into the deep? that is, to bring Christ up from the dead.

(77) "But what does Scripture say? The word is very near you, in your mouth and in your heart."[124] And to these the Savior also kindly points out the matters pertaining to the kingdom of God, that they may not seek it outside themselves, nor say, "Behold here or behold there."[125] For he says to them, "The kingdom of God is within you."[126]

(78) And as long as we preserve the seeds and principles

---

120. Jn 8.37.
122. Cf. Mt 7.8.
124. Cf. Rom 10.6–8; Dt 30.12–14.
126. Lk 17.21.

121. Cf. Jn 8.40.
123. Cf. Jn 1.1.
125. Cf. Lk 17.21.

of the truth that have been sown in our soul, the Word has not as yet departed from us. But if we utterly destroy them with a profusion of evil, then he will say to us, "I go," so that, even if we seek him, we will not find him, but we will die in our sin, being overtaken in it and taken away by means of it by those appointed to demand back the soul, according to him who says, "Fool, this night do they require your soul of you."[127]

### *"You Will Die in Your Sin"*

(79) But we must also not pass by without examining the statement, "You will die in your sin." If it is taken in the ordinary sense, it is clear that sinners will die in their sin, but the just in their justice. But if the expression, "You will die," is taken in relation to death, the enemy of Christ,[128] since the one who dies has committed a sin which leads to death,[129] then it is clear that those to whom these words were spoken had not yet died.

(80) And you will ask how these who did not believe when they were alive will die at some time. But someone will reply and say to this that at that time not yet to believe was not as yet a sin to death, and those to whom the Word had not yet come had not committed the sins to death. They were, nevertheless, living in sickness of their soul, and that sickness was to death.[130]

(81) The Physician, therefore, also seeing that they were deadly ill said, after he had despaired of healing them, "I go, and you will seek me, and you will die in your sin." We made the statement that their sickness was to death inasmuch as we have learned from Jesus that there is a difference between sicknesses.

(82) Now Lazarus too was sick, but the Physician knew that his sickness was not to death, wherefore he said, "This sickness is not to death."[131] For this reason, even if we contact diseases and become ill ourselves, let us be careful that

127. Lk 12.20.
128. Cf. 1 Cor 15.26.
129. Cf. 1 Jn 5.16.
130. Cf. Jn 11.4.
131. Jn 11.4.

we not be sick to death, our sickness progressing from that which can still be cured to that which is incurable.

(83) But at the same time, perhaps the statement, "Where I go you cannot come," which is subjoined to the statement, "And you will die in your sin," will be clearer. For, whenever anyone dies in his sin, he cannot go where Jesus goes, for no one who is dead can follow Jesus. "For the dead will not praise you, Lord, nor all who go down into Hades. But we, the living, will praise the Lord."[132]

(84) In addition, you will compare Ezechiel's statement, "The soul that sins, the same shall die,"[133] with the statement, "You will die in your sin," for sin is the death of the soul. I do not think, however, that this is true of every sin, but of the sin that John says is to death.[134]

(85) But at the same time he also distinguishes between one sin, which is the death of the soul, and another, which is its sickness. Now, it may be that there is yet another third sin, which is the loss of the soul, being the sin, that is, which is referred to in the words, "What will a man be profited if he gain the whole world but lose his soul, or forfeit it?"[135] and also in the words, "If anyone's work be burned up, he will suffer loss."[136]

(86) He says, therefore, to those who will die in sin, "I go, and you will seek me, and you will die in your sin; where I go you cannot come." But to Peter he says, "Where I go you cannot follow me now, but you will follow later."[137] For it is possible for one who is a disciple of Jesus not to be prepared now to follow him when he departs to the Father, but later, by diligently walking in his steps, to follow the Teacher and draw near the Word of God.

(87) Now it is likely that, on the basis of our conjectures about the end, someone will focus on the statement, "Where I go you cannot come," and reply that it is possible not to be able now, but to be able later. And if indeed there is a present age[138] and another to come, these to whom he has said,

132. Cf. Ps 113.25–26 (LXX).
133. Cf. Ez 18.20.
134. Cf. 1 Jn 5.16.
135. Cf. Mt 16.26; Lk 9.25.
136. 1 Cor 3.15.
137. Cf. Jn 13.36.
138. Cf. Gal 1.4.

"You cannot come," cannot go where Jesus is during the present age (and the time which remains until its completion is great), that is, where truth and wisdom and the Word are, for this is where Jesus is.

(88) But I know that some are overcome by their own sin not only in this age, but also in the age to come, as those of whom the Word says, "If anyone blasphemes against the Holy Spirit he has forgiveness neither in this age nor in the one to come."[139] If, however, there is no forgiveness in the coming age, neither is there any in the ages which come after it as well.[140]

### Heracleon's Understanding of Where Jesus Is Going

(89) When Heracleon related the text about the treasury, he made no comments on it. But on the statement, "Where I go you cannot come," he asks, *How can they come to a state of incorruption while they are in ignorance, unbelief, and sins?*

(90) Not even here does he pay attention to what he himself says. For if those who are in ignorance, unbelief, and sins cannot come to a state of incorruption, how have the apostles, who were once in ignorance, unbelief, and sins come to a state of incorruption? Those, therefore, who were in ignorance, unbelief, and sins can come to a state of incorruption if they should change, for it is possible for them to change.

The Jews therefore said: Will he kill himself,
because he he says: Where I go, you cannot come?
(John 8.22)

### The Esoteric Traditions of the Jews

(91) It is worthwhile to examine on what basis the Jews, having been disturbed by the statement, "Where I go, you cannot come,"[141] say, "Will he kill himself, because he says, Where I go, you cannot come?" even if we grant that they said, "Will he kill himself?" in a very straightforward manner.

---

139. Cf. Mk 3.29; Mt 12.32; Lk 12.10.
140. Cf. Eph 2.7.     141. Jn 8.21.

(92) How can those who are capable of killing themselves, even if they do not destroy themselves nor go where the one who destroys himself goes, not be able to go where the one who destroys himself goes? We must say, then, on this subject, to those who listen carefully and on a deeper level to what the Jews say in the Gospels, that it is obvious that they made many remarks in accordance with certain secret and esoteric traditions, as if they knew things other than those that were common and trite.

(93) And whenever we observe those things by the comparison of their words, then we will investigate if they said this too about the Savior because they perceived something more profound. Now it is certain that they were speaking with esoteric and uncommon words in reference to [Jesus] casting out demons by Beelzebub, the prince of demons.[142]

(94) For, to be sure, they had learned something about demons and their prince whose name was Beelzebub. But such things are not to be found at all in their books that are extant.

(95) The Savior's testimony about Beelzebub, too, is not false when he says, "If I by Beelzebub cast out demons, by whom do your sons cast them out?"[143] For he says these things because he recognizes that there is a certain Beelzebub, and that whoever casts out demons by Beelzebub brings about a kind of division, as it were, of Satan against himself.

(96) They erred, therefore, when they said that the Savior cast out demons by Beelzebub, but they had grasped that there is a certain Beelzebub, who is prince of demons.

(97) But also when they say of Jesus that he is John risen from the dead, or some one of the prophets, it is, to be sure, because they hold a doctrine of the soul such as we examined in our discussion about John,[144] that they assume such things about the Savior. And it is likely also that they knew

---

142. Cf. Lk 11.15; Mt 12.24. I have accepted Wendland's suggestions for emending this sentence. The text, as it stands, is unintelligible.
143. Mt 12.27; cf. Lk 11.19.
144. See Book 6.62–87 (FOTC 80:185–93).

either from traditions or esoteric books, many other things that the multitudes did not know.

(98) Let us look, therefore, also at the question, "Will he kill himself?" Can they have intended something that was not the common and simple meaning, as when one releases himself from life either by hanging, or by sword, or by whatever means those who commit suicide use? And can this be the case, especially since they think that when he kills himself he will depart to a place to which it would be impossible for them to go? And—if we do not have scruples about the terms, but when we look to the realities[145] we do not discover other terms to use for the realities—perhaps, if I may put it this way, Jesus killed himself in a more divine manner, which we set forth as follows. The souls of all those released from the body are taken away when those who have been appointed to this task require them. [But] it is likely that those who have been appointed to this service are better than the souls, for the statement, "Fool, this night do they require your soul from you,"[146] indicated something such as this.

### "No One Takes My Life from Me, but I Lay It Down of Myself"

(99) But if someone replies that this can be said in reference to inferior souls, but certainly not also of those who are superior and have lived properly, let him consider whether the Lord does not declare something extraordinary about himself that sets him apart from all who have lived in the body when he says, "No one takes my life from me, but I lay it down of myself; I have power to lay it down, and I have power to take it up again."[147]

(100) For let us imagine someone who leaves the body when he wishes, and departs from it apart from a means that leads to death, whether by violent means or diseases, and comes back again whenever he wishes, and who uses the body that he left behind as an instrument. We will say of such a person that his soul was not required of him.

---

145. Preuschen marks a corruption in the text between this word and the following phrase. I have followed Blanc's text in this sentence.
146. Lk 12.20.   147. Cf. Jn 10.18.

COMMENTARY ON JOHN, BOOK 19  191

(101) And it is fitting, indeed, in the case of Jesus' soul, to speak in this way of the death that occurred. It was fitting also, when he wished to tell his disciples of the extraordinary nature of his departure from here, for him to have said, "No one takes my life from me, but I lay it down of myself."[148] For neither Moses, nor any of the patriarchs or prophets, nor any of the apostles said this [except] Jesus, since all men's souls are taken from them.

(102) Now when this is understood, it is clear that what is said in the eighty-seventh Psalm, "Free among the dead,"[149] can be a figure of the person of the Savior. If you pay attention to what has been written of his departure from here in the Gospels, you will discover that our interpretation of his exodus is not at variance with what has been recorded. For if he had died as the thieves who were crucified with him, when the soldiers broke the bones of those who were suffering,[150] we would not say that he laid down his life of himself, but [that he died] in a way common to those who die.

(103) But as it is, "Jesus cried with a loud voice and yielded up the spirit."[151] And as a king who has left the body and has powerfully and authoritatively effected what he considered proper to do, immediately "the veil of the temple was rent from the top even to the bottom, the earth quaked, the rocks were rent, the tombs were opened, and many bodies of the saints who had slept were raised, and they came out of the tombs after his Resurrection and entered the holy city, and appeared to many."[152] When the centurion and those with him guarding Jesus saw the earthquake, and the things that happened they were very frightened and said, "Truly this was the Son of God."[153]

(104) Perhaps, then, just as it was in the traditions about Christ that he was to be born in Bethlehem and that he was to arise from the tribe of Juda according to the sound interpretations of the prophetic words, so also was it in the traditions concerning his death, that he would remove himself

148. Cf. Jn 10.18. 149. Ps 87.5 (LXX).
150. Cf. Jn 19.32. 151. Cf. Mt 27.50.
152. Cf. Mt 27.51–53. 153. Mt 27.54.

from life in the manner in which we said. And it is likely that the Jews knew that the one who was thus to depart was to go to a region where not even those who apprehend these things could go. Consequently, they were not speaking literally when they said, "Will he kill himself, because he says, Where I go, you cannot come?" but in accordance with some tradition about Christ. And although the Jews say these things, they say them with uncertainty, for the question, "Will he kill himself?" expects a negative answer.

(105) It is not strange that they disagree about Christ, when even in the words above, those in the crowd who heard Jesus' words said, "This is truly the prophet. But others said, This is the Christ. And some said, For does Christ come out of Galilee? Did not the Scripture say that the Christ comes of the seed of David and from Bethlehem, the village where David was?"[154] At that time also "there was a dissension in the crowd because of him."[155]

(106) But in addition, a little after those words, it is written, "The servants answered, Never did a man speak like this."[156] So also the Pharisees said to those marvelling at his speech, "Have you also been led astray? Has any one of the rulers believed in him, or of the Pharisees? But this crowd, which does not know the law, is accursed."[157]

(107) It was at this time also that Nicodemus said, "Does our law judge a man unless it first hear from him and know what he does? They answered, Are you also from Galilee? Search and see that a prophet neither comes from nor arises out of Galilee."[158]

(108) And how could those who heard him say, "I am the light of the world; he who follows me will not walk in darkness, but will have the light of life,"[159] understand him to mean literally that he would kill himself? How could they think this of him to whom the Pharisees had said, "You testify of yourself; your testimony is not true,"[160] whom Jesus an-

154. Cf. Jn 7.40–42.
156. Jn 7.46.
158. Cf. Jn 7.51–52.
160. Jn 8.13.

155. Cf. Jn 7.43.
157. Cf. Jn 7.47–49.
159. Jn 8.12.

swered, saying, "Even if I testify of myself, my testimony is true, because I know whence I came and where I go. You judge according to the flesh, I judge no one.

(109) And even if I do judge, my judgment is true, because I am not alone, but I and the Father who sent me. And in your law it is written that the testimony of two men is true; I am the one who testifies of myself, and the Father who sent me testifies of me."[161]

(110) And how is it plausible to think of him killing himself after he has said in this very noble manner, "You know neither me nor my Father. If you had known me, you would also have known my Father."[162]

(111) For it is likely that they also took the statement, "I go, and you will seek me and you will die in your sin. Where I go you cannot come,"[163] in a similar manner to these words. It was to these latter words that the Jews responded, "Will he kill himself, because he says, Where I go you cannot come?" Moreover his power to die of his own free will, having left the body behind, is made very clear also in the statement, "I go."

(112) Perhaps it was because of the statement, "I go," that he added, "and you will seek me." For it is likely also that those who happen to be present with him when he departs from life in this manner seek him. But because they die in their sins without even blushing after all these things they say of him, not without doubt, "Will he kill himself?" For where he goes they cannot go.

(113) I think, however, that they are putting forward rather maliciously what had come to them in the tradition about the death of Christ. And, so as not to glorify the one who thus departs from life, they said, "Will he kill himself?"

(114) For it was possible to speak hesitantly, but with a hint of his glory in the presence of death, and say something like this, "Will his soul depart when he himself wishes, when the body has been left behind?" It was for this reason that he said, "Where I go you cannot come."[164]

161. Cf. Jn 8.14–18.
163. Jn 8.21.
162. Jn 8.19.
164. Jn 8.21.

(115) But at the same time also, because of what we have said about how he has departed life, you will take note of the passage, "And when Jesus went up to Jerusalem he took the twelve privately, and said to them on the way, Behold we are going up to Jerusalem, and the Son of Man will be betrayed to the chief priests and scribes and they will condemn him to death. And he will be delivered to the Gentiles to mock and scourge and crucify him, and he will be raised on the third day."[165]

(116) And if someone objects on the basis of the words, "From that time he began to show to his disciples that he must go up to Jerusalem, and suffer many things from the chief priests and Pharisees and scribes, and be killed,"[166] along with the words, "The Son of Man will be betrayed into the hands of men, and they will kill him, and on the third day he will be raised,"[167] you shall say that all those who said, "Crucify him, crucify him,"[168] killed him, along with those who were liable for his death, although he anticipated the soldiers who came to break his legs, and cried out with a loud voice and expired.[169]

(117) But you will compare with this the statement, "Everyone who finds me will kill me,"[170] and the statement, "Everyone who kills Cain will be punished sevenfold."[171] For how "will everyone who finds Cain kill him," when only one person would have killed him, that is, the one who found him first. Or how "will everyone who killed Cain be punished sevenfold," since many would not have killed him? For the word "everyone" is used as if there were a crowd.

(118) Peter too, perhaps, took what the Savior said in a way that was too human when he said, "Far be it from you, Lord; this shall not happen to you."[172] And the Savior rebuked him because he had not taken what he said correctly, and said, "Get behind me, Satan. You are a stumbling block

---

165. Cf. Mt 20.17–19.
166. Cf. Mt 16.21.
167. Mt 17.22–23.
168. Lk 23.21.
169. Cf. Jn 19.32–33; Mt 27.50; Mk 15.37.
170. Gn 4.14.
171. Gn 4.15.
172. Mt 16.22.

to me because you are not thinking about the things of God, but the things of men."[173]

(119) But consider also if what Paul said is not similar to this, "He delivered himself for us as a sacrifice to God."[174]

(120) It is only in this way, at any rate, that one will be able to maintain the words about the high priest forever according to the order of Melchisedeck,[175] and the Lamb of God who takes away the sin of the world,[176] who is offered as a sacrifice to God, not by impious men, but by a pious high priest.

(121) We have published these remarks, therefore, in investigating to the best of our ability the intent of those who said, "Will he kill himself, because he says, Where I go you cannot come?" after they had heard such great words spoken previously by Jesus.

(122) It is likely, however, that some will take offence at our interpretation as forced and will think that they spoke more literally when they said, "Will he kill himself?" thinking that Jesus would kill himself, and would be in the region of those who have killed themselves and who are to be punished for this. The Jews, however, cannot go there because they are not liable to the penalty for that same sin against themselves.

(123) But let these objectors themselves also consider if the Jews could have thought that Jesus said these things, condemning himself as about to go off to a place of punishment where they could not go because they were better than him, as it were, so far as this interpretation is concerned. Or will it be logical to say that if indeed Jesus made this statement with this in mind and with the intention of killing himself, that he thought it was better to destroy himself than not to do it?

(124) Heracleon, however, takes the question, "Will he kill himself?" to have been asked in the literal sense, and says that the *Jews said these things because they were entertaining evil thoughts and consid-*

---

173. Cf. Mt 16.23.
175. Cf. Heb 6.20.
174. Cf. Eph 5.2.
176. Cf. Jn 1.29.

ered themselves to be better than the Savior, and assumed that they would go off to God into eternal rest, but that the Savior would go to corruption and death once he had slain himself, where they reckoned they themselves would not go.

(125) He says in these very words, *"The Jews thought the Savior said, When I have slain myself, I will go to corruption, where you cannot come."* Now I do not know how he could say, *"When I have slain myself, I will go to corruption"* of the one who said, "I am the light of the world,"[177] and what follows.

(126) But if someone should say that the Savior did not say these things, but that the Jews supposed it, it is clear that he will say that the Jews have thought on the subject that [although he knew that][178] those who have slain themselves perish, nonetheless he did these things believing that he would perish and be punished, which would be silly in all respects.

> And he said to them: You are from below, I am from above. You are of this world, I am not of this world. (John 8.23)

(127) And in the words above he said, "He who is of the earth is of the earth and speaks of the earth. He who comes from heaven is above all. What he has seen and heard, to this he bears testimony."[179] If, therefore, "he who is of the earth speaks of the earth," and "he who comes from heaven testifies to what he has seen and heard," you will inquire whether perhaps "to be of the earth" is the same as "to be from below," or whether it is different.

(128) But at the same time you will observe that even there he did not say, "He who is of heaven is of heaven and speaks of heaven," for perhaps the Savior was not of heaven, especially insofar as he was "firstborn of all creation."[180] For concerning the phrase "of heaven,"[181] the second man was

---

177. Jn 8.12.
178. Wendland's suggestion. Preuschen marks a lacuna in the text.
179. Jn 3.31–32.
180. Col 1.15.
181. Preuschen says the text is in disorder at this point, and thinks words may have been lost after "heaven."

of heaven as also Paul says somewhere, "The first man was of the earth, earthly; the second man was of heaven."[182]

(129) And here you will observe whether he is possibly saying the same thing in the expression "You are from below," and, "You are of this world," or whether to be of the earth is different from being of this world. And you will make the same inquiry also in the expression, "I am from above," and, "I am not of this world." For it is worthwhile to see what it is to be "from above," and what it is to be "not of this world."

### Who Is from Below, Who Is from Above?

(130) Consider, therefore, whether he who has received his origin from material substance and bodies is not of the earth because he has forsaken the better things. Insofar as this person is of the earth, he speaks of the earth,[183] since he cannot see or speak of anything higher. The same person is also from below.

(131) The concept, however, of being from "below" is one thing, and that of being "of the earth" another. For just as the expression "below" is understood in reference to a place, so it is also understood in reference to doctrines and a way of thinking, and everyone who employs such doctrines and manner of thought that are from below, is from below.

(132) But the visible world too, since it is material because of those who need material life, has places that differ. In relation to things that are immaterial, invisible and incorporeal these are all "below," not so much in a local sense as in comparison with the things that are invisible.

(133) But so far as [places] of the world being compared with places of the world is concerned, some places would be those that are below and others those that are above. For the things of the earth are below, but the things of heaven are above, so that according to this, the one from below is necessarily of this world, but the one who is of this world is not necessarily from below.

182. 1 Cor 15.47.   183. Cf. Jn 3.31.

(134) Consider if the citizen of the heavens[184] can perhaps be of this world, without, however, being from below in the local sense. But even this person is from below when compared with spiritual beings. For every citizen of things that are seen, and pass away, and are temporary is from below even if, in a comparison of places, he happen to be from the highest.

(135) It is possible, however, for one who is from below, and of this world, and of the earth, to change and become one who is from above and is no longer of this world, and for another to be of this world but [also] of heaven.

(136) He says, therefore, to the disciples, "You were of the world, and I chose you out of the world, and you are no longer of the world."[185] For if the Savior came to seek and save the lost,[186] he came to transfer those who are below and who have been enrolled as citizens among the things that are below to the things that are above.

(137) For he is also the one who descended into the lower parts of the earth because of those in the lowest parts of the earth.[187] But he also ascended above all the heavens and prepared a way for those who desire it and who have genuinely become his disciples that leads to the things that are above all the heavens, that is to the things that are incorporeal.

(138) But pay attention, if you also desire to learn from Scripture who it is who is from below, and who it is who is from above. Since each person's treasure is where his heart is,[188] if someone stores up treasure on earth,[189] by the very act of storing up treasure on earth he is from below. But if someone stores up treasure in heaven,[190] that person is born from above and assumes "the image of the heavenly."[191] And in addition, when this person has passed through all the heavens, he is found to have reached the most blessed goal.

(139) But there would also be the works of each person

---

184. Cf. Phil 3.20.
186. Cf. Lk 19.10.
188. Cf. Mt 6.21.
190. Cf. Mt 6.20.

185. Cf. Jn 15.19.
187. Cf. Eph 4.9–10.
189. Cf. Mt 6.21.
191. Cf. Jn 3.3; 1 Cor 15.49.

[to consider], as I said,[192] so that one might say that the one who is from below does the works of the flesh,[193] but the one who is from above produces the fruits of the spirit.[194] And again one might say that the one who is of this world has love for this world, since, according to John, he who has the love of God [is from above].[195] He is not of this world, however, who does not love the world nor the things in the world,[196] but who says, "God forbid that I should boast, except in the cross of my Lord Jesus Christ, by whom the world has been crucified to me and I to the world,"[197] and who is capable of loving the Lord his God with his whole heart, and with his whole soul, and with his whole mind,[198] for such love is not oppressed by love for the world and the things in the world. For it is impossible for love for the world to coexist with love for God, as it is impossible for light and darkness to coexist with one another, or Christ and Beliar, or for the temple of God to exist along with the temple of idols.[199]

(140) Since, however, those who are below differ in relation to one another, the statement is made in the superlative, "They have placed me in the lowest pit,"[200] as is also the statement, "He who descended into the lowest parts of the earth, this is also the one who ascended."[201] Wherefore all those who descend into the lower parts of the earth, that is, Hades, will fall down before Christ, since the saying is true, "There is no one in death who is mindful of you. And who will confess you in Hades?"[202]

(141) But if someone should object about him descending into the lower parts of the earth, you will observe that the expression "they will fall down before" is said in the case of those who descend into the earth, for although [all] will

---

192. Preuschen thinks this clause is corrupt.
193. Cf. Gal 5.19.
194. Cf. Gal 5.22.
195. Suggested by Preuschen in his apparatus. There is a lacuna in the text after "God."
196. Cf. 1 Jn 2.15.
197. Cf. Gal 6.14.
198. Cf. Mt 22.37; Dt 6.5.
199. Cf. 2 Cor 6.14–16.
200. Ps 87.7.
201. Cf. Eph 4.9–10.
202. Ps 6.6.

fall down to Christ [and] bow the knee at the name of Jesus,[203] some will fall down to him earlier and others later.

(142) And perhaps those on the earth will fall down and be subjected before others, for it belongs to the worse to be subordinated later, wherefore "the enemy death is destroyed last."[204]

(143) After this you will inquire if just as there is a difference among the things that are below because something is said to be lowest, so also there is a difference among the things that are above, especially since there is an inheritance of the kingdom of heavens. All the heavens that are inherited are above, but they are not all alike in being above.

(144) But also when you have given it your attention you will discover not simply a difference in the case of the spiritual descent of the soul because of wickedness and evil opinions, and its spiritual ascent, [but][205] you will come to apprehend more fully souls descending in a spiritual manner.[206]

(145) But consider if, at the same time, you[207] will not understand the saying about Jesus' soul in a more mystical manner and not spatially, "Having ascended above all the heavens."[208] For the spiritual ascent of that soul has leaped over all the heavens and, so to speak, already reached God himself.

### The Spiritual World

(146) But there is also another world in which there are things that are not seen, besides the manifest and perceptible world that consists of heaven and earth, or of heavens and earth. Now this in its entirety is an invisible world, a world which is not seen, and a spiritual world on whose ap-

---

203. Cf. Phil 2.10.   204. 1 Cor 15.26.
205. Accepting Brooke's suggestion.
206. Preuschen thinks the text of the latter part of this sentence is corrupt.
207. Brooke's text prints second person singular; Preuschen's third person singular. Since neither mentions a problem in the apparatus, I have assumed that Preuschen's is a misprint.
208. Eph 4.10.

pearance and beauty the pure in heart will look, being prepared in advance by beholding it to seek God, so that they may also see him, to the degree that God is disposed by nature to be seen.

(147) But you will inquire if, in some sense, the first-born of all creation[209] can be a world, and especially in so far as he is "the manifold wisdom."[210] For by being the principles[211] of absolutely everything according to which all things made by God in wisdom have come to be (as the prophet says, "You made all things in wisdom"[212]), in himself he would himself also be a "world" that surpasses the world of sense perception in its diversity and excels it as much as the principle stripped of all the material of the whole world differs from the material world, a world constituted, not on the basis of matter, but on the participation of the things that have been set in order in the Word and Wisdom, which set matter in order.

(148) And see if the one who says, "I am not of this world,"[213] can be the soul of Jesus which is a citizen of that whole world, traversing it in its entirety and leading his disciples to it.

(149) That world has nothing below even as this world has nothing above, to one who examines it as to its exact nature. For how can this world, whose creation is a throwing down, have anything above? For one must not hear the phrase, "Before the throwing down of the world,"[214] in just any way, [but][215] advisedly because the saints coined the ex-

209. Cf. Col 1.15.
210. Cf. Eph 3.10.
211. λόγοι.
212. Ps 103.24.
213. Jn 8.23.
214. Jn 17.24; Eph 1.4. I have rendered καταβολή as "throwing down" rather than the more usual "foundation." Origen takes the word to refer to the fall of souls from their original state of pure spiritual existence in the presence of God to their present state in the material world. The best commentary on his understanding of this term is his own discussion of it in *princ.* 3.5.4, where he says, "A descent therefore, of all alike from higher to lower conditions appears to be indicated by the meaning of this word καταβολή" (trans. Butterworth, 241).
215. My addition.

pression "throwing down" to express such a concept, although they could have said, "Before the creation of the world," and not have used the expression "throwing down.".

(150) The whole world, therefore, and the things in it are included in the "throwing down." But the genuine disciples of Jesus, whom he chose out of the world[216] that, by bearing their own cross and following him,[217] they might no longer be of the world, come to be outside the throwing down of the world in its entirety.

> Therefore I said to you that you will die in your sins.
> For if you do not believe that I am he, you will die in
> your sins. (John 8.24)

(151) When did he say to them, "You will die in your sins," or when did he declare, "You will seek me, and you will die in your sins"?[218] And what causes men to die in their sins other than not believing that Jesus is the Christ?[219] For he himself says, "If you do not believe that I am he you will die in your sins."

### He Who Believes in Christ Will Not Die in His Sins

(152) Now, if the one who does not believe that Jesus is the Christ will die in his sins, it is clear that the one who does not die in his sins has believed in the Christ. But he who dies in his sins, even if he says that he believes in the Christ, has not believed in him so far as truth is concerned, and if faith is mentioned but it lacks works, such faith is dead, as we have read in the epistle that is in circulation as the work of James.[220]

(153) Who, then, is the one who believes or who has been convinced by being well disposed according to the Word and has been united with him so that he does not fall into the sins that are said to be to death,[221] according to these words, nor does he sin[222] in any way that is contrary to

---

216. Cf. Jn 15.19.
218. Jn 8.21.
220. Cf. Jas 2.17.
222. Cf. 1 Jn 5.18.

217. Cf. Mk 8.34.
219. Cf. 1 Jn 5.1.
221. Cf. 1 Jn 5.16.

the upright Word in accordance with the statement, "Everyone who believes that Jesus is the Christ has been born of God."[223]

(154) But you will perceive even more what is meant by the statement, "For if you do not believe that which I am, you will die in your sins,"[224] in relation to the things that the first born of all creation is recapitulating.[225]

(155) For example, he who believes that justice is something would not be unjust,[226] and he who has believed in wisdom because he has contemplated what wisdom is, would not say or do anything foolish; furthermore,[227] he who has believed in the Word that was with God in the beginning[228] in that he has contemplated him, would do nothing unreasonable.

(156) Furthermore, he who believes that "he is our peace,"[229] would not contrive anything warlike and factious. In addition, if Christ is not only the "wisdom of God," but also the "power of God,"[230] he who believes in him insofar as he is power would not be powerless concerning good things.

(157) And because we think of him as endurance and strength on the basis of the saying, "And now what is my endurance? Is it not the Lord?"[231] and the expression, "My strength,"[232] and the statement, "The Lord is my substance,"[233] we will have to say that if we give in to troubles, we do not believe in him insofar as he is endurance; and if we are weak, we have not believed in him insofar as he is strength.

(158) And if we should [thus] collect the remaining as-

---

223. Cf. 1 Jn 5.1.
224. M. Harl (*Origène*, 174) notes that Origen interprets Jn 8.24 as if it read, "If you do not believe that which I am," i.e. he read the word ὅτι as if it were ὅ τι. On the basis of such a reading he can then introduce the "aspects" of Christ.
225. Cf. Col 1.15.
226. Origen appears to be using Platonic terminology here. Cf. Plato, *Phaedo* 65d.
227. Accepting Wendland's suggestion.
228. Cf. Jn 1.1. Origen understands λόγος here as Reason.
229. Cf. Eph 2.14.  230. Cf. 1 Cor 1.24.
231. Ps 38.8.  232. Ps 117.14.
233. Cf. Ps 38.8.

pects of Christ, we will discover without difficulty from what has been said how he who does not believe in Christ will die in his sins.[234] For because he is in opposition to the things that Christ is in his aspect, he dies in the sins themselves.

> Therefore they said to him, Who are you?
> (John 8.25)

(159) It follows that those who heard what the Lord said with great authority should ask who he is who says these things. For when the Savior declares, "If you do not believe that I am he, you will die in your sins,"[235] he appeared to be greater than man, and to be some more divine nature.

(160) Therefore, they ask, "Who are you?" as if there would be an answer when they ask, such as, "I am the Christ," or "I am the prophet," or "I am Elias,"[236] or perhaps, "I am an angel of God." For should he happen not to be any one of these or even someone similar to them he would not have spoken such words legitimately.[237]

---

234. Cf. Jn 8.24.
235. Jn 8.24.
236. Cf. Jn 1.19–21.
237. The remainder of Book 19, which covered Jn 8.25–36 is lost.

# BOOK TWENTY

AMBROSE, most devout and zealous for learning in the Lord, as we dictate the twentieth book on the Gospel according to John, we pray that we may receive thoughts that are full and solid, so to speak, and that have nothing hollow about them, from the fullness of the Son of God, in whom all the fullness was pleased to dwell.[1] We pray [that] the gospel may be revealed in the things we examine, and that we may neglect nothing that needs to be examined and to be believed in the writings that serve as memoirs, and that we may neither claim too much, as one ought not, nor misconstrue the mind of Jesus our Savior. May God, therefore, send the Word himself to us, revealing himself, that we may become beholders of his depth, if the Father grants.

> I know that you are seed of Abraham, but you seek
> to kill me, because my word has no place in you.
> (John 8.37)

*Seed of Abraham*

(2) For those who do not understand what is meant by the word "seed" and the word "child," the statement, "I know that you are seed of Abraham," will seem to be in conflict with what will be added immediately and addressed to the same people, "If you are Abraham's children, do the works of Abraham."[2]

(3) So that these things may be perceived, then, let us first see the difference between "seed" and "child" in the literal sense.[3] Now, it is clear that the seed of someone has the

---

1. Cf. Col 1.19.   2. Jn 8.39.
3. Cf. Diogenes Laërtius, VIII. 30.

principles of the procreator in itself still at rest and reserved. The child exists, however, once it has been formed and prepared for birth, when the seed has been transformed and has molded the material surrounding it provided by the woman and the collected nourishments. And if some portion [of seed] is someone's child in the proper sense [of the word "child"], as in the case of physical children, it exists from seed, but if something is seed, it does not necessarily become a child.

(4) But once we have made these assumptions, if it should be necessary to consider the statement literally, "I know that you are seed of Abraham," it would appear at any rate to follow that those to whom the sentence is addressed are also children of Abraham, it being conceded that the child continues to be seed, and that the term is not being used precisely.

(5) But on the other hand, since the children of Abraham are determined from custom and works, never from any generative principles[4] that are sown along with certain souls, in my opinion, it is necessary to designate those who are seed of Abraham by a characteristic mark. And if, indeed, all men are not seed of Abraham in the physical sense, it is clear [also] in relation to what we are now explaining concerning the question, "Who are the seed of Abraham?" that not all men have come into human life with completely identical generative principles which were sown in their souls.

(6) But it is possible, for a few who have distinguished the things that precede the birth and the things that accompany the birth of each one more carefully, to grasp the cause of these things in accordance with judgments that are great and difficult to explain,[5] that are contemplated by those who have received the mind of Christ, that they may perceive the things given them by God.[6] And since such things

---

4. σπερματικοὶ λόγοι, "generative principles," was a technical expression in Stoic philosophy for the generative principles in organisms.
5. Cf. Wis 17.1.
6. Cf. 1 Cor 2.16, 12.

would trouble some people who have an inkling of these matters but do not understand them thoroughly, we will expose ourselves to danger concerning such matters where it is precarious to mention and disclose such things, even if one speaks the truth.[7]

(7) Now, it is precarious because the administrator of the mysteries of God[8] must seek the proper time for the presentation of such doctrines so as [not] to harm the hearer, and at the same time also consider carefully the measure [of the presentation], whether it is too little or too much, measured by the correct Word,[9] even if the time is right. In addition, he must examine very carefully whether those to whom such doctrines are delivered are fellow-servants, or are servants of someone other than the Lord of Lords.[10]

(8) And the text that declares, "Who, then, is the faithful and wise administrator whom his Lord will appoint over his household to give to his fellow-servants their measure of grain in due season?"[11] shows that the administrator of God's mysteries must examine all these matters. All men, therefore, are not seed of Abraham, for they do not have the principles implanted in their souls which are capable, if cultivated, of producing children of Abraham.

(9) Someone may raise a problem in relation to these matters, asserting that the one who is seed of Abraham is culpable if he should not also become Abraham's child. But how would the one who does not even have the basis to be seed of Abraham, whence comes the ability to become Abraham's children, reasonably be blamed if he does not do the works of Abraham?[12]

---

7. Cf. *Selecta in Psalmos*. Psal. 1 (PG 12.1080A) where Origen remarks that when speaking of God the danger is not insignificant even if one speaks the truth, and H. Chadwick, *The Sentences of Sextus*, Texts and Studies, N.S. V (Cambridge, 1959), 114–15, who points out that Origen's statement is a quotation of maxim 352 of Sextus.
8. Cf. 1 Cor 4.1.
9. Origen has Lk 12.42 in mind, and is thinking of the administrator measuring out allotments of grain.
10. Cf. 1 Tm 6.15.
11. Cf. Lk 12.42.
12. Cf. Jn 8.39.

### Seed of the Just

(10) We will reply to these objections by using the literal sense as a ladder, as it were, and seeking the traces of the truth in the letters in this passage. If someone who is not a child of Abraham were seed of no just man, he would be blameless even if he were a sinner because he would have no opportunity for doing good from his seeds. But, as it is, just as in the case of physical bodies, one is seed of numerous just men, and another of fewer, as will be clear from the comparison of the things that we will relate, so it will be possible to say the equivalent in the case of the anagogical sense.

(11) Abraham was born the twentieth from the first-formed man, for there were ten generations from Adam to Noah,[13] and ten from Noah to Abraham.[14] And Abraham's brothers were Nachor and Aran, for the three were sons of Thare.[15] Nachor and Aran, therefore, were not seed of Abraham. Not even Abraham himself was seed of Abraham.

(12) The three, however, were seed of just men. Consequently, if the just men descended from Adam are further investigated, among which of them must Abraham be numbered? He was seed of Seth whom God raised up in place of Abel;[16] and of Enos, who "hoped to call upon the name of the Lord God";[17] and of Henoch, "who was well-pleasing to God two hundred years after he begot Mathusala";[18] and of Noah, of whom it is said, "A just man, perfect in his generation; Noah was well-pleasing to God";[19] and of Sem, whose God appears first to have been called "the Lord God," in Genesis, which is clear from the statement, "Blessed be the Lord God of Sem."[20] These three sons of Thare, however, were the seed of the rest[21] [of Adam's descendants] in addition to these.

13. Cf. Gn 5.
14. Cf. Gn 11.11–26.
15. Cf. Gn 11.26.
16. Cf. Gn 4.25.
17. Gn 4.26.
18. Cf. Gn 5.22.
19. Cf. Gn 6.9.
20. Gn 9.26.
21. Preuschen prints ἀδίκων (unjust) here, which is Wendland's addition to the text. I have omitted it for, although some such word would

(13) What we said, therefore, about the seed of Abraham must be understood of the seed of Sem, Noah and the just men who preceded them, whose distinctive properties Abraham, Nachor, and Aran seem to have taken up in common germinally when they were born. Abraham, however, must be understood to have cultivated the generative principles of all the just men before him that he had in himself, and to have added to these his own distinctive holy quality so far as his own distinctive seed is concerned, in which those after him who are called "seed of Abraham" could participate. Aran, on the other hand, must be understood to have paid very slight attention to himself and the ancestral seeds in himself, whence he could produce Lot, who even for a certain time was redolent of salvation. And Nachor must be understood to have been inferior to both brothers.

(14) It is possible, therefore, to be seed of Noah while not being seed of Abraham, especially since, in light of the story about the flood, those born after Noah have descended from him. And, if this is the case, then it is possible also to be seed of Henoch, and certainly also seed of Enos and Seth. It is unclear to us, however, in the case of the many who are inferior[22] to Noah, who is seed of Sem, who is of Cham, and who is of Japheth and of those even more inferior. It is not possible, however, that one participate in no way at all in the seed of the just.

(15) But I wonder whether it is possible for one who is not of Abraham's seed, although he has the resources that Abraham had from the seed of his predecessors, to become such that, although he is not of Abraham's seed, he is like Abraham.

(16) For just as Abraham became Abraham, although he was not of the seed of Abraham, but the seed of those mentioned previously, so it is possible that someone, by cultivat-

---

make the μέν ... δέ contrast stronger, I do not think it is necessary. Blanc does not have ἀδίκων in her text, but renders παρὰ τούτους "différents de ceux-là." Cf. Book 13.289, 293.

22. κατωτέρω. Blanc renders this "postérieurs," which may be correct. It seems to me, however, that there is an implicit value judgment in Origen's statement.

ing the better seeds which were sown in himself, become another Abraham, not at all being of Abraham's seed, but himself being sufficient to sow seed even as Abraham.

### Spiritual Seeds

(17) But let us give ear to all these things, referring what is said, not to physical bodies and men, but to certain spiritual realities and principles that are more or less numerous in which those descending into, or entering into, and perhaps also somehow even ascending into birth participate in different ways.

(18) You will consider whether the statement, "When they went, they went and wept, bearing their seeds,"[23] can have reference to such seeds that are actually specified as belonging to those who receive them into themselves. For, if anyone is able, let him contemplate the tearful journey of certain souls as they come to birth bearing the seeds of just men greater or fewer in number, and likewise of unjust men.

(19) And, as one contemplates this, let him reflect on farmers, as it were, in turmoil over the seeds that they hold, [considering] how they may cultivate some [I mean the better ones] and not sow others, since indeed they come also with inferior seeds.

(20) For what is likely to be the nature of the weeping of those of whom the Word says, "When they went, they went and wept, bearing their seeds"?[24]

(21) There is indeed good hope among those who go and weep, bearing their own seeds, for they are the ones in general who, "when they come shall come in joyfulness, bearing their sheaves."[25]

(22) But perhaps there were others who came, of whom

---

23. Ps 125.6.   24. Ps 125.6.
25. Ps 125.6 (LXX; Douay 125.7). Gregory Thaumaturgus, it seems to me, makes a play on Origen's discussion here of this verse in his *pan. Or.* 17. If this is so, it places the composition of this book prior to Gregory's departure from Origen's school in Caesarea. See above, Introduction, pars. 25ff.

you might say, "When they went, they went and laughed, bearing their seeds," for whom it will follow, "But when they come, they shall come in weeping, bearing their sheaves." Of these you might say, "They were begotten like the grass on housetops, which was withered before it was plucked up, with which the reaper did not fill his hand, nor the one gathering the sheaves his bosom. And those passing by did not say, The blessing of the Lord be upon you."[26]

(23) And consider, if it is possible, that it was in relation to this more profound and mystical meaning that our Savior said, "Blessed are those who weep now, because they shall laugh,"[27] and, "Woe to you that laugh now, for you shall mourn and weep."[28]

(24) To the extent, however, that someone born later is the seed of just men, he bears more principles of justice. This is why it has been written, "The seed of Abraham his servants; the sons of Jacob his chosen."[29] Perhaps this is also why it is said of John, "Among those born of women, no one is greater than John the Baptist."[30]

(25) Now consider, since you are engaged in these topics, if the reason God deprives someone of seeds is not to prevent the evil seeds of those sown, who lack the resources that come from better seeds, from increasing on the earth, so that he may cultivate what comes from superior seeds. It was to destroy the seed of Cain that the flood occurred,[31] since those born from him could have nothing to cultivate except only the seeds that come from Adam.

(26) The book entitled the Wisdom of Solomon proves that the flood occurred to destroy Cain's seed in these words, "But when the unjust man fell away from her (and it is clear that wisdom is meant) in his anger, he perished by the fury wherewith he murdered his brother, on whose account, when water destroyed the earth, wisdom saved it again, steering the course of the just man in cheap wood."[32]

---

26. Cf. Ps 128.6–8.
28. Lk 6.25.
30. Cf. Lk 7.28.
32. Wis 10.3–4.

27. Cf. Lk 6.21.
29. Ps 104.6.
31. Cf. Gn 6.13.

(27) The destruction of the Sodomites and their land seems to me to show the same thing, whose "barren and smoking land exists yet as a testimony of their wickedness, and plants that bear fruits that do not ripen."[33]

(28) It was the work of the good God, indeed, to destroy the land of the Sodomites and to dry up all its remaining moisture, so that there might no longer be a vineyard of the Sodomites, nor a vine-branch of Gomorrah, nor grapes of gall, nor a cluster of bitterness, nor wine, the wrath of dragons and the incurable wrath of asps.[34]

(29) But you will say the same thing also of the Egyptians, of whom it has been said, "He killed their vineyard with hail and their mulberry trees with hoar-frost,"[35] for killing the vineyards of the Egyptians and the mulberry trees of the impious was a work of the good God.

(30) We have made these remarks, which are set forth in our examination of the saying about the seeds of Abraham or of someone of the just, to show how and in what manner the Savior says to the same people, "I know that you are Abraham's seed," and, "If you are Abraham's children, do the works of Abraham."[36]

(31) If God grants it, however, we will speak more appropriately of Abraham's children doing the works of Abraham, when we have reached the examination of that text.[37]

*Seeds are Generative Principles*

(32) It is possible, therefore, for one who happens to be seed of Abraham also to become his child by exercising diligence. It is also possible, however, by neglect and poor husbandry, to cease even to be his seed. There was still hope for these, however, to whom the saying was addressed, since Jesus knew that they were still seed of Abraham, and saw that they had not yet lost the ability to become children of Abraham. For since it was possible for them to become children of Abraham in addition to being his seed, he said to

33. Wis 10.7.
35. Ps 77.47.
37. See below, sections 66ff. on Jn 8.39.
34. Cf. Dt 32.32–33.
36. Cf. Jn 8.39.

them, "If you are Abraham's children, do the works of Abraham."[38]

(33) But, just as some are seed of Abraham, so others, as Daniel says, are "seed of Chanaan, and not of Juda,"[39] and others, as Wisdom [says], are "cursed seed from the beginning."[40]

(34) Now we will also say on these matters that, just as with physical seeds one occasionally emerges from a large number of seeds because of its capacity for greater action, so too can the same thing be observed among spiritual seeds.

(35) What I mean will be clear from the following comments. Because the sower has in himself both ancestral and kindred principles, when his own principle prevails and is brought to birth, what is born is like the sower. But when the principle of the sower's brother, or father, or uncle—sometimes even of his grandfather—[prevails], consequently those who are born are like one or the other of these.

(36) It is also possible to see the principle of the wife, or the wife's father, or brother, or grandfather prevailing in the course of the agitation in the mingling when all the seeds are shaken together until one of the generative principles prevails.

(37) Now transfer these things to the soul that has been filled with spiritual seeds which have come from some of those called its fathers, and because of the great mobility of the ruling principle and its care in the case of such a representation, let them emerge as if they were certain generative principles of the fathers. When these are cultivated one will be a child of Abraham (now it is clear that the same one is also a child of Noah), and another a child of Noah, but it does not follow that he is also a child of Abraham. Another will also be a child of Chanaan, and another a child of one of the just or unjust men.

(38) But we have not all come with seeds that are equal and the same. Neither, however, has anyone come devoid of saving and holy seeds, unless perhaps someone should

38. Jn 8.39.
39. Sus 56.
40. Cf. Wis 12.11.

change our mind by adducing immediately on this subject God's help, which does not give up as hopeless even the worst men, who have come into life without the best seeds. He would change our mind on the basis of the statement, "God is able of these stones to raise up children to Abraham."[41]

(39) Now, we would have accepted everything that has been said about Abraham's seed and those who resemble him, if we had accepted that the following statements were not made in the literal sense, "I was not sent except to the lost sheep of the house of Israel," and, "I have not found so great faith, not even in Israel,"[42] and all the statements which are similar to these.

(40) These, however, to whom the Word speaks are not likely to receive the Word since he cannot proceed into them because of the surpassing superiority of his greatness, since they are still only seed of Abraham.

(41) But if, in addition to being seed of Abraham, they had cultivated the seed of Abraham and given it over to greatness and growth, the word of Jesus would have proceeded in the greatness and growth of the seed of Abraham.

(42) And you will add that to the present time the Word does not continue in those who have not advanced beyond being seed of Abraham nor come into the state of being his children.

(43) But these also wish to kill the Word, and to crush him, as it were, because they do not contain his greatness.

(44) It is always possible to see those who do not contain the Word because their vessels are too small wishing to kill the unity of the Word's greatness, since they can contain his members after he has been destroyed and crushed.

(45) If the Word should in this way come to be in those who will destroy him, as it were, he will say, "All my bones were scattered."[43] If indeed, then, anyone of us is seed of Abraham, and the Word of God does not continue in him still, let him not seek to kill the Word, but by changing from

---

41. Mt 3.9.  42. Mt 15.24; Lk 7.9.
43. Cf. Ps 21.15.

being seed of Abraham to having become a child of Abraham, he will be able to contain the Word of God whom he did not contain till then.

> I speak that which I have seen with the Father;
> and you, therefore, do the things that you have heard
> from the Father. (John 8.38)

### Those Who Hear the Father

(46) Just as we might say that some men have been eyewitnesses of the Word from the beginning, of whom Luke says, "According as they have delivered them to us, who from the beginning were eyewitnesses and ministers of the Word,"[44] so we will say that the Savior is an eyewitness of the things with the Father. In accordance with this it is said, "No one has known the Father except the Son,"[45] since they are no longer eyewitnesses to whom the Son has revealed him.

(47) Now, the text before us clearly reveals the fact that the Savior is an eyewitness of the things with the Father when it says, "I speak those things that I have seen with the Father." But you may ask if there will be a time when the angels themselves will see the things with the Father, no longer seeing them through a mediator[46] and a servant. On the one hand, insofar as he who has seen the Son has seen the Father who sent him,[47] one sees the Father in the Son, but there will be a time when one will see the Father and the things with the Father as the Son sees them. Then he will be an eyewitness, as it were, of the Father and of the Father's things in a manner similar to the Son, and will no longer conceive of the things concerning God, of whom the Son is the image, from the image.

(48) And I, at least, think that this is the goal when the Son delivers the kingdom to God and the Father, and when God becomes all in all.[48]

---

44. Lk 1.2.
46. Cf. Gal 3.19.
48. Cf. 1 Cor 15.28.

45. Cf. Mt 11.27; Lk 10.22.
47. Cf. Jn 14.9.

(49) The Savior, speaks, therefore after he has seen [the things] with the Father. The Jews, however, who have believed in him, have not seen [the things] with the Father, but have heard from the Father, so that they might do what they have heard. For this reason the Lord says to them, "And you, therefore, do the things that you have heard from the Father."

(50) But someone might ask when the Jews who have believed in the Lord have heard from the Father. And another will reply, because he has understood the saying in a simple manner, "You do the things that you have heard from the Father," that they heard from the Father when the Father uttered, through Moses and the prophets, the things which have been recorded in the law and the prophets that must be done. Whoever uses this saying against the heterodox proves clearly that the Father of Christ is no other than the God who gave the law and the prophets.

(51) [But] another adduces also the statement, "Everyone who has heard from the Father, and has learned, comes to me, not that anyone has seen the Father, except the one who is with the Father, he has seen the Father."[49]

(52) This person will say that there are some souls that have taken on bodies that were instructed by the Father and heard him before they were born, who also come to the Savior. Those Jews who believed in him and are now being questioned belonged to this group, to whom he said, "You, therefore, do the things that you heard from the Father." This same person will say in addition that these are those who are also called seed of Abraham.

(53) Someone might reply to this by declaring that the statement, "Everyone who has heard from the Father, and has learned comes to me,"[50] shows that the one who has heard from the Father, and has learned from him by all means comes to the Savior. On the other hand, the statement, "And you, therefore, do the things that you have

---

49. Cf. Jn 6.45–46.
50. Jn 6.45.

heard from the Father," which is made to those Jews seeking to kill the Son of God, to whom it is said, since they are not as yet children of Abraham, "If you are children of Abraham, do the works of Abraham,"[51] proves that these do not as yet have the fruits of having come to the Savior. But another will respond to the one who replies in this way by declaring that the clause, "Everyone who has heard from the Father, and has learned"[52] is not identical with the clause, "And you, therefore, do the things that you have heard from the Father." For the one, in addition to having heard from the Father, because he has learned, by all means comes to the Savior, but those who have heard, but have by no means also learned, are, not as yet, children of Abraham.

(54) Now we would ask those who also introduce the natures into the clause, "Because my word has no place in you,"[53] and explain, according to Heracleon, that *it has no place because they are unfit either in their essence or will*, how those who are unfit in their essence have heard from the Father?

(55) But we would also ask whether these were ever Christ's sheep, or if they belonged to others.[54] And if they belonged to others, how did they hear from the Father when it is clearly said, as they think, to those belonging to others, "For this reason you do not hear, because you are not of my sheep."[55]

(56) Unless, perhaps, because they are hard pressed, they involve themselves in another absurdity by saying that those who belong to others have heard from the Father, but these same people do not hear from the Savior. But if they were of the Savior's own household, and of the blessed nature, how did they seek to kill him? And how did the Savior's word have no place in them?

---

51. Cf. Jn 8.39.
52. Jn 6.45.
53. Jn 8.37.
54. Cf. Jn 10.1.
55. Cf. Jn 10.26.

> They answered and said to him, Abraham is
> our father. (John 8.39)

### *They Cannot Be Sons of God*

(57) These would appear to have replied as if they had understood the statement about who their father was in a much more lowly manner than the Lord meant it.

(58) For Jesus was referring to God when he declared, "And you, therefore, do the things that you have heard from the Father."[56] They, however, make an humbler assertion about the father of their own nation, when they say, "Abraham is our father."

(59) But someone may come to their defense as having answered appropriately, and say that they reply, "Abraham is our father," because they are modest and do not make themselves out to be sons of God, since Jesus has reference to God when he says, "You do the things that you have heard from the Father."[57]

(60) It is clear, however, that the Savior refutes this, too, as a false statement by his reply, "If you are children of Abraham, do the works of Abraham."[58]

(61) In addition, however, it would not be improper for one to raise the following question in reference to these matters. Since the Savior does not agree that they are children of Abraham, how can he say to them, "And you, therefore, do the things which you have heard from the Father,"[59] when the phrase, "from the Father," has reference to God?

(62) For if he who is not a child of Abraham [although][60] . . . he is among those after Abraham, is blameworthy, as these to whom the saying is addressed, by how much more will he not be a child of God.

(63) But consider if we can also say regarding this question, that it has not been said, "And you, therefore, [do] the

---

56. Jn 8.38.  
57. Jn 8.38.  
58. Cf. Jn 8.39.  
59. Jn 8.38.  
60. Accepting Blanc's conjecture of καίπερ. The text is damaged at this point. The entire translation of this sentence is, consequently, conjectural.

things that you have heard" from your father, [or] from our father, but "from the Father." Whoever the Father may be, he is by no means the father of those who are not children of Abraham nor of those who have not been formed from the seed of Abraham to be Abraham's children.[61] Or, can the words, "the things that you have heard from the Father"[62] be taken as equivalent to the words, "from my Father"? Now that the latter is the case will be clear from the statement, "I speak that which I have seen with the Father,"[63] which is the same as saying, "with my Father."

(64) In what follows also we are taught of whom God is the Father, for it is because of them that the Savior also says, "If God were your Father you would love me."[64]

(65) Now, it is clear that those who were seeking to kill the Son did not love him, and because they did not love him they would not be called sons of God. Consequently, it is clear that the statement, "And you, therefore, do the things which you have heard from the Father,"[65] cannot be the same as saying "from your father."

> Jesus says to them, If you are children of Abraham, do[66] the works of Abraham. (John 8.39)

(66) Let those who fasten on to one of Abraham's works, such as the statement, "Abraham believed God, and it was reckoned to him for justice,"[67] and think that this is what is

---

61. For Origen's distinction between Abraham's children and Abraham's seed see above, sections 2–31.
62. Jn 8.38. 63. Jn 8.38.
64. Jn 8.42. 65. Jn 8.38.
66. The imperfect is generally accepted as the correct reading today rather than the imperative which Origen has. The manuscript evidence is divided. The earliest texts, which come from Egypt, testify to each reading. The papyrus manuscript P$^{66}$ (c.200) and the important velim manuscript Vaticanus (4th century), in the original hand, have the imperative, as Origen. The papyrus manuscript P$^{75}$ (3rd century) and the important Sinaiticus (4th century) in the original hand, have the imperfect. Sinaiticus has been changed by a later scribe to read the imperative, and Vaticanus has been changed to read the imperfect.
67. Rom 4.3; Gn 15.6; Jas 2.23.

referred to in the command, "Do the works of Abraham" (even if it be conceded to them that faith is a work, which would not be conceded by those who accept the saying as authoritative, "Faith without works is dead,"[68] nor by those who understand that to be justified by faith differs from being justified by works of law) explain why it was not said in the singular, "If you are children of Abraham, do the work of Abraham," but in the plural, "Do the works of Abraham." This is equivalent, I think, to saying, "Do *all* the works of Abraham."

### The Works of Abraham

(67) But if this is equivalent to saying, "Do *all* the works of Abraham," the man who has a wife, and who wishes to show himself to be a child of Abraham by doing the works of Abraham in accordance with the Savior's explanation, need not literally have sexual intercourse with a handmaid,[69] nor take another wife in old age after the death of his wife.[70] We also learn from this quite clearly that we must interpret the whole story of Abraham allegorically, and make each thing he did spiritual, beginning with the command, "Go forth from your land, your kindred, and your father's house, into the land that I will show you."[71] This statement is made not only to Abraham, but also to everyone who will be his child.

(68) For prior to the time we receive the divine command, we each have a certain land and kinship that is not good, as well as a house of our fathers before the Word of God encounters us. It is because[72] of all these things, according to the word of God, that we will have to go forth, if indeed we hear the Savior saying, "If you are children of Abraham, do the works of Abraham." For it is in this way, when we have left our land, that we will arrive at that land which

---

68. Jas 2.26. The canonicity of the Epistle of James was still debated by some in Origen's time.
69. Cf. Gn 16.1–4.   70. Cf. Gn 25.1.
71. Gn 12.1.
72. Preuschen marks a corruption at this point in his text, but says nothing about it in his apparatus. Blanc notes this, and says something seems to be missing.

God will show us, which is truly good and really abundant, and which the Lord God appropriately gives to those who have done what has been commanded in the words, "Go forth from your land."[73]

(69) And when we have left the kinship that is not good we will become a great nation, even greater than a human nation; and when we have despised the house of the father who is not to be praised, we will be blessed and our name will be magnified. We will be blessed to the extent that those who bless us will be blessed by God, and those who curse us will be under a curse, and every tribe of the earth will be blessed in us. At this time the Word may say of us too, "he went," as was said of Abraham, "And Abraham went as the Lord said to him."[74] And I think that in the beginning, Lot will accompany us for a while. The statement, "And Lot went with him,"[75] is symbolic of this. And when we have gone up into the land of Chanaan, we will go through the land as far as the place of Sichem,[76] thus advancing in the ascent of thought until we come to the high oak.[77]

(70) And the Lord God who appeared to Abraham will appear to us, and he will promise to give the land around the high oak to the spiritual seed of our soul.[78]

(71) Now it is also the duty of him who has understood the command, "Do the works of Abraham," to build an altar to the Lord who appears to us, too, where the high oak is, and afterwards to depart from the place of the high oak toward the mountain. The mountain is east of Bethel, which means "house of God."[79] There he will pitch his tent with Bethel to the west and Hai to the east.[80] Hai means "feasts."[81]

(72) And, as such a person advances, he will later build a second altar to the Lord, when he is now able also to call upon the name of the Lord.[82] And next, the one who will be a child of Abraham will depart from there, when he has

73. Gn 12.1.
74. Gn 12.4.
75. Gn 12.4.
76. Cf. Gn 12.6.
77. Cf. Gn 12.6.
78. Cf. Gn 12.7.
79. Cf. Lagarde OS 182.93.
80. Cf. Gn 12.8.
81. Cf. Lagarde OS 181.76.
82. Cf. Gn 12.8.

somehow become more suited for command and understands for how many wars he must prepare himself, and he will encamp in the wilderness.[83]

(73) After these things, he will experience a trial of famine in the land, and will go down into Egypt to sojourn there, that the famine which prevails upon the land may not also prevail against him.[84] And he will go down into Egypt with his beautiful wife, having made certain agreements with her, so that the Egyptians may treat him well because of her,[85] and he may acquire in Egypt "sheep, and cattle, and asses, and menservants, and maidservants, and mules, and camels."[86]

(74) It would be the task of a wise man, capable of skillfully plumbing the depths even of Scripture,[87] to speak of each of these matters, by examining every story related to Abraham in general, and the entirety of the things written about him, "which things are allegorical,"[88] [which] we, as spiritual persons, shall attempt to perform spiritually.[89]

(75) But consider if our examination of the matters related to this passage does not prove that to become a child of Abraham is the part of a wise man who has also been adorned with every virtue.

(76) For why must we speak of the amount of wisdom needed to understand the works of Abraham, and of the amount of power needed to perform them? And what sort of wisdom or power do we need, except Christ, who is "the power of God and the wisdom of God"?[90]

(77) What has been written, therefore, is, "If you are children of Abraham, do the works of Abraham," but subsequently you might say, in addition, If you are children of Isaac, do the works of Isaac, and likewise of Jacob, and of each of the holy fathers.

(78) On the contrary, however, each person who sins is generically a child of the devil, since everyone "who com-

---

83. Cf. Gn 12.9 (LXX).
84. Cf. Gn 12.10.
85. Cf. Gn 12.11–13.
86. Cf. Gn 12.16.
87. Cf. 1 Cor 2.10.
88. Gal 4.24.
89. Cf. 1 Cor 2.12–15.
90. 1 Cor 1.24.

mits sin has been born of the devil."[91] But in addition, more specifically, he is a child as well either of Cain, or Cham, or Chanaan, or Pharao, or Nabuchodonosor, or some other impious person.

(79) Consequently, you will say that each person will go to his own fathers when he is delivered from this life, for we must consider that at the time of departure it is said, not only to Abraham, but to all men, "But you will go to your fathers."[92] "With peace,"[93] however, is not said to all men at this time, but only to the saints; and the words, "having been maintained[94] to a good old age," are addressed to those who have been perfected and have enjoyed a long spiritual life, since "understanding for men is grey hairs,"[95] and "old age is a crown of boasting,"[96] and the spiritual grey hairs that adorn them are a glory to truly godly elders.

> But now you seek to kill me, a man who
> has spoken the truth to you, which I have heard
> from God. (John 8.40)

*The Jews Seek To Kill Jesus As a Man*

(80) Those who seek to kill him seek to kill a man, since even if they should kill him, God is not killed. And if they seek to kill him, when they have not yet killed him they plot against him as against a man, not thinking that the one against whom they plot is God, for no one would continue to plot against him if he were convinced that the one against whom he plots is God.

(81) Now, it is always possible, perhaps, to see those who plot against the Word of God. They seek to kill and utterly destroy him, because they assume that he is a man, that is, human and mortal. Or, they attack his more human and visible aspect. Granted, however, that they may kill the Word's body, it is clear that, after this, they can do nothing more.

---

91. Cf. 1 Jn 3.8.   92. Gn 15.15.
93. Gn 15.15.
94. τραφείς, the reading of Codex Alexandrinus in the LXX. Rahlf's edition of the LXX has ταφείς, "buried," at Gn 15.15.
95. Wis 4.9.   96. Prv 16.31.

(82) For this reason we must not fear those who kill the body, but afterwards can do nothing more, nor must we fear those who kill the body, but cannot kill the soul of the Word.[97]

(83) But if some word is such that both its body and soul can be destroyed because they deserve destruction, we must fear the Word who is able, as God, to destroy and obliterate both soul and body, whether in Gehenna, or however he wishes. For the Lord Jesus kills with the spirit of his mouth the word that opposes and exalts itself over everything that is called God or is worshipped,[98] and destroys it with the appearance of his coming.

(84) And these people whom the Word addresses seek indeed to kill a man who has told them the truth that he has heard and received from God.

(85) Nevertheless, even if we adopt a simpler understanding so far as this passage is concerned, the Savior clearly taught that what the Jews sought to destroy was not God, but a man, who indeed was destroyed. For it is not permitted to say that God dies. For this reason the Word in the beginning with God,[99] who also was God the Word, did not die. But since it has been written that "the Word became flesh,"[100] you will ask whether the Word that once became flesh, also did or did not become a man in having become flesh.

(86) For if he became a man, it is possible to seek to destroy him. But if the Word that became flesh did not become a man, then because he was not destroyed, he has been restored to what he was before he became flesh, and likewise each [word] is restored [to that primitive state].[101]

---

97. Cf. Mt 10.28; Lk 12.4.
98. Cf. 2 Thes 2.8, 4; Is 11.4.
99. Cf. Jn 1.1.
100. Jn 1.14.
101. I take the masculine singular ἕκαστος to be a reference to the λόγος (i.e. reason) that dwells in each person. In this sense λόγος is the equivalent of soul. On Origen's belief in the existence of souls prior to bodies, see *princ.* 1.8.4; 2.9.1–8, and FOTC 80.146, note 302.

## This Abraham did not do. (John 8.40)

*"Abraham Your Father Rejoiced To See My Day"*

(87) If Abraham has not done what he could not possibly have done, the words, "This Abraham did not do," will seem to have been spoken without purpose. For some would say to this that the statement, "This Abraham did not do," is made in vain, since he did not do what by no means occurred during his time, for Jesus did not exist during his time.

(88) But since I assume that the statement, "This Abraham did not do," has been made in praise of Abraham, as it were, I would say that, in accordance with the word that teaches, "Abraham your father rejoiced that he might see my day, and he saw it and was glad,"[102] it is possible that there was also a man in Abraham's time who spoke the truth that he heard from God,[103] and that Abraham, in truth, did not seek to kill this man.

(89) And note that there is no time when the man understood figuratively in relation to Jesus was not present in life, both after the time of the story about him and before. This is why I think that everyone who has once been illuminated and tasted the heavenly gift, and has become a participant in the Holy Spirit, and tasted the good word of God and the powers of the age to come, and has fallen away again, renews himself to repentance, whether he crucified the Son of God previously, or crucified him again, and made him a mockery, either before or after the bodily sojourn of our Savior that is recorded.[104]

(90) For does not the one who sins now, after his illumination and God's other benefits to him, crucify the Son of God again by his own sins to which he has returned, although he does nothing that in the common literal use of language could be said to be a crucifixion of the Son of God? And did this not also happen earlier, and did not he

---

102. Jn 8.56.
104. Cf. Heb 6.4–6.
103. Cf. Jn 8.40.

who sinned after he had heard divine words crucify the Son of God in advance?

(91) And if one agrees to accept what has been written in *The Acts of Paul* as said by the Savior, "I am about to be crucified again,"[105] just as he accepts that the statement, "I am about to be crucified again," is made after the sojourn, so also would he accept that it could be said, "Now I am about to be crucified," before the sojourn, whenever the same causes are present.

(92) For why was he not also crucified previously, as he is about to be crucified "again"? But consider if the saying, "I have been crucified with Christ,"[106] can be applied not only to the saints after his coming, but also to those previous saints, so that we may not say that the saints after his coming surpass Moses and the patriarchs.

(93) And let the statement, "I no longer live, but Christ lives in me,"[107] be made not only by those after his coming, but also by those who preceded it. I note also in relation to the Savior's saying, "The God of Abraham, and the God of Isaac and the God of Jacob, but he is not the God of the dead but of the living,"[108] that perhaps Abraham and Isaac and Jacob are living because they, too, were buried with Christ and arose with him,[109] but by no means at the time of Jesus' physical burial or his physical Resurrection. These are our remarks on the statement: "This Abraham did not do."

(94) But what does "this" mean, other than to seek to kill a man who has spoken the truth that he has heard from God?[110] We explain it then as follows. The spiritual economy related to Jesus has always been present with the saints.

(95) And if, contrary to the more usual approach, you refer these words anagogically to Abraham, understood in a more mystical manner, as we have assumed elsewhere, you

---

105. See E. Hennecke, *New Testament Apocrypha*, ed. by W. Schneemelcher, trans. by R. McL. Wilson, Vol II (Philadelphia: Westminster), 324.

106. Gal 2.19.   107. Gal 2.20.
108. Cf. Mt 22.32.   109. Cf. Col 2.12; Rom 6.4.
110. Cf. Jn 8.40.

## You do the works of your father. (John 8.41)

### He Who Sins Is of the Devil

(96) So far as this statement is concerned, it is not clear whom he wishes to say is the father of the Jews who have believed in him and have not as yet known the truth; for he says all these things to them.

(97) If it were not added a little later, "You are of your father the devil, and you wish to do the desires of your father,"[111] we would not have known clearly the meaning of the statement.

(98) Now, it is not strange that, to those Jews who had believed in him, but had not yet remained in his word that they might truly become his disciples and know the truth so as to be made free by it, he said, "You do the works of your father," and, as is added in what follows, "You are of your father, the devil."[112]

(99) For although what is said in this way of those who have believed in him and were, in some way, disciples, yet to be sure they were not already called disciples of Jesus in truth, seems harsh, nevertheless, we must understand also what John says in the catholic epistles about sons of God and sons of the devil. For he says, "He who commits sin is of the devil, for the devil sins from the beginning.

(100) "The reason the Son of God appeared was that he might destroy the works of the devil. Everyone who has been born of God does not commit sin, for his seed abides in him, and he cannot sin, because he has been born of God.

(101) "In this the children of God are manifest, and the children of the devil. No one who is unjust is of God, nor one who does not love his brother."[113]

---

111. Jn 8.44.
112. Jn 8.44.
113. Cf. 1 Jn 3.8–10.

(102) Since, therefore, these words are such, notice if it is not clearly stated that everyone "who commits sin is of the devil."[114]

(103) In so far as we commit sins, we have not as yet put off the generation of the devil, even if we are thought to believe in Jesus. Consequently Jesus says to those Jews who have believed,[115] "You do the works of your father," "father" meaning the devil because of the statement, "You are of your father the devil."[116]

(104) Now, if everyone "who commits sin is of the devil,"[117] everyone who is not of the devil does not commit sin.

(105) In addition, if "the reason the Son of God appeared was that he might destroy the works of the devil,"[118] to the extent that he has not yet destroyed the works of the devil in us, because we have not presented ourselves to him who destroys the works of the devil, we have not as yet put aside being children of the devil, since it is our fruits that show whose sons we are.[119]

*"That You May Become Sons of Your Father Who Is in Heaven"*

(106) These words make it very clear that one is not a son of the devil as a result of creation, nor is any man said to be a son of God because he was so created. It is also clear that one who was previously a son of the devil can become a son of God. Matthew also reveals this when he records that the Savior spoke as follows, "You have heard that it was said, You shall love your neighbor and hate your enemy. But I say to you, you shall love your enemies, and pray for those who persecute you, that you may become sons of your Father who is in heaven."[120]

(107) For note that by [obeying] the commands, "Love your enemies," and "Pray for those who persecute you," he

---

114. 1 Jn 3.8.
115. Cf. Jn 8.31.
116. Jn 8.44.
117. 1 Jn 3.8.
118. 1 Jn 3.8.
119. Cf. Mt 7.16.
120. Cf. Mt 5.43-45. In paragraphs 106 and 107 Origen is arguing against Gnostic determinism.

who previously was not a son of the Father in heaven, subsequently becomes his son. In addition, it is clear that every person, on attaining the age of reason, is either a child of God or a child of the devil, because it is said, "In this the children[121] of God and the children of the devil are manifest."[122] It was said earlier of the children of the devil, "He who commits sin is of the devil,"[123] and of the children of God, "Everyone who has been born of God does not commit sin, because his seed abides in him and he cannot sin because he has been born of God."[124] One either commits sin or does not commit sin. No one is between committing sin and not committing sin. If one commits sin, he is of the devil; if one does not commit sin, he has been born of God.

(108) What is said in the same epistle about those who are in the Son of God and those who have not seen him follows closely the statement in these verses about the children of God and the children of the devil. For John says, "Everyone who abides in him does not sin; everyone who sins has not seen him."[125]

(109) If, then, everyone who abides in him does not sin, he who sins does not abide in the Son. And if everyone who sins has not seen him, he who has seen him does not sin.

(110) You will also note[126] at the same time because[127] of the words "has seen him," what John had in mind [when] he said, "Everyone who sins has not seen him," that those who see the Son of God can always partake of the ability not to sin at all as a result of having seen him.

---

121. Accepting the correction of Ferrarius in line with the text of 1 Jn 3.10. The text of Origen has "works" both places "children" appears in 1 Jn 3.10.

122. 1 Jn 3.10 (as corrected by Ferrarius). See note 121.

123. 1 Jn 3.8.

124. 1 Jn 3.9.

125. 1 Jn 3.6.

126. Accepting the future indicative of M in place of Preuschen's alteration to the aorist imperative. The ἔτι φήσεις (future indicative) of paragraph 111, which parallels this statement suggests that the future is correct.

127. Following the reading of M with Blanc: διὰ τό. Preuschen has διὰ τοῦ, following Wendland's emendation.

(111) You will say further, that the statement, "You do the works of your father," might be said sometimes to the sons of the devil, and sometimes to the sons of God. For those who sin do the works of their father the devil, but those who live a good life do the works of God their father.

(112) Now, it is likely that someone will be troubled because of these words and fear that the same person may, by doing good and bad works alternately, be a child of God because of the good works, but a child of the devil because of the opposite works. But in addition to being very irrational, this is not meant by the words.

(113) For John declares, "Everyone who has been born of God does not commit sin, because his seed abides in him, and he cannot sin because he has been born of God."[128]

### The Dignity of Being Born of God

(114) Everyone, therefore, who has been born of God does not commit sin. It has not indeed been written that everyone who has been born of the devil does not do justice, but, "he who commits sin is of the devil."[129]

(115) Again, it has not been recorded, 'He who does justice is of God,' in the same way as it is said, "He who commits sin is of the devil."[130] Give careful attention to the differences in the propositions,[131] and note how John has proposed them very precisely so that one might marvel at how accurately and, as some would say, logically, he has set them forth. He has not set forth the same things concerning those who are of the devil, and those who are of God. Now, he would have set them forth in a similar manner if he had written, 'He who does justice is of God,' just as he wrote, "He who commits sin is of the devil,"[132] or had he written, 'Everyone who has been born of the devil does not do justice,' just as he wrote, "Everyone who has been born of God does not commit sin."[133]

128. 1 Jn 3.9.
129. 1 Jn 3.8.
130. 1 Jn 3.8.
131. Cf. *Jo.* II.34–35 (FOTC 80.103).
132. 1 Jn 3.8.
133. 1 Jn 3.9.

(116) Perhaps he has also provided a very wise interpretation by using the word "is" in the case of the one who is "of the devil," and not using it in the case of those who are of God, and likewise by writing "has been born" in the case of those [who are born] of God, and not using this word in the case of those who are of the devil.

(117) For he exalted the one who is of God when he applied the expression "has been born" to him, but if he had also said this of the one who is of the devil, it would have indicated something worse than the statement, "he is of the devil."

(118) But also, if he had used the word "is" in the case of the one who is of God, in the same way as he applied it to the one who is of the devil, he would have presented something inferior so far as the one who is of God is concerned, for to have been born of God is much better than to be of God. Now someone will say that some of the created beings are of God, and have by no means been born of God. These assuredly have a lower rank in the universe than those said to have been born of God.

(119) Having arrived at the distinction between the statements, "He is of the devil," and "He has been born of God," you will ask whether there is someone who has been born of the devil, who by all means also is of the devil, since not everyone who is of the devil has been born [of the devil]. Furthermore, you will ask if there is someone who is of God, but who has not also been born of God, since not everyone now who is of God has been born of God.

(120) The one who has been born of God, however, is characterized as not committing sin because God's seed abides in him, and from the power of that seed which exists in him the characteristic of no longer being able to sin appears in him.

(121) Now, it is also said in the final words of the epistle, "That everyone who has been born of God does not sin, but he who has been born of God guards himself, and the wicked one does not touch him."[134]

134. Cf. 1 Jn 5.18.

(122) Now, if the one who is born "of God guards himself and the wicked one does not touch him," the one who does not guard himself so that the wicked one may not touch him has not been born of God, and everyone whom the wicked one touches, has not been born of God, for the wicked one touches those who do not guard themselves.

### The Children of Abraham Do the Works of Abraham

(123) But because the statement, "You do the works of your father," is added to the words about Abraham, when nothing has intervened, we ask whether this has been recorded because of the first command that was given to Abraham.

(124) Now, the first divine word to him is as follows, "Go forth from your land, and from your kindred, and from your father's house, and depart into the land that I will show you."[135]

(125) Therefore, Abraham went forth from his father's house, the very thing that those who are reproved for having incorrectly said, "Abraham is our father"[136] have not done.

(126) For if the children of Abraham do the works of Abraham, and the first of these works is to go forth from his own land, and from his own kindred, and from his own father's house, and to depart into the land that God shows him, then this is why those to whom this word is addressed are reproved as not being children of Abraham, for it is clear that they are reproached because they have not gone forth out of their father's house, since they still belong to the wicked father and still do the works of that father.

(127) Now that we have made these remarks on this saying, I think we have clearly refuted those who think they can prove from this source that some are sons of the devil as a result of creation.[137]

---

135. Cf. Gn 12.1.   136. Jn 8.39.
137. Cf. above, paragraphs 106 and 107, and note 120. Although Heracleon is not mentioned in pars. 96–117, pars. 168–70, where Heracleon's views on the same subject are explicitly set forth, show that Origen is arguing against Heracleon in this entire section.

> They said to him, We have not been born of fornication;
> we have one Father, God. (John 8.41)

### *This They Say Vindictively*

(128) I ask whether those Jews who are said to have believed in him[138] do not respond rather vindictively, because they were reproved as not being children of Abraham, by hinting in a veiled manner that the Savior was born of fornication. They assume this as probable because they do not accept his famous and widely discussed birth from the Virgin.

(129) For indeed it appears very irrational to me that they uttered these words in response to his saying. For if their statement, "We have not been born of fornication," be understood in its literal sense, it is appropriate neither to what precedes nor to what follows.

(130) Furthermore, since the Savior said that God was his Father,[139] and acknowledged no man as his father, it is likely because of the statement, "We have not been born of fornication," that, to give offense, they in turn add, "We have one father, God." It is as if they were saying, "We are the ones who have one Father, God, rather than you, who claim to have been born of a virgin, though you were born of fornication. You boast that you have been born of a virgin by saying that you have God alone as your one Father. We who acknowledge God as our Father do not deny that we also have a human father.

(131) But someone will say that these words, understood in this way, cannot be the words of the Jews who had believed in him. We must say in reply, however, that since the words addressed to them in the beginning, "If you continue in my word, you are my disciples indeed, and you will know the truth,"[140] were spoken as if they were capable either of continuing in Jesus' word or not continuing in it, it was not impossible that some of those who were reproved had not continued in his word, and, because they had not contin-

---

138. Cf. Jn 8.31.
139. Cf. Jn 5.18.
140. Jn 8.31.

ued, replied in a vindictive and offensive manner, "We have not been born of fornication; we have one father, God."

(132) Now it seems to me that their answer is also rather contentious. For although they had said earlier, "We are seed of Abraham,"[141] and had acknowledged this more clearly, as it were, in the statement, "Abraham is our father,"[142] once they heard Jesus' response, "If you are the children of Abraham, do the works of Abraham,"[143] they asserted that one greater than Abraham was their father by saying, "We have one father, God."

### All Who Are Not Born of God Are Born of Fornication

(133) It may be, however, since some men are of the devil, and others have been born of God, that we would be correct in saying that all who have not been born of God have been born of fornication.

(134) For those of the devil, whom he either begets or makes, are not of the bride, but of the whore, matter. And because these have craved bodily things and been engrossed in them, they join themselves to the whore, matter, and become one body with her.[144] Those who have been born of God separate themselves from the whore, matter. They join themselves to the Lord[145] and are united with the Word who was in the beginning with God,[146] and with his wisdom, which "he created as a beginning of his ways for his works,"[147] so that they might become one spirit with her.[148] "For he who joins himself to a whore is one body, but he who joins himself to the Lord is one spirit."[149]

---

141. Jn 8.33.
142. Jn 8.39.
143. Jn 8.39.
144. Cf. 1 Cor 6.16.
145. Cf. 1 Cor 6.17.
146. Cf. Jn 1.1.
147. Cf. Prv 8.22.
148. I.e. wisdom, which is a feminine noun in Greek, and consequently, when personified, is treated as a feminine person.
149. Cf. 1 Cor 6.16–17.

COMMENTARY ON JOHN, BOOK 20     235

Jesus said to them, If God were your Father, you would love me; for I have proceeded and come from God.
(John 8.42)

*If You Love Christ, God Is Your Father*

(135) Since those who introduce the natures use this saying, and explain it to mean that if God were your Father you would have recognized me as one of your family and a brother, and furthermore you would have loved me as your own, consequently we must address an additional question to them. Was there a time when Paul hated Jesus?

(136) And did he hate him when he was ravaging and persecuting the Church of God?[150] And did the first divine revelation speak the truth indeed when it asked him, "Saul, Saul, why do you persecute me?"[151]

(137) If, then, the [conditional] proposition is true, "If God were your father, you would love me,"[152] it is clear that the [conditional] contrary to this is also true: If you do not love me, God is not your Father. God is not the Father, therefore, of those who do not love Jesus. And there was a time when Paul did not love Jesus. There was a time, then, when God was not Paul's Father.

(138) Paul, therefore, was not a son of God by nature, but later became a son of God, since we would also consider true the consequent derived from the conditional proposition,[153] namely, "But in fact, God is your Father, Paul, therefore you love Jesus."

(139) But, in addition, since the [conditional], "If God were your Father, you would love me," was true prior to Paul's faith, it would be fitting to admit that Jesus said [then], as it were, "But in truth, you do not love me, therefore God is not your Father, Paul."[154]

---

150. Cf. Gal 1.13.    151. Acts 9.4.
152. Jn 8.42.
153. συνημμένου. This was the meaning of the term in Stoic logic. See LSJ sv. συνάπτω, III.3; Blanc, *Origène* IV, 382–83; Benson Mates, *Stoic Logic*, 135.
154. See R. E. Heine, "Stoic Logic as Handmaid to Exegesis and Theology in Origen's Commentary on the Gospel of John," JTS, n.s. 44 (1993): 103–7.

(140) Now, at what other time does God become one's Father than at the time one keeps his commandments? It is because of these commandments that one who was not formerly a son of the Father in heaven becomes his son, when the Father leads the one who becomes his son to regeneration, and is called his Father.

(141) It is also possible to apply the following words recorded in the Gospel according to Matthew to these matters. "You have heard that it was said, You shall love your neighbor, and hate your enemy.

(142) "But I say to you, You shall love your enemies and pray for those who persecute you, that you may become sons of your Father in heaven."[155]

(143) For note the clause, "that you may become sons of your Father in heaven," which indicates that one who was not formerly a son of the Father in heaven becomes his son.

### "That You May Become Sons of Your Father in Heaven"

(144) And when you have also carefully observed that "your" is added to "Father" (for it is written, "That you may become sons of your Father"), you will ask whether this was said in the simpler sense, or the "your" is added because the copies are in error. For we would have made no investigation had it been written, "That you might become sons of the Father in heaven." For one to become a son, however, not simply of the Father in heaven, but of his own Father, seems to contain a contradiction.

(145) For if he is his Father [already], he does not later become his son; but if he becomes his son, he was not [previously] his Father.

(146) At the same time, however, you will consider why some of those assumed to have believed are said to be servants of God, and others are called his sons. Perhaps it is not some random command, but certain extraordinary achievements that make the one who has achieved them become a son of God.

---

155. Cf. Mt 5.43–45.

## COMMENTARY ON JOHN, BOOK 20

(147) Since there are many precepts in the Gospel according to Matthew, observe that the promise, "That you may become sons of your Father in heaven,"[156] is added to the words, "But I say to you, You shall love your enemies and pray for those who persecute you."[157]

(148) For indeed, likeness to God and imitation of him who loves everything that exists, who detests nothing that he has made and cares for all things (since all things belong to him, the master who loves souls[158]), are demonstrated by loving one's own enemies and praying for those who persecute one.

(149) But how would the added promise, "That you may become sons of your Father in heaven,"[159] be appropriate to the words, "It was said, You shall not commit adultery, but I say to you that everyone who looks at a woman to desire her has already committed adultery with her in his heart"?[160] Or how would it be appropriate to those words about the loss of one of one's members so his whole body may not go into hell?[161]

(150) Furthermore, if the promise, "That you may become sons of your Father in heaven,"[162] were added to the words, "It was said to those of old, You shall not swear, but you shall perform your oaths to the Lord; but I say to you not to swear at all,"[163] it would obviously have caused much difficulty.

(151) But now, just as the Father in heaven makes the sun rise on the evil and the good,[164] so each of God's sons, having love in himself like a sun, makes this rise also upon those who are evil whenever he loves his enemies. And again just as God sends rain upon the just and the unjust,[165] so the saint sends down prayer, a kind of rain as it were, upon those who, because they persecute him, are below him, since he prays even for such people.

---

156. Mt 5.45.
157. Cf. Mt 5.44.
158. Cf. Wis 11.24, 26.
159. Mt 5.45.
160. Cf. Mt 5.27–28.
161. Cf. Mt 5.29–30.
162. There is a space for two or three letters at this point in the MS.
163. Mt 5.33–34.
164. Cf. Mt 5.45
165. Cf. Mt 5.45

These are our remarks to clarify the words we have been considering, "If God were your Father, you would love me."

### "Behold, the Lord Proceeds from His Place"

(152) Now let us also consider the statement, "I have proceeded and come from God." It seems useful to me to juxtapose to these words the following words from Micheas: "Hear my words, you people, and let the earth and all who are therein pay attention; and the Lord shall be among you for a witness, the Lord from his holy house. Wherefore behold, the Lord proceeds from his place, and will come down and tread upon the high places of the earth, and the mountains will be shaken under him, and the valleys will be dissolved like wax before fire and like water tumbling down in a waterfall."[166]

(153) Now, consider whether the statement, "I have proceeded from God," is equivalent to the statement, "The Lord proceeds from his place," since, when the Son is in the Father, being in the form of God before he empties himself,[167] God is his place, as it were.

(154) And if indeed one considers him who, before he has emptied himself, is in the essential form of God, he will see the Son who has not yet proceeded from God himself, and the Lord who has not yet proceeded from his place.

(155) But when one compares the condition that resulted from having taken up the form of a servant after he had emptied himself,[168] with that former condition of the Son, you will understand how the Son has proceeded from God and has come to us,[169] and has come out, as it were, of the one who sent him, even if, in another manner, the Father has not left him alone, but is with him,[170] and is in the Son just as also the Son is in the Father.[171]

---

166. Cf. Mi 1.2–4.
167. Cf. Phil 2.6–7.
168. Cf. Phil 2.7.
169. Cf. Jn 8.42.
170. Cf. Jn 8.29.
171. Cf. Jn 14.10.

(156) For unless you understand that the Son is in the Father in a different way than he was before he proceeded from God, it will seem contradictory that he has both proceeded from God, and, after he has proceeded from God, is still in God.

(157) Others, however, interpret the statement, "I proceeded from God," to mean, "I have been begotten by God." These must say consequently that the Son has been begotten of the Father's essence, as one might understand this also in the case of those who are pregnant, and that God is diminished and lacking, as it were, in the essence that he formerly had, when he has begotten the Son.

(158) These people must also say, as a consequence, that the Father and the Son are corporeal, and that the Father has been divided. These are the doctrines of people who have not even dreamed of an invisible and bodiless nature that is pure essence.

(159) Now, it is clear that these people locate the Father in a physical place, and understand that the Son has come into life by exchanging one place for another in a material sense, and not by exchanging one condition for another, as we have understood it.

> For I have not come of myself, but he sent me.
> (John 8.42)

(160) I think that these words were spoken because there were some who came of themselves and had not been sent by the Father. Jeremias also teaches us of such men who promise some teaching or prophecy, where it is written, "I did not send the prophets, and they ran."[172]

(161) But if certain powers also come to men, although they are not sent by the Father, consider if some of them have proceeded from God and have erred in the fact that they were not sent by him.[173]

---

172. Jer 23.21.
173. Origen is making a distinction between the two verbs in Jn 8.42: to have proceeded from God, and to have been sent by him.

(162) We must also not fail to examine the passage in regard to the doctrine of the soul, for perhaps the soul of Jesus was in God and his fullness when it was in its own perfection, and, after it had proceeded from there by being sent by the Father, it took up a body from Mary.[174] Other powers, however, did not proceed from God in this way, that is, they were neither dispatched nor sent forth by the will of God.

> Why do you not know my speech? Because you cannot hear my word. (John 8.43)

### Be Opened

(163) The reason my speech is not known to you, he says, is that you cannot hear my word. First, then, we must acquire the ability to hear the divine word, so that subsequently we may also be able to know all Jesus' speech.

(164) For it is possible that, although one previously could not hear Jesus' word, he could later attain the ability to hear it, since one cannot hear insofar as he has not yet had his hearing healed by the Word who says to the deaf, "Be opened."[175]

(165) But whenever the fetter responsible for the deafness is destroyed, then one will be able to hear Jesus, at which time he can also know his speech. Or, let those who think that the teaching concerning the natures[176] is also confirmed through these words tell us whether those whom he later healed were able to hear when they were still deaf, or were unable.

(166) Now, since it is clear that "they were unable," it is evident that it is possible to change from not being able to hear Jesus' words to hearing them, and that the inability to hear is not the result of a nature which is incurable. We

---

174. On Origen's doctrine of the preexistence of souls see section 86 above and the note there.
175. Cf. Mk 7.34.
176. The word is singular, but Origen must be referring to the Gnostic doctrine of the different natures.

must apply these words especially to the heterodox who rejoice in allegories and refer the story about the healings anagogically to the healings of the soul, when every sickness and every weakness is relieved by Jesus.[177]

(167) I think hearing is used here in the sense of understanding what is said, and knowing in the sense of agreeing, once one has comprehended and been enlightened by the light of knowledge concerning what is said.

### Heracleon: The Deaf Are of the Devil

(168) Heracleon, however, assumes that *the reason for their inability to hear Jesus' word and to know his speech is explained in the statement,* "You are of your father the devil."[178] He says, at any rate, in his own words, *"And why can you not hear my word, other than that you are of your father the devil?" This means "of the essence of the devil," and further makes their nature clear to them.* He had rebuked them previously[179] because *they were neither children of Abraham,*[180] *otherwise they would not have hated him, nor of God, because they did not love him.*

(169) Now if the statement, "You are of your father the devil," were taken as we explained it above, and he had said, "Because you are still of the devil, you cannot hear my word," we too would have accepted Heracleon's interpretation.

(170) But now it is clear that he means that *some men are of the same essence as the devil, being of a different essence than those whom they call psychics or pneumatics,* as his followers maintain.

> You are of your[181] father the devil, and you wish to do the desires of your father. (John 8.44)

### The Ambiguity of the Text

(171) The text is ambiguous. One meaning suggested by it is that the devil has a father, and, so far as the literal meaning is concerned, those addressed by this word appear to be derived from this father.[182] There is another [possible

---

177. Cf. Mt 4.23.      178. Jn 8.44.
179. Accepting προελέγξας with Blanc and others.
180. Cf. Jn 8.39.
181. This pronoun is in the text of neither John nor Origen.
182. The text of John could possibly be read: "You are of the father of the devil." This takes the second genitive phrase to express relationship, rather than being in apposition with the first genitive phrase.

meaning], however, which is preferable, namely, "You are of this father, concerning whom the title 'devil' is predicated."

(172) What is said, therefore, would be ambiguous, even if the first genitive article were removed, but the meaning of the phrase would appear much more clearly. He, however,[183] who agrees that there is some father of the devil whose sons Jesus would appear to say these are to whom the saying is addressed, will use the following additional words, "When he speaks a lie, he speaks of his own, because he is a liar and his father.[184] He will say that the lie is the devil, but another, in addition to him, is the father of the lie.

(173) But this conclusion will not be correct, for the lie, instead, will refer to the antagonist of him who said, "I am the truth."[185] This is the antichrist, whose father is a liar, being the devil.

(174) But someone may likely take offence at the antichrist being a lie,[186] since he will no longer be culpable if, in substance, he is nothing other than a lie. If one compares with this what is said in Ezechiel about one who, because of evil, has changed so he has become destruction, "You have become destruction, and you shall not exist forever,"[187] he will support in the same way the possibility that someone may be of the lie, not by his substance from creation, but having become such and having been endowed with such a nature, if I may use a novel expression, by change and his own choice.

(175) Someone, to avoid as nonsense the assertion that the antichrist is a lie, will say that the statement, "When he speaks a lie, he speaks of his own,"[188] refers to all who lie, for

183. I follow Brooke and Blanc in rejecting Wendland's insertion of a negative.
184. Jn 8.44. Again John's text can be read this way. The final genitive third person pronoun, however, is usually taken to refer to the lie, and not to the devil, i.e., "he is a liar and the father thereof."
185. Cf. Jn 14.6.
186. Origen means that this constitutes the antichrist's essence or substance from creation.
187. Cf. Ez 28.19.
188. Jn 8.44. This could also be rendered, "Whenever the lie speaks, he speaks of his own." This may be the way Origen understood the statement.

whenever the lie in each liar speaks, "he speaks of his own," namely the lie. But in addition, the statement, "His father is a liar,"[189] refers to the fact that each one who brings forth a lie from his own mouth is father of the lie that he speaks. Such an interpretation indeed will not be completely lacking in persuasion. Let these remarks be made as relevant to the ambiguity of the statement we are expounding.

### The Desires of the Devil

(176) But, since we discussed this statement in anticipation when we were explaining the words, "You do the works of your father,"[190] and we brought together from many places the words that appeared useful to us for the interpretation, we will not now spend further time on the passage.[191] But if someone has been born of the devil by committing sin,[192] and has not nullified his birth from him, he wishes to perform, not one, but many desires of such a father. And since the desires in every son of the devil have been born from the desires that are in the devil, it is clear that the desires of that person are thoughts of matter and corruption, which one might properly say are hostile to God.[193]

(177) It is not absurd, therefore, to assert that the desires of the devil are murders, and acts of injustice and covetousness, since he has engendered desires very similar to these in his sons. But it is also not absurd to say, in general, that the desires of the devil are unclean acts which are opposed in nature to cleanness, and it is not difficult to believe that from these desires of the devil arise the desires for unclean things in the children of the devil.

(178) But one might be hesitant to agree in addition to the assertion that prostitution is a desire of the devil, or adultery, or pederasty, or effeminacy (even if he be at a loss how these desires arise in men apart from the desires in the

---

189. Cf. Jn 8.44.  190. Jn 8.41.
191. See above, sections 96ff.
192. Cf. 1 Jn 3.8, pars. 117–19 above, and *hom. in Ex.* 8.6 (FOTC 71.329).
193. Cf. Rom 8.7; 2 Pt 1.4.

devil, as far as the literal meaning is concerned) as if something general about human desires is being presented, namely that men wish to do the desires of their father, so that everything that they desire contrary to law was earlier the desire of their father.

(179) For such is the meaning of the words, "You wish to do the desires of your father." But we must say in reference to these matters that the devil desires, let us say, that this boy be corrupted, and that this woman commit adultery, and that these men visit prostitutes, and, by the power of these desires, he makes the desire to do the things that he wishes to effect serve him so that, according to this, one could say that the one who causes the prostitution or adultery practices prostitution and commits adultery before the human involved.

(180) And you will say the same thing also about every sin, that is to say, the devil does not desire money, but he desires to make people lovers of money and passionately desirous of material things. And those who love money, even if all they do is wish for it, will to carry out this desire of his.

(181) This is why we must pay attention to everything we wish to do, and examine whether what we wish to do comes from the desires of the devil, that we may cease wishing to do those things that we have perceived to be of the desires of the devil. We know that everyone who wishes to do the desires of the devil by no means has God as Father, but has become a child of the devil, and been formed from wishing to do the desires of the worse one, and is in the image of the wicked father, from whom the images of that earthly man come and receive their imprint. For that first man was of the earth.[194]

(182) Because, therefore, the first man fell away from the superior things and desired a life different from the superior life, he deserved to be a beginning neither of something created nor made, but "of something molded by the Lord, made to be mocked by his angels."[195] Now, our true sub-

---

194. Cf. 1 Cor 15.47–49.   195. Jb 40.19 (LXX).

stance too is in our being according to the image of the Creator,[196] but the substance resulting from guilt is in the thing molded, which was received from the dust of the earth.[197]

(183) And if, forgetful, as it were, of the superior essence in us, we subordinate ourselves to that which is molded from dust, even the superior part will take on the image of the earthly. But if, once we have understood what has been made according to the image and what has been received from the dust of the earth, we should completely incline to him in whose image we have come into existence, we will also be according to the likeness of God,[198] having abandoned every passionate desire for matter and bodies, and even for some of those beings who are according to the likeness.

(184) But since, according to the divine Scriptures, desire belongs to those things that are morally indifferent, since the Scriptures do not know the precision of meanings among the Greeks who make such distinctions, so that they call willing, which they define as rational longing, honorable, but desire, which they say is irrational longing or excessive longing, they call bad, we must say that every created nature wishes to do the desires of its own father, just as every nature also does the works of its own father.[199] The one is of

196. Cf. Col 3.10.  197. Cf. Gn 2.7.
198. Cf. Gn 1.26.
199. Origen is reflecting here the words in John 8.44, 41 when he refers to doing "the desires of its own father" and "the works of its own father." A similar definition of "desire" appears in a fragment containing Origen's comments on Rom 7.8 (A. Ramsbotham, "The Commentary of Origen on the Epistle to the Romans. III," JTS 14 [1913]: xxxviii, 13–14), and in Clement, *paed.* I.13.101.1 and *str.* II.20.119.3, and the same definition of "willing" appears in Clement, *fr.* 41. The definitions come from Stoic ethics. They appear verbatim, i.e. willing is rational longing and desire is irrational longing, in the third century work of Diogenes Laertius (*Diogenis Laertii Vitae Philosophorum*, ed. H. S. Long [Oxford, 1964], II. 7.113, 116), and in the (perhaps) second century work of Pseudo-Andronicus (*Andronici qui fertur libelli*, Περὶ Παθῶν, *Pars Prior de affectibus*, ed. X. Kreuttner [Heidelberg, 1884], 12.4, 20.5). The same definitions are repeated in the fifth century work of Stobaeus (*Ioannis Stobaei, Anthologii* II. ed. C. Wachsmuth [Berlin, 1958], II.164, 166, 170, 172), and the definition of "desire" occurs in the tenth century lexicon of Suidas (*Suidae Lexi-*

a father who is holy and unbegotten (and this is God), and the other is of an evil father, who exists as a father from nothing. For some father did not cause evil to subsist in him; it was the act of turning away from God that engendered it.

(185) It is clear, therefore, that what is now being examined in relation to the statement, "And you wish to do the desires of your father," has reference to the devil, since the statement, "You are of your father the devil," precedes it, and the statement, "He was a murderer from the beginning" follows.

*If We Do the Works of God, and Wish To Do His Desires, We Are Sons of God*

(186) Now the words, "You wish to do the desires of your father," might also appropriately be addressed, not only to each of the children of the devil, but also to each of the children of God. For certain desires are also said to belong to God, although they are called his purposes.

(187) For example, it is said in the eighteenth Psalm, "The judgments of the Lord are true, justified in themselves, more to be desired than gold and very precious stone."[200] Even if [we should read], as some of the copies have, "the objects of desire are beyond gold and very precious stone,"[201] you will agree that it is fitting that one desire the objects of desire, just as the objects of blessing are worthy to be blessed, and the objects of love of being loved.

(188) Therefore, as the objects of blessing are blessed more by God, and the objects of love are loved more by God, so also the objects of desire would reasonably be desired more by God, if we understand desire in the more positive sense, as we discussed it previously.[202] But the Savior also

---

con *Graece et Latine,* ed. G. Bernhardy [Halis et Brunsvigae, 1853], II. 406–7). See also C. Blanc, SC 290, 388–90, who discusses the use of these terms in the LXX, and also traces their prior distinctions in Plato and Aristotle.

200. Ps 18.10–11.

201. Blanc, *Origène* IV, 250–51, notes that the Sahidic version, according to a study of A. Rahlfs, supports this variant.

202. See above, section 184.

says, "With desire I have desired to eat this pasch with you, before I suffer."²⁰³

(189) Now, the text in hand is sufficient [to show] that there is also an inferior desire, but we must also add, no less, the saying, "Whoever looks on a woman to desire her has already committed adultery with her in his heart."²⁰⁴ Now, he who desires by no means desires what is absent, just as he who wishes does not wish for things that are absent.

(190) Now, we have treated this in advance because of the objects of God's desire, and the desires of the perfect.

(191) Any son, then, of anyone wishes to do the desires of his own father, and any son of anyone does the works of his father. In the same way, the Savior wishes to do the desires of his own Father, and does the works of his own Father.

(192) "The man of sin, the son of destruction,"²⁰⁵ also wishes to do the desires of his own father, and does the works of his own father. In our case too, the works of men are always either of God or of the devil, and what we wish to do is either the desire of our good Father in heaven or of his enemy, the devil.

(193) If we do the works of God and wish to do his desires, we are sons of God; but if we do the works of the devil, and wish to do what he desires, we are of our father, the devil.

(194) Let us pay attention, then, not only to what we do, but also to what we desire. For even to wish to do the desires of the devil is sufficient to be his son. Perhaps this is why the words, "You wish to do the desires of your father," are added after the statement, "You do the works of your father,"²⁰⁶ so that we may learn that if we merely wish to do what the devil desires we will be called sons of the devil.

(195) Now, someone may plausibly respond to these remarks that, therefore, to wish to do the desires of God is sufficient to be his son, even if the performance of God's works be lacking.

(196) But we must reply that the one who wishes to do

---

203. Lk 22.15.
204. Cf. Mt 5.28.
205. Cf. 2 Thes 2.3.
206. Jn 8.41.

the desires of God must also perform the works of God, for, as Paul says, not only to will, but also to act is of God,[207] since acting certainly accompanies willing the good as a yoke-fellow (for also, "to those who love God, all things work together for good"[208]). He who made all things very good[209] would not leave willing the good imperfect. But neither is it possible to conceive of willing the good unless action that is good in relation to such willing is joined with the good willing.

(197) The activity, however, related to willing would frequently be hindered by providence, with good reason, when it is necessary to restrain the action related to willing what is inferior on behalf of some general good, or any good whatever.

### Men Do Not Differ with Respect to Their Essense

(198) Now Heracleon says on these words, *"Those to whom the word was addressed were of the essence of the devil,"* as though the essence of the devil is another essence over and above the essence of other rational creatures.

(199) But in this remark he appears to me to have been in a state of mind like that of one who asserts that there is one essence of the eye that overlooks and another of the eye that sees, and one essence of the ear that misunderstands, and another of the ear that hears correctly.

(200) For just as in these matters the essence is not different, but some reason for misunderstanding and overlooking supervenes, so, since everything has been disposed by nature to follow reason, the essence, as a consequence, is the same whether it accepts reason or refuses it.

(201) For we could not say, in the case of us humans, in what respect that which follows reason differs from that which does not, although after understanding what is said, one makes a decision and assents to what is said, and another rejects it.

(202) Now, we have frequently said that if this impossibility be allowed (I mean that the devil is of a different essence and is incapable of experiencing better things), we will construct a defense for him that removes him from all responsi-

---

207. Cf. Phil 2.13.  208. Rom 8.28.
209. Cf. Gn 1.31.

bility for his wickedness, and will lay the blame on the one who invested him with being and created him, which is the most absurd thing conceivable.

(203) Now, the absurdity will be evident to one who has considered the essence of human souls, and has observed that, just as it is inconceivable that there are some human bodies that differ from other human bodies, some being of one essence and others of another, so also it is inconceivable that there are souls that differ from souls, and intelligence that differs from intelligence, and thought that differs from thought.

(204) But you will say the same thing also in the case of reason and the faculties in the soul, both of memory and the imagination. For if one man differs from another in essence, the faculties of the soul also must differ, and, let us say, one memory differs [from another], and one thought differs from another.

(205) But let us examine the teaching concerning these faculties that may also be conceived and thought of in a similar way, so that, in like manner, we may agree with, suspend judgment, or reject what they call spiritual and what they call earthly. For did a similar change occur in different essences, or was the change similar because this change was of the same essence with that which resulted?

(206) To say, therefore, that the same types of imaginations, agreements, thoughts, and memories have occurred in different essences is irrational. But it is foolish to say that some things are partly of the same essence, as though over and above one essence there is also another essence in them.

(207) For let them produce, alongside these faculties in those whom they say are spiritual, some other essence which neither thinks, intends, nor has memory or imagination, which is superior to thinking and intending, or among the earthly is similar or inferior, for they will not say superior.

(208) It is likely, however, that they will reply that, just as it is possible for the dissimilar essence of gold, silver, tin,

lead, and wax to be stamped in the same manner by the same seal, so it is possible, from the same impressions, that similar types appear in those with different essences and in those imagined. And they will say the same thing also in the case of purpose, thought, and memory.

(209) But see whether, even though this argument seems to be very persuasive, because the comparison is dissimilar, it can mislead and deceive rather than persuade the one who understands the example accurately. For, in the case of the image, I can show that, whether the imprint is in gold or in silver, the imprint *qua* imprint is similar, but it shows a specific character of having been done in gold in distinction from having been imprinted in silver or the other materials.

(210) So, then, let them show us the distinctive feature of the one who has received an impression that is better, or worse, or inferior, and let them also attempt to describe the essence that differs from those who have received the mark of the imprints in a similar manner. For since they have not shown it, they will assert it, but they will not prove it.

(211) Let these remarks be made on Heracleon's statement that *the words, "of your father the devil" mean, "of the essence of this father."* Again Heracleon makes a distinction in reference to the statement, "You wish to do the desires of your father,"[210] and says that *the devil does not have a will, but has desires.*

(212) The inconceivability of his argument is self-evident, for anyone would admit that he wills wicked things. And, although we do not have [texts] in hand at present to cite as evidence, you yourself will collect [such texts] to see if "willing" has been applied to the devil anywhere in Scripture.

(213) After this, Heracleon says that *these words were not addressed to the earthly people who are sons of the devil by nature, but to the psychics who become sons of the devil by adoption.* It follows from this that some can be called sons of God by nature, and some by adoption.

(214) And he says indeed that *these who are not such by nature become children of the devil by loving the desires of the devil and doing them.*

(215) He also makes a distinction, namely that *one must understand the term "children" in a threefold manner: first by nature, second by*

---

210. Jn 8.44.

*choice, third by merit. What has been begotten by some parent,* he says, *is a child "by nature," and is properly called a child; a child "by choice" results when someone, by doing the will of another of his own choice, is called a child of him whose will he does; others are called children "by merit" in the sense that some are said to be children of hell, others of darkness, others of lawlessness, and others to be offspring of serpents and vipers.*[211]

(216) *For these things,* he says, *do not give birth to anyone because of their own nature, for they are deadly and destroy those cast into them, but because some have done their works, they are said to be their children.* But after he made such a distinction, he did not support his interpretation from the Scriptures in any way.

(217) We would reply to him, however, that if it is not by nature but by merit that some are called children of hell, and darkness, and lawlessness (for these are things that are deadly and destroy rather than bring things into existence), how does Paul say somewhere, "We were by nature children of wrath, even as the rest"?[212] Or let them tell us how wrath, whose children we were, is not destructive and especially deadly by itself.

(218) Again he says that Jesus says that *these are now children of the devil, not because the devil begot certain ones, but because they became like the devil by doing his works.*

(219) But how much better it is to declare of all the children of the devil, that they become like him by doing his works, and that they are not called children of the devil because of their essence and their constitution independent of their works?

> He was a murderer from the beginning, and he did not stand in the truth, because truth is not in him.
> (John 8.44)

### The Devil Is a Murderer

(220) It is true that one who has killed a man in whatever manner is a murderer in the common sense of the word. The term murder, however, is also a morally neutral[213] term in the sense in which Phinees committed murder in the zeal of God when he killed the Israelite man and the Madianite woman when the Israelite committed fornication with her.[214]

---

211. Cf. Mt 23.15, 33.   212. Cf. Eph 2.3.
213. μέσος, "middle", in the Stoic sense of midway between good and bad.
214. Cf. Nm 25.6–12.

Phinees would not be said to be a murderer in a blameworthy sense, nor would David when he [smote] Goliath "in the name of the Lord of hosts, the God of the army of Israel."[215] [Because of this ambiguity in the term murderer], we must ask about the true life of man and his death, which is opposed to this true life, that we may understand what murderer means in the blameworthy sense.

(221) So far as the literal sense is concerned, you will mention that Adam and Eve were not destroyed so long as they had not sinned, but died immediately on the day in which they ate of the forbidden tree. No one other than the murderous devil killed them when he deceived Eve through the serpent, and Eve gave to her husband of the tree and the man ate.[216]

(222) The statement, "I shall not die, but live, and shall declare the works of the Lord,"[217] must be understood, however, in respect to the deeper aspects of what it teaches, along with the following remarks the Savior made to the Sadducees in the Gospel according to Matthew, remarks which are very mysterious to those capable of understanding what is said. "Concerning the resurrection of the dead, have you not read what was spoken by God, saying to you, I am the God of Abraham, and the God of Isaac, and the God of Jacob? God is not God of the dead, but of the living."[218] Similar words are found in the Gospel according to Luke, "Now even Moses has revealed that the dead are raised, as he says at the bush, the Lord God of Abraham, and the God of Isaac, and the God of Jacob; he is not the God of the dead, but of the living, for all live in him."[219]

(223) In addition, these words occur in the Gospel according to Mark, "Concerning the dead, have you not read in the book of Moses that they are raised, as God spoke to him at the bush, saying, I am the God of Abraham, and the God of Isaac, and the God of Jacob? He is not the God of the dead, but of the living."[220] When you have understood

---

215. Cf. 1 Kg 17.45.
216. Cf. Gn 3.1–6.
217. Cf. Ps 117.17.
218. Cf. Mt 22.31–32.
219. Cf. Lk 20.37–38.
220. Cf. Mk 12.26–27.

these sayings you will see that if one is now alive after being raised from the dead, then Abraham, Isaac, and Jacob were dead before they were alive. No one, however, is said to be dead in the proper sense of the word who has not previously been alive.

(224) But notice also the statement, "In Adam all die, and in Christ all shall be made alive."[221] In these words neither is the neutral sense of death indicated by the words, "In Adam all die," nor the morally indifferent sense of life, which also is neither good nor bad in and of itself, by the words, "In Christ all shall be made alive." By observing these words you will perceive the life of man according to the image.[222] And when you have understood what his life is, you will perceive in what manner the murderer killed the living man, and that he will correctly be called a murderer, not because he killed some particular individual, but because he killed the whole race insofar as "in Adam all die."

(225) Now, he committed this murder, having begun even from the beginning, and because of this murder of Adam, each one who has reflected on it and on his own body and to whom it is related, will make the following remark because he considers himself unfortunate since he himself has died in Adam, "Wretched man that I am, who will deliver me from this body of death?"[223] He considers also in what way these words were spoken, "You have brought me down into the dust of death,"[224] and, "You have humbled us in a place of affliction,"[225] and "the body of our lowliness."[226]

(226) Now, there is also something very mysterious, on account of which he who is a murderer from the beginning is ruler of this world (I mean, of course, of the earthly region), where those men are whom he has killed. On the one hand, then, the murderer has killed us, but, by the grace of God, we have been buried with Christ and raised with him, if indeed we have become conformed to his Resurrection and walk in newness of life.[227]

---

221. Cf. 1 Cor 15.22.
222. Cf. Gn 1.26.
223. Rom 7.24.
224. Ps 21.16.
225. Ps 43.20.
226. Phil 3.21.
227. Cf. Rom 6.4.

(227) Now, the murderer rules those who have perished, and he rules the dead, but he can rule no one who is alive.

(228) And if you pay more attention also to what has been written of the dead, such as in the words, "For this reason Christ died and arose, that he might be the Lord both of the dead and of the living,"[228] you will see in what manner the devil is no longer even Lord of the dead because of the death of Jesus, for Jesus died that he might be Lord also of the dead.

(229) Insofar as man lives, then, he does not bear the image of the earthly. But when he dies and is destroyed by the murderer, and at the same time does [not] maintain the image of God, he takes up, in addition, the image of the earthly and of the dead, for the earthly man is dead, just as the heavenly man is alive, and God is not God of the dead, but of the living.[229]

(230) This is why, if we have arisen with him and are walking in newness of life, he is our God.[230] But if we are still among the dead, he is not God of the dead, and will not be our God.

### Those Who Are Dead in Christ

(231) Related to our examination of matters pertaining to him who was a murderer from the beginning, is the consideration of those who are dead, but who are dead in no other than Christ, and who will also rise first. In the Epistle to the Corinthians, they are spoken of as follows: "For the trumpet shall sound, and the dead shall rise incorruptible, and we shall be changed."[231] And in the Epistle to the Thessalonians, "For this we say to you by the word of the Lord, that we who are alive, who remain to the coming of the Lord, shall not precede those who sleep, because the Lord himself will come down from heaven with a shout of command, with the voice of an archangel, and the trumpet of God, and the dead in Christ shall rise first, then we who are alive, who are left, will be taken up together with them in

---

228. Cf. Rom 14.9.
229. Cf. 1 Cor 15.49; Mt 22.32.
230. Cf. Rom 6.4.
231. Cf. 1 Cor 15.52.

the clouds to meet the Lord in the air, and so shall we always be with the Lord."[232]

(232) We think that those who have been perfected and who no longer commit sin are alive in Christ, and that the dead in Christ are those who are favorably disposed to the Christian faith, and who prefer to live a good life, but who have not, in fact, actually succeeded, but still sin, either in ignorance of the accurate, true word of justice, or in weakness, because their decisions are overcome by the flesh, which lusts against the spirit.[233]

(233) And it is in conformity with these matters that Paul, conscious of himself, says, because he has already succeeded, "We who are alive."[234] But those whom we said to be dead have special need of the resurrection, since not even those who are alive can be taken up in clouds to meet the Lord in the air before the dead in Christ first rise. This is why it has been written, "The dead in Christ shall rise first, then we who are alive,"[235] etc.

(234) But you will consider if it is also because of the murder committed by the devil that the things which exist upon the cursed earth in the works of Adam, who was cast out of "the paradise of pleasure,"[236] [have arisen, and that, apart from this], they would not exist.

(235) But he was a murderer from the beginning of the present things, and, I think, after he had become the "beginning of what the Lord molded,"[237] he envied those who were created "that they might have being."[238]

(236) In this way "death entered the world by means of envy,"[239] since [the devil] always commits murder among those whom he finds alive until all enemies have been put under the feet of the Son of God, and his last enemy, death, has been destroyed.[240]

---

232. Cf. 1 Thes 4.15–17.
233. Cf. Gal 5.17.
234. 1 Thes 4.17.
235. 1 Thes 4.16–17.
236. Cf. Gn 3.17, 23.
237. Cf. Jb 40.19.
238. Wis 1.14.
239. Cf. Wis 2.24.
240. Cf. 1 Cor 15.25–26.

### "And He Did Not Stand in the Truth"

(237) But let us also consider the statement, "And he did not stand in the truth." He, and he alone,[241] would reasonably be thought to have stood in the truth, who firmly holds sound teachings and, because of the firmness of the teachings, is unshaken in his judgments in every season, and is shaken by no circumstance or bodily provocation such as severe pains, or excessive desire of sexual pleasures, or by any cause whatsoever, which would remove him from the good even for a short time.

(238) And let this word be applied also to those natures that do not consist of flesh and blood, for it can also be said appropriately in the life of such beings that those that live a good life have stood in the truth, but if one does not so live, "he has not stood in the truth."

(239) But I wonder whether to have stood in the truth is something single and simple, and not to have stood in it is something complex and manifold. Some may be compelled to stand in the truth on bases that are trembling and shaking, if I may put it this way, who have not yet attained this, and there may be others who have not experienced this, but who are exposed to the danger of coming to be in this situation, like the one who says, "My feet were almost moved."[242] There may be yet others who have even fallen in the truth, of whom I think it is said, "Everyone who falls on this stone shall be broken."[243]

(240) The Lord, urging Moses to stand on this, that is, in the truth, said to him, "Behold there is a place by me, and you shall stand upon the rock."[244] For if the rock was Christ,[245] and Christ says, "I am the truth,"[246] perhaps the statement, "You shall stand upon the rock,"[247] can be equivalent to, "You shall stand upon the truth." But this is only possible for one eventually and with difficulty after many trials.

---

241. Lit.: Everyone, and only he.
242. Ps 72.2.
243. Cf. Mt 21.44.
244. Cf. Ex 33.21.
245. Cf. 1 Cor 10.4.
246. Cf. Jn 14.6.
247. Ex 33.21.

(241) At any rate, up to the time of the statement, "Behold there is a place beside me, and you shall stand upon the rock,"[248] Moses had not yet stood upon the rock. And if one were to consider carefully human nature, which cannot easily be pure of false teachings, he will see that just as "every man is a liar,"[249] so not every man has stood in the truth.

(242) For if someone is no longer a liar, or has stood in the truth, such a one is not a man, and, consequently, God may say to him and those like him, "I said, you are gods and are all sons of the Most High,"[250] nor will the statement be added, "But you, indeed, die as men."[251]

(243) If, then, someone else also has not stood in the truth, it is clear that the devil, that murderer from the beginning, has not, and the reason he has not stood in the truth has been expressed as follows, "Because truth is not in him."

(244) And the reason why truth is not in him is that he has been deceived and accepts lies, and he has himself been deceived by himself. On this basis he is reckoned to be worse than the rest of these who are deceived, since they are deceived by him, but he creates his own deception himself.

### *"Because Truth Is Not in Him"*

(245) Now it is worthwhile to ask in what sense it is said, "Truth is not in him." Is it, for example, that he never has a true opinion, but everything he ever thinks is false? Or is it that he does not participate in Christ, since those who participate in Christ participate in the one who said, "I am the truth"?[252]

(246) For those who participate in him participate in him also insofar as he is truth, and this is why truth is in them. Now, in addition, a third such difficulty in the passage could also be proposed. Some will wonder if it is necessary to say that truth is not in one who admits a lie at any time,

---

248. Cf. Ex 33.21.
250. Ps 81.6.
252. Cf. Jn 14.6.

249. Ps 115.2.
251. Cf. Ps 81.7.

even if he should hold the lie along with many things that are true.

(247) For as that which consists of countless things that are true is false if even one falsehood is interwoven, so in the case of him who holds one false opinion along with many true ones, as if such is interwoven, one would say, consequently, that truth is not in this person. Now I am portraying the person who accepts one lie along with many things that are true.

(248) These three positions will seem, at least, to be reasonable. One will say that the statement, "Truth is not in him," has been made in the sense that he does not participate in Christ, against whom, indeed, he even wages war. And another will say that it was made because he thinks there is nothing true [in him], but that he is deceived in everything. And the reason he is the devil and is wicked and worse than anyone else whoever who sins is that, among the multitude of sinners there may be something true also in the midst of the many things that are mistaken, but there is nothing true in the devil.

(249) A third party will agree with the rest and say that it is impossible that any rational being hold a false opinion about everything, and accept the truth about nothing, even in a small degree.

(250) When the devil thinks of himself, he would, at least, hold as a true opinion that he is rational, and that such a being is man, and such an angel, and such is a body, and what sort of body, and that something else differs from a body.

(251) But even if the latter[253] should not present our last argument, nor even consider it, indeed his first arguments are sufficient to show that the assertion that he holds no true opinion cannot be true of the devil.

(252) We, therefore, understand the statement, "He did not stand in the truth," neither to indicate a particular kind of nature, nor to mean that it was impossible for him to have stood in the truth.

253. I. e., the third interlocutor.

Heracleon, on the other hand, says on these words, *"For his nature is not of the truth, but is of the opposite to the truth, namely of error and ignorance."*

(253) *"For this reason,"* he says, *"he can neither stand in truth nor have truth in himself, because he possesses falsehood as his own from his own nature and is unable by nature ever to speak truth."* He goes on to say that *not only is he a liar, but he is also the father of falsehood,* taking the words "his father" in a peculiar sense to refer to his nature, since it consists of error and falsehood.

(254) But all these things rescue the devil from all blame, accusation, and censure. For no one would reasonably blame, accuse, or censure one who is not disposed by nature to the better things. *The devil, therefore,* according to Heracleon, *is unfortunate rather than blameworthy.* One must see, however, that just as the devil has not stood in the truth because truth is not in him, so also those who are of their father the devil have not stood in the truth, because truth is not in them.

(255) And all who still commit sin are such, even if they say they belong to Christ, "For everyone who commits sin has been born of the devil."[254]

## When he speaks a lie, he speaks of his own, for he is a liar and the father thereof. (John 8.44)

### *The Liar Speaks of His Own Resources*

(256) We mentioned this saying previously in relation to the statement, "You are of your father the devil,"[255] and we made the comments that occurred to us in relation to it when we were investigating what the lie is and its father. Let our present remarks be compared with those previous comments.[256]

(257) I think every evil and deceitful spirit is a lie, and whenever anyone of these speaks, it speaks from its own resources and by no means from the resources of God. And the father of these [spirits] is the liar, the devil.

(258) We will now present what moved us to say that every inferior spirit is false. It is written in the Third Book of

254. Cf. 1 Jn 3.8.  255. Jn 8.44.
256. Cf. above, sections 171ff.

Kings that at the time Micheas was called by Achab to prophesy concerning whether he should go to Ramoth Galaad for war or stay,[257] he said, "I saw the God of Israel sitting on his throne, and all the host of heaven stood around him on his right and on his left.

(259) "And he said, Who will deceive Achab, king of Israel, and he will go up and fall in Ramoth Galaad? And he spoke in this manner.[258] And a spirit came forth and stood before the Lord and said, I will deceive him.

(260) "And the Lord said to him, By what means? And he said, I will go forth and will be a false spirit in the mouth of all these prophets of yours."[259]

(261) And in the Second Book of Paralipomenon, the same Micheas says to Achab and Josaphat, "Hear the word of the Lord. I saw the Lord sitting on his throne, and every power of heaven stood at his right and at his left. And the Lord said, Who will deceive Achab, king of Israel, and he will go up and fall in Ramoth Galaad? And he spoke in this manner. And a spirit came forth and stood before the Lord and said, I will deceive him. And the Lord said, By what means? And he said, I will go forth and be a false spirit in the mouth of all his prophets."[260]

(262) These words show clearly, then, that if any spirit is the lying spirit, all similar spirits would be lying spirits, indebted to their lying father for being lying spirits in accordance with their falsehood and evil, and not because this belongs to their essence.

(263) Whenever, then, the Holy Spirit or an angelic spirit speaks, it does not speak from its own resources, but from the word of truth and of wisdom. This is made clear also in the Gospel according to John where he teaches about the Paraclete and says, "He will receive from me, and will announce to you."[261]

(264) Whenever the lie speaks, however, it speaks from its

---

257. Cf. 3 Kgs 22.15.
258. Omitting ἐν σοί with Preuschen.
259. Cf. 3 Kgs 22.19–22.   260. Cf. 2 Chr 18.18–21.
261. Jn 16.14.

own resources. The lying spirit in the Third Book of Kings also spoke from its own resources when it deceived Achab.

(265) But notice that the term "liar" has been applied in the same way to the devil, who gave birth to the lie, and to man. For it is [not][262] said here of man, "Because he is a liar and the father thereof," but it is said in the Psalms, "And I said in my ecstasy, Every man is a liar."[263]

(266) Now, we have presented these comments that we may flee being men with all our strength, and hasten to become "gods,"[264] since, indeed, insofar as we are men, we are liars, just as also the father of the lie is a liar.

(267) Now, it is in the same way that we participate in one and the same name and in the reality indicated by the name. I am referring to us, so long as we continue to be men, and to the devil, who is said to be a liar.

> But because I speak the truth, you do not believe in me. (John 8.45)

*It is Possible To Believe in Some Respects without Believing Entirely*

(268) If we recall that this word is addressed to those Jews who have believed in him, who are the recipients of the promise that if they remain in Jesus' word then they are truly his disciples and will know the truth which makes them free,[265] we will question how he says to such people, "But because I speak the truth, you do not believe in me."

(269) Consider if it is possible that someone believe in the same person so far as some particular aspect is concerned, but not believe so far as another is concerned. Take, as an example, those who believe in the Jesus crucified in Judea in the time of Pontius Pilate, but who do not believe in the one born of the Virgin Mary. These believe and disbelieve in the same one.[266]

---

262. Wendland's addition.  263. Cf. Ps 115.2.
264. Cf. Ps 81.6.  265. Cf. Jn 8.31–32.
266. Perhaps he is referring to Jewish Christians, some of whom, at least, did not accept the virgin birth.

(270) Take, as another example, those who believe in the Jesus who performed the recorded wonders and signs in Judea, but who do not believe in the Son of the one who made heaven and earth. These believe and disbelieve in the [same] one.

(271) Again, consider in turn those who believe in the Father of Jesus Christ, but who do not believe in the Creator and maker of this universe. These believe and disbelieve in the same one.

(272) But there are also those who believe in the maker of heaven and earth, but who do not believe in the Father of Jesus who was crucified in the time of Pontius Pilate. These believe and disbelieve in God.

(273) So, then, that there not be a discrepancy that trips us up, as if the writer of the Gospel had not seen such a discrepancy, you will say that he who says to the Jews who have believed in him, "But because I speak the truth, you do not believe in me," addressed these words to those who believe so far as one aspect is concerned, and disbelieve so far as another is concerned.

(274) It is likely that they believed in him on the basis of what was seen because of his marvelous deeds, but they did not believe in his deeper sayings. And the statement, "Because I speak the truth, you do not believe in me," is appropriately joined with the statement, "You shall know the truth,"[267] which is said to those who have not known the truth. It is as if he said, "Insofar as I perform marvelous deeds, you believe in me, but insofar as I speak the truth, you do not believe in me."

(275) Now you may see this even at present in many people who marvel at Jesus whenever they consider the story about him, but who no longer believe when a teaching that is deeper and greater than their capacity is disclosed to them, but instead suspect it to be false. For this reason let us take heed so that the Word may never say to us too, "Because I speak the truth, you do not believe in me."

267. Jn 8.32.

Which of you convicts me of sin? (John 8.46)

(276) Whenever the Word presents his meaning clearly so that none of his hearers can contradict him, he might also make these remarks to shame those who do not agree: If you do not convict what I am saying as sinful, you could reasonably be required to agree.

(277) Now, so far as the literal meaning is concerned, the text also involves the Savior's boldness, since no man could say with the confidence that he had not sinned, "Which of you convicts me of sin?" It is only our Lord "who did not sin,"[268] "who has been tempted in all things like as we are, without sin,"[269] who is able to address these words to all who have ever known him.

(278) Now, I understand the words, "which of you," to be said, not only to those present, but also to the whole human race, as if we were to understand it to mean, Who of your race? Or, what sort of man will be able to convict me of sin? But be assured that there is no one.

(279) Because, however, of the command, "Become imitators of me as I also am of Christ,"[270] so far as it is possible for human nature, we must strive in every way to regain such boldness of a pure conscience in relation to all men, that we may say to each person who knows us, in relation to those times subsequent to the beginning of our faith, "Which of you convicts me of sin?"[271] It is not possible, however, to say this from the time that we have attained reason.

(280) The Savior, however, might have said this not only to men, but also to the devil and the powers subordinate to him because they can say nothing to convict him of sin.

(281) And this indeed is in conformity with the statement, "The prince of this world comes, and he finds nothing in me."[272]

(282) But we too, by much diligence, after a period of time, can regain the confidence so that, at the time of our

---

268. 1 Pt 2.22.  
269. Heb 4.15.  
270. 1 Cor 11.1.  
271. Jn 8.46.  
272. Cf. Jn 14.30.

exodus we may say to the devil and his angels who seek an opportunity against us, "Which of you convicts me of sin?"

> If I speak truth, why do you not believe in me?
> (John 8.46)

(283) It is worthwhile to see what underlies this question. And we will see this, although those to whom the word was addressed did not respond in the proper way when they expressed their opinion.

(284) For one might say, "We do not believe because we do not see how what he says is truth, and we are not aware that our eyes, which by nature are perceptive of truth, have not yet been purified. And since we are such, we are not of God; if we are not yet of God, our eyes, too, which are capable of perceiving the truth have not been purified, but they have been covered over, or made corporeal, or obscured by evil."

(285) But when we contemplate what believing is in the proper sense, insofar as "everyone who believes that Jesus is the Christ has been born of God,"[273] and when we perceive how far short we fall of believing in this manner, let us respond as follows, exhorting the Physician of the eyes of the soul[274] by his wisdom and beneficence to do everything to uncover our eyes, which are still covered by the shame we feel because of evil, according to what is said somewhere, "Our shame has covered us."[275] For he will listen to us when we confess the reasons we do not yet believe, and help us as those who are sick and in need of a physician,[276] and work with us that we may receive the gift of believing, which is placed third in Paul's catalogue of gifts, after the word of wisdom and the word of understanding, to which he adds, "To another, faith in the same Spirit."[277] He says of this gift also in other passages, "For it has been given to you by God not only to believe in Christ but also to suffer for him."[278]

---

273. 1 Jn 5.1.
274. Cf. Prv 14.30.
275. Jer 3.25.
276. Cf. Mt 9.12.
277. 1 Cor 12.9.
278. Cf. Phil 1.29.

(286) But it will also be clear to the attentive person from its effect, that the gift of God, which consists in believing in nothing but the truth alone, is no ordinary gift, since there are numerous different teachings being proclaimed by many who promise that their teachings are true. For this discernment is already the work of a trustworthy money-changer,[279] and you would not err if you were to call such a person perfect, since it is also written in the Epistle to the Hebrews, "But solid food is for the perfect, who by practice have their senses exercised to the discerning of good and evil."[280]

> He who is of God hears the words of God; you do not hear them because you are not of God. (John 8.47)

### We Were by Nature Children of Wrath

(287) Those who introduce the fable concerning different natures and say that there are sons of God by nature who also, by their original constitution, are uniquely capable of receiving the words of God because of their kinship with God, appear to prove their point from this passage, too.

(288) By means of this text, occupying themselves with it as they do, they mislead those who are uncritical and incapable of replying to their persuasive use of the text and who do not see that its interpretation is as follows. If, indeed, as many as received "the true light which enlightens every man coming into this world,"[281] have not received it because they are of God (for if they have received it because they are of God, it would not have been written of them, "But as many as received him, he gave them power to become children of God, to those who believe in his name"[282]), then it is clear that those who are not of God do not have any power at all to become children of God before they have received the true light. Moreover, once they receive the true light they do not yet become children of God, but they receive power

---

279. Cf. Book 19.44 and our note there.
280. Heb 5.14.   281. Jn 1.9.
282. Jn 1.12.

to become children of God because they have received the light. Then, when they have come to be of God, they also hear his words, and no longer only simply believe, but now also perceive the realities of religion in a more discerning manner.

(289) [But] those who do not aspire to be such do not become children of God, nor do they come to be of God, and this is why they do not hear his words nor understand their meaning. They continue in the condition that precedes being children of God, the condition of those who have only believed and are slaves of God because they have received the spirit of slavery to fear[283] and have not been zealous to go forward and advance so that they might also receive the spirit of adoption by which those who have it cry, "Abba, Father."[284]

(290) For the fact that no one at all is a son of God from the beginning is clear from Paul's statement in which he also includes himself, "We were by nature children of wrath."[285] It is also clear from the statement, "But I say to you, Love your enemies and pray for those who persecute you, that you may become sons of your Father who is in heaven."[286]

(291) For if Paul was "by nature a son of wrath,"[287] who, more than Paul so far as his constitution is concerned, was not a son of wrath before he received power to become a child of God,[288] and before he became a child of God?

(292) And if the only way one becomes a son of the Father who is in heaven is by loving one's enemies and praying for those who persecute one,[289] it is clear that no one hears the words of God because he is of God by nature, but because he has received power to become a child of God and has made proper use of this power, and because he has loved his enemies and prayed for those who abuse him, and has become a son of the Father who is in heaven.

283. Cf. Rom 8.15.  284. Rom 8.15.
285. Eph 2.3.
286. Cf. Mt 5.44–45. Cf. above, sections 144ff.
287. Cf. Eph 2.3.  288. Cf. Jn 1.12.
289. Cf. Mt 5.44–45.

(293) At that time he is also of God, and hears and understands God's words and assimilates their knowledge. This is not a distinguishing feature of slaves,[290] but of children of God who have nullified their birth [from the devil][291] in every respect, and have received their birth from God through "the spirit of adoption."[292]

### He Who Hears the Words of God Is a Child of God

(294) But at the same time we must carefully consider how to take the words, "He hears the words of God," which resemble the words, "My sheep hear my voice."[293]

(295) For if we take the verb "to hear" to refer to simple assent, even natural men[294] who believe for a time will be of God, since they have the Word's testimony that some believe for a while.[295]

(296) But if we take the verb "he hears" to refer to keeping the commandments, it is clear that one will not be a son of God if he sins even in one point.[296] This will not cause difficulty for us who say that one becomes a son of God by change, but it will for them because they cannot at all demonstrate that they themselves are sinless along with those who hold the same doctrines as they do.

(297) But if we take the verb "he hears" to refer to understanding and apprehending, let them point to someone who hears all the words of the New Testament in this way, that we may say that he is a son of God, if his interpretation of the Holy Scriptures should not be liable to refutation. For, so far as these matters are concerned, we too, if we imagine that the one who is already a son of God is someone great and marvelous, will not be convicted of having taken the words,

---

290. Cf. Rom 8.15.
291. Wendland's suggestion. Brooke makes a similar suggestion. Preuschen and Blanc indicate that something is missing in the text. There is support for the concept, at least, in section 176 above.
292. Cf. Rom 8.15.
293. Cf. Jn 10.27.
294. οἱ ψυχικοί. Cf. the use of this term in 1 Cor 2.14; 15.44, 46.
295. Cf. Lk 8.13.
296. Cf. 1 Jn 2.3; Jas 2.10.

"He who is of God hears the words of God," in a manner unworthy of those who are of God.

(298) Furthermore, it will also be possible to prove something from opposites which would seem to be paradoxical. Now the paradox is this, that someone is more a son of God than is another son of God, and that someone is twice as much a son of God as another.

(299) We will demonstrate how this is proven from its opposite as follows. The second "woe to the scribes and Pharisees" in the Gospel according to Matthew is as follows. "Woe to you, scribes and Pharisees, hypocrites, because you traverse sea and land to make one proselyte, and, when he is made, you make him twice as much a son of hell as yourselves."[297]

(300) According to this, then, neither are some sons of hell by nature, nor are the sons of hell equally sons of hell, since one is twice as much a son of hell as another.

(301) But, if one is twice as much a son of hell as another, why not also of destruction, death, darkness, and the other things of which those who sin in various degrees are sons?

(302) Now, if this is so in the case of the latter, why will not some also be twice as much sons of light as others, and sons of life, and sons of wisdom, and thus sons of God?

(303) But, if someone becomes twice as much a son of God as another, why is it not worthy to think that the Firstborn of all creation[298] is many and multiple times more[299] a son of God than the other sons of God, even those who no longer have a spirit of slavery to fear, but have received the spirit of adoption?[300]

(304) Perhaps, therefore, since the words of God are so many, including not only those which have been recorded, but also the secret ones "which it is not granted to man to utter,"[301] and those of which John says, "I do not think the world itself could contain the books written,"[302] everyone

---

297. Mt 23.15.   298. Cf. Col 1.15.
299. Origen joins three superlative quantitative adverbs here which are impossible to translate together into readable English.
300. Cf. Rom 8.15.   301. 2 Cor 12.4.
302. Jn 21.25.

who hears words of God of whatever kind is already of God. To whatever extent, however, one hears more words of God, he will accordingly come to be of God so many times more. Consequently, if one must so spell it out, someone who has heard all the words of God, if indeed this should happen to someone who receives the spirit of adoption,[303] becomes a son of God in a way that is perfect and unsurpassable since he is of God in every way, altogether, and totally.

(305) Now, we must take the words "altogether and totally" quite candidly as equivalent to all teachings, and all knowledge, and all mysteries, so as to say that the one who knows all mysteries and all knowledge, and, together with these, the achievements of perfect love[304] has come to be of God altogether and totally.

(306) And consider if it is possible, in consequence of the statement, "We know in part, and we prophesy in part,"[305] for such a one to say, "And we are sons of God in part"? And again, "When that which is perfect has come, and that which is in part has been abolished,"[306] can one say that that which is perfect in regard to becoming a son of God will come when that which is in part for one to have become a son of God is abolished?

(307) But do not leave unexamined also the question if it is ever possible, in part, to be a son of the superior portion that concerns divine things and, in part a son of its opposite, or if this is an impossibility. You will compare with this in what way many sons are said to be sons of one father. Is it because of the ancestors and their descendants, or is it related to this conjecture we have put forward?

(308) Since, therefore, we have received power to become children of God,[307] let us do everything that we may come to be of God and hear his words, and advance even to be of God, that we may advance also in hearing words of God, always clearly understanding more of them until we receive all the words of God, or as many, at least, as it is possi-

303. Cf. Rom 8.15.
305. Cf. 1 Cor 13.9.
307. Cf. Jn 1.12.

304. Cf. 1 Cor 13.2.
306. Cf. 1 Cor 13.10.

ble for those considered worthy of the spirit of adoption[308] to receive both now and later.

(309) But as often as we do not hear the words spoken by God, that is, we do not understand them, so often must we assume that we are reproved as not being of God. For he who does not hear the words of God does not hear them because he is not of God, and he is not of God on his own account, although sometimes he has already received power to become a child of God[309] and is able to become a son of the Father in heaven by loving his enemies and praying for those who abuse him.[310]

> The Jews answered and said to him: Are we not correct in saying that you are a Samaritan and have a demon? (John 8.48).

### Jesus Is the Good Samaritan

(310) It is likely that some frequently made these remarks about the Savior to one another in secret and called him a Samaritan because, like the Samaritans, he falsified Jewish traditions. "For the Jews do not have dealings with the Samaritans,"[311] since they disagree with them on many doctrines.

(311) But it is possibly worthwhile to ask how, since the Samaritans deny the age to come and do not accept the continued existence of the soul, they dared to say the Savior was a [Samaritan] when he taught so many things about resurrection and judgment.

(312) But perhaps they say this to reproach him, and not at all because he teaches the same doctrines as the Samaritans. And it is likely that some thought that his teachings about the age to come, and judgment, and resurrection came, not from his own views on these subjects, since he himself held the Samaritan view that nothing is in store for men after this life, but from pretense, and that his remarks about resurrection and eternal life were made in accor-

---

308. Cf. Rom 8.15
309. Cf. Jn 1.12.
310. Cf. Mt 5.44–45; Lk 6.28.
311. Jn 4.9.

## COMMENTARY ON JOHN, BOOK 20

dance with what is generally approved and pleasing to the Jews.

(313) And they said he had a demon because of his teachings, which exceeded human limits, as when he said that God was his Father[312] and that he had descended from heaven,[313] and that he himself was the bread of life that was much greater than the manna, so that the one who eats this bread will live forever,[314] and ten thousand other things with which the Gospels are filled.

(314) Now, it is also possible that they said, "You have a demon,"[315] because of what they believed about Beelzebub, since some of them thought he "cast out demons by Beelzebub, the prince of demons,"[316] and had Beelzebub in himself, as it were.

(315) His enemies, therefore, will know in what respect they say that he has a demon, but we believe him who declares, "I do not have a demon."[317] For a demon cannot open the eyes of the blind or perform these signs which also have been recorded. And traces and remnants of these signs continue to occur in the name of Jesus up to the present in the churches.[318]

(316) One might next investigate why indeed, when the Jews (not those who had believed in him) who answered him apply two slanders to him, namely, "You are a Samaritan," and, "You have a demon," he does not respond to both, but only to the charge, "You have a demon," when he says, "I do not have a demon."[319]

(317) And see if it is possible that the message of the parable in the Gospel according to Luke is related to this. It is about the man who went down from Jerusalem to Jericho and fell among thieves, whom the priest and the Levite passed by, but the Samaritan came upon him on his journey, saw him, had compassion, approached him and bound up his wounds, pouring on oil and wine.[320]

---

312. Cf. Jn 5.18.
313. Cf. Jn 6.38.
314. Cf. Jn 6.32–35.
315. Cf. Jn 8.48.
316. Cf. Lk 11.15.
317. Jn 8.49.
318. Cf. *Cels.* 1.2, 46; 7.8.
319. Jn 8.49.
320. Cf. Lk 10.30–34.

(318) For if someone, in discussing this parable, should be able to prove that the things said about the Samaritan who healed the man who was half-dead and had fallen among thieves refer to no one other than the Savior, he will also show why the Savior did not deny that he was a Samaritan.

(319) But someone else, when he has observed the distinction Paul makes between Jews and those under the Law,[321] and has referred those under the Law anagogically to the Samaritans, and has understood that the Savior, more than Paul, became all things to all men that he might gain all men,[322] will say that because he became as one under the Law for those under the Law, he also became a Samaritan, as it were, and in accordance with this he did not deny that he was a Samaritan.

(320) Moreover, a third person who has understood the meaning of the name Samaritan, which means guard,[323] will say that, although the Jews called him a Samaritan in another sense, because he understood what the name means, he did not deny it. He knew that he was the guard of human souls, and that it was said of him, "Behold, he who guards Israel shall neither slumber nor sleep,"[324] and, "The Lord is the guard of the little ones."[325]

(321) The Hebrews, however, call a guard *somer*, and thus they also hand on in their tradition that the Samaritans first received this name because the king of the Assyrians sent them to be guards of the land of Israel after the captivity, that is, that other Israel besides Judah, which was taken captive into Assyria because of their many sins.[326]

---

321. Cf. 1 Cor 9.20.
322. Cf. 1 Cor 9.22.
323. Cf. Lagarde, *OS* 66, 3.
324. Ps 120.4.
325. Ps 114.6.
326. Cf. 4 Kgs 17.

> Jesus answered, I do not have a demon, but I
> honor my Father, and you dishonor me. I do not
> seek my own glory; there is one who seeks and
> judges. (John 8.49–50)

(322) If the tree planted "beside the running waters" is such that it produces its fruit "in due season" and its leaf does not fall off, but all that it does prospers,[327] what must we think about our Savior Jesus other than that he, being the tree of life insofar as he is wisdom, and wisdom is "a tree of life to all those who lay hold on her,"[328] both bears fruit, and has other leaves in addition to the fruit that are such that not even one of them falls off.

(323) This is why one must take no word of Jesus in an ordinary manner, and especially these words which his holy disciples considered worthy of being recorded. One must apply every test even to those words assumed to be clear, and not despair that even concerning his word that is thought to be straightforward and simple, something worthy of that holy mouth will be discovered by those who seek correctly.

(324) But, if we perhaps find nothing,[329] we must blame ourselves and not Jesus' word for not breathing forth from his fullness doctrines full of truth and wisdom.[330]

### *Jesus Alone Can Say That He Does Not Have a Demon*

(325) Now I have made these remarks because I intend to examine the saying, "I do not have a demon." By means of this saying all of us who read the Gospel are taught something that we did not know before reading the Gospel. But we must now consider what this is.

(326) It is a prevailing view in the Scriptures that sinners do many things contrary to reason for no other reason than that they have become receptive of the activity of an evil spirit or the will of an unclean demon.

---

327. Cf. Ps 1.3.  
328. Cf. Prv 3.18.  
329. Cf. Mt 7.7.  
330. Cf. Jn 1.16.

(327) Those, therefore, who said that ill-temper was demonic, and likewise also backbiting, did not hesitate to ascribe even things thought to be the least of sins to demons.[331]

(328) And it is likely also that in countless other things demons delude us and influence us to act according to their will. And it is possible that, just as no one among men is "clean from defilement,"[332] and there is no "just man on the earth who will do good and will not sin,"[333] so also there is no one who has always been free of demons and has never fallen victim to their influence.

(329) Wherefore, by interpreting the healings in the Gospel allegorically, in which there are also exorcisms of demons, we will say that the demons are always exorcised by Jesus from all those who are no longer influenced by demons because they have been healed by the Word.

(330) I, therefore, understand it to be a statement that only Jesus can make, who alone has despoiled the principalities and powers and exposed them publicly, and has triumphed over them on the tree,[334] having set the cross as a sign of victory against every opposing power, to say, "I have neither had a demon, nor do I have one, nor will I," in the same way as he says, "The prince of this world is coming, and he has nothing in me."[335]

(331) Now we too can make this statement and say, "I do not have a demon," but we will be reproved in the same manner as those were who denied that they were demon-possessed, and by their very deeds proved that they lied.

(332) Or is it not proof that we are demon-possessed whenever we cry out ablaze with anger and wrath in a state of madness, or frenzied and neighing, as it were, we mount even our own wives like lusty stallions[336] and cast behind us the words of God about freedom from passion?

(333) Moreover, if we are downcast and gloomy and depressed by grief and lack the splendor proper to rational be-

---

331. Cf. Hermas, *Shepherd, Mand.* v.1, 3; 2, 8; ii, 3.
332. Cf. Jb 14.4.
333. Cf. Eccl 7.20.
334. Cf. Col 2.15.
335. Cf. Jn 14.30.
336. Cf. Jer 5.8.

ings, and forget that no sparrow falls into a trap apart from God, and that the judgments concerning each thing that happens to men are just, how shall we explain this unless we say that we suffer these things because a demon has conquered us and has disturbed our ruling principle?

(334) But also, how would we explain fear of things that are not fearful, and excessive joy for things that are worth nothing other than ascribing these to the activities of demons who have filled those who cannot say truthfully, "I do not have a demon"?

(335) But it is likely that someone will disconcert us by introducing the holy patriarchs into the examination, or the sacred servant, or the marvelous prophets, or the mightiest apostles of our Savior Jesus, so that these too then might say, like Jesus, "I do not have a demon." It is possible to ask them in response, And did these ever sin? Or is the statement false, "For all have sinned and are deprived of the glory of God"?[337] And is this statement not true, "No one is clean from defilement"?[338] And was it not carefully stated, "There is no just man on the earth who will do good and will not sin"?[339] But it is clear that all the Scriptures are true, and that not even those who changed to the virtuous life were always able to say from the beginning, "I do not have a demon." The statement of that man considered to be the Savior alone was from the beginning. This is why he alone honored the Father in the most appropriate and true manner, for no one who honors something that God does not honor, honors the one who esteems the things he honors as unworthy of honor.

(336) For in what way must we say that he who has not received the spirit of adoption at all honors the Father?[340]

### "I Honor My Father"

(337) And no one who sins has the spirit of adoption, for he who has been born of God does not sin.[341] And how does

337. Rom 3.23.
339. Cf. Eccl 7.20.
341. Cf. 1 Jn 5.18.

338. Cf. Jb 14.4. Cf. *princ.* 4.4.4.
340. Cf. Rom 8.15.

he honor the Father who holds glory from men[342] in honor, or silver, or earthly wealth, or the beauty of flesh and blood, or anything in general that belongs to matter and corruption?

(338) It is clear, then, in what way the Savior's statement, "I honor the Father," is intended. This is something we must strive to say, so far as possible, as our conscience bears witness to us in the Holy Spirit, rendering honor to whom honor [is due],[343] and not imparting it to another.

(339) And he who was sent by God when the fullness of time had come, to be born of woman and to be born under the law,[344] so that he is under the law that says, "Honor your father and your mother, that it may be well with you,"[345] says well, "But I honor my Father," since he has no other Father than God in heaven.

(340) But we too will make this statement when we have become aware of the washing of regeneration,[346] and have received its washing to become sons of God, and no longer call anyone father on earth[347] because we have become sons of the Father in heaven and brothers of the one who said, "I go to my Father and your Father, and to my God and your God."[348]

(341) It is clear, then, that since Jesus said with complete validity and accuracy, "I do not have a demon, but I honor my Father," each of his imitators, so far as each is able, because he can do all things in Christ Jesus who strengthens him,[349] will himself also say, "I do not have a demon, but I honor my father." But who, when he is with the dead and dwells among tombs, can say, "I do not have a demon"?

(342) Or who, when he honors something other than God and his Word and the things commanded by the Word, when he gives honor to another, when he ought to give it "to whom honor" is due,[350] would say as a disciple of Jesus, "But I honor my Father"?

---

342. Cf. Jn 5.44.
343. Cf. Rom 9.1; 13.7.
344. Cf. Gal 4.4.
345. Cf. Ex 20.12; Eph 6.2.
346. Cf. Tit 3.5.
347. Cf. Mt 23.9.
348. Cf. Jn 20.17.
349. Cf. Phil 4.13.
350. Rom 13.7.

## "And You Dishonor Me"

(343) The statement, "And you dishonor me," follows these words and is addressed to those who have dishonored him and said to him, "Are we not correct in saying that you are a Samaritan and have a demon?"[351] They thought that their incorrect statement was correct. For they denounced the Savior because they thought incorrectly that he was a Samaritan and had a demon.

(344) But we must think that the statement, "And you dishonor me," was made not only to those at that time, but also to those who always dishonor him by what they do contrary to the upright word of God, and those who dishonor Christ who is justice by the unjust things they do, and those who dishonor the power of God, which the Savior is, "for Christ is the power of God,"[352] by the things that they execute weakly and feebly.

(345) "You dishonor me" would also be said to anyone who despises wisdom, since Christ also is wisdom.[353]

(346) But also if it were necessary that someone be at peace with all men, so far as he himself were concerned, so that he could utter that word of the prophet, "I was peaceful with those who hate peace,"[354] he would also have to be a recipient of the peace of God, which surpasses all understanding and guards the heart and thoughts of the one who has received it.[355]

(347) But if someone should be polemical, and biting, and accusing, and a devourer of his neighbor,[356] and have his ruling principle filled with the discord of the passions, it would be said to this man too, "You dishonor me." For Christ is our peace.[357]

(348) And, in addition, since "everyone who does evil hates the light, and does not come to the light,"[358] but he is light who said, "I am the light of the world,"[359] it is clear that

---

351. Jn 8.48.
352. Cf. 1 Cor 1.24.
353. Cf. 1 Cor 1.24.
354. Ps 119.7.
355. Cf. Phil 4.7.
356. Cf. Gal 5.15.
357. Eph 2.14.
358. Cf. Jn 3.20.
359. Jn 8.12.

he who does evil dishonors Christ by dishonoring the light. This person, too, will hear the words, "And you dishonor me."

(349) But why must I prolong the discourse further by disclosing and proving who they are who are reproved by Jesus and hear him say, "You dishonor me"? It is clear who they are from what has been explained and from what can subsequently be associated with these explanations.

### "But I Do Not Seek My Own Glory"

(350) Let us see next what the statement means, "But I do not seek my own glory; there is one who seeks and judges." God, who gave his own Son for us, seeks the glory of Christ in each of those who have received him. He will find it in those who attend to themselves and work out the opportunities for virtue that have been implanted in them, but he will not find it in those who are not such. When he does not find it, he will judge those in whom he does not find the glory of his own Son, and will say to them, "Because of you my name is continually blasphemed among the nations."[360]

(351) But someone may object because of the words, "There is one who seeks and judges," and question if one ought to take this to refer to God, since the Savior has clearly said, "For the Father judges no one, but he has given all judgment to the Son, that all may honor the Son as they honor the Father."[361]

(352) But consider if it is possible to use the following statement as a response to this objection. "I can do nothing of myself; as I hear, I judge, and my judgment is just, because I do not seek my own will but the will of him who sent me."[362]

(353) For if our Savior judges as he hears from the Father, and seeks, not his own will but that of the Father who sent him, and this is why his judgment is just, perhaps, in a more proper sense, the judgment that he who hears judges

---

360. Is 52.5.
362. Jn 5.30.
361. Jn 5.22–23.

is not the judgment of him who hears, but the judgment of him who speaks to the one who hears.

(354) But even if he should say, "My judgment is just,"[363] listen to what is said in the same Gospel, "All my things are yours."[364] For if what the Savior has said is true, "All my things are yours," it is obvious that the judgment, too, of which he says, "My judgment is just,"[365] is the Father's judgment.

(355) Now, if it is the Father's judgment, the objection that concerns the words, "But I do not seek my own glory; there is one who seeks and judges" can be solved.

(356) And what is said in the words, "But I do not seek my own glory," contains a hint of humility, which befits the Savior. For it would not have been very fitting for him to demand his own glory and, in addition, to pass judgment on those who did not give it. It would be proper, however, for the Father who had given glory to the Son to demand it from those who withhold it, and to judge them in reference to it.

(357) But perhaps the Savior, too, since he is an imitator of the Father, seeks the glory of God from those who learn the things of God, and should he not find the glory of the Father in some, he would judge them, since he has authority to pronounce judgment because he is the Son of Man.[366]

(358) Heracleon, however, does not refer the words, "There is one who seeks and judges," to the Father, when he makes the following comments. *"He who seeks and judges is the one who avenges me, the servant who has been appointed for this, who does not bear the sword in vain,*[367] *the avenger of the king. Now this is Moses, as he said to them earlier, when he said, 'On whom you have hoped.'"*[368]

(359) Then he continues, *"It is Moses who judges and punishes, that is, the lawgiver himself."*

(360) Next Heracleon poses a problem for himself when he says, *"How then does he not say that all judgment has been delivered to him?"*[369]

363. Jn 5.30.
364. Cf. Jn 17.10.
365. Jn 5.30.
366. Cf. Jn 5.27.
367. Cf. Rom 13.4.
368. Jn 5.45.
369. Cf. Jn 5.22.

(361) Assuming to solve the problem, he says, *"He speaks correctly, for the judge judges by doing the will of this one as a servant,*[370] *as it manifestly occurs also in the case of men."*

(362) But how he attributes judgment to someone else as inferior to the Savior, that is, to the Demiurge as he understands it, he cannot demonstrate in this way, since it has clearly been written, "For the Father judges no one, but he has given all judgment to the Son,"[371] and, "He has given him authority to pronounce judgment, because he is the Son of Man."[372]

> Truly, truly I say to you, if anyone shall keep my word, he will not see death forever. (John 8.51)

### The Last Enemy, Death

(363) Just as there is a life that is indifferent, being neither good nor bad, and in which we say the impious live along with the irrational animals, and another life that is [not in]different,[373] but good, of which Paul says, "Our life is hidden with Christ in God,"[374] and our Lord himself says of himself, "I am the life,"[375] so you will say that corresponding to the indifferent life is indifferent death, and that some evil and hard death is the enemy to him who said, "I am the life."[376] He who dies this latter death is in that death,[377] of which it has been written, "The last enemy, death, is destroyed."[378]

(364) And we must assume that it is of this particular death that the Apostle says, "Wherefore, as through one man sin entered the world, and through sin, death, and so death passed to all men, because all have sinned, for until the law, sin was in the world (for sin is not imputed when there is no law), but death reigned from Adam to Moses, even over those who have not sinned in the likeness of Adam's transgression."[379] And a little further on, he adds,

---

370. Cf. Mt 7.21.  
371. Jn 5.22.  
372. Jn 5.27.  
373. Accepting Wendland's emendation. The text Preuschen prints, "Which is different but good," makes no sense in the context.  
374. Cf. Col 3.3.  
375. Cf. Jn 11.25.  
376. Cf. Jn 11.25.  
377. Cf. 1 Jn 3.14.  
378. 1 Cor 15.26.  
379. Cf. Rom 5.12–14.

"For if by one man's transgression death reigned through that one man, much more will those who receive the abundance of grace and righteousness reign in life through the one man, Christ Jesus."[380]

(365) For what is that death, which has come into the world through sin, if it is not the last enemy of Christ that will be destroyed? And what is that death, which passed to all men because all have sinned, if it is not this very death that also reigned from Adam to Moses?

(366) Now Moses, that is, the law, continued until the sojourn of our Lord Jesus, and ruled "by one man's transgression," "through that one man," until "those who have received the abundance of grace and righteousness should reign in life through the one Christ Jesus."

(367) Whoever, then, has kept the word of the Only-Begotten and Firstborn of all creation[381] will never see this death, since it is the nature of the Word to prevent death from being seen.

(368) And this is how we must understand the words, "If any man keep my word, he shall not see death forever." It is as if he who speaks these words had given those who hear them light as a gift and said, If anyone keeps this light of mine, he will never see darkness.

*"Who Is the Man Who Shall Live and Not See Death?"*

(369) For there can be no darkness for one who keeps the light. If, however, one should lose this light, the one who has lost it consequently sees darkness immediately. It was in this way, then, that the life also came into being in the Word who was in the beginning with God.[382]

(370) Wherefore the beginning (that is wisdom, which says, "God created me as the beginning of his ways for his works"[383]) will teach and say of the Word who was in it, in whom life came into being, "If anyone shall keep my word, he will not see death forever." For whoever shall keep the Word will, at the same time keep also the life that came into

---

380. Cf. Rom 5.17.  381. Cf. Col 1.15.
382. Cf. Jn 1.1, 4.  383. Cf. Prv 8.22.

being in him and is inseparable from him, which life is, at the same time, also the light of men, which shines in the darkness and is not overcome by it.[384]

(371) If, then, the prophet should inquire, as it were, and say, "Who is the man who shall live and not see death?"[385] we, having learned from our Savior, will answer and say, The man "who shall live and not see death" is the man who keeps the word of the one who said, "If anyone shall keep my word, he will not see death forever."

(372) But, at the same time, I ask whether in this passage "forever" is to be taken with both clauses,[386] so that the whole sentence would read as follows: If any man keep my word forever, he will not see death.

(373) For indeed one is not likely to see death as long as he keeps the word of Jesus; but no sooner has one lost it than he has seen death.

(374) But if one can also have recourse to the deeper doctrines, and understand how a man might say, "You have brought me down to the dust of death,"[387] and Paul, "Who will deliver me from the body of this death?"[388] he will see how, as long as the word is kept, the one who keeps it does not see death. When, however, someone has become discouraged in his attention to the word and his keeping of it, or has become careless about keeping it and has no longer kept it, then he has seen death, and it is the fault of no one other than himself.

(375) We must, at any rate, consider this to be a dogma and an eternal law, as the statement, "If anyone shall keep my word, he will not see death forever," will always be made to us who have received the word.

(376) But, if I may put it this way, just as darkness, when it has been beheld too long, destroys the sight of the beholder, so death, when it has been beheld by the one who has not kept the word, is fatal to and deadens the sight that has

---

384. Cf. Jn 1.4–5.
385. Ps 88.49.
386. For this meaning of ἀπὸ κοινοῦ ληπτέον see LSJ s.v. κοινός V.4.
387. Ps 21.16.   388. Rom 7.24.

beheld it, blinding it, so that, for this reason, the one who opens the eyes of the blind is needed.[389]

(377) And I, at least, think this is why the blind, of whom the blind in the Gospel were a symbol, lost their sight, that is, they have seen death because they did not keep the word.

> The Jews said to him, Now we know that you have a demon. (John 8.52)

(378) The majority, even of the wise, think that every kind of sin, of which one form[390] is also the sin against reason, has no other source than mistaken judgments. But those who have believed in the Holy Scriptures as divine think that the things men do contrary to right reason are not accomplished apart from demons, or some such hostile powers.

(379) The Jews, too, therefore, assumed that it was the result of the activity of a demon that Jesus said, "Truly, truly I say to you, If anyone shall keep my word, he will not see death forever."[391]

(380) And they had this impression because they had neither kept the word, nor perceived the meaning of what was said. For he who understood the death that those who sin die to be some enemy to the Word declared that this death is not seen forever by the one who has kept his word. But those who suppose that what is said is about the common death, think that the one who says that everyone who has kept his word will not die forever has lost his wits, since Abraham and the prophets died.

---

389. Cf. Jn 9.32.
390. Accepting with Blanc the emendation, ἓν εἶδος, of Klostermann and Corsini. Preuschen prints ἐν εἴδει, which is the reading of M.
391. Jn 8.51.

> Abraham died, and the Prophets, and you say: If anyone shall keep my word, he will not taste death forever. Are you greater than our father Abraham who is dead? And the prophets are dead. Whom do you make yourself? (John 8.52–53)

### "Abraham Your Father Rejoiced That He Might See My Day, and He Saw It and Was Glad"

(381) If, according to the simpler interpretation, as we ourselves have also explained it, the sense of the Jews' assumption appears evident when they responded to the Savior's word by saying that Abraham and the prophets had died, none the less we must not leave unexamined texts that are parallel to this.

(382) For did they think it was without reason that the Savior said, "If anyone shall keep my word, he will not see death forever,"[392] and, therefore, they made some obvious response to his word?

(383) Or, did they think he had not spoken of the common death, and thinking of Abraham and the prophets, as also of themselves who were once in the worse death, say, because they neither accepted his word nor thought it to be so great as the speaker promised, "Now we know that you have a demon"?[393]

(384) We have made a similar examination more extensively above concerning other words of his, and responses to them. Take, for example, the Samaritan woman. After Jesus said to her, "[Give me] to drink,"[394] he later added the following words. "If you had known the gift of God, and who

---

392. Jn 8.51.
393. Jn 8.52.
394. Cf. Jn 4.7. Origen's discussion of Jn 4.1–12 was in Book 12, which has not been preserved. Fragments 52–55 treat Jn 4.6, 9, and 12. Frags. 53 and 54 (on Jn 4.9, 12) are probably not from Origen (See R. E. Heine, "Can the Catena Fragments of Origen's Commentary on John be Trusted?" *VC* 40 [1986]: 119). Frag 55 (also on Jn 4.12) is similar, though in summary form, to the comments in Book 13.37–39. Book 13 begins with Jn 4.13. Origen's discussion of Jn 4.13–15 is found above in Book 13.3–42.

## COMMENTARY ON JOHN, BOOK 20

he is who says to you, Give me to drink, you would have asked him, and he would have given you living water.

(385) "And the woman says to him, Lord, you do not have a bucket, and the well is deep; whence do you have living water?"³⁹⁵ And again, "Sir, give me this water, that I may not thirst nor come here to draw."³⁹⁶

(386) For it would not be plausible that the Samaritan woman answered him in regard to water that is perceptible to the senses, and that she asked him for literal water so that she would no longer thirst nor come to draw water from the well of Jacob which was perceptible to the senses.

(387) As another example, take the Lord's words, "The bread that I shall give for the life of the world is my flesh."³⁹⁷ When "the Jews strove with one another saying, How can this man give us his flesh to eat?"³⁹⁸ we showed that the hearers were not so foolish as to suppose that the speaker was inviting the hearers to approach him and eat of his flesh.

(388) It is likely indeed that, in the case of the words we are now examining, the Jews said, "Abraham died, and the prophets," after they had learned how "through one man sin entered the world, and death through sin, and so death passed to all men because all have sinned,"³⁹⁹ and had seen in addition that "death reigned over those who sinned in the likeness of Adam's transgression."⁴⁰⁰ Their response was about the death that results from sin, which passed to all men because all have sinned.

(389) But although they had learned about these matters, inasmuch as they did not accept Jesus' words, they did not know what comes next, nor that "the gift is not as the offence."⁴⁰¹

(390) But neither, perhaps, could they infer that "if the many died by the offence of the one man, how much more

---

395. Cf. Jn 4.10–11.
396. Jn 4.15.
397. Cf. Jn 6.51. The Book containing Origen's discussion of Jn 6 has perished, nor are there any fragments on this chapter.
398. Cf. Jn 6.52.   399. Rom 5.12.
400. Cf. Rom 5.14.   401. Rom 5.15.

has the grace of God, and the gift which came by the grace of the one man Jesus Christ, abounded to many."[402]

(391) In addition, they did not understand in what way the gift was not like the death "which resulted from the one man's sin," for they had not as yet been instructed that "the gift followed many offenses and resulted in justification."[403]

(392) But neither did they see that "those who receive the abundance of grace and of the gift shall reign in life through one man Jesus Christ."[404]

(393) They reflected on the death of Abraham and the prophets, understanding that Samuel, too, when he was under the earth because of death, was brought up by a medium who thought the gods were somewhere below the earth and who said, "I saw gods ascending from the earth."[405] They had not, however, comprehended the life of Abraham and the prophets, nor that the God of Abraham, Isaac, and Jacob was not the God of them as men who were dead, but as men who were alive.[406] Because they assumed that the prophets were dead, they built their tombs, and for this reason they are said to be unhappy.[407]

(394) Therefore, although Abraham died, nevertheless he was alive[408] and no longer saw death, since he had seen the day of Jesus and rejoiced and was glad.[409]

(395) Now, I think it was also for this reason that in response to the statement, "Abraham died," our Savior, to teach that Abraham was alive, said, "Abraham your father rejoiced that he might see my day, and he saw it and was glad."[410]

(396) But if someone prefers that the words about Abraham not have this meaning, let him tell us whether he who once saw the day of our Savior, and rejoiced and was glad because of this, thereafter sees death, or after he has seen the day of the Savior and rejoiced and been glad, having

402. Cf. Rom 5.15.
403. Cf. Rom 5.16.
404. Cf. Rom 5.17.
405. Cf. 1 Kgs (1 Sm) 28.7–13.
406. Cf. Mt 22.32.
407. Cf. Mt 23.29.
408. Cf. Rom 14.9.
409. Cf. Jn 8.56.
410. Jn 8.56.

been considered worthy of such a sight because he was worthy of it, he was later deprived of what he saw.

(397) For if each of these assertions is absurd, then when Abraham saw the day of Jesus, at the same time that he saw it he also heard his word and kept it, and he no longer sees death.[411] The Jews were also incorrect when they said, "Abraham died," as if he were still among the dead.

(398) You will say the same thing also of the prophets. For if he is not the God of the dead, but of the living,[412] just as he is the God of Abraham, Isaac, and Jacob, so he is also the God of the rest of the prophets, and the prophets are alive. For these too kept the word of the Son of God, when the word of the Lord came to Osee, or the word came to Jeremias, or the word came to Isaias, for no other Word of God came to any of these than he who was in the beginning with God, his Son, God the Word.[413]

(399) Now, if anyone has kept this word, the prophets certainly have, so that from the time they received the word they have no longer seen death.

(400) Therefore, just as the Jews' statement, "Now we know that you have a demon,"[414] is false, so also is their statement, "Abraham is dead, and the prophets." For they neither knew that he who gave commands to demons had a demon (for no one knows what does not exist), nor were Abraham and the prophets still among the dead when the Jews said, "Abraham died, and the prophets."

### Seeing Death and Tasting Death

(401) Next, we ask why in the world, after the Savior had said of everyone who keeps his words, "He will not see death forever," following the words previously examined, when it would have been appropriate for the Jews to have responded to the words, "He will not see death forever," by saying,

---

411. Cf. Jn 8.51, and paragraphs 363–77 above.
412. Cf. Mt 22.32.
413. Cf. Hos 1.1; Jer 14.1; Is 2.1; Jn 1.1; and Origen, *Jo.* II.1–3 (FOTC 80.95, note 3).
414. Jn 8.52.

"And you say, If anyone shall keep my word, he will not see death forever," they did not say this, but said what the Savior did not say. For he did not say, "If anyone shall keep my word, he will not taste death forever,"[415] which they cite as said by our Lord.

(402) And consider if it is not because there is a difference between not "seeing" death and not "tasting" death that the other evangelists unanimously have spoken of those who stood near Jesus not tasting death until they should see the Son of Man coming in his kingdom. Matthew says, "Truly, truly I say to you there are some of those standing here who will not taste death until they see the Son of Man coming in his kingdom."[416]

(403) Mark says, "Truly, truly I say to you that there are some of those standing here who will not taste death until they see the kingdom of God that has come in power."[417]

(404) And Luke says, "Truly there are some of those standing here who will not taste death until they see the Son of Man in his glory."[418]

(405) For, just as taste and sight are different perceptions so far as the body is concerned, so, in accordance with the divine perceptions mentioned by Solomon, the visual and contemplative power of the soul is one thing, but that which is capable of tasting and apprehending the quality of spiritual foods is another.[419]

(406) And, since the Lord is capable of being tasted, being food for the soul, insofar as he is the bread of life which came down from heaven,[420] and is capable of being seen, insofar as he is wisdom, of whose beauty he confesses to be a lover who says, "I became a lover of her beauty,"[421] and he commands us, "Love her, and she will preserve you,"[422] for this reason it is said in the Psalms, "Taste and see that the Lord is good."[423]

415. Cf. Jn 8.51.
416. Cf. Mt 16.28.
417. Cf. Mk 9.1.
418. Cf. Lk 9.27.
419. Cf. Wis 7.22–23.
420. Cf. Jn 6.51.
421. Wis 8.2.
422. Prv 4.6.
423. Ps 33.9.

(407) And, just as the Lord is capable of being tasted and seen, so also is his enemy, death, capable of being tasted and seen.

(408) These words prove that death is capable of being tasted, "There are some of those standing here who will not taste death,"[424] etc., and the following prove that it can be seen, "If anyone shall keep my word, he will not see death forever."[425]

(409) Now he who utters words contrary to the words of eternal life[426] tastes death; and not only does he taste it, but he is also filled with death as food.

(410) The promise is that some of those standing in the spiritual place designated by Jesus will not taste death, for observe carefully that the three Gospels together have said, "There are some of those here standing,"[427] or, "There are some of those standing here."[428] They have also recorded of these, "They will not taste death until they see the Son of Man coming in his kingdom,"[429] or, "in his glory,"[430] or, "until they see the kingdom of God that has come in power."[431]

(411) And, since the one who stands can fall, it has been said, "Let him who thinks he stands beware lest he fall."[432] This is why it is not written of all who stand, but of some, "Truly I say to you, there are some of those standing here."[433]

(412) The one who stands, therefore, does not taste death if he continues to stand, and the one who has received and keeps the word will not see death.

(413) Since, therefore, there is a difference between tasting death and seeing death, the Jews, as unintelligent hearers, confused the saying of the Lord, and instead of "he will not see death,"[434] said, "He will not taste death," thereby descending in their statement to the inferior sensation. But

---

424. Mt 16.28.
425. Jn 8.51.
426. Cf. Jn 6.68.
427. Mt 16.28; cf. Lk 9.27.
428. Cf. Mk 9.1.
429. Cf. Mt 16.28.
430. Cf. Lk 9.27. This reading is found in codex D, the fifth century witness to the Western text of the New Testament.
431. Mk 9.1.
432. 1 Cor 10.12.
433. Mt 16.28.
434. Cf. Jn 8.51.

you will ask if, just as it is possible to see death and taste death, so also in relation to the other senses, it is possible to hear death, or smell death, or touch death. For if the hands of the apostles "have handled [something] of the word of life,"[435] have the hands of false apostles and deceitful workmen, who transform themselves into angels of justice,[436] handled something of the word of death? And if Christ's sheep hear his voice,[437] perhaps those who are not his sheep, to whom he would say, "You are not of my sheep,"[438] hear the voice of death.

(414) [And] consider if there is not a smell of death in the wounds that come from sin, concerning which it has been said, "My wounds stink and rot."[439] The smell of death was also on Lazarus before he arose from the dead. It was because the disciples did not wish to smell it that they said to the Savior, "Lord, he already stinks, for it is the fourth day."[440]

(415) But on the question concerning the spiritual smell of death, or the smell of life, it will be necessary to observe carefully the following apostolic word. "We are a good odor of Christ to God in every place, among those who are saved, and among those who perish; to some an odor of death to death; but to others an odor of life to life."[441] For the people who are in Christ are a good odor of Christ in every place and by no means a bad odor.

(416) Now, just as a good corporeal odor is said to destroy some animals,[442] so, because of the evil which occurred earlier, the good odor of Christ too may be an odor of death to their death for some, but for others it proves to be an odor of life to life.

---

435. Cf. 1 Jn 1.1.
436. Cf. 2 Cor 11.13–15.
437. Cf. Jn 10.27.
438. Cf. Jn 10.26.
439. Ps 37.6.
440. Jn 11.39. It is Martha, and not the disciples, who makes this statement in the Gospel of John.
441. Cf. 2 Cor 2.15–16.
442. Cf. Origen, *Cant.* I.4 (ACW 26.81).

(417) These present comments seemed to us to be necessary in the examination of tasting death and of seeing or not seeing death.

*"Are You Greater Than Our Father Abraham?"*

(418) Next, because they do not perceive how far Christ surpasses the patriarchs and the prophets, nor do they even believe that he who teaches such great things is the Christ, they raise a further objection, asking, "Are you greater than our father Abraham who died?"

(419) And they do not see that he who was born of the Virgin is not only [greater] than Abraham, but that he is also greater than everyone among those born of women.[443] Nor do they see that the one prophesied by the prophets is greater than all the prophets, and that he who made them alive is greater than those who die, although he did not make himself such, but received it from the Father.

(420) "For as the Father has life in himself, so also he has given to the Son to have life in himself."[444] He cannot do a single thing of himself, and he seeks, not his own will, but the will of the one who sent him.[445] The question, "Whom, then, do you make yourself?" was not the question of men who had perceived that Jesus had not made himself what he was.

(421) For this reason, too, it seems to me, he responded to this question by teaching who made him what he was in the words, "If I shall glorify myself, my glory is nothing; it is the Father who glorifies me."[446]

(422) But since the twentieth volume of the commentaries on the Gospel according to John has reached a suitable stopping point with these words let it be concluded here, so that, if God reveals the things that follow to us, we may contemplate them in the next book, beginning with the words, "Jesus answered, If I shall glorify myself, my glory is nothing."[447]

---

443. Cf. Mt 11.11.
445. Cf. Jn 5.30.
447. Jn 8.54.

444. Cf. Jn 5.26.
446. Jn 8.54.

## BOOK TWENTY-EIGHT

THOSE WHO INVESTIGATE the natures of numbers have said that six is the first perfect number, being equal to its own parts, both from the combination of what is doubled from the unit, one and two, which is three, a prime number, and the doubling of the number arrived at, now I mean from the two, for when the two has been multiplied by three it makes six.[1]

(2) But they say the second perfect number is twenty-eight, being composed both of the compound of the doubling beginning from the unit until the first number results, and the doubling of the number arrived at. For four is the number doubled from the unit in the order one, two, four.

(3) Now, the combination of these numbers is seven, which is itself also a prime number, since it is measured by the unit alone; and when four is multiplied by seven, it makes twenty-eight, also itself equal to its own parts.[2]

(4) Now for this reason I think [the number][3] that is related to the preparation of the tent of witness is grasped by Moses who was instructed in "all the wisdom of the Egyptians,"[4] for the curtains are twenty-eight cubits in length.

(5) And, indeed, the tent of witness which was prepared for the glory of God had to contain the number twenty-eight among the special numbers.[5]

(6) Since, holy brother Ambrose, we have reached this section of the commentaries on the Gospel according to

---

1. Cf. Philo, *Op.* 3. Preuschen demonstrates the scheme as: $6=(1+2)\times 2$, or $6=1+2+3$.
2. I.e. $28=(1+2+4)\times 4$, or $28=1+2+4+7+14$ (Preuschen).
3. My addition, based on Wendland's suggestion. Preuschen indicates that the text is corrupt at this point.
4. Cf. Acts 7.22.
5. Cf. Ex 26.2.

John (for, if God grants, this will be the twenty-eighth volume on the Gospel), let us call upon God, who is perfect and is the provider of perfection through our perfect high priest Jesus Christ,[6] that he might grant that our mind discover the truth about the matters that will be investigated and their composition, and thus let us proceed to what follows.

### Jesus says, Take away the stone. (John 11.39)
*Jesus Does Not Take the Stone Away Himself*

(7) Here Jesus himself does not take away the stone that lies upon the cave, but says, "Take away the stone." In Genesis, on the other hand, when "there was a large stone on the mouth of the well, and the custom was to gather all the flocks there and roll back the stone from the mouth of the well, and gather and water the sheep, and restore the stone to the mouth of the well in its place,"[7] and when this had not yet taken place because the flocks had not been gathered,[8] Jacob, when he saw "Rachel, the daughter of Laban his mother's brother, and the sheep of Laban his mother's brother, himself approached and rolled back the stone from the mouth of the well and watered the sheep of Laban his mother's brother."[9] Inasmuch as there is this difference, we wish to examine both stones together so that we may grasp the reason that here Jesus himself did not take away the stone from the cave, but said, "Take away the stone," yet in Genesis Jacob himself rolled the stone away from the mouth of the well.

(8) Consider if we can say that, because the cave was a tomb, Jesus himself must not touch the stone upon the cave, but only command those suitable for the work to take the stone away. On the other hand, Jacob himself had to grasp the stone that was lying on the mouth of the well and keeping those sheep, from which would come the spotted sheep,

---

6. Cf. Heb 2.17.
8. Cf. Gn 29.8.
7. Cf. Gn 29.2–3.
9. Cf. Gn 29.10.

294                            ORIGEN

even the portion of Jacob,[10] from drinking, and when he had approached the stone he had to roll it back from the mouth of the well that the sheep of Laban his mother's brother might be watered.

(9) And it was necessary, indeed, that Jacob himself approach the well, but that Jesus stand outside the cave.

(10) But if you can, direct your attention to why, in the case of the cave, the stone lying upon it is not rolled away, but is taken away, but in the case of the well, it is not taken away completely, but only rolled away. It was fitting by all means that the stone be taken away in the case of the tomb, and not rolled back, but that, in the case of the well, the stone only be rolled away.

(11) For it has been said before that . . .[11]

### Believe and See the Glory of God

(12) Let us believe [that we may see the][12] glory of God, having considered the greatness of the faith that is reckoned for righteousness.[13]

(13) But if someone who thinks he has believed has not yet seen the glory of God, let him learn that he is exposed as not having believed because[14] he has not yet seen the glory of God, for he does not lie who says not only to Martha but to everyone, whoever he be, "If you believe, you will see the glory of God."[15]


## Therefore, they took away the stone. (John 11.41)

### The Imitator of Christ

(14) The delay in the removal of the stone lying upon the cave resulted from the dead man's sister, for she hindered, as it were, those whom Jesus commanded when he said,

---

10. Cf. Gn 30.42.
11. There are 41 lines missing from M at this point.
12. The translation offered here is conjectural, based on Jn 11.40, since part of the sentence is missing.
13. Cf. Gn 15.6.
14. The text has δι' ὧν, which seems to me to make no sense.
15. Jn 11.40.

"Take away the stone," by saying, "He already stinks, for it is the fourth day."[16]

(15) And if Martha's unbelief had not been checked when Jesus said to her, "Did not I say to you, that if you believe, you will see the glory of God?"[17] those who heard the words, "Take away the stone,"[18] would not have taken away the stone.

(16) For come, let us suppose that when Jesus said, "Take away the stone," the dead man's sister had not responded nor said, "He already stinks, for it is the fourth day."[19] What, then, would have been written subsequently than this, "Jesus says, Take away the stone; therefore, they took away the stone"?

(17) But now, between the words, "Take away the stone," and, "therefore, they took away the stone," the words of the dead man's sister hindered the removal of the stone. And it would not have been taken away at all even later had not Jesus answered and said to her unbelief, "Did I not say to you that if you believe, you will see the glory of God?"[20] It is good, then, that nothing intervene between Jesus' command and the action enjoined by his bidding.

(18) And I, at least, think that it is appropriate for such a person to say that he has become an imitator of Christ.[21]

(19) For as God spoke to this one, and "they were made, he commanded and they were created,"[22] so Christ spoke to the believer and the latter performed it; the Son of God commanded and the believer fulfilled the command, having set nothing above the command, nor having penalized himself by disobedience in the time between the command and the deed. For we must believe that the period of delay concerning the commandment is a time of disobedience for the one who later does what was commanded.

(20) Now, this is also why the son in the Gospel parable whose father commanded him to go into the field and work,

16. Jn 11.39.  
17. Jn 11.40.  
18. Jn 11.39.  
19. Jn 11.39.  
20. Jn 11.40.  
21. Cf. 1 Cor 11.1.  
22. Cf. Ps 32.9.

because he did not do it immediately, but went when he had later repented, did not do the will of his father in the time prior to his repentance.[23]

(21) Wherefore, we must remember the saying, "Delay not to be converted to the Lord, nor defer it from day to day,"[24] and the saying, "Do not say, Go and come again, and tomorrow I will give; do good while you are able."[25]

(22) We must believe, therefore, that it is a condemnation of Martha that the words, "Therefore they took away the stone,"[26] were written later. They should have been said next to the words, "Jesus says, Take away the stone."[27]

And Jesus lifted up his eyes and said. (John 11.41)

*"Lift Up Your Eyes on High"*

(23) We must carefully observe and examine what has been written concerning[28] the position of Jesus' eyes in relation to certain people. For example, in the Gospel according to Luke, when Jesus was about to deliver the beatitudes and the teaching that follows them, "he lifted up his eyes to his disciples and said."[29] And in the present passage, "he lifted up his eyes and said."

(24) For we are taught by the previous statement that Jesus's disciples are not below, because the teacher's eyes are lifted up to those to whom it was worthy that he lift up his eyes. The statement now being examined teaches us that he changed his thought from his conversation with those below and lifted it up and exalted it, bringing it in prayer to the Father who is over all.

(25) But in addition, if indeed Paul is an imitator of Christ along with those who are near him,[30] the one who

23. Cf. Mt 21.28–31.  
24. Cf. Sir 5.7.  
25. Prv 3.28.  
26. Jn 11.41.  
27. Jn 11.39.  
28. Following Klostermann and Blanc, Preuschen prints the words "what has been written concerning" in the lemma.  
29. Lk 6.20.  
30. 1 Cor 11.1.

prays zealously and in imitation of Christ's prayer, lifting up the eyes of his soul, and bringing them up in this way from deeds, memory, thoughts, and reasonings must thus address to God the great and heavenly words of prayer concerning great and heavenly matters.

(26) But if someone shall reply to these remarks that the tax collector wished not even to lift up his eyes, and beat his breast and said, "God be merciful to me, a sinner,"[31] we must reply that just as we must not apply to all people nor always the sorrow that is according to God, which works repentance without regrets unto salvation,[32] but only to that one and everyone who has done things worthy of such sorrow and who changes his mind in relation to them, and we must apply it with due limit and not excessively lest in excessive sorrow he be swallowed by Satan,[33] so perhaps it is not proper for everyone to wish not even to lift up his eyes, as neither is it proper to stand afar off.[34]

(27) But let each one judge himself concerning such matters,[35] and "let a man prove himself, and so," not only "let him eat of the bread and drink of the cup,"[36] but also let him lift up his eyes, and let him lift them up during prayer, and when he subjects himself to God and humbles himself to him, let him speak.

(28) And if we think that it is proper for one who lives in any way whatever to wish not even to lift up his eyes like the tax collector, it is fitting to say that along with wishing not to lift up his eyes he must also stand afar off from the temple.[37]

(29) Now, what temple would this be, except the Church of the living God? Paul also calls this Church the house of God when he says, "But if I tarry, that you may know how one ought to behave in the house of God, which is the Church of the living God, the pillar and ground of the truth."[38]

(30) [Therefore], as it is not proper for everyone not to

31. Lk 18.13.
32. Cf. 2 Cor 2.7.
33. Cf. 2 Cor 2.7.
34. Cf. Lk 18.13.
35. Cf. 1 Cor 11.31.
36. Cf. 1 Cor 11.28.
37. Cf. Lk 18.13.
38. 1 Tm 3.15.

use the bread, and not to drink of the cup, and [not][39] to be far from the house of God and the Church, so it is not proper for everyone not to wish to lift up his eyes.

(31) But if someone does not lift up his eyes when it is proper for him to lift them up, he sins; and [the same is true] if someone lifts them up when it is proper not to lift them up.

(32) The tax collector in the Gospel, therefore, acting properly, did not wish even to lift up his eyes,[40] but on the other hand, the disciple who is present with Jesus would reasonably lift them up when he is given the command, "Lift up your eyes and see the fields, that they are already white to harvest."[41]

(33) The prophet, too, says, "Lift up your eyes on high."[42] But in addition, in the one hundred and twenty-second Psalm, which is the fourth song of the gradual psalms, the prophet, when he has lifted up his eyes to God in a fitting manner, says, "To you who dwell in heaven I have lifted up my eyes. Behold as the eyes of servants are on the hands of their masters, as the eyes of a handmaid are on the hands of her mistress, so our eyes are on the Lord our God, until he have mercy on us."[43]

(34) And if we must also show more clearly for whom it is now proper to imitate Jesus by lifting up his eyes, in that he also lifts up his eyes, and for whom this is not proper, but who, like the tax collector, should not only stand far away from the temple but also not wish to lift up his eyes, we will quote the words of Daniel about the lawless elders who lusted after Susanna. The words are as follows: "And they perverted their own mind and turned their eyes away that they might not look to heaven, nor remember just judgments."[44] These words should be taken along with the following remarks made about Susanna, "But she, weeping, looked up to heaven, for her heart trusted in the Lord."[45] For notice in

---

39. Wendland omits the negative.
40. Cf. Lk 18.13.
41. Jn 4.35.
42. Cf. Is 40.26.
43. Ps 122.1–2.
44. Sus (Theod.) 9.
45. Sus (Theod.) 35.

these words that those who perverted their own mind turned their eyes away that they might not look to heaven, but she who trusted in the Lord looked up to heaven consequent to her trust in the Lord.

(35) It was fitting, therefore, for her who was about to pray boldly about her chastity to look up to heaven and lift up her eyes. On the other hand (if, by way of supposition, after the elders had "perverted their own mind and turned aside their eyes that they might not look to heaven nor remember just judgments," they repented, after they had attempted to seduce the woman, but failed to attain their desire, and after this they prayed) it would be fitting for the elders also not to wish to lift up their eyes, indeed also to stand far off, like the tax collector, and beat their breasts and say, "God, be merciful to me, a sinner."[46]

(36) And it would be proper, when one lifts up his eyes and lifts them up properly to heaven, also to lift up holy hands, especially when he offers up prayer without anger and contention.[47]

(37) For in this way, when the eyes are lifted up through thought and contemplation, and the hands are lifted up in deeds which lift up and exalt the soul, as Moses lifted up his hands,[48] one may consequently say, "The lifting up of my hands is as the evening sacrifice";[49] the Amalikites and all the unseen enemies will be worsted, and the Israelite reasonings in us will prevail.[50]

(38) So many related thoughts have been disclosed to us on this point in relation to the statement, "Jesus lifted up his eyes and said."

---

46. Lk 18.13.
47. Cf. 1 Tm 2.8.
48. Cf. Ex 17.11.
49. Ps 140.2.
50. Cf. Ex 17.11.

> Father, I give you thanks that you have heard me.
> I knew that you always hear me; but because of the
> crowd standing around I said it, that they may believe
> that you have sent me. (John 11.41–42)

### 'Before You Have Spoken, I Will Say, Behold, I Am Here'

(39) If indeed God makes some such promise as follows concerning the prayer of those who pray in a worthy manner who live in the flesh and do not wage war according to the flesh,[51] "And while you are still speaking, I will say, Behold, I am here,"[52] what ought we think that he says in the case of our Savior and Lord, other than, 'Before you have spoken, I will say, Behold, I am here.' For "he lifted up his eyes and spoke" at the same time.[53]

(40) But what did he say? If it is thus possible in such matters to make a guess consistent with the statement, 'Before you have spoken, I will say, Behold, I am here,' that which is said to the Savior would surely be something more than that which was written in the promise to just men, "While you are still speaking he will say, Behold I am here."[54]

(41) What, then, did he say? He proposed to utter a prayer, but because the one who said to him, 'Before you have spoken, I will say, Behold, I am here,' anticipated his prayer, in place of the prayer that he intended to offer, he addresses thanksgiving to the one who anticipated his prayer. Consequently, as if the thoughts that he had not uttered in prayer had been heard, he says, "Father, I give you thanks that you have heard me."[55]

(42) Therefore, he was about to pray about the resurrection of Lazarus when the only good God and Father[56] antici-

---

51. Cf. 2 Cor 10.3.
52. Cf. Is 58.9.
53. Jn 11.41.
54. Cf. Is 58.9.
55. Jn 11.41. Cf. H. Freedman and M. Simon (eds.), *Midrash Rabbah* (London: The Soncino Press, 1939), III, 303, Exodus 25, 3: "R. Abba said: They were even spared the utterance of their wish, for God fulfilled the thought still in their heart and they tasted their heart's desire."
56. Cf. Mt 19.17.

COMMENTARY ON JOHN, BOOK 28        301

pated his prayer and heard the words about to be spoken in his prayer. The Savior offers up thanksgiving for these things in place of prayer in the hearing of the crowd that stood around him. He was doing two things at the same time. He was giving thanks for the things he had obtained concerning Lazarus, and establishing faith in the crowd that stood around him, for he wished to receive them, since this was why he had been sent from God and had sojourned in life.

(43) Now, he knew that he had been heard because he saw in his spirit that Lazarus' soul had been restored to his body, having been sent up from the region of souls.

(44) For we must not think that Lazarus' soul continued to be present in his body after its exodus and, because it was present, immediately heard Jesus when he cried and said, "Lazarus, come forth."[57] Or, if indeed someone assumes this about Lazarus' soul and accepts as true the absurdity that the soul which has been released from the body continues to hover near the dead man, let him tell us how Jesus was heard by the Father, if Lazarus' body remained dead and his soul had been separated from the body but continued to hover near it, as someone who says this would assume.

(45) For supposing that this be granted, we would say that Jesus, when he was about to be heard, was not heard, seeing that the soul continued to dwell in the body. Now I think something similar happened also when Jesus raised the daughter of the ruler of the synagogue after he prayed about it, for he asked that her soul return and dwell again in her body.[58]

(46) And you shall also inquire whether it is the same or not concerning the widow's son who was being carried out,[59] that you may discover the orderly sequence in these accounts in all the passages, for it is not proper that we make such great digressions.

(47) But perhaps also Jesus, who was so great, saw Lazarus' soul itself being brought either by those appointed

57. Jn 11.43.      58. Cf. Lk 8.55.
59. Cf. Lk 7.12.

to such matters, or by the will itself of the Father who heard Jesus, and when he saw it entering through the place from which the stone had been removed, he said, "Father, I give you thanks that you have heard me."[60]

(48) Now, it was because he had both asked and obtained for countless others before this that he gives thanks not only for Lazarus, but also for those earlier ones. He says in relation to Lazarus, "Father, I give you thanks that you have heard me,"[61] and in relation to the earlier ones, "And I knew that you always hear me."[62] All this, he says, I have said "because of the crowd standing around, that they might believe that you have sent me."[63] We have explained these words in relation to the literal meaning and the resurrection of Lazarus.

(49) On the other hand, the anagogical sense concerning the passage is not difficult in consequence of what we have already explained. For he asked that the one who had sinned, after becoming his friend, and had become dead to God return to life by divine power. And he obtained it and saw movements of life in such a one for which he gave thanks to the Father.

(50) Now a crowd stood around such a dead man, although they did not yet believe that God sent Jesus, nor that this Word from God had sojourned with men. This crowd stood around and marvelled that someone who had become foul-smelling from sins to death[64] and was dead to virtue, should return to virtue. The crowd also marvelled that they would believe at some time in the Word who made him alive, as the Word from God who had sojourned with men.

---

60. Jn 11.41.
61. Jn 11.41.
62. Jn 11.42.
63. Cf. Jn 11.42.
64. Cf. 1 Jn 5.16.

And after he said these things, he cried
with a loud voice: Lazarus, come forth. The dead
man came out bound feet and hands with strips
of cloth, and his face was bound with a napkin.
Jesus said to them: Loose him and let him go.
(John 11.43-44)

### Jesus' Loud Cry

(51) Jesus lifted up his eyes and was heard when he was still about to pray, and he gave thanks in place of a prayer, when he perceived that Lazarus' soul had entered the body and was in need of the strength that would result from Jesus' command to him to come forth from the tomb.

(52) Wherefore, after the thanksgiving to the Father, he used a loud voice which infused Lazarus with power. The latter was in need of a loud cry to call him forth from the tomb because his hearing was not yet sharp.

(53) Now, we must consider this, too, to be a work worthy of Jesus, not only to pray that the dead might live, but also to shout to him and summon the one within the cave and the tomb to the things outside it.

(54) Now, we ought to be aware that there are some Lazaruses even now who, after they have become Jesus' friends, have become sick and died, and as dead persons they have remained in the tomb and the land of the dead with the dead, and later they were made alive by Jesus' prayer, and were summoned from the tomb to the things outside it by Jesus with his loud voice. He who trusts in Jesus comes forth wearing bonds worthy of death from his former sins, and still bound around his face, so that he can neither see nor walk, nor do anything because of the bonds of death, until Jesus commands those who are able to loose him and let him go. And let everyone who is able to say, "Or do you seek proof of Christ who speaks in me?"[65] attempt, at least, to become such that Christ might cry out in a loud

---

65. Cf. 2 Cor 13.3.

voice in him and say to the one who stirred after he died, but not quickly, and for this reason needs Jesus' cry, "Lazarus, come forth."[66]

(55) Consider the one who has fallen away from Christ and returned to the Gentiles' life after he has received knowledge of the truth and been enlightened, and tasted the heavenly gift, and become a partaker of the Holy Spirit, and tasted the good word of God and the powers of the age to come,[67] to be in Hades with the shades and the dead, and to be in the land of the dead or the tombs.

(56) Whenever, therefore, on behalf of such a person, Jesus comes to his tomb and, standing outside it, prays and is heard, he asks that there be power in his voice and words and cries out with a loud voice, and summons him who was his friend to the things outside the life of the Gentiles and their tomb and cave.

### The Bonds of the Dead

(57) Now and then we see someone following Jesus in the following manner. Such a one comes forth because of Jesus' voice, but he is still tied and bound with the cords of his own sins. He is alive because he has repented and has heard Jesus' voice, but because he has not yet been released from the bonds of sin, he cannot immediately walk with free feet, but neither has he been released to perform the things that excel, his feet and hands being bound with strips of cloth as the bonds of the dead.

(58) Such a person, because of the death which is in him clinging to the bonds on his hands and feet, has covered his face with ignorance and bound it round himself.

(59) Since,[68] then, Jesus did not wish that he merely live and remain in the tomb, he has come bound to the things of life outside the tomb, as was said before. And because he

66. Jn 11.43.
67. Cf. Heb 6.4–6.
68. Preuschen thinks the text is corrupt in this section. There are several ambiguities that appear unsolvable on the basis of the present text. The translation offered is tentative.

COMMENTARY ON JOHN, BOOK 28        305

has not been able to come forth from the tomb insofar as he is bound, Jesus says to those who can serve him, "Loose him and let him go."[69] I think he was not[70] in agreement with the teaching about conversion after one has sinned. But such a one has come forth from the tomb still too weak to live by himself and control the active, efficient, and contemplative powers of his soul. His feet and hands are still bound with bandages, and his face is bound with a napkin.

(60) But because the command of Christ is like that of a master, when Jesus said to those able to release him, "Loose him and let him go,"[71] his feet and hands were released, and the veil lying upon his face was removed and put away.[72] He advances so far that he anticipates that even he himself may become one of those who recline with Jesus.[73]

(61) Next, because of the statement, "The dead man came out bound feet and hands with strips of cloth," we must say that there is a distinction among those who have been bound feet and hands. It is [not] the same to have begun to be bound because one is dead, so that even the bonds bear the name of death (for as a matter of fact, the bandages of the dead are bonds), with one being bound as a result of the judgment of the Lord, who entered to see those reclining and saw one not wearing a wedding gar-

---

69. Jn 11.44. Cf. pars. 124–26 below. There is a large amount of literature on Origen's views on the forgiveness of post-baptismal sins. See, for example, P. Galtier, "Les péchés 'incurables' d'Origène," *Greg* 10 (1929): 177–209; R. C. Mortimer, *The Origins of Private Penance in the Western Church* (Oxford, 1939), 22–30; J. Daniélou, *Origène*, 80–83; K. Rahner, "La doctrine d'Origène sur la pénitence," *RechSR* 37 (1950): 47–97, 252–86, 422–56; H. J. Vogt, *Das Kirchenverständnis des Origenes* (Köln: Böhlau, 1974), 155–69; H. Crouzel, *Origen*, 229–33.

70. Blanc deletes the negative. Origen seems clearly in these paragraphs to allow for repentence and forgiveness for post-baptismal sins. The question, it seems to me, is what he means here by "the teaching about conversion after one has sinned." If he is alluding to the common second century view that such was not allowed, then the negative is correct. If, on the other hand, he means one *can* repent of sin after baptism, then the negative is incorrect.

71. Jn 11.44.
72. Cf. 2 Cor 3.14–15.
73. Cf. Jn 12.2.

ment,[74] and said of him, "Bind his feet and hands and cast him into outer darkness."[75]

(62) Now, it is possible that a distinction needs to be made in the passage between the statement, "And his face was bound with a napkin," and the statement that a veil lay upon Moses' face when he spoke to the people.[76] For the napkin lying on Lazarus' face covered his eyes, which were dead, but Moses' veil was covering his face for an accommodation because of those people who were incapable of looking at his glory.

(63) But you will ask of the one [not] wearing a wedding garment, of whom it is said, "Bind him feet and hands, and cast him into outer darkness,"[77] whether he will continue always to be bound and in outer darkness (for it is not added, "for the age," or "for the ages"), or whether he will be released sometime.

(64) For the text concerning him indicates nothing about his future release.[78]

(65) But it does not seem safe to me to express an opinion about him when one has grasped nothing at all about him, especially insofar as nothing has been written of him.

(66) And because of the statement, "Jesus says to them: Loose him," you will ask who the "them" are. For it has not been recorded that it was said to the disciples, nor to the crowd standing around, but neither has it been recorded that it was said to the Jews who were with Mary and were comforting her. Now, one may assume, because of the statement, "Angels came and ministered to him,"[79] and because of the anagogical sense related to the passage, that the command, "Loose him and let him go," could, perhaps, even be addressed to angels.

---

74. Cf. Mt 22.11.
75. Mt 22.13.
76. Cf. Ex 34.33–35.
77. Cf. Mt 22.13.
78. The general sense of this sentence is clear, but its expression is awkward, and may be corrupt.
79. Mt 4.11.

## "But I Go That I May Awaken Him"

(67) I ask further if Jesus has fulfilled the words, "But I go that I may awaken him," which are subjoined to the statement, "Lazarus our friend is asleep."[80]

(68) I wonder, therefore, if, when Jesus spoke with a loud voice and cried, "Lazarus, come forth"[81] (for it would not be absurd to say that the loud voice and the cry have awakened him), it can also be asserted in addition that the statement, "I go that I may awaken him,"[82] has been fulfilled in this action rather than when the Father made Lazarus' soul return to his body which was laid away in the tomb after he heard[83] the Son's prayer.

(69) For one may say that when the Father heard the Son pray, he raised Lazarus from the dead. On the other hand, he who spoke with a loud voice and cried, "Lazarus, come forth,"[84] fulfilled what he had promised earlier in the words, "But I go that I may awaken him."[85]

(70) If the one who affirms this makes a distinction between the statement, "Lazarus our friend is asleep,"[86] and, "Lazarus is dead,"[87] he will say that he made a promise related to the statement, "He is asleep," when he said, "But I go that I may awaken him."[88] He did not, however, append the statement, 'I go that I may raise him from the dead,' to the words, "He is dead."

(71) But he who refutes the apparent distinction in these statements and shows that the resurrection of Lazarus from the dead was the common work of the Son who prayed and the Father who heard, will use what the Lord said to Martha in the words, "I am the resurrection and the life,"[89] and will

---

80. Jn 11.11.
81. Jn 11.43.
82. Jn 11.11.
83. Wendland's emendation, which Preuschen accepts, must be incorrect. The participle must be accusative, in agreement with "the Father," as it is in M. The following statement in the text shows clearly that Origen is thinking of the Father hearing the Son's prayer.
84. Jn 11.43.
85. Jn 11.11.
86. Jn 11.11.
87. Jn 11.14.
88. Jn 11.11.
89. Jn 11.25.

quote in addition the words, "For as the Father raises the dead, and gives life, so also the Son gives life to whom he will."[90]

> Many, therefore, who came to Mary from the Jews, and saw the things that Jesus did, believed in him.
> (John 11.45)

### Many Believed in Him

(72) And whom, indeed, would this not impel to believe in Jesus' preaching, and truly so, of those who have been greatly overwhelmed by evil, by death and its stench, as it were, who, by the most extreme change, at the command of the Word and with his cooperation, have shaken off not only the great stench that comes from sin, but also the bonds that restrain the active and efficient power of the soul, and further, apart from these, the contemplative power, too?

(73) For those who saw Jesus when he was so mighty in such affairs, those who boasted that they were busy concerning the word of God, but who had not yet received the fullness of the word, especially as many as had come to a dead man, as it were, for whom all hope had been abandoned and who had themselves abandoned hope regarding such a one, but who had come to comfort the sister who was suffering pain at the loss of her brother, would be astounded and would believe. Perhaps it was because of these people more than the man who suffered these things that when Jesus came to the cave of the dead man, "he lifted up his eyes and said, Father, I give you thanks that you have heard me. And I knew that you always hear me."[91]

(74) For from the statement, "But because of the crowd standing around I said it, that they may believe that you have sent me,"[92] it is clear that it was because of these people rather than Lazarus that he uttered this thanksgiving to the Father.

90. Jn 5.21.
91. Jn 11.41–42.
92. Jn 11.41.

(75) He busied himself concerning Lazarus, therefore, because of the crowd standing around, that many of the Jews who came to Mary and saw the things that he did might believe in him.

(76) But hear the words about these people also not only in the literal sense.

> But some of them went to the Pharisees and told them the things that Jesus had done.[93] (John 11.46)

(77) The text has a certain ambiguity. Were those who went to the Pharisees and told them the things Jesus had done from those many Jews who saw the things that he had done and believed in him, and wished to win over those who were hostile to him by the announcement about Lazarus? Or, were they the others, besides the many who also believed, who, as they were not impelled to faith concerning Jesus by what had happened, intended, insofar as they were able, to stir up the wicked jealousy in the Pharisees against him[94] by the announcement about Lazarus.

(78) The Evangelist seems to me rather to intend this latter as the meaning.

(79) For this reason he also adds, "The chief priests, therefore, and the Pharisees assembled," etc.[95] He called those "many," therefore, who believed because they saw the things concerning Lazarus;[96] and it is as if he said that those who did not believe were fewer when he said, "But some of them went," etc.[97]

---

93. I follow Blanc in taking this sentence to be a lemma. Preuschen prints it as part of par. 76.

94. This is the sense of the passage. Something may have been omitted in the manuscript tradition. Preuschen indicates a problem in the text, and Wendland suggested an emendation. The emendation would not alter the meaning of the sentence as I have given it, but only the way it is worded.

95. Jn 11.47.
96. Cf. Jn 11.45.
97. Jn 11.46.

### Those Who Saw Believed

(80) But notice also what will be said. Can we compel consent inasmuch as it has not been said, 'Many, therefore, of the Jews who came to Mary and saw the things that he had done believed in him,' but it has been written, "Many, therefore, who came to Mary from the Jews, and who saw the things that he had done believed in him"?[98]

(81) And I am moved especially because of the anagogical meaning to raise the issue whether perhaps all who saw, that is, who saw and understood what Jesus had done, believed in him; those, however, who went to the Pharisees and told them what Jesus had done, since it is not testified that they saw, perhaps lacked what is praised in those who believed, namely that "they saw."[99]

(82) For if indeed these too had seen, it could have been written that some of them went to the Pharisees and told them what they saw Jesus do, or what they saw and what Jesus did.

(83) But as it is, the expression, "they saw," has not been used at all of these people, but of those who believed, who also had come to Mary and saw what Jesus did. It was also because of these people, I think, that he said, "But because of the crowd standing around I said it, that they may believe that you have sent me."[100]

(84) But at the same time consider, too, if one can say of this that only those who came to Mary and saw what Jesus did and believed in him, since they were indeed many, constituted the crowd that stood around Jesus, on whose account he said, "Father, I give you thanks that you have heard me; but I knew that you always hear me."[101]

(85) For if he spoke these words "because of the crowd

---

98. The distinction Origen is making, which is difficult to express clearly in English, is that in John's text the participles that have been translated "who came" and "who saw," are in agreement with "many," and not with "the Jews."
99. Cf. Jn 11.45–46.
100. Jn 11.42.
101. Jn 11.41–42.

that was standing around,"[102] that they might believe that the Father had sent him, he also spoke them that the crowd standing around might believe. But if some of them had not believed, he would not have said to the Father, as if some men were ignorant of what was about to happen, "But because of the crowd standing around, that they may believe that you have sent me."[103] Perhaps only those who came to Mary and saw what he did and believed in him constituted the crowd that stood around Jesus, and the rest neither saw what he did, nor had stood around him.

> The chief priests, therefore, and the Pharisees assembled the sanhedrin and said: What are we going to do, for this man does many signs? If we let him alone, all will believe in him, and the Romans will come and take away our place and nation. (John 11.47–48)

### The Blindness of the Chief Priests and the Pharisees

(86) So far as the literal meaning is concerned, the Pharisees and the chief priests saw that it was possible, because of the greatness of the prodigious miracles that Jesus had performed, that all the Jewish people might be drawn away to faith in him, and once drawn away, they might despise the corporeal service of the Levites and priests in the place.[104] They saw consequently that such a thing could become a provocation to the Romans, inasmuch as the Jews did not treat the place with respect, [to think that] both the place they assumed to be holy and the whole nation of the Jews

---

102. Jn 11.42. Origen is attempting to see a basis in the text of John for distinguishing between those who went to the Pharisees, and those who believed in Jesus. He is trying to eliminate the former from the crowd that stood around Jesus. His point seems to be that the crowd around Jesus, exclusive of the unbelieving Jews, should be understood as the subject of the purpose clause, as well as the subject of the causal clause in Jn 11.42. This, of course, seems obvious enough even to a casual reader. What is not so obvious, and what probably cannot be established, is that this crowd in Jn 11.42 should not be understood as composed of both groups of people mentioned in Jn 11.45–46.
103. Jn 11.42.     104. I.e. the temple.

were under the Savior since they no longer wished in any way to preserve the confession that they were Jews.

(87) Accordingly, since they preferred the service and the place and the preservation of the nation above all the things thought to be superior to these, they plotted against Jesus that they might not permit him to live.

(88) And so, likewise, I think the phrase "this man,"[105] was used to diminish his glory, for they also did not believe in what was said above about him being God, when they wished to stone him as though for blasphemy and said to him, "You, being a man, make yourself God."[106] At that time he answered in accordance with his own benevolence, teaching that everyone to whom the word of God was addressed is called a god by God, and that the prophetic Scripture that made this declaration cannot be broken and destroyed.[107]

(89) Now, it is possible from what is said by the Pharisees and chief priests to perceive both the inconsistency and the blindness of their evil. It was inconsistent because they bore witness to him that he had performed many signs, and yet they thought it possible to plot against the one who had performed such great signs as if he could do nothing on behalf of himself when plotted against. On the other hand, this very thing was no less blind, for it were better to be in the favor of one who performs many signs than [to be a part of] the plot of those who do not wish to permit him to live, unless perhaps they thought that he performed signs while assuming that they were not the result of divine power, so that, for this reason, he could not do all things, nor could he deliver himself from their plot.

(90) They watched, therefore, so as not to let him live,[108] thinking because of this that they would be a hindrance to those believing in him, and to the Romans who were about to take away their place and nation.

(91) But seeing that "the Lord brings to nought the counsels of nations, and rejects the designs of peoples,"[109] no

105. Jn 11.47.
106. Jn 10.33.
107. Cf. Jn 10.34–35.
108. Cf. Jn 11.48.
109. Cf. Ps 32.10.

less did they not permit him [to live], but God raised him up and permitted him [to live], and all the nations served him,[110] and the Romans came and took away their place.

(92) For where is that which they call a sanctuary? And they also took away the nation, casting them out of the place, and scarcely permitting them to be where they wish even in the Diaspora.

(93) But if we must venture also into the anagogical meaning of the matters related to these words, we will say that the Gentiles received the place of those of the circumcision. "For by their transgression salvation has come to the Gentiles, to stir them to envy."[111] "Romans" was substituted for "Gentiles," since those who are ruled were specified by those who ruled.

(94) But the nation also was taken away by the Gentiles, for the people have become not a people,[112] and those of Israel are no longer Israel, and the seed did not reach the point that they became children.[113] It was because of Jesus' many signs that these things occurred, and because the Father permitted him [to live], in that he was mightier than the plot of the chief priests and Pharisees who took counsel against him.

(95) But the chief priests and all the physical worship among the Jews, and the Pharisees and all the teaching of the law according to the letter, plot against Jesus, the truth.[114] The type, in order to exist, wishes to hinder the manifestation of the truth,[115] just as the flesh lusts against the spirit[116] for the same reason.

(96) But because the spirit that lusts against the flesh is stronger, as also the true high priesthood of our Savior and his spiritual teaching, he destroys the council of the high priests and Pharisees who took counsel against him.

(97) Now we must assume that these things are happening now too, and that it is possible to see them in those who,

---

110. Cf. Ps 71.11.
111. Cf. Rom 11.11.
112. Cf. Hos 1.9; 1 Pt 2.10.
113. Cf. Rom 9.6–8, and the discussion of Jn 8.37–39 in Book 20.2ff.
114. Cf. Jn 14.6.
115. Cf. 2 Cor 4.2.
116. Cf. Gal 5.17.

through the preservation of physical Judaism, wish to destroy the spiritual teaching of Christ.

> But one of them, Caiphas, being the high priest that year said to them: You know nothing. Neither do you consider that it is expedient for us that one man should die for the people, and the whole nation not perish. But he did not say this of himself, but being the high priest of that year, he prophesied that Jesus was to die for the nation, and not only for the nation, but also to gather together into one the children of God who were dispersed. (John 11.49–52)

### Not All Who Prophesy Are Prophets

(98) The fact that someone prophesies does not make that person a prophet.[117] Caiphas, indeed, being high priest of that year, prophesied that Jesus was to die for the nation, and not only for the nation, but also to gather together into one the scattered children of God. He was by no means also a prophet.

(99) And although Balaam prophesied the things recorded in Numbers, when he said, "Whatever word God puts in my mouth, this I shall speak,"[118] and spoke the words beginning with the statement, "He sent for me from Mesopotamia,"[119] etc., it is clear that he was not a prophet, for it is recorded that he was a seer.[120]

(100) If, therefore, someone is a prophet, he no doubt prophesies, but if someone prophesies he is not necessarily a prophet.

(101) It is as if I should say something like this of any of the other virtues: If someone is just, he pursues justice; it by no means follows that if someone pursues justice, he is just.

(102) You will understand this if you have given attention

---

117. Cf. the shorter version of this chapter in Frag. 85, and the discussion in R. E. Heine, *VC* 40 (1986): 120–24. For the general theme, cf. *Did.* 11.8. The *Apostolic Constitutions* 8.2 cites the example of Caiphas as proof that not everyone who prophecies is holy.

118. Cf. Nm 22.38.   119. Nm 23.7.
120. Cf. Jos 13.22.

to the statement, "You shall pursue justice justly,"[121] unless "justly" has been affixed without meaning to the words, "You shall pursue justice." For I think it is possible to pursue justice, but not justly. For those also who do something that is proper in itself, let us say for the poor, to be glorified by men,[122] have done something just; not, however, by reason of habitual justice, but from vanity.

(103) Now, I think that analogous to "You shall pursue justice justly,"[123] one might say, 'You shall pursue prudence prudently,' and, 'You shall pursue courage courageously,' and, 'You shall pursue wisdom wisely,' and one might make similar statements concerning the other virtues.

(104) Now, we have made these remarks to compare something similar to someone prophesying who is by no means a prophet.

(105) I think this is why it is said repeatedly of the prophets in the prophecies, "Jeremias the prophet said,"[124] and any other expression that may be similar to these words. Those who are knowledgeable about names say that the fact someone has done something pertaining to a physician, or has done something which contributes to health, does not make that person a physician. Nor does the fact that someone has done something related to architecture make that person an architect.

(106) Now, it is possible, on the basis of what is recorded about Caiphas when he prophesied about the Savior, to make clear that even a wicked soul is capable of prophesying sometimes.

(107) For the evangelists denounce the wickedness of Caiphas, who was high priest the year when our Savior brought the dispensation to its completion, when he suffered for man. For Matthew says, "Then one of the twelve, who was called Judas Iscariot, went to the chief priests and said, What are you willing to give me, and I will deliver him to you? And they appointed him thirty pieces of silver."[125] And a little later Matthew says, "Behold Judas, one of the

121. Dt 16.20.
122. Cf. Mt 6.2.
123. Dt 16.20.
124. Cf. Jer 51.31 (LXX).
125. Mt 26.14–15.

twelve, came, and with him a large crowd with swords and clubs, from the chief priests and elders of the people."[126]

(108) We understand, therefore, that Caiphas also was among these chief priests, since testimony has been given that he was high priest of that year.[127] But later Matthew says clearly, "And those who had apprehended Jesus led him to Caiphas the high priest, where the scribes and elders were assembled."[128]

(109) And after a few words he adds, "And the high priest and the council sought false witness against Jesus, that they might put him to death; and they did not find any, although many false witnesses came forward. But finally two came forward and said, This man said, I am able to destroy the temple of God and rebuild it in three days. And the high priest stood up and said to him, Have you no answer to the testimony these bring against you? But Jesus remained silent. And the high priest said to him, I adjure you by the living God that you tell us if you are the Christ, the Son of God. Jesus says to him, You have said it. But I say to you, hereafter you will see the Son of Man sitting on the right hand of the power and coming on the clouds of heaven. Then the high priest tore his robes saying, He has blasphemed. What further need do we have of witnesses? Behold, now you have heard the blasphemy. What do you think? And they answered and said, He deserves death."[129]

(110) Then again after some other words, "And when he was accused by the chief priests and elders he answered nothing."[130]

(111) And again a little later, "But the chief priests and elders persuaded the crowds that they should ask for Barabbas and have Jesus put to death."[131]

(112) Then, after the Resurrection of the Savior when Mary Magdalene and the other Mary were returning, "be-

---

126. Mt 26.47.
127. Cf. Jn 11.49. The word rendered "chief priests" and "high priest" is the same in Greek. I have followed the Douay version and translated it chief priests when it is plural, and high priest when it is singular.
128. Mt 26.57.     129. Cf. Mt 26.59–66.
130. Mt 27.12.     131. Mt 27.20.

hold some of the guard entered the city and reported to the chief priests all that had happened. And they assembled with the elders and took counsel and gave a large sum of money to the soldiers saying, Say that his disciples came at night and stole him while we were asleep. And if this should get to the governor, we will persuade him and keep you out of trouble."[132]

(113) And Luke has recorded that "Satan entered Judas, called Iscariot, who was of the number of the twelve, and he went off and conferred with the chief priests and officers how he might deliver him to them."[133] Then after a few words, he says, "Jesus said to the chief priests and officers of the temple and the elders who came to him, Have you come out with swords and clubs as against a thief?"[134] And after a few words, "They apprehended him and led him away and entered the house of the high priest."[135] And further after a few words, "The chief priests and scribes stood and accused him vehemently."[136]

(114) And again after a few words, "When it was day, the elders of the people were assembled, and the chief priests and scribes, and they brought him into their council."[137]

(115) Mark says that "Judas Iscariot, one of the twelve, went to the chief priests to betray him. And when they heard it they were glad and promised to give him money."[138] And after a few words, "While Jesus was still speaking, Judas Iscariot, one of the twelve, came, and with him a large crowd with swords and clubs, from the scribes and Pharisees and elders."[139]

(116) And after a few words, "They brought Jesus to Caiphas the high priest, and all the chief priests and scribes and elders assembled."[140]

(117) Then again after a few words, "The high priest stood up and asked Jesus saying, Have you no answer to what these men testify against you? But he remained silent

---

132. Cf. Mt 28.11–14.
133. Cf. Lk 22.3–4.
134. Cf. Lk 22.52.
135. Cf. Lk 22.54.
136. Cf. Lk 23.10.
137. Cf. Lk 22.66.
138. Cf. Mk 14.10–11.
139. Cf. Mk 14.43.
140. Cf. Mk 14.53.

and made no reply. Again the high priest asked him a second time saying, Are you the Christ, the Son of the Blessed? And Jesus answered and said to him, You have said that I am, and you will see the Son of Man sitting on the right hand of the power, and coming with the clouds of heaven. And the high priest immediately tore his robes."[141]

(118) Then, after a few words, "At daybreak the chief priests with the elders and the scribes, and the whole council, held a consultation, and bound Jesus and led him off to the courtyard, and delivered him to Pilate."[142] Then, after a few words, "The chief priests accused him of many things,[143] but he made no reply."[144]

(119) And John says that "they led Jesus from Caiphas to the praetorium."[145]

(120) We have set these words out more fully to prove the abundance of Caiphas' evil through the numerous testimonies of all the Gospels, and to show that although he contended against Jesus, none the less he prophesied. John has clearly taught us, therefore, that he prophesied.

### Does Everyone Who Prophesies Prophesy by the Holy Spirit?

(121) You will ask, no doubt, whether if someone prophesies he prophesies by the Holy Spirit, even though some may think what is said has no pertinence to the investigation.

(122) But surely it is worthy of investigation, since David, after his sin against Urias, fearing that the Holy Spirit be taken from him, says, "Do not take your Holy Spirit from me."[146] And if someone accepts in addition the saying, "For the Holy Spirit of discipline will flee deceit, and will withdraw from foolish thoughts,"[147] it will appear clearly to be proven that the Holy Spirit flees from the soul that has dealt treacherously, even if he was there previously before the deceit and sin.

---

141. Cf. Mk 14.60–63.
143. Mk 15.3.
145. Cf. Jn 18.28.
147. Wis 1.5.

142. Cf. Mk 15.1.
144. Cf. Mk 15.5.
146. Ps 50.13.

(123) Consequently, it is worthwhile to investigate the following question concerning the Holy Spirit. Can he also be in a sinful soul, so that one may say that if "no one can say Jesus is Lord except by the Holy Spirit,"[148] and many of the sinful are disposed toward Jesus as toward the Lord, then the Holy Spirit is in these people, too?

(124) And perhaps since those who sin after obtaining him would not obtain forgiveness, this is why it is said of those who have sinned in some way before [they obtained] the Holy Spirit, "Every sin and blasphemy shall be forgiven the sons of men,"[149] but concerning those who have fallen after they obtained the Holy Spirit, "But he who has blasphemed against the Holy Spirit has no forgiveness, neither in this age nor in the age to come."[150]

(125) For he who sins when the Holy Spirit is present in his soul blasphemes against him who is present by his sinful deeds and words.

(126) Now, someone will say that what has been recorded as follows in the Epistle to the Hebrews was said in reference to this. "For it is impossible to renew again to repentance those who were once illuminated, and who have tasted the heavenly gift and become partakers of the Holy Spirit, and who have tasted the good word of God and the powers of the age to come, and who have fallen away, since they crucify to themselves the Son of God and make him a mockery."[151] For notice in these words the phrase, "who have become partakers of the Holy Spirit."

(127) But on the contrary, although Caiaphas prophesied, the Holy Spirit, none the less, was not in him because it was said, "For the Spirit was not yet, because Jesus was not yet glorified."[152]

(128) And if indeed the Spirit was not even in the apostles before Jesus was glorified, how much less was he in Caiaphas?

(129) But after the Savior arose "he breathed on" the dis-

---

148. 1 Cor 12.3.
149. Cf. Mt 12.31; Mk 3.29.
150. Ibid. Cf. pars. 54–59 above.
151. Heb 6.4–6.
152. Cf. Jn 7.39.

ciples "and said to them, Receive the Holy Spirit," etc.[153] Someone will boldly apply, then, what will be said to the fact that Caiphas did not prophesy from the Holy Spirit. And likewise, therefore, he will say that evil spirits, too, can bear witness to Jesus and prophesy of him or bear witness to him, as that spirit which said, "We know who you are, the holy one of God."[154] And there were those, too, who exhorted him that he not command them to depart into the abyss, and said, "Have you come to destroy us?"[155]

(130) The following words have also been written in the Acts of the Apostles, "And it came to pass as we went to prayer, a certain girl having a spirit of Python met us, who brought her masters much gain by divining. She followed Paul and us, and cried out saying, These men are servants of the most high God who preach to you the way of salvation."[156]

(131) He, therefore, who makes use of these words will say that the word of the Python falls short of prophecy in no way, since it bears witness to the apostles, and urges that those who hear them believe in the way of salvation that is being preached.

(132) And since we also cited the words of Balaam, see if it can also be said of him that he did not speak from God, but from an angel. For it says, "The angel of God stood in the way to divert him. And he had mounted his ass, and his two servants were with him. And the ass saw the angel of God set against it in the way, and his sword drawn in his hand, and the ass turned aside from the way and went into the field. And Balaam struck the ass with his rod to direct it in the way, and the angel of God stood in the ruts of the vineyards with a wall on each side."[157]

(133) Then after a few words, "When the ass saw the angel of God it settled down under Balaam."[158] And again after a few words, "The angel of God said to him: Why did you strike your ass this third time? And behold I have come

---

153. Jn 20.22.
155. Cf. Lk 8.31.
157. Cf. Nm 22.22–24.
154. Cf. Mk 1.24.
156. Cf. Acts 16.16–17.
158. Nm 22.27.

to withstand you, because your way is perverse and contrary to me; and when the ass saw me she turned aside from me this third time; and if she had not turned aside from me now I would have slain you and preserved her. And Balaam said to the angel: Lord, I have sinned, for I did not know that you stood against me to meet me in the way; and now if it does not please you, I will turn back. And the angel of God said to Balaam: Go with the men; but the word that I speak to you, take care that you speak this."[159]

(134) For observe that it is an angel who says, "The word that I speak to you, take care that you speak this."

(135) But you will say that a little later "God appeared to Balaam and Balaam said to him, I have erected seven altars, and I have placed a calf and a ram upon the altar. And God put a word in Balaam's mouth and said: Return to Balac, and thus you shall speak."[160]

(136) But notice also how both statements are true, both what is said by the angel in the words, "The word that I speak to you, take care that you speak this,"[161] and what is related by the Scripture, that "God put a word in Balaam's mouth and said."[162]

(137) But we marked the words, "The spirit of God came upon him,"[163] with an obelus, because we found neither that statement nor anything resembling it in the other translations.

(138) And again, in turn, after a few words the Scripture says, "God met Balaam and put a word in his mouth and said, Return to Balac, and you shall say these things."[164]

(139) Now, he who ventures into all these matters will say that it has also been said in the case of Saul, "An evil spirit of God troubled him."[165] But in addition, a false spirit came forth and was in the mouth of all the prophets of Achab,

---

159. Cf. Nm 22.32–35.
161. Nm 22.35.
160. Nm 23.4–5.
162. Nm 23.5.
163. Nm 23.7. Origen is referring to his work on the text of the Old Testament, which is called the Hexapla. Only fragments of this massive work survive.
164. Nm 23.16.
165. Cf. 1 Kgs (1 Sm) 16.14.

322   ORIGEN

when the Lord said, "Who will deceive Achab?"[166] And a false spirit came forth and said, "I will deceive him."[167]

(140) Let these matters, then, be investigated in these passages, if anyone is able to consider for himself the things that are in conformity with the words quoted about how Caiphas prophesied. But perhaps we must also say the following in regard to his prophecy. Since he was not holy, although he prophesied, [yet he did not prophesy by the Holy Spirit].

### How Caiphas Prophesied

(141) But just as how Caiphas prophesied is worthy of investigation, so you will also investigate how the messengers of Saul prophesied when they were sent to David, and after them, Saul, in the First Book of Kings.

(142) For it has been written, "And it was told to Saul saying, Behold David is in Anoth in Ramatha. And Saul sent messengers to take David, and they saw the company of the prophets, and Samuel presided over them.

(143) "And a spirit of the Lord came upon the messengers of Saul, and they also prophesied. And it was reported to Saul, and he sent other messengers and they also prophesied.

(144) "And Saul became very angry, and went to Armathaim, and came as far as the great well that is also on the way to Sophein, and he asked and said, Where are Samuel and David? And they said, Behold at Anoth Ramatha.

(145) "And he went from there to Anoth Ramatha. And a spirit of God came upon him, and he went, walking and prophesying, until he came to Anoth Ramatha. And he stripped off his garments and prophesied before Samuel, and he fell down naked all that day and all night. Because of this they said, Is Saul also among the prophets?"[168]

(146) Now, I think these things must also be cited in order to reveal how sinners prophesy, and whether they

---

166. 3 Kgs (1 Kgs) 22.20.   167. 3 Kgs (1 Kgs) 22.21.
168. Cf. 1 Kgs (1 Sm) 19.19-24.

prophesy by the Holy Spirit, or from some other power that is not false in so far, at least, as it bears witness to the truth.

(147) Moreover, in the First Book of Kings, the diviners of the idols are found pointing out things about the ark, and that whenever cows that have given birth to their firstborn go the way of Jesus of Bethsames they indicate that the plague on the Philistines has come from God.[169]

(148) Nor must we pass over in silence the things about the divining spirit and Samuel in these passages, from which Saul learned that on the next day he would be destroyed together with his sons.[170]

(149) He who is able to make a distinction concerning differing powers, I mean inferior and superior powers and those in between too, should there be such, will see the precision concerning these matters in these passages.

(150) Moreover, the one who wants Caiphas to have prophesied from an inferior power will say that it is not strange that an evil power has made these remarks, since indeed even the devil, in the words the evangelists have recorded that he addressed to the Lord, is found not to be completely ignorant of the fact that Jesus is the Son of God.

(151) Now, the same person will also say that there is some evil set forth by the power that causes these things to be prophesied of the Savior. For the goal of this power was not to make the hearers believe, but to provoke the chief priests and Pharisees in the council against Jesus, that they might kill him. This was not to act in accordance with the Holy Spirit.

(152) For consider if either Caiphas or that which inspired him to prophesy does not want to incite the hearers to kill Jesus through the words, "You neither know, nor do you consider that it is expedient for us that one man should die for the people, and the whole nation not perish."[171]

(153) Indeed, is he who says, "It is expedient for us," which was part of his prophecy, telling the truth or lying?

---

169. Cf. 1 Kgs (1 Sm) 6.2–9.
170. Cf. 1 Kgs (1 Sm) 28.7–19.
171. Cf. Jn 11.49–51.

For if he is telling the truth, then Caiphas and those who struggled against Jesus in the council are saved, since Jesus died for the people, and they obtain that which is expedient. But if it is absurd to declare that Caiphas and those in the council against Jesus are saved, and that they obtained that which was expedient when Jesus died, it is clear that it was not the Holy Spirit which inspired these words to be spoken, for the Holy Spirit does not lie.

(154) But the one who wishes that which inspires Caiphas to be speaking the truth even in this—I mean when he declares, "It is expedient for us that one man should die for the people"—will understand the words, "it is expedient for us," in a deeper sense because of the statement about the goal. He will make use of the words, "that by the grace of God (or, apart from God) he might taste death for all,"[172] and he will give attention to the words, "for all," and to the words, "apart from God for all."[173]

(155) He will also use the statement, "Who is the Savior of all men, especially of the faithful."[174] And because this is "the Lamb of God who takes away the sin of the world,"[175] he understands in a particular way the words "to take away the sin of the world," and not of a part of it.

(156) But he who says that the statement, "It is expedient for us that one man should die,"[176] is true, will also say that everything in the passage is a true prophecy, beginning with the clause, "You know nothing,"[177] for the Pharisees and chief priests who did not recognize Jesus, who is Truth,[178] Wisdom, Justice,[179] and Peace ("for he is our peace"[180]), knew nothing.

---

172. Heb 2.9.
173. Origen discusses this textual variant in Heb 2.9 in Book I.255–56 (FOTC 80.85–86). See my note there.
174. 1 Tm 4.10.
175. Jn 1.29. Cf. the discussion in Book 6.284–85 (FOTC 80.245).
176. Jn 11.50.
177. Jn 11.49.
178. Cf. Jn 14.6.
179. Cf. 1 Cor 1.30.
180. Eph 2.14.

*"The Lamb of God, Who Takes Away the Sins of the World"*

(157) But also these who knew nothing did not consider in what manner it was expedient even for them that this one man, insofar as he is man, should die for the people, for Jesus is a man when he dies.

(158) Wherefore also he himself says, "But now you seek to kill me, a man who has spoken the truth."[181]

(159) And since he who dies is a man, but the truth, and wisdom, and peace, and justice, and him of whom it is written, "The Word was God,"[182] were not man, the Word which was God, and the truth, and wisdom, and justice did not die, for the Image of the invisible God, the Firstborn of all creation[183] does not admit of death.

(160) But this man, the purest of all living creatures, died for the people. He took away our sins and infirmities,[184] since he was able, by taking up all the sin of the whole world into himself, to bring it to nought, and destroy and obliterate it, because he committed no sin, nor was guile found in his mouth, nor did he know sin.[185]

(161) And I think that it is in accordance with this too that Paul has said, "Him who knew no sin, he has made sin for us, that we might become the justice of God in him."[186] For he made him to be sin who did not know sin, so that he who had sinned in no respect has taken up the sins of all, even if one must dare to say that he, much more than his apostles who said, "We have become as the refuse of the world, and the offscouring of all until now,"[187] has become the refuse of the world and the offscouring of all.

(162) Now, there are many Greek and barbarian stories in circulation concerning the solution of certain grievous things that frequently prevail among the human race, such as plagues, or harmful cessations of the winds, or famines. Such things are solved when the evil spirit that causes them

---

181. Cf. Jn 8.40. See above, Book 20.80–86.
182. Jn 1.1.
183. Cf. Col 1.15.
184. Cf. Mt 8.17; Is 53.4.
185. Cf. 1 Pt 2.22; 2 Cor 5.21.
186. 2 Cor 5.21.
187. 1 Cor 4.13. See above, Introduction, pars. 99–101.

is rendered impotent, as it were, because someone gives himself for the common good. The Greeks and barbarians do not disown or reject the concept of such a person. This is not the time to examine whether such things are true or not.

(163) But never yet has a story been told of one who was able to take responsibility for purification on behalf of the whole universe,[188] that the whole universe might be cleansed, since it would perish had he not taken responsibility to die on its behalf. Nor can such a story be told, since Jesus alone has been able to take up into himself on the cross the burden of the sin of all on behalf of the whole universe[189] apart from God,[190] and to bear it in his great strength.

(164) And in fact, he alone knew how to bear infirmity, as the prophet Isaias says, "Who was a man with a wound, and who knew how to bear infirmity."[191]

(165) And this man indeed took our sins and has borne infirmity because of our iniquities, and the chastisement due us has come upon him, that we might be disciplined and regain peace.[192]

(166) For this is the way I understand the statement, "The chastisement of our peace was upon him."[193] And perhaps also, since "by his bruise we were healed,"[194] we who were healed by the bruise of the cross that came to him may say, "May I never boast except in the cross of the Lord Jesus Christ, by whom the world has been crucified to me and I to the world."[195] The Father delivered this Jesus for our sins, and because of them, "he was lead as a sheep to slaughter, and was dumb, as a lamb before its shearer."[196]

---

188. κόσμος. Origen is using this word in its broadest possible sense, to mean the entire created universe, including all spiritual beings, as well as mankind. See Introduction, pars. 88-98.
189. For τὰ ὅλα (plural) used to mean the universe, see the examples given by Lampe under ὅλος 2.a.
190. Cf. Heb 2.9.
191. Is 53.3.
192. Cf. Is 53.4–5.
193. Is 53.5.
194. Is 53.5.
195. Cf. Gal 6.14.
196. Cf. Is 53.7.

(167) In his humility, in regard to which "he humbled himself and became obedient unto death, even the death of the cross,"[197] his judgment was taken away. For this is the way I understand the statement, "In humility his judgment was taken away,"[198] since the next[199] words are, "In humility his judgment was taken away." And he was led to death because of the iniquities of the people of God.

(168) This man died, then, for the people, and for this reason the whole nation did not perish.

(169) And consider if you can take the name "people" in reference to those of the circumcision, and the name "nation" in reference to the rest.[200]

(170) For this man died not only for the people, but also that the whole nation might not perish, as if he had said that the designated nation and all the Gentiles would perish.

(171) Next, after this is the statement, "He did not say this of himself." I think we learn from this that we men say some things of ourselves, there being no power that inspires us to speak, but there are other things that we say when some power prompts us, as it were, and dictates what we say, even if we do not fall completely into a trance and lose full possession of our own faculties, but seem to understand what we say.[201]

(172) Now, it is possible for us, while we understand what we say on our own, not to understand the meaning of the words that are spoken, just as now Caiphas the high priest

---

197. Phil 2.8.
198. Is 53.8.
199. Origen seems to mean that these words are next in Is 53, after the statement about the lamb dumb before its shearer (Is 53.7–8).
200. Cf. Jn 11.50.
201. One of the major arguments against the late second century Montanist prophets and prophetesses of Phrygia was that they uttered their prophecies while in a trance and not in full possession of their faculties. Their opponents argued that this type of prophecy was foreign to the tradition of prophecy in the Old Testament and in the Church (See R. E. Heine, *The Montanist Oracles and Testimonia* PMS 14 [Macon, GA: Mercer, 1989], 28–39). Origen's statement reflects the vocabulary and concern of that debate.

did not speak of himself, and did not understand the meaning of what he said, since a prophecy was spoken.

(173) In Paul, too, there are certain teachers of the law "who understand neither the things they say, nor whereof they affirm."[202]

(174) But such is not the wise man of whom Solomon says in Proverbs, "A wise man will understand the words from his own mouth, and on his lips he will bear prudence."[203]

(175) Now, it seems to me that fortuitous circumstance also is sometimes the cause of prophesying, as is true in the present case of Caiphas. He was high priest of that year [in which] Jesus was to die for the people that the whole nation might not perish. For although others were high priests, as is clear from what we presented previously, no one prophesies except the high priest of the year in which Jesus was to suffer.

(176) And it was fortuitous circumstance that caused the messengers of Saul to prophesy when they were sent to David, along with Saul himself.[204] For it is as if the fact that they were seeking David became the cause of their prophecy, such as it was, as has been recorded.

(177) But Balaam too would not have taken up his parable and said, "He summoned me from Mesopotamia,"[205] etc., had he not seen Israel encamped.[206] And every time he sees another part of the encampment, he is moved by the newness of what he sees to speak about Israel.

(178) Jesus, then, was to die for the nation that was other than the scattered children of God, as is clear from the statement, "Jesus was to die not only for the nation, but also to gather together in one the scattered children of God."[207]

---

202. 1 Tm 1.7.
203. Cf. Prv 16.23. This verse is cited against the Montanist prophets by Jerome in the prologue to his *Commentary on Isaiah* (See Heine, *Montanist Oracles*, 159).
204. Cf. 1 Kgs (1 Sm) 19.20–24.
205. Nm 23.7.
206. Cf. Nm 24.2.
207. Cf. Jn 11.51–52.

### The Scattered Children of God

(179) Now is the appropriate time to investigate who the scattered children of God in addition to the nation were. Now, concerning these matters, those who introduce [the doctrine of] the natures, since they do not judge all things spiritually, will say that the children of God are those who are, according to their view, spiritual. For it follows to say to those who think that there are natures, that they even understand the spiritual ones contrary to the meaning of the Apostle who teaches that "the spiritual man judges all things and is judged by no one."[208]

(180) Consequently, the one who does not judge all things either is not spiritual, or is not yet spiritual.

(181) But also, since the spiritual man is judged by no one, if someone is judged by someone he either is not spiritual, or is not yet spiritual.

(182) Perhaps, then, it is better to say that someone who was not formerly spiritual becomes spiritual who is now also a son of God in the proper sense.

(183) It is time, therefore, to see who those now called children of God are, if they are not those who are "spiritual" in the view of those who introduce [the doctrine of] the natures. See if you can conceive of the scattered children of God who are other than the nation as those who were already righteous in God when these words were spoken, being either the patriarchs, or the prophets, or some other elect people of God who had previously died, or even those who were already healthy at that time. For he speaks as follows of those who are healthy and are not sick, "The healthy have no need of a physician, but those who are sick,"[209] and in the same way he says of those who are just, "I have not come to call the just, but sinners, to repentance."[210]

(184) Jesus, therefore, was to die for the nation, that it

---

208. Cf. 1 Cor 2.15. Origen may be referring to Heracleon's exegesis in this section. The position he is attacking, at least, is a Gnostic position.
209. Mt 9.12.
210. Lk 5.32.

might not perish, but on the other hand, for the children of God who were in dispersion, that they might be gathered together into on[e,²¹¹ and in him] there might be one flock, one shepherd,²¹² at which time, I think, the Savior's prayer is fulfilled, when he says, "As you and I are one, that they also may be one in us."²¹³

(185) And is there anything more profound to say of Israel, not of nature, but of race, of whom it was written, "Israel is my firstborn son,"²¹⁴ when Israel was in dispersion? You yourself will also understand that these are the scattered children of God for whom Jesus was to die in order to gather them together into one.

> From that day, therefore, they took counsel together to kill him. (John 11.53)

### From What Sort of Spirit Caiphas Prophesied

(186) After Caiphas [spoke] the words previously expounded, the chief priests and the Pharisees gathered the council together and plotted what they were to do to our Savior. Spurred on by his words, they took counsel together to kill the Lord.

(187) For this reason you will inquire from what sort of spirit Caiphas prophesied that Jesus was to die for the nation, and whether the Holy Spirit was at work in such a man and became the cause of the plot against Jesus, or whether it was not, then, the Holy Spirit, but another which was able both to speak in the impious man and to move those like him against Jesus. None the less, he also perceived something in relation to Jesus, as we examined earlier according to our ability.

(188) The person, then, who wishes to defend the Holy Spirit, since he appears to have been the reason the chief priests and Pharisees, moved by the words of Caiphas, took counsel together to kill Jesus, says that such a thing is not

---

211. Cf. Jn 11.52.  
213. Cf. Jn 17.21.  
212. Cf. Jn 10.16.  
214. Cf. Ex 4.22.

foreign to holiness, since neither did Jesus act in a manner unworthy of himself when he came "to cause the falling and rising of many in Israel,"[215] and declared, "I have come into this world for judgment, that those who do not see may see, and those who see may become blind."[216]

(189) For as we lack a word of wisdom[217] to defend how he who confesses that he came into this world for judgment has not acted in a manner unworthy of himself, so also [we lack such a word to defend] the fact that the chief priests and Pharisees took counsel together to kill Jesus in accordance with the words of the Holy Spirit spoken through Caiphas.

(190) On the one hand, then, concerning the statement, "I have come into this world for judgment,"[218] we have said as much as we can in the commentaries on the passage.[219] But let the following comments be made concerning the statement now before us. Just as those who deliberately put the worst construction on things misrepresent the holy meaning of the Scriptures, a meaning spoken for the benefit of those who seek to be benefitted by it, so that there appear even to be occasions for the fabrication of the impious teaching of those who prattle about injustice in regard to the Most High,[220] so the Pharisees and the chief priests, because they did not understand correctly the prophecy about our Savior that Caiphas spoke—a prophecy that is true in that it is better for us that one man die for the people and the whole nation not perish— but thought the meaning and intention of his counsel was something else, took counsel together from that day to kill Jesus.

(191) Now, I say these things in conformity with the interpretation that it was the Holy Spirit who prophesied through Caiphas. I do not in the least maintain that this was

---

215. Cf. Lk 2.34.
216. Jn 9.39.
217. Cf. 1 Cor 12.8.
218. Jn 9.39.
219. Origen's comments on Jn 9 are lost. They would have appeared in Books 21–27, which covered Jn 8.54–11.38.
220. Origen may have Marcion in mind. He insisted that the Old Testament must be taken in its literal sense and not allegorized, and thereby regarded the God of the Old Testament as unjust.

the case, but leave it to the readers to decide what one must recognize as correct concerning Caiphas, and the fact that he has been moved by the Spirit.[221]

> Jesus, therefore, no longer walked openly among the Jews, but went into a country near the desert, into a city called Ephrem, and there he remained with his disciples. (John 11.54)

*Jesus' Withdrawal*

(192) I think that these words and those like them have been recorded because the Word wishes to turn us back from rushing too hastily and irrationally to struggle unto death on behalf of the truth[222] and to suffer martyrdom.

(193) For, on the one hand, it is right not to shun the confession nor to hesitate to die for the truth if one has been caught in the struggle about confessing Jesus.

(194) But, on the other hand, it is no less right also not to provide an opportunity for such a great trial, but to avoid it by every means, not only because the outcome of such an act is unclear to us, but also so that we may not be responsible for causing those who would not, in actual fact, have become guilty of pouring out our blood, to have become more sinful and impious [by doing so], if we act in our own interest and take no thought for those who plot against us unto death. These people will experience greater and more serious punishment because of us, if we are self-centered and

---

221. I have omitted the word "feet." Preuschen marks the passage as possibly corrupt. The text, as printed in Preuschen, would mean: "and the fact that he has been moved under the feet of the Spirit."

222. Cf. Sir 4.28. On the view of martyrdom presented here (192–203) cf. par. 244 below; *comm. in Mt.* 10.23; ibid. 16.1; *Cels.* 1.65; Clement, *str.* 4.10.76–77; ibid. 4.9.71–73.1. The last reference is of particular interest, for there Clement presents some words of Heracleon on martyrdom in which Heracleon, while disallowing an exaggerated importance to martyrdom, does allow for the possibility if it is necessary and dictated by reason. In the previous reference, Clement presents essentially the same view of martyrdom as Origen presents here, and argues, like Origen, that the one who does not avoid martyrdom when it is possible to do so is responsible for the guilt of his executioner.

do not consider the things of others,²²³ and deliver ourselves to be killed when this necessity has not overtaken us.²²⁴

(195) For if indeed he, too, who has caused someone to sin by having impelled the sinner to it shall himself pay the penalty for those who sinned in some way because of himself, how will he not also give an account of that man's sin, when he could have avoided it so that such a one might not have become a traitor against Christianity and an enemy of the religion according to Jesus, when he did not avoid it, but even provoked it? [And will not this be true] even if he be worthy of ever so much honor and acceptance for his eagerness to suffer martyrdom and his courage in relation to it in order that God might be worshipped and the Savior be confessed by him?

(196) But the Scripture that says, "They were seeking, therefore, to arrest him, and no one laid a hand on him, because his hour had not yet come,"²²⁵ will prove that such things have been written for our sake, that we, having Jesus as an example, might also become imitators of him in such matters.

(197) For since, according to this saying, no one laid a hand on him because his hour had not yet come although he was present and did not flee, so also he²²⁶ would not have been arrested had he remained²²⁷ without withdrawing at this time when his hour was not yet at hand.

(198) For this reason, we must heed not only the words, "If they persecute you in this city, flee to another," etc.,²²⁸ but also the fact that when the chief priests and Pharisees took counsel together to kill Jesus,

(199) he prudently walked openly no longer among the

---

223. Cf. 1 Cor 10.24.
224. Cf. Clement *str.* 4.10. See W. Tabernee, "Early Montanism and Voluntary Martyrdom," *Colloquium* (May 1985): 33, and Heine, *VC* 40 (1986): 125.
225. Jn 7.30.
226. I have accepted the MS reading, with Brooke: κατέσχητο. Preuschen emended this to κατεσχέθημεν.
227. Accepting Brooke's emendation.
228. Cf. Mt 10.23, and Clement, *str.* 4.10.76; Origen, *comm. in Mt.* 10.23; *hom. in Jud.* 9.1.

Jews, nor did he withdraw into another city filled with crowds, but withdrew into some obscure city.

(200) For it has been written, "Jesus, therefore, no longer walked openly among the Jews, but he went from there into the country near the desert, into a city called Ephrem."

(201) And he did not go there alone, indeed, but so as to give no opportunity to those seeking him, he also took his disciples with him, and "there he remained with his disciples."

(202) Such is also what is written in the Gospel according to Matthew, when "Jesus had heard that John was delivered up, he withdrew into Galilee, and left Nazareth, and came and dwelt in Capharnaum on the sea coast, in the borders of Zabulon and Nephthalim."[229] Also at the time he anticipated that he would be arrested he watched that he not suffer this by himself, nor be found in Jerusalem or in the temple where he frequently taught, or in any other such place, "for he went forth with his disciples over the brook Cedron, where there was a garden into which he and his disciples entered."[230]

(203) And so he withdrew at that point of time and was not in public, so that the chief priests and Pharisees needed Judas when they wished to arrest him, who, because he was his disciple, inquired into the places of his retreat.

(204) Wherefore at that time "Judas took a band of soldiers and servants from the chief priests and Pharisees and went there with torches and lanterns and weapons."[231]

(205) Now in this passage of the Gospel it is made clear that if he had wished not to be captured, he would not have been restrained. He was restrained, however, because he humbled himself and became obedient to those restraining him, even to the cross.[232]

(206) When, therefore, he went forth and said to those who entered the garden, "Whom do you seek? They answered him, Jesus of Nazareth."[233] And when "he said to

---

229. Cf. Mt 4.12–13.
231. Cf. Jn 18.3.
233. Jn 18.4–5.
230. Cf. Jn 18.1.
232. Cf. Phil 2.8.

them, I am he, they went backward and fell to the ground."[234]

(207) After that, because he wished to take upon himself the dispensation in suffering, he asked them again, "Whom do you seek? And they said, Jesus of Nazareth."[235]

(208) And after a few words, "the band of soldiers and the tribune and the servants of the Jews arrested Jesus," since he was willing, "and bound him,"[236] when he delivered himself to the bonds. For if he had not wished to suffer, he would have said again, "I am he," and so great a crowd would have fallen back, and all would have fallen to the ground.[237]

(209) Now, in the same way that he teaches us through such things to withdraw in persecutions and plots against us, so in others you would find him withdrawing also from things the world holds to be good, so that through these examples, too, he might teach us to flee honors and positions of superiority in the world.

(210) For once, when Jesus "knew that they would come and take him by force to make him king, he withdrew into the mountain,"[238] not, however, with the disciples, but alone. He did not present an opportunity even to those who loved him and would wish, along with those wanting to make him king, that he might now become their king in a worldly sense as well.

### Salvation Has Come to the Gentiles

(211) These remarks have been made concerning the literal sense and the teaching of the letter of the Gospel about withdrawal. The following comments might be made concerning the anagogical meaning. Long ago Jesus walked boldly among the Jews when the Word of God dwelt among them through prophets. For "thus says the Lord" was Jesus' boldness. But now Jesus no longer walks boldly among the Jews, but has departed from there, and the Word of God is

234. Jn 18.6.
236. Cf. Jn 18.12.
238. Cf. Jn 6.15.

235. Jn 18.7.
237. Cf. Jn 18.6.

not among the Jews. And when he departed from there (now I mean from the Jews), he entered the country near the desert[239] of which it is said, "Many are the children of the desolate, more than of her who has a husband,"[240] to whom it is also said, "Rejoice, O barren one, who does not give birth; sing forth and shout, you who do not suffer birth pangs."[241]

(212) The city near the desert, which Jesus entered when he no longer walked boldly among the Jews, is Ephrem.

(213) Now Ephrem means "fruitfulness."[242] He was the brother of Manasses, the elder of the people "from forgetfulness."[243]

(214) For after the people "from forgetfulness" have been left behind, the fruitfulness of the Gentiles has come about, when God "turned" the rivers in Israel "into a desert, and the sources of the waters" there "into dry ground" and "their fruitful land into barrenness, for the wickedness of those who dwell in it."[244] But he "turned the desert" from the Gentiles "into pools of waters," and "their dry land into sources of waters.

(215) And he has placed there the hungry, and they made a city for their habitation," the Church.[245] There he sowed fields, according to the seed that fell upon the beautiful and good ground and produced a hundredfold, and he planted vineyards, for the Lord's disciples are branches, which also "yielded fruit of produce, and he blessed them and they were multiplied exceedingly."[246]

(216) But the Lord who saves men and beasts[247] did not

---

239. Cf. Jn 11.54.
240. Gal 4.27; Is 54.1. The word rendered "desert" in Jn 11.54 is the same in Greek as the word rendered "desolate" here. Cf. the similar interpretation given to Jesus' withdrawal in *comm. in Mt.* 10.23, and the same use of Is 54.1.
241. Is 54.1.
242. See Lagarde, *OS* 164,67.
243. Cf. Gn 41.51–52; Lagarde, *OS* 8,27; 195,63.
244. Cf. Ps 106.33–38.
245. Cf. Ps 106.35–36.
246. Cf. Ps 106.37–38; Lk 8.8; Jn 15.5.
247. Cf. Ps 35.7.

even consider those who were more irrational among them to be insignificant, for it has been written, "And he did not diminish their cattle."[248]

(217) And the Jews "were diminished and afflicted by the oppression of evils and sorrow, and contempt was poured forth upon those who," because of Abraham, "were princes, and he made them wander in a place that was untravelled and out of the way."[249]

(218) But after those people, God "helped the poor people from the Gentiles out of poverty, and he established his family like a flock of sheep whom the upright angels will see and rejoice at, and all iniquity shall stop her mouth."[250]

(219) And there is added to these words that are prophesied mystically in the one-hundred-sixth Psalm, "Who is wise, and will keep these words, and they will understand the mercies of the Lord?"[251]

(220) For since the Lord is merciful to those from the Gentiles, the wise man will keep these words because he has understood the mercies of the Lord.

(221) "Jesus," therefore, "no longer walks openly among the Jews, but has departed from there into the country" of the whole world, "near the desert" of the Church, "into the city which is called Ephrem," that is, "fruitful," "and there he has remained with his disciples."

(222) And to this moment, Jesus is with his disciples near the desert in the city called Ephrem, for he is present in "fruitfulness."

(223) And at the birth, indeed, of this Ephrem, our Lord, magistrate of the grain,[252] who begot him, who humbled himself and became obedient unto death, even death of the cross,[253] might say, "God increased me in the land of my humility."[254]

---

248. Ps 106.38.
249. Cf. Ps 106.39–40.
250. Cf. Ps 106.41–42.
251. Ps 106.43.
252. Cf. Gn 47.12.
253. Cf. Phil 2.8.
254. Cf. Gn 41.52.

338                           ORIGEN

> And the Pasch of the Jews was at hand: and many of
> the Jews from the country went up to Jerusalem
> before the Pasch to purify themselves. They sought
> Jesus, therefore, and talked with one another, standing
> in the temple: What do you think? Is he likely to come
> to the feast? (John 11.55–56)

*The Pasch of the Lord and the Pasch of the Jews*

(224) We must not think that the Pasch of the Lord and the Pasch of the Jews are the same.[255] For the one, according to the law, is the Pasch of the Lord, but the other is the Pasch of the lawless Jews.

(225) For this reason we must carefully observe when it is the Pasch of the Lord, and other days of the Lord that are mentioned, and when these are not of the Lord but of those who are rebuked for their sins.

(226) For example, it is written in Exodus following some other words related to the first commandment about the Pasch, "And you shall eat it with haste; it is the Pasch of the Lord."[256] And according to the second commandment, "If your sons say to you, What is this service to you? And you shall say, This sacrifice is the Pasch of the Lord, when he visited the houses of the sons of Israel in Egypt."[257]

(227) But, on the other hand, the Lord says in Isaias that the new moons and Sabbaths and fasting and Sabbath rest and feasts are not his, but belong to those who sin.[258]

(228) And if [this is so] in regard to the feasts, it is clear that [it is so] also in regard to the Pasch, for it is one of the feasts. And it is written as follows, "I will not abide your new moons, and your Sabbaths, and your great day; my soul hates [your] fasting and Sabbath rest, and your new moons, and your feasts."[259] And in one of the twelve [prophets] it is written, "I have hated, I have rejected your feasts."[260]

(229) According to the passage being expounded, more-

---

255. Cf. Book 10.67–84 (FOTC 80.270–73).
256. Cf. Ex 12.11.                 257. Cf. Ex 12.26–27.
258. Cf. Is 1.13–14.               259. Cf. Is 1.13–14.
260. Cf. Am 5.21.

COMMENTARY ON JOHN, BOOK 28

over, it was not the Pasch of the Lord, but of the Jews; for plots were made against our Savior during it.

(230) This is why I think the following words were addressed to them prophetically in respect to their Pasch, "I have hated, I have rejected your feasts,"[261] for it was not a work of God's feast, but a polluted work that they performed when they killed Jesus during the Pasch.

(231) But before this Pasch of the Jews many from the country went up to Jerusalem to purify themselves.[262]

(232) Now, in anticipation I would say that the many did not understand how they might purify themselves. Wherefore, supposing that their Pasch offered service to God, they had so great a need to purify themselves, because they would become more polluted than they were before they purified themselves. For the Jews who delivered Jesus to Pilate said to him, "It is not lawful for us to kill anyone."[263] Because of these men Pilate said to the Savior, "Am I a Jew? Your own nation, and the chief priests have delivered you to me."[264]

(233) And those indeed who said they had gone up to purify themselves cried out, saying to Pilate, "Do not release this man, but Barabbas. Now Barabbas was a robber."[265]

(234) And again, "The Jews answered, We have a law, and according to the law he ought to die, because he made himself Son of God."[266] And again, "The Jews cried out, saying to Pilate, If you release this man, you are not Caesar's friend; everyone who makes himself a king speaks against Caesar."[267] And again, "The Jews cried out, Away with him, away with him; crucify him."[268]

(235) And those who had gone up before the Pasch to purify themselves[269] said during the Pasch itself, "We have no king but Caesar."[270] And that which the Savior said to the disciples when he prophesied and said, "The hour is coming

261. Cf. Am 5.21.
262. Cf. Jn 11.55.
263. Jn 18.31.
264. Cf. Jn 18.35.
265. Cf. Jn 18.40.
266. Cf. Jn 19.7.
267. Cf. Jn 19.12.
268. Cf. Jn 19.15.
269. Cf. Jn 11.55.
270. Jn 19.15.

when everyone who kills you will think he offers service to God,"[271] has been fulfilled, beginning with himself.

(236) For those who thought he deserved to die thought they were offering service to God, and they had gone up to Jerusalem before the Pasch to purify themselves.

(237) But the true purification was not before the Pasch but during the Pasch, when Jesus died as the Lamb of God for those who were purifying themselves, and took away the sin of the world.[272]

(238) These Jews were seeking Jesus, not to be benefitted, but to kill him. He might have said to them, "But now you seek to kill me, a man who has spoken the truth to you, which I have heard from God."[273]

(239) And they stood in the temple itself and said to one another of Jesus, "What do you think? Is he likely to come to the feast?"[274]

(240) But Jesus did not feast where these had stood, but in the large upper room that had been swept and put in order, where with desire he had desired to eat the Pasch with his disciples before he suffered.[275]

(241) But you may say that even now they stand in the temple seeking Jesus, relying thus on the sacred Scriptures, but because they have not known the one who has come, they seek to revile him, and to confess another than him to be the Christ.[276]

(242) But consider if you can also say that other Jews go up to Jerusalem and enter the city of God from the country outside Jerusalem, and that these come that they may purify themselves, so that when Christ, the Pasch, is sacrificed, they can feast not "with the old leaven, nor with the leaven of evil and wickedness, but with the unleavened bread of sincerity and truth."[277]

(243) And such people indeed will seek Jesus as they stand in the temple of the Scriptures and question one another if Jesus will come to the feast.

271. Cf. Jn 16.2
272. Cf. Jn 1.29.
273. Cf. Jn 8.40.
274. Jn 11.56.
275. Cf. Mk 14.15; Mt 12.44; Lk 22.15.
276. Cf. Lk 7.19.
277. Cf. 1 Cor 5.7–8.

COMMENTARY ON JOHN, BOOK 28   341

> And the chief priests and Pharisees had given commands that if anyone knew him, where he was, he should reveal it, that they might arrest him.
> (John 11.57)

*Those Who Plot against Jesus Do Not Know Where He Is*

(244) Observe how it has been testified that he has withdrawn, that we too might know to do such at the proper time. And notice indeed that neither the chief priests nor the Pharisees knew where he was, and because they did not know, they gave commands that if anyone should know where he was, he should reveal it to them and they would seize him.

(245) But you will say in addition that those who plot against Jesus do not know where he is.

(246) This is why they give commands that are other than those of God, "teaching as doctrines the commandments of men."[278]

(247) And the commands [which] the Pharisees and the chief priests, who belong to the corporeal Jews, give are against Jesus, for they want certain ones to make Jesus known to them that they may get him in their power and deliver him up.

(248) You will also say that everyone who diligently investigates the matters concerning Christianity to refute it and accuse it is a Pharisee, and not a good high priest. He is one who gives commands of other words by which he thinks he will teach himself the things concerning Jesus, so that when Jesus has become known to him, he may arrest him, and insult him and kill him.

(249) But indeed since the twenty-eighth volume of the commentaries on the Gospel according to John has reached a suitable stopping point, let us conclude its explanation. We will begin the explanation of what follows in the twenty-ninth volume, if God grants.

278. Mt 15.9.

# BOOK THIRTY-TWO

SINCE WE are being prosperously guided by God through Jesus Christ, let us continue walking the great way of the Gospel, which is also a living way for us,[1] if we may both[2] know and travel it so that we come even to its end.

(2) Now, however, let us attempt to set foot on the thirty-second encampment, as it were, among the things that will be said. And may the pillar of the shining cloud of Jesus be present with us, leading us forward when that is necessary, and stopping when that is necessary,[3] until we go completely through the whole Gospel also in our dictation of the matters related to the Gospel, holy brother Ambrose [and] man [of God],[4] neither losing heart from the length of the journey, nor growing weary because of our weakness, but endeavoring to walk in the tracks of the pillar of truth.[5]

(3) But God himself would know whether or not he is willing that our mind, through our dictations, complete the journey of Scripture through the whole Gospel according to John.

(4) May it be only that we, whether at home in the body or absent from it and at home with the Lord,[6] not walk outside the gospel, so that we too may enjoy the works and words that bring blessings in God's delightful paradise.[7]

---

1. Cf. Jn 14.6.
2. εἰ καί here does not express concession, as is usually the case. The construction here is καί ... καί (both ... and), joining the two verbs.
3. Cf. Ex 14.19–20.
4. Cf. 1 Tm 6.11.
5. Cf. 1 Tm 3.15.
6. Cf. 2 Cor 5.6, 8.
7. Cf. Jn 13.17; Rv 2.7.

And during supper, the devil having already put into the heart of Judas Iscariot, the son of Simon, to betray him, knowing that the Father had given all things into his hands, and that he came from God, and goes to God, he rises from supper, and lays aside his garments, and having taken a towel, he girded himself. Then he put water into a basin and began to wash the disciples' feet and to wipe them with the towel with which he had girded himself. (John 13.2–5)

*The Washing of the Disciples' Feet*

(5) In the homilies on the Gospel according to Luke, we compared the parables with one another, and asked what "breakfast" means according to the divine Scriptures, and what "supper" represents according to them.[8]

(6) And now, therefore, let it be said that breakfast is the first nourishment, which is suited for catechumens, and precedes the completion of the spiritual day in this life. Supper, on the other hand, is the final nourishment, and is served to those who have already advanced further in their understanding.

(7) Someone might also explain it differently and say that breakfast refers to the meaning of the Old Scriptures, but supper refers to the mysteries which have been hidden in the New Testament.

(8) But these remarks have been made as a preface to ex-

---

8. While we have 39 homilies of Origen on Luke in the Latin translation of Jerome, the comparison to which Origen refers is not among them. Since the term "supper" (δεῖπνον) occurs only in Lk 14.12, Lk 14.16–24 (3 times), the parable of the Great Supper, and once in Lk 20.46, which is not a parable, and the term "breakfast" (ἄριστον) occurs only in Lk 11.38 and 14.12 in that Gospel, it appears most likely that the discussion to which Origen alludes here was in a homily on Lk 14. The homilies preserved in Jerome's translation skip from Lk 12 (Hom. 35) to Lk 17 (Hom. 36). The Greek fragments 211 and 212 on Luke deal with Lk 14.16 and 14.18–20, but contain no investigation of the significance of the words "breakfast" and "supper." There were either additional homilies on Luke by Origen besides those Jerome had in his manuscript, or Jerome omitted some. If the latter is true, he gives no indication in his preface to the homilies on Luke that he has omitted some.

amining how, during supper, Jesus arises from supper, and when he has put water into the basin, he begins to wash the disciples' feet.

(9) For I think that those who eat with Jesus and partake of food with him in the day at the end of this life need a certain cleansing, not indeed concerning any of the first [parts] of the soul's body, if I may call it this, but they need, so to speak, to wash well those [parts] that are final and last, and which of necessity come into contact with the earth.

(10) Only Jesus can perform this first cleansing, but the second can [also] be done by his disciples to whom he said, "You also ought to wash one another's feet; for I have given you an example that as I have done to you, you also should do."[9]

(11) It seems to me that the Evangelist has not preserved the literal sequence concerning the washing in these words, that he might raise our understanding to the spiritual sense of the things in the passage, since those who need to wash their feet wash them before supper and before they recline to eat. The Evangelist, however, passed over that proper time for washing in his account, and now, after he has reclined to eat, Jesus arises from supper, that the teacher and Lord might begin to wash the disciples' feet after they have eaten.

(12) For they had washed before supper and were all clean in accordance with the saying, "Wash yourselves, be clean, take away the evils from your souls before your eyes," etc.[10] But after that washing they needed a second water for their feet only, that is, the lowest parts of the body.

(13) For it is impossible, I think, that no part of the soul, including even its most extreme and lowest parts, be filthy, even when someone may appear to be perfect among men.

(14) The majority, therefore, even after the washing, are filled with the dirt of sins in their head, or a little lower than this, but those who are genuinely Jesus' disciples, inasmuch as they anticipate also dining with him, have only their feet that need to be washed by the Word.

9. Cf. Jn 13.14–15.   10. Cf. Is 1.16.

(15) Now, when one observes the differences between sins, and perceives those sins as they appear to the exact and vigorous nature of the Word, but which the majority do not consider even to be sins, he will see what sins they are for which the feet need to be washed by Jesus.

(16) And if such are the defilements related to the feet, what shall we do who have never drawn near to the supper with Jesus, and who are defiled not only in our feet? Jesus says to Peter, who at that time did not know the mystery of the washing of the feet cleansed by Jesus, but who would know later,[11] "If I do not wash you, you have no part with me."[12]

(17) You will ask what this means. Does it mean that you do not have a part at all if I do not wash you, a good man? Or, does it mean that you do not have a part with me, the teacher and Lord, but with those who are less than me, among whom are those who, after they have washed themselves, have not eaten supper with me nor had their feet washed by me, or who have eaten supper, but have not had themselves washed?

(18) But because of the statement, "Behold I stand at the door and knock; if anyone open the door to me, I will come in to him and will eat supper with him, and he with me,"[13] I wonder if perhaps Jesus neither eats breakfast with anyone (for there is no need of an introduction and first doctrines), nor anyone eats breakfast with him, but he who eats with him eats supper only, for Scripture says, "A greater than Solomon is here"[14] of whom it has been written, "And this was Solomon's breakfast,"[15] which is related in the Third Book of Kings.

### He Did Not Wash Judas' Feet

(19) I would also venture to say, as consistent with the statement, "If I do not wash you, you have no part with me,"[16] that he did not wash Judas' feet, [because] the devil

11. Cf. Jn 13.7.
12. Jn 13.8.
13. Cf. Rv 3.20.
14. Cf. Mt 12.42.
15. Cf. 3 Kgs (1 Kgs) 2.46e (LXX).
16. Jn 13.8.

had already put into his heart to betray the teacher and Lord, since the devil found him not clothed in the full armor of God, and not having the shield of faith with which one can quench all the fiery darts of the wicked one.[17]

(20) For since it is written, "the devil having already put," I understand that the Scripture also teaches about this in the seventh Psalm, when it says that an archer also prepares fiery darts for those who do not keep their heart with all watchfulness.[18]

(21) Now, the text of the Psalm is as follows. "Unless you be converted, he will brandish his sword; he has bent his bow and prepared it, and has prepared instruments of death in it; he has prepared his darts for those that burn. Behold, he has been in labor with injustice, he has conceived sorrow and brought forth iniquity."[19]

(22) Everyone, therefore, will agree that the statement, "Behold he has been in labor with injustice, he has conceived sorrow and brought forth iniquity," can be referred to the devil. But it is absurd not to think likewise that the following words also are said of him, "Unless you be converted, he will brandish his sword; he has bent his bow and has prepared it, and in it he has prepared vessels of death," for no other has prepared vessels of death in his bow which he has bent than him by whose envy death entered into the world.[20]

(23) From these darts, therefore, which the devil has prepared for those who burn, he put it in the heart of Judas Iscariot, son of Simon, who had already been struck at the supper, but not with the result that it was pleasing to him, since the food and wine of this supper could not exist in a heart that had been struck by the devil with a missile in order to betray him who, perhaps, was the host, since it does not appear clearly in these words who it was who gave the supper, as Scripture says in the preceding words, "They made him a supper there, and Martha served, but Lazarus was one of those reclining with him."[21]

17. Cf. Eph 6.13–16.
18. Cf. Prv 4.23.
19. Ps 7.13–15.
20. Cf. Wis 2.24.
21. Cf. Jn 12.2.

(24) In the case of Judas, therefore, it has been written, "The devil having already put it into his heart that Judas Iscariot, son of Simon, should betray him."[22] Consistently with this you might say of each of those wounded in the heart by the devil, the devil having already put it in the heart of so-and-so that he should commit fornication, and of so-and-so that he should commit fraud, and of so-and-so that, mad for fame, he should submit to the idolatry of those who seem to have rank, and so in the case of the other sins that the devil puts into that heart that is not armed with the shield of faith, by which shield of faith one can quench not one, or two, but all the fiery darts of the wicked one.[23]

(25) Since, therefore, the economy of suffering was approaching, inasmuch as Judas Iscariot, son of Simon Iscariot, who had been wounded by the devil, was about to betray him, while the supper was in process, Jesus, it says, "knowing that the Father had given all things into his hands, and that he came from God, and goes to God, rises from supper."

*All Things Have Been Given into Jesus' Hands*

(26) The things, therefore, that were not formerly in Jesus' hands are given into his hands by the Father. And it is not some things and not others that are given into his hands, but all things. David, too, seeing in the Spirit, says in relation to this, "The Lord said to my Lord, Sit at my right hand until I make your enemies your footstool."[24]

(27) For Jesus' enemies were also a part of the "all things" that Jesus knew, so far as it was in the power of foreknowledge, to be given to him by the Father. But, that we may perceive more clearly what the statement means, "The Father had given all things into his hands," let us turn our attention to the statement, "For, as in Adam all die, so also in the Lord all shall be made alive."[25]

(28) But even though the Father has given "all things" into his hands, and in Christ "all shall be made alive," the justice of God is not confounded, nor the fact that each is

22. Cf. Jn 13.2.
24. Ps 109.1.
23. Cf. Eph 6.16.
25. Cf. 1 Cor 15.22.

treated as he deserves. This is made clear when the words, "but each in his own order,"[26] are added to the words, "so in Christ shall all be made alive."[27]

(29) And again in turn you will perceive the different orders of those who will be made alive in Christ when the statement, "The Father had given all things into his hands," is fulfilled, when you understand it in conjunction with the statement, "Christ the firstfruits, then those who are Christ's in his coming, then the end."[28] This end will be present with Christ in his coming when "he will deliver the kingdom to God and the Father,"[29] having previously destroyed "every principality and every authority and power."[30]

(30) Now, I think it is with these that the wrestling occurs.[31] Once every principality and authority and power has been destroyed so that there is no longer any principality and authority and power with which to wrestle, for this reason too, there will be no more wrestling.

(31) It is Paul's addition to these words, "For he must reign until he has placed all his enemies under his feet,"[32] that moves me to take "every principality and every authority and power"[33] that is destroyed to be the powers with which the wrestling occurs. Then, "the last enemy, death, is destroyed."[34]

(32) This agrees, at least, with the statement, "The Father had given all things into his hands," which the Apostle states more clearly when he says, "But when he said that all things have been subjected, it is clear that he who subjected all things to him is excepted."[35]

(33) But if all things have been subjected, and it is clear that all things have been subjected except the one "who subjected all things to him," then he too, of whom it is written, "He exalted himself before the Lord almighty,"[36] will belong to those things subjected to him, having been conquered, so

26. 1 Cor 15.23.
27. Cf. 1 Cor 15.22.
28. 1 Cor 15.23–24.
29. Cf. 1 Cor 15.24.
30. 1 Cor 15.24.
31. Cf. Eph 6.12.
32. 1 Cor 15.25.
33. 1 Cor 15.24.
34. 1 Cor 15.26.
35. 1 Cor 15.27.
36. Cf. Jb 15.25.

that he yields to the Word, is subjected to the image of God,[37] and becomes Christ's footstool.

(34) He sees, therefore, the economy [of suffering] already proceeding towards its good goal because of the statement, "The devil having already put it into his heart that Judas Iscariot, son of Simon, should betray him, he knew that the Father had given all things to him."[38] He had given them into the hands that hold all things, so that all things might be under his control, or the Father had given all things into his hands, that is into his actions and virtuous deeds, for he says, "My Father works until now, and I work."[39]

(35) Now, it was because of the creatures that went forth from God that he went forth from God. He came to be outside of God, although he had not previously wished to go forth from the Father, so [that] the creatures that had gone forth might come into his hands in the way and order of Jesus, and by following him they might be disciplined to go to God, and they will be with God because they follow him.[40]

(36) Therefore, it was once said to Peter, "Where I go, you cannot [follow] me now, but you will follow later,"[41] for Peter still possessed that which did not permit him to follow the Word immediately at that time.

(37) Now, you must understand that the same thing, but in an analogous manner that is appropriate, will be said to each of the "all things" which the Father has given into the Son's hands. For to each of the "all things" it will be said, "But you will follow me later."

(38) But if they shall not follow at the same time, the "later" in the statement, "but you will follow later," which applies to each of those who will follow him, does not refer to the same time.

(39) Consider the following with me also concerning all

---

37. Cf. Col 1.15.   38. Cf. Jn 13.2–3.
39. Jn 5.17.
40. This rather obscure statement seems to be a reference to Origen's doctrine of the fall of souls, and the voluntary acceptance of a body by Christ's soul, which did not fall, that he might lead the fallen souls back to God. Cf. *princ.* II.8.
41. Cf. Jn 13.36.

the things that are destroyed either when he has destroyed every principality, or every authority, or every power,[42] and in general, "until he has put all his enemies under his feet; the last enemy, death, shall be destroyed."[43]

(40) "Jesus, therefore, knowing that the Father had given all things into his hands, and that he came from God and goes to God," and "knowing" so far as we have discussed these matters[44] as we explained them when we presented our opinion on the words, "he came from God," and "he goes to God," "rises," it says, "from the supper."[45] Let us understand this with the words which follow thereafter.

### "I Am Meek and Lowly in Heart"

(41) And see if you can say on these words that, unaffected by circumstances, eating supper with the disciples cheered him; but with regard to circumstances and necessity, because of the disciples he rises from supper and, for a certain time, stops eating until he has cleansed the disciples' feet, since they could have no part with him unless he wash them.

(42) Let us consider, therefore, what is said after the words, "he rises from supper." "He lays aside his garments," it says, "and having taken a towel, girded himself."

(43) Now on these words too we would ask those who are not willing to ascend from the literal meanings and understand the foods of the soul which are presented in these words spiritually: What prevented him from washing the disciples' feet clothed?

(44) This is not a problem at all, however, if we consider, in a manner worthy of Jesus, the garments that he wore while eating and rejoicing with the disciples, should we reflect on what adornment the Word that became flesh wears.[46]

(45) But he puts aside this garment that exists in a kind of robe woven of phrases with phrases and sounds with

---

42. Cf. 1 Cor 15.24.  43. Cf. 1 Cor 15.25–26.
44. Preuschen marks this section of the text as corrupt.
45. Cf. Jn 13.3–4.  46. Cf. Jn 1.14.

sounds, and is unveiled to a greater extent with the form of a servant,[47] which is made clear through the words, "Having taken a towel, he girded himself," both that he might not be completely naked, and that, after washing the disciples' feet, he might dry them with a more appropriate cloth.

(46) And notice in these words how the great and glorified Word that became flesh humbles himself to wash the disciples' feet. For it says, "He puts water into a basin."

(47) Abraham, therefore, "when he lifted up his eyes and looked, and, behold, men stood above him; and when he saw them he ran to meet them from the door of his tent, and bowed down to the ground, and he said: Lord, if I have found favor in your sight, do not pass by your servant,"[48] did not himself take water, nor did he offer to wash their feet as strangers who had come to him, but he says, "Let water be drawn, and let them wash your feet."[49]

(48) But neither did Joseph bring water to wash the feet of his eleven brothers, but the man over Joseph's house "brought Simeon out to them, and brought water to wash their feet."[50]

(49) But he who said, "I came not as one who reclines at table, but as one who serves,"[51] and justly says, "Learn of me, because I am meek and lowly in heart,"[52] himself puts water into a basin. For he knew that no one could wash the disciples' feet as himself in such a way that, because of the washing, they would have a part with himself.[53]

(50) And the water, in my opinion, was such a Word that cleansed the feet of the disciples when they came to the basin Jesus set before them.

(51) Next, I ask why do you suppose it was not written, 'He washed the disciples' feet,' but was said, "And he *began* to wash the disciples' feet."

(52) For is it the custom of the Scriptures to prefix "he began" without a reason, as in the usage of the majority? Or

47. Cf. Phil 2.7.
48. Cf. Gn 18.2–3.
49. Gn 18.4.
50. Gn 43.23–24.
51. Cf. Lk 22.27.
52. Mt 11.29.
53. Cf. Jn 13.8.

did Jesus then "begin to wash the disciples' feet," and not stop when he had washed their feet at that time?

(53) For later he washed them and completed the washing, since they were defiled, according to the saying, "You will all be made to stumble in me in this night,"[54] and what was said to Peter, "The cock will not crow until you deny me three times."[55]

(54) For, when these sins occurred, the defiled feet of the disciples were again in need of washing, which he had begun to wash when he rose from supper, [but] he completed the washing when he cleansed them that they might no longer be defiled.

(55) And so also then did he begin to dry the disciples' feet, but he finished drying them when he also finished washing them.

> He comes, therefore, to Simon Peter. He says to him, Lord, are you going to wash my feet? Jesus answered and said to him, What I do you do not know now, but you will know afterwards. Peter says to him, You shall never wash my feet. Jesus answers him, If I do not wash you, you have no part with me. Simon Peter says to him, Not only my feet, but also my hands and head. Jesus says to him, He who has bathed has no need but to wash his feet, but he is wholly clean, and you are clean, but not all. For he knew the one betraying him; because of this he said, You are not all clean.
> (John 13.6–11)

### Peter's Rashness

(56) If an example should perhaps be necessary, we will make opportune use of what Peter now says to show that someone, with the best intention, can, in ignorance, say things that are not at all beneficial to himself.

(57) For if to have one's feet washed by Jesus was expedi-

---

54. Mt 26.31.
55. Cf. Jn 13.38.

ent in order to have a part with him, but Peter, because he did not understand that this was expedient, first objected, as it were, and said, so as to put him to shame, "Lord, are you going to wash my feet?" and a second time, "You shall never wash my feet," and if what he said was a hindrance to the act that would cause him to have a part with the Savior, it is clear that although he said this to the teacher with a sound and reverent intention, he spoke in a way harmful to himself.

(58) Now, life is full of errors of this kind, of people who intend what they believe to be best, but out of ignorance say, or even do, things which take them in the opposite direction.

(59) Such indeed are those who declare, "Touch not, taste not, handle not,"[56] concerning everything that is meant for destruction and human consumption,[57] based on some teaching which, very generally, falls far below the divine statement, "You shall die as men."[58]

(60) But why [must] we speak of those tossed about in heresies and carried about by every wind at the cunning of men,[59] who babble that destructive things bring salvation, and who glorify lies about Jesus as if to reverence him?

(61) Now, Scripture has frequently recorded that Peter was such a person as to profess hastily what appeared to him to be better. Take as an example how he spoke without examination and due consideration of the prophecy concerning the disciples when Jesus said, "You will all be scandalized in me in this night." Jesus presented the reason for this in the statement, "For it has been written, I shall smite the shepherd, and the sheep of the flock will be scattered."[60] For without examination respecting this, and without due con-

---

56. Cf. Col 2.21.
57. Origen clearly has Col 2.22 in mind, but he has changed the grammatical structure of the statement in Col and made its meaning more obscure. Col 2.22 speaks of "destruction by consumption," which is probably also what Origen means.
58. Cf. Ps 81.7.
59. Cf. Eph 4.14.
60. Mt 26.31; cf. Zec 13.7.

sideration of Jesus' declaration, Peter said, "Although all shall be scandalized in you, I shall not be scandalized."[61]

(62) I think it was this rashness still present in his soul at that time that caused him to sin more than the measure of the stumbling of the others when he denied Jesus three times before the crowing of the cock.[62]

(63) For this reason, once he understood, his previous rashness of this kind became an aid to the greatest things, so that he became very strong and patient. This is made clear when Paul said to him "before all, If you, being a Jew, live like the Gentiles and not like the Jews, how do you compel the Gentiles to live as the Jews?" etc.[63] He, however, maintained a firm silence and very patiently did not offer a reason on the subject. This will be discussed more appropriately in the Epistle to the Galatians.

(64) And in the Acts of the Apostles his settled condition, after he had been transformed into the same image,[64] will be apparent to those who give attention and devotion to each passage.

(65) And now, therefore, they all offered their feet to Jesus when he rose from supper and placed his garments aside and girded himself with the towel that he had taken and put water in the basin and began to wash the disciples' feet and to dry them with the towel with which he had girded himself. Consistently with their preconception about Jesus, they perceive that so great a man would not, wishing to burden the disciples, as the majority might say, wash their feet without a reason, but would perform something useful which they would wait to know later, thinking perhaps that he might do these things as a symbol of something. It was only Peter who, seeing the obvious, and offering no other reason than reverence for Jesus, did not present his feet to be washed, but first attempted to hinder him with the words, "Lord, are you going to wash my feet?" And after this,

61. Cf. Mt 26.33; Mk 14.29.
62. Cf. Mt 26.34, 75.
63. Gal 2.14.
64. Cf. 2 Cor 3.18.

when he had to be persuaded with the words, "What I do you do not know now, but you will know afterwards," he says, "You shall never wash my feet."

(66) In addition, when the other disciples entrusted themselves to Jesus and offered no resistance, this man, by what he says, although he seemed well intended, not only accuses Jesus of beginning to wash the disciples' feet without a reason, but also accuses his companions.

(67) For if he, as he thought, acted properly when he wanted to hinder Jesus, but those did not see it, he accused those who, contrary to what was proper, presented their feet to Jesus. And if he had thought one must not resist what is reasonable, and he had supposed that what happened when the disciples' feet were washed by Jesus was reasonable, he would not have resisted what happened.

(68) He appears, therefore, to have assumed rashly that Jesus' will concerning washing the disciples' feet was not reasonable. And if one must examine in Scripture even those things thought to be most insignificant, someone may ask why, since Peter was listed first in the number of the twelve—perhaps because he was more honored than the rest, since Judas, too, who had been relegated to the last places by his wicked disposition, was truly last of all—Jesus did not begin with Peter when he began to wash the disciples' feet and to dry them with the towel with which he had girded himself.

### *"He Who Has Bathed Has No Need To Wash"*

(69) We must reply that, just as a physician begins his healing with the urgent cases and those suffering most severely when he ministers to the sick masses with his skill as a physician, so he who washes the dirty feet of the disciples begins with those that are dirtier. It may be that he came to Peter last because he needed his feet washed least of all.

(70) And it may also have been that the nearly clean condition of his feet contributed to his apparent resistance.

(71) But if Jesus' statement, "He who has bathed has no

need to wash, but is wholly clean; and you are clean, but not all," be put to the test, perhaps one might suggest the following meaning. The disciples had already washed their feet, and after their bathing no longer needed that Jesus wash them,[65] and in addition, Peter himself was already clean even before Jesus washed his feet.

(72) But if someone should ask about these matters why then, when he said, "He who has bathed has no need to wash, but is wholly clean," Jesus washed the disciples feet, since they did not need to wash, we must reply to him, "To everyone who has, it will be given and added."[66]

(73) Since, therefore, the disciples were clean, Jesus adds to their cleanness also the washing of their feet. He would have washed neither those who had not bathed nor those who were not wholly clean, but consequently speaks of those clean in this manner, for even if someone among the sons of men be perfect, if the cleanness that comes from Jesus be lacking, if I may put it this way, he will not be considered clean.

(74) Now, I am expounding these matters later, since they have come to mind after the earlier things were explained, for we preserve even the order of the things that enter our mind. First it[67] perceived that the dirty feet of the disciples needed washing by Jesus, but now it sees that he washed their feet because they were clean so far as men are concerned, but not also with God, for without Jesus no one is clean with God even if previously he was thought to have cleansed himself by a certain diligence.

(75) Now, the Holy Spirit and the power of the Most High can dwell in those who have already become clean so far as men are concerned, as though they were a garment, and who have bathed in regard to the baptism of Jesus, and who have had their feet washed by him.

(76) Because, therefore, Peter did not consider the prin-

---

65. Following Blanc's suggestion.
66. Cf. Mt 25.29.
67. There is no expressed subject of the verb. Presumably it is to be understood as "mind" from the preceding clause.

ciple of Jesus' intent when he began to wash the disciples' feet and to dry them with the towel with which he had girded himself, he says to him, "Lord, are you going to wash my feet?" He said this to raise difficulties and put him to shame. But Jesus "answered and said to him, What I do you do not know now, but you will know afterwards," teaching that this act was a mystery.

*"How Beautiful Are the Feet of Those Who Preach Good Things"*

(77) But what was it that Jesus was doing when he washed the disciples' feet? Was he, by washing their feet and drying them with the towel with which he had girded himself, making them beautiful,[68] since they were about to preach the good things?

(78) For I think the words spoken prophetically of the apostles were fulfilled when Jesus washed the disciples' feet, namely, "How beautiful are the feet of those who preach good things."[69]

(79) And if he makes the disciples' feet beautiful by washing them, what shall we say of the true beauty that appears in all those who have themselves baptized by Jesus in the Holy Spirit and fire?[70]

(80) Now, the feet of those proclaiming good things became beautiful, so that, when they were washed and cleansed and dried by Jesus' hands, they might be able to walk on the holy way and travel over him who said, "I am the way."[71]

(81) For he alone, and everyone who has had his feet washed by Jesus, travels over this way, which is living and which brings one to the Father. This way admits no feet that are defiled and not yet clean.

(82) Moses, therefore, had to loose the sandals from his feet since the place to which he had come, on which he stood, was holy ground;[72] and the same was true of Josue the son of Nun.[73]

---

68. Cf. Rom 10.15; Is 52.7.
69. Rom 10.15; cf. Is 52.7.
70. Cf. Mt 3.11.
71. Jn 14.6.
72. Cf. Ex 3.5.
73. Cf. Jos 5.15.

(83) But that Jesus' disciples might travel this living and animate way, it was not enough that they only be without sandals for the journey (Jesus had given this command to his disciples[74]), but indeed, to travel this way they also had to be washed by Jesus when he had put aside his garments. Perhaps, on the one hand, it was so that he might make their feet, which were clean, cleaner, but on the other hand, perhaps it was to take up the filth on the disciples' feet into his own body by means of the towel with which alone he was girded.[75] For he himself bears our infirmities.[76]

(84) Notice, therefore, that when he was to wash the disciples' feet, he chose no other time than when the devil had already put it into the heart of Judas Iscariot, son of Simon, to betray him,[77] and the economy [of suffering] on behalf of men was about to take place.

(85) For prior to this the time was not appropriate for Jesus to wash the disciple's feet. For who would wash away the filth of their feet in the interval up to the Passion? It was also not appropriate at the time of the Passion, for there was not another Jesus who would wash their feet.

(86) But neither was it appropriate after the economy [of suffering], for by this time it was the hour of the Holy Spirit, who visited the disciples who had become clean and had had their feet washed, and by this time had their feet prepared and made beautiful to preach the good things in the Spirit.[78]

(87) The following, then, is the meaning of the statement, "What I do you do not know now, but you will know afterwards." For me to wash your feet is symbolic of the bases of your souls being purified, that they may be beautiful, since you are to preach the good things,[79] and to approach the souls of men with your feet clean.

(88) But you do not now know this mystery, inasmuch as you do not yet contain knowledge of it. Such knowledge will more appropriately be present in you when I have washed

---

74. Cf. Mt 10.10.
76. Cf. Mt 8.17; Is 53.4.
78. Cf. Rom 10.15; Is 52.7.
75. Cf. Jn 13.4.
77. Cf. Jn 13.2.
79. Cf. Rom 10.15; Is 52.7.

your feet, and after this you will know, when you understand this mystery and are enlightened with a knowledge of something that is not contemptible and insignificant.

(89) But when Jesus speaks these words to Peter, the disciple makes a reply that lacks understanding, but which proceeds from an image of honor and reverence for Jesus, an image that is nevertheless mistaken.

*"If I Shall Not Wash You, You Have No Part with Me"*

(90) Wherefore, since Peter's answer was disadvantageous for him, Jesus, who in a manner appropriate to his own goodness, prevents those things from becoming true which would prove harmful to the one who speaks them, does not permit Peter's answer to become true.

(91) For Peter, on the one hand, said, "You shall never wash my feet," and declared, although Jesus chose to wash his feet, that he would not be washed by him, and that he would not ever be washed. But, on the other hand, he who sees that it is more advantageous that Peter speak falsely in this than that he speak the truth, shows the advantage to him who had made this statement in its not having to be true, when he says, "If I shall not wash you, you have no part with me."

(92) If then, when Peter declared, "You shall never wash my feet," and if he spoke the truth in this he would not have a part with Jesus, but would have a part if he spoke not the truth in relation to which he had already spoken rashly, what else ought he do than not speak the truth?

(93) Jesus showed him to be a liar when he washed his feet so that speaking the truth regarding this not cause him to forfeit having a part with him.

(94) For it has been written, "Every man is a liar."[80] This saying is appropriately applied to those who have made rash and reckless statements about what they will do when it is disadvantageous for them if they continue in what has been ill-decided.

80. Ps 115.2.

(95) For if we show them that they will not have a part with Jesus when they have kept the rash assertion in their declaration, but that they will be able to be hopeful if they reject what they previously said, we will remove them from continuing in their ill-made decisions, even if such a statement was once made with an oath because of excessive rashness.

(96) And we will say that just as Peter, who said, "You shall never wash my feet," was prevented from continuing in what he had professed so that he might have a part with Jesus, so you too, who have erred in hasty judgment and recklessly made such and such a promise, would do better if you would desist from continuing in your ill-made decision and would more sensibly do such and such.

(97) But having understood both the statement, "What I do you do not know now, but you will know afterwards," and the statement, "If I shall not wash you, you have no part with me," let those who, from a sense of reverence, do not wish to interpret this and statements like it spiritually, admit such a form of Gospel investigations, or if they are not willing, let them show how it is reasonable that the one who said to the teacher, out of reverence for Jesus as they would say, "You shall never wash my feet," heard that he then would have no part with the Son of God, as though not [to have wished] his feet to be washed by Jesus involved a very great sin.

(98) For, on the one hand, the statement, 'If you shall commit this mistake, you will have no part with me,' [would] have a place, if it were said of manifest sins. But the statement, "If I shall not wash you, you have no part with me," makes no sense at all in respect to one who insisted when Peter did not wish to have his physical feet washed.

(99) [And] when he washes his feet, an action so banal[81] it is not proper to speak of it, the teacher will appear to have

---

81. The text is corrupt here. The MS reads ἡμερώτατα ἅ, ὅπερ (tamest things which, which). Brooke emended this to ἠλιθώτατα ἅπερ (most foolish things which). Preuschen emended it to <ἀν>ημερώτατά [ἅ], ὅπερ (wildest things, which). None of the three seem very satisfactory to me. I have loosely rendered the MS reading.

answered the disciple who honored him, which is very strange.

(100) For this reason let us present our feet to Jesus who even now rises from supper, puts his garments aside, takes a towel and girds himself, puts water into a basin and begins to wash our feet as disciples, and to dry them with the towel with which he girded himself when, for our sake, he came into our midst as one who serves.[82]

(101) For if we shall not do this, we will have no part with him, nor will our feet be beautiful.[83] This is especially important seeing that we are zealous for the greater gifts[84] and wish to be included with those who preach the good things.

(102) But because Peter is rash, after he heard the words, "If I shall not wash you, you have no part with me," when he was asked to present his feet to Jesus, he then wanted to exceed what Jesus requested and offered not only his feet to be washed by Jesus, but also his hands as well. Jesus did not now wish their hands to be washed when they were eating bread, since he despised those who said, "Your disciples do not wash their hands when they eat bread."[85] And in addition to his hands, Peter wished to offer his head, which Jesus wished no longer to be covered, on which already rested the image and glory of God.[86]

(103) For it is sufficient for us, whenever we come to the same point of time with the disciples of Jesus, to offer our feet alone to him who will wash and dry them. "For he who has bathed has no need to wash, but he is wholly clean." But if someone is not wholly clean, he has not bathed.

### "To Everyone Who Has, It Will Be Added"

(104) But someone may ask if he who has bathed has no need to wash, but is clean, and if Jesus' disciples were clean because they had bathed, why does Jesus put water into the basin and begin to wash the disciples' feet?[87]

(105) We have addressed this point partially in anticipa-

---

82. Cf. Lk 22.27.
83. Cf. Rom 10.15.
84. Cf. 1 Cor 12.31.
85. Cf. Mt 15.2.
86. Cf. 1 Cor 11.7.
87. Cf. Jn 13.5.

tion, and now we will add the following remarks to those earlier ones.

(106) The expression "we have need" is applied to those things that are necessary for life. Consequently, applied to material things, it means that one does not need most things, but only those of which Paul says, "but having food and clothing, we shall be satisfied with these things."[88] Those things, on the other hand, that are accumulated in wealth and luxury are the result of abundance among those who live luxuriously. They are not considered to be necessary and absolutely essential, but to be superfluous. So, therefore, there are also things that are necessary for us in the realm of divine matters, which bring us into life and cause us to be in the one who says, "I am the life."[89] But what supersedes these things would be said to supersede need. It is said of such things, "Delight in the Lord, and he will give you the requests of your heart."[90] These include all the things that are considered in relation to the paradise of luxury, and in relation to wealth and glory, the things in the left hand of wisdom according to him who said, "For length of life and years of life are in her right hand, but in her left hand are wealth and glory."[91] One would say that these go beyond necessity.

(107) Perhaps to have one's feet washed by such a great Teacher and Savior after one has bathed belongs to this category. For the gift of God exceeds need, as also in the holy resurrection of the dead there is the state of being in the glory of the sun, moon, or stars.[92]

(108) He who is clean, therefore, and has bathed has no need to wash, but he washes, in accordance with what was explained previously, since, "to everyone who has it will be added,"[93] and as John says, "And let him who is clean be cleansed in addition, and let him who is holy be sanctified."[94]

88. Cf. 1 Tm 6.8.
89. Cf. Jn 11.25; 14.6.
90. Ps 36.4.
91. Prv 3.16.
92. Cf. 1 Cor 15.41–42.
93. Cf. Mt 25.29.
94. Cf. Rv 22.11.

(109) But the words, "You are clean," have reference to the eleven, to which are added the words, "not all," because of Iscariot, for he knew the one who was to betray him, who was already unclean. This was so first, because he was not concerned for the poor, but was a thief, and having the money-box, he carried what was put in it,[95] and later, because "during supper, the devil having already put into the heart of Judas Iscariot, son of Simon, to betray him,"[96] he did not reject what was put in his heart.

(110) Wherefore the eleven who had bathed and were clean became even cleaner when they had their feet washed by Jesus, but Judas, who was already unclean (for it says, "He who is filthy, let him be filthy still"[97]), became filthier and unclean when Satan entered him after the morsel.[98]

> When, therefore, he had washed their feet, and taken his garments, and reclined again, he said to them, Do you know what I have done to you? You call me Teacher and Lord; you speak correctly, for so I am. If, then, I, your Lord and Teacher, have washed your feet, you also ought to wash one another's feet. For I have given you an example that as I have done to you, you also should do. (John 13.12–15)

*Jesus Has Washed the Feet of His Disciples As a Teacher*

(111) It is likely that those who perceived the magnitude of Jesus' power, and understood what he had done when he washed the disciples' feet, that is, that by washing their most extreme and ordinary parts, even the bodies mingled with earth, he might cleanse [their inner bodies] of which those bodies were a symbol, were amazed and would not have dared also to perform so great a deed themselves in the washing. They would have thought themselves to be too insignificant to wash the feet of the inner and secret man[99] of those who embrace the same teachings of God, unless Jesus

---

95. Cf. Jn 12.6.
96. Cf. Jn 13.2.
97. Rv 22.11.
98. Cf. Jn 13.27.
99. Cf. Rom 7.22; 2.29.

had assumed the form of the host and urged them to do this through the words we are expounding, when he was about to teach them the words spoken after they had eaten.

(112) For on the one hand, the words, "Do you know what I have done to you?"[100] were addressed in a persuasive and hortatory manner to the knowledge of what was occurring.

(113) This must be read either as a question, that the greatness of what has occurred might be manifest, or as a command,[101] that he might arouse their mind to receive its knowledge by giving attention to the deed.

(114) But on the other hand, the following words have been spoken in a most instructive manner with persuasion. "You call me Teacher and Lord, and you speak correctly, for so I am. If, then, I, your Lord and Teacher, have washed your feet, you also ought to wash one another's feet."

(115) Jesus, therefore, washed the feet of the disciples insofar as he was their teacher, and the feet of the servants insofar as he was their Lord.

(116) For the dust from the earth and from worldly things is cleared away by teaching, since it reaches nothing else than the extremities and lower parts of the disciples. But those things that defile the feet are also removed by the lordship of the ruler, since he has authority over those who still receive common defilement because they still have the spirit of bondage.[102]

(117) Someone not thinking clearly might say that Jesus washes the feet of the disciples and servants insofar as he is door, or shepherd, or physician. I think, however, that the disciples' feet need to be washed by the teacher insofar as they have not yet received the sufficiency, but still lack that sufficiency referred to in the statement, "It is sufficient for the disciple that he be as his teacher."[103]

(118) And this is the goal of the teacher, *qua* teacher, for

---

100. Jn 13.12.
101. The words in Jn 13.12 can be read either as a question or a command. They are usually taken as a question.
102. Cf. Rom 8.15.
103. Mt 10.25.

the disciple: to make the disciple as himself, that he may no longer need the teacher, *qua* teacher, although he will need him in other respects.

(119) For as the goal of the physician, whom the sick need, but the well have no need of a physician,[104] is to stop the sick from being sick so that they no longer need him, so the goal of the teacher is to achieve for his disciple what is called "sufficient" in the statement, "It is sufficient for the disciple that he be as his teacher."[105]

(120) But concerning the Savior, who is Lord, it is possible immediately to see something that surpasses other lords, who have no desire that the servant become as his lord.

(121) But such is the Son of the Father's goodness and love. For although he was Lord, he produced in his servants the state of being as their Lord, when they would no longer have the spirit of bondage again to fear, but would receive the spirit of adoption, in which they cry, "Abba, Father."[106]

(122) Before the disciples become as their teacher and Lord, therefore, they need to have their feet washed because they are deficient disciples and still possess the spirit of bondage to fear. But whenever anyone of them becomes as his teacher and Lord, in accordance with the statement, "It is sufficient for the disciple that he be as his teacher, and the servant as his Lord,"[107] he can then imitate the one who washed the disciples' feet, and wash the disciples' feet as the teacher, whom God appointed in the Church after the apostles, who received the first place in the Church, and the prophets, who received the second place.[108]

(123) But if the statement, "You shall serve your brother,"[109] can be applied to those who are inferior, and the statement, "Become lord of your brother,"[110] to those like Jacob, who are superior, it is clear that when the slave has become as his lord he washes the feet of those who serve the teaching with him, since I do not think the statement, "You call

---

104. Cf. Mt 9.12.
106. Rom 8.15.
108. Cf. 1 Cor 12.28.
110. Gn 27.29.

105. Mt 10.25.
107. Mt 10.25.
109. Gn 27.40.

me Teacher and Lord, and you speak correctly, for so I am," has any meaning that is deeper and over and above that which the majority have perceived. For Jesus will not say to all who say to him, "Lord, Lord,"[111] "You call me Lord, and you speak correctly."[112]

### All Do Not Say "Lord, Lord" Correctly

(124) They do not say "Lord" correctly, therefore, who will say on that day, "Lord, Lord, have we not eaten in your name, and drunk in your name, and cast out demons in your name, and performed miracles?"[113]

(125) Jesus will indeed then say to them, "Depart from me; I never knew you, because you are workers of iniquity."[114] Now he would not have said, "Depart from me," to those who say "Lord, Lord" correctly.

(126) Furthermore, the words, "Not everyone who says to me, Lord, Lord, will enter the kingdom of heaven,"[115] show that not everyone who says, "Lord, Lord," will be confirmed by him as the apostles now are, to whom he said, "You speak correctly, for so I am."[116]

(127) And indeed evil truly was no longer their lord, but the Word, and, in general, the Lord, total virtue, which is animate and living.

(128) But also, since "no one can say Jesus is Lord, except in the Holy Spirit,"[117] we also perceive in this what it means to say, "Jesus is Lord." He who says, "Jesus is Lord," in the Holy Spirit speaks correctly.

(129) Now, although he who speaks correctly certainly speaks in the Holy Spirit, you will raise a question about the present words, "and you speak correctly," when they are compared with the words, "For the Spirit was not yet, because Jesus was not yet glorified."[118]

(130) To say "Jesus is Lord" correctly, therefore, is the proper work of one who genuinely serves the Word. Analo-

---

111. Mt 7.22.
112. Cf. Jn 13.13.
113. Cf. Mt 7.22; Lk 13.26.
114. Cf. Mt 7.23; Lk 13.27.
115. Mt 7.21.
116. Jn 13.13.
117. 1 Cor 12.3.
118. Jn 7.39.

gous to this, it belongs to the disciple properly to address the Savior as "Teacher." He would say in response, "For so I am." The Word will not make this response to one who serves sin, and is a disciple of lies.

*The Universal Obligation To Wash One Another's Feet*

(131) It is possible, however, that even one who is a saint needs the washing of feet, since even the widow who is enrolled into ecclesiastical honor is examined, along with her other good works, also about this, "If she has washed the feet of saints."[119] For I think it would be ridiculous to stop at the literal meaning and, for a widow who, let us say, has all the marks that characterize a holy widow and lacks only this, not to be appointed into ecclesiastical honor, although she had frequently, when she was prosperous and possessed what was necessary, been gracious, through her maids and household servants, to strangers or those, in general, who needed to experience some philanthropic deed from her.

(132) And do not be surprised if you have to interpret the statement anagogically, "If she has washed the feet of saints,"[120] since older women, analogous to older men, are commanded also to be teachers of what is good.[121]

(133) But consider if it is not also difficult for anyone who is a disciple of Christ, who wishes to fulfill the command that says, "You also ought to wash one another's feet," since he is obliged to desire to perform the work of washing his brothers' feet which are physical and perceptible to the senses. Consequently, the faithful [are obliged] to do this in whatever station of life they happen to be, whether bishops and presbyters, who seem to be in ecclesiastical prominence, or even men in other positions of honor in the world. This means that the master comes to wash the feet of the believing servant, and parents the feet of their son. This custom either does not occur, or it occurs exceedingly rarely and among those who are very simple and rustic.

(134) Now, in relation to these matters, we must remem-

119. 1 Tm 5.10.  120. 1 Tm 5.10.
121. Cf. Ti 2.3.

ber also what was said on the words, "If I shall not wash you, you have no part with me,"[122] and in addition, the words, "Do you know what I have done to you?"

(135) Indeed, it is fitting that Jesus has given us an example of washing feet analogous to those words spoken figuratively by the bride in the Song of Songs, "I have washed my feet; how shall I defile them?"[123]

(136) Notice also the words, "That as I have done to you, you also should do," in comparison with the words, "If I shall not wash you, you have no part with me."[124]

(137) But if someone should object and say that even if this is interpreted allegorically, none the less it also occurred literally, we must also listen, with a view to spiritual interpretation, to the text that declares, "If, then, I, your Lord and Teacher, have washed your feet, you also ought to wash one anothers' feet. For I have given you an example, that as I have done to you, you also ought to do." We must say to such a person, Since, then, the words, "If I shall not wash you, you have no part with me,"[125] which were spoken to Peter, who had said, "You shall never wash my feet,"[126] occurred literally, we too, in accordance with the literal sense, will address those who do not reverently present their feet to us that we may wash them, and dare to say to such people, "If I shall not wash you, you have no part with me."

(138) And if he does not thereupon respect what I have said, consider what you must say to the further difficulty concerning whether one must also keep that text in an absolute manner.

(139) Even I myself would agree, then, that it will be the duty for one to wash the feet of some disciple of Jesus at some time or other, and for the latter to offer his feet to be washed by him, the one to perform the act out of love and graciousness, and the other to permit it.

(140) But if we shall say that each one who is not conscious of having performed this act, and thus washed the

---

122. Jn 13.8.
123. Song 5.3.
124. Jn 13.8.
125. Jn 13.8.
126. Jn 13.8.

feet of the saints, has not paid his debt in respect to a certain obligatory command, namely, "You ought to wash one anothers' feet,"[127] it is time, perhaps, to say that nearly all are debtors to this command.

> Truly, truly I say to you: a servant is not greater that his lord, nor an apostle greater than the one who sent him. If you know these things, blessed are you if you do them. I do not speak of all of you, I know whom I have chosen; but that the Scripture may be fulfilled: he who eats . . .[128] bread lifted up his heel against me. (John 13.16–18)

### "The Disciple Is Not above His Master"

(141) It seems to me that these words, too, pertain to the necessity of interpreting the words about footwashing allegorically. For the statement, "If you know these things, blessed are you if you do them," has reference to that washing, since nothing to be done has been mentioned previously, except the washing of feet.

(142) But the lessons in that passage, that is, how the disciples' feet are defiled although they have already bathed, and in what manner they are washed, are truly the proper work of the blessed, since the Word wills that they know them, and Jesus wishes that they do them.

(143) For it is not right to pronounce so great a word as "blessed" on just anyone who happens to be present, since even a household slave washing his master's feet would appear to be blessed by this very act, as would also a flatterer and a hypocrite. For the act of washing the feet of Jesus' disciples that we are explaining, is the act of someone great, who also has Jesus within himself, and is blessed in general.

(144) But we must know that there is a corresponding teaching to this saying. In the Gospel according to Matthew there is the statement, "The disciple is not above the teacher, nor the servant above his lord. It is enough for the

127. Jn 13.14.
128. Preuschen notes that "with me" has fallen out of the text.

disciple that he be as his teacher, and the servant as his lord."[129] And in the Gospel according to Luke, "The disciple is not above the teacher; but let everyone be made perfect as his teacher."[130]

### "I Do Not Speak of All of You"

(145) We must investigate the statement that follows, "I do not speak of all of you." To what previous words shall we refer this statement? Someone, then, will say that it refers to the words, "Blessed are you if you do them," for Judas was not blessed. I do not think, however, that these words are correctly referred to this.

(146) For this is entirely true of Judas and of anyone else, even the most worthless person, 'Blessed are you so and so, if you do these things.' It is as if I should say to an undisciplined man, even if he will not hear what is said nor show self-control, 'Blessed are you if you show self-control,' and to a man who despises wisdom, even if he treads upon this choice, 'Blessed are you if you take up wisdom and instruction.'

(147) Perhaps, then, we should refer the statement, "I do not speak of all of you," to the words, "A servant is not greater than his lord."

(148) For since "whoever commits sin is a servant of sin,"[131] and Judas committed sin, he was a servant of sin, especially since the devil had put it into his heart to betray the Savior.[132]

---

129. Mt 10.24–25.  130. Cf. Lk 6.40.
131. Jn 8.34.
132. Cf. Jn 13.2. In pars. 148–50 Origen employs two of the types of argument in Stoic logic (See B. Mates, *Stoic Logic* [Berkeley: University of California Press, 1961], 101 for the two models that I cite below). In par. 148 he uses a type 1 undemonstrated argument:

> If the first, then the second
> The first.
> Therefore, the second.

Origen's argument is:

> If one commits sin, then he is a servant of sin.
> Judas committed sin.
> Therefore, he was a servant of sin.

(149) And since he was a servant of sin, he was not a servant of the Word of God.

(150) Consequently, he was no longer an apostle of Jesus, for he had already come to belong to the devil, since he had put it into his heart to betray the Savior.

(151) Wherefore, after the statement, "A servant is not greater than his lord, nor an apostle greater than the one who sent him," the Savior said, "I do not speak of all of you," to deny that Judas was his servant and apostle.

### "I Know Whom I Have Chosen"

(152) Next, let us consider the statement, "I know whom I have chosen." Literally, this means, I know who each one is whom I have chosen; therefore, I also know who Judas is, and he does not escape my notice, although the devil has already put the things against me into his heart.[133] But it also has the following meaning because of the customary usage in Scripture of the expression, "I know," and of similar words in this text. "I have known" is also such an expression.[134]

(153) Somewhere the Savior says he will say to those who shall say, "We have eaten in your name, and have drunk, and

---

Pars. 149 and 150 follow the pattern of a type 3 argument:
    Not both the first and the second.
    The first.
    Therefore, not the second.

Origen's argument in par. 149 is:
    One cannot be a servant of sin and a servant of the Word of God.
    Judas was a servant of sin.
    Therefore, he was not a servant of the Word of God.

In par. 150, he argues, on the same model:
    One cannot be an apostle of Jesus and belong to the devil.
    Judas belonged to the devil.
    Therefore, he was not an apostle of Jesus.

133. Cf. Jn 13.2.
134. Origen has mentioned two Greek words for "to know" in this sentence (οἶδα and ἔγνων). Their distinctions are not expressible in English translations without cumbersome paraphrases, and, in addition, they are frequently used interchangeably in Greek. Only οἶδα occurs in the passage he is discussing (Jn 13.16–18); the other word occurs in Jn 13.12.

have cast out demons,"[135] "I never knew you,"[136] and, "I do not know where you come from."[137] If these statements are taken literally, it will appear that we are assuming things that violate the Savior's honor.

(154) But perhaps, since "the Lord knows those who are his,"[138] he does not know those who are not his. And just as he says of some, "I never knew you,"[139] so he might also have said of Judas, if [he had never been his],[140] "I never knew you."[141] But if Judas had been his and had fallen away, it might be said to him, "I do not know where you come from."[142]

(155) Now, therefore, since the devil had already put the things against Jesus into Judas' heart,[143] Jesus did not know him. This is why he did not say, 'I know all those present,' but, "I know whom I have chosen," as if he had said, "my elect."

(156) But I do not say of all who are present, "I know whom I have chosen." And what is happening is brought about by that one of you who will betray me, that the Scripture may be fulfilled which says, "He who eats my bread lifted up his heel against me."

*"He Who Eats My Bread Lifted up His Heel against Me"*

(157) Now, the saying from the fortieth Psalm, which is as follows, has been paraphrased: "For even the man of my peace, in whom I hoped, who eats my bread, has kicked powerfully against me."[144]

(158) The Savior says, therefore, that this statement was made of Judas and himself. You will ask in respect to this statement how Judas was a man of peace, and how the Savior hoped in him.

(159) I think, therefore, that these words make clear that Judas had once genuinely believed. For if he had never been

---

135. Cf. Mt 7.22; Lk 13.26.
136. Mt 7.23.
137. Lk 13.27.
138. 2 Tm 2.19; cf. Nm 16.5.
139. Mt 7.23.
140. Wendland's suggestion. The text is corrupt.
141. Mt 7.23.
142. Cf. Lk 13.27.
143. Cf. Jn 13.2.
144. Ps 40.10.

a son of peace, Jesus would not have sent him with the rest of the apostles and said to him, too, (for he is recorded to have said to the twelve), "Say, Peace be to this house. And if there is a son of peace there, your peace shall rest upon him; otherwise your peace shall return to you."[145]

(160) For observe also how much later the devil put the things against the Savior into his heart,[146] although a little earlier testimony has been given that he was a thief.[147]

(161) But I would not think that he would have been entrusted with the money-box if he were a thief from the beginning. He was trusted with it, therefore, because he was worthy of being trusted, although it was foreknown that he would fall away.

(162) And he was so great a man of Christ's peace that Jesus once had high hopes in him, as in a good apostle, for hear the words, "In whom I hoped."[148]

(163) Now, I think that he also shared the most nourishing secret teachings with the apostles, having received them from Jesus, of which Jesus said, "He who eats my bread."

(164) And the statement, "He has kicked powerfully against me,"[149] has been paraphrased as, "He lifted up his heel against me," since the verb "he has made powerful" has the same meaning as the verb, "he lifted up."[150]

(165) And if it is necessary to explain the expression, "He lifted up his heel against me," and, "He has kicked powerfully against me,"[151] we will say that he who stretches out his foot against someone does this, and that Judas was such a person when he trampled on the Son of God.[152]

(166) He was also eating his bread with Jesus when Jesus dipped the morsel and took it and gave it to Judas Iscariot son of Simon.[153]

---

145. Cf. Lk 10.5–6.
146. Cf. Jn 13.2.
147. Cf. Jn 12.6.
148. Ps 40.10.
149. Ps 40.10.
150. The two verbs are ἐμεγάλυνεν, which means "to make great or powerful," and ἐπῆρεν, "to lift up." The first verb, with its object, could be rendered: "He has made his kick great."
151. Ps 40.10.
152. Cf. Heb 10.29.
153. Cf. Jn 13.26.

(167) [And] Judas lifted up his heel against the teacher when Satan entered him after the morsel.[154]

(168) But you yourself, too, will join in examining if it is possible also for the statement, "the iniquity of my heel shall encompass me,"[155] to have reference to Judas, when it is examined together with the statement, "He lifted up his heel against me," since Judas had a part with Jesus, and was called his possession and apostle, but is figuratively said to have become a heel because of his end.

> I tell you this now, before it comes to pass, that when
> it comes to pass you may believe that I am he.
> (John 13.19)

### The Perfection of Faith

(169) This text refers to what was said previously. "I do not speak of all of you; I know whom I have chosen; but that the Scripture may be fulfilled: he who eats bread with me lifted up his heel against me."[156] For this is what will be, that the Scripture may be fulfilled concerning him who lifts up his heel against me, who is eating my bread with me. I tell you before it comes to pass, that whenever what is to be fulfilled of the things that have been prophesied in Scripture comes to pass, you may believe that I am he of whom these things have been prophesied, because of the one who eats bread with him having lifted up his heel against him.

(170) But someone may ask how the words, "I tell you now before it comes to pass," and I tell you "in order that when it comes to pass you may believe that I am" the Christ who has been prophesied, are addressed to the disciples whose feet Jesus washed, as if they had not yet believed that he himself were the Christ.

(171) Consider if we can preserve the intention of him who said, "that when it comes to pass you may believe that I am he," without condemning such great disciples of Jesus because they have not yet believed.

154. Cf. Jn 13.27.  
155. Ps 48.6.  
156. Jn 13.18.

(172) He who accepts the doctrines of wisdom, sometimes, in addition to the first doctrines, because of which he is already wise, takes up second doctrines in reference to which he was not formerly wise, and he will be wiser, just as also it is said, "For when a wise man has heard these things, he will be wiser."[157]

(173) Just as if words of this sort, then, were addressed to a wise man, and it were added, 'These words make you wise,' we would not at all assume that it meant wise from not being wise, but even wiser from being wise, as progress supervenes and proceeds to perfection, in the same way, assume with me that the believer, too, can come to have more faith.

(174) In fact, the apostles once approached the Lord and said to him, "Lord, increase our faith."[158] They did not thereby condemn themselves as unbelievers. For indeed the word "increase" clearly shows that they had faith that would admit an addition.

(175) If, then, we are in agreement on these matters, observe with me that additions of things that convince add to faith when they follow things that have previously convinced. Consequently, the disciples, too, in addition to the things that had convinced them, needed to receive this in addition, namely to see the Scripture fulfilled which says, "He who eats my bread lifted up his heel against me,"[159] because what was prophesied proved that he was the one of whom these things were prophesied.

(176) And understand the words, "that you may believe," as capable of being equivalent to the words, "that you may be increased in faith,"[160] while you continue to believe and are susceptible to no impulse that will produce change.

(177) And if, indeed, faith were not great in magnitude or much in multitude, Paul would not have said, "If I should have all faith."[161]

---

157. Prv 1.5.  
158. Lk 17.5.  
159. Jn 13.18.  
160. Wendland's suggestion. The text is corrupt. Brooke's suggested emendation would mean: that you may be active, or perhaps, effective.  
161. Cf. 1 Cor 13.2.

(178) For just as the man who is perfect and who possesses all the virtues, having assumed each virtue in its totality, possesses perfect wisdom and perfect self-control, and so also piety and the other virtues,[162] so, too, one might say that to possess all faith is to be perfect in the virtue of believing.

(179) Now, I do not make these remarks in the strict sense, so that wisdom will be designated imperfect, or self-control, or piety, or the other virtues, but loosely so that even those who are progressing in each virtue are given the same name as the perfect virtue.

(180) For in this manner one who errs in certain things so that he needs rebuke is said to be wise, not, in truth, if he hates those who rebuke him, but, indeed, rather if he loves them, as has been written, "Rebuke a wise man and he will love you."[163]

(181) So also he is said to be wise, who is receptive of other doctrines of wisdom and does not yet possess the second doctrines, just as it is also said, "Give opportunity to a wise man and he will be wiser."[164]

(182) But indeed, we have come to these matters to show that it is possible for one who already believes to learn certain things that he may believe once more, and by means of additional teachings have his faith increased.

*Those Who Possess All Faith*

(183) Now, if we wish to know who it is who possesses all faith,[165] let us assume as an example that the articles that save the believer by being believed are collectively, let us say, one hundred in number. And let us say that the one who accepts these one hundred articles without doubt and firmly believes in each of them has all faith. The one, however, who is deficient in a certain number of the articles that save by being believed, or is deficient in his certainty about the articles that he believes, although he is a believer, falls short

---

162. Origen is here expressing the Stoic ideal of the wise man, i.e. that the perfect man possesses all the virtues.
163. Prv 9.8.   164. Prv 9.9.
165. Cf. 1 Cor 13.2.

of possessing all faith to the extent that he is deficient in so many numbers, or so far as he has shrunk from certainty concerning either all or some of the articles believed. This is true even if, in the present example, it be granted that someone can believe some articles with certainty, and that he can believe in other articles, but not with certainty. Admittedly, it would be granted that it is impossible to prove that the one who is imperfect in [one article] has no certainty at all, because each of those of little faith,[166] if I may so designate them according to the Scripture, and each of those who have not yet assumed certainty in respect to the articles which are believed, does not maintain an equal distance from certainty in respect to the articles which are believed.

(184) Now it follows from these considerations, because of the saying, "Let it be done to you according to your faith,"[167] and, "Faith has saved you,"[168] that for each one salvation, too, turns out to be proportionate to the quantity and quality of his faith according to the recompense in the just judgment of God, if indeed there is some difference in this too among those who are saved, so that the statement, "With what measure you measure it will be measured to you again,"[169] is applicable both to the measures of faith and to the measures of the recompense from God and salvation.

(185) Now, he who has grasped the principle of these matters will see how reasonably the words, "Judge not that you may not be judged,"[170] and, "Judge nothing before the time, until the Lord come,"[171] are addressed to men incapable of judging.

(186) Again, in turn, since I said, as an example, that if the articles that save by being believed are one hundred, the one who believes in all one hundred with certainty possesses all faith, but the one who is deficient in faith in respect to some of the hundred, or is deficient in certainty in respect to the articles that he believes, in one way or another does

---

166. Cf. Mt 6.30; 8.26; Lk 12.28.
167. Cf. Mt 9.29.
168. Cf. Mt 9.22.
169. Cf. Lk 6.38.
170. Mt 7.1.
171. 1 Cor 4.5.

not possess all faith, we will set forth the following things for the sake of clarity.

(187) "First of all believe that God is one, who created all things, and fashioned them and made all things to exist out of what did not exist."[172]

(188) And one must also believe that Jesus Christ is Lord, and believe in all the truth about him in relation to his divinity and humanity.

(189) And one must also believe in the Holy Spirit, and that, because we possess free will, we are chastened for our sins, and rewarded for our good actions.

(190) For instance, then, if someone, hypothetically, should seem to believe in Jesus, but should not believe that the God of the law and of the gospel is one, whose glory the heavens declare, since they were made by him, and the work of whose hands the firmament proclaims, since it is their work,[173] this person would be deficient in the greatest article of faith.

(191) Or again, if someone believes that he who was crucified in the time of Pontius Pilate visited the world in respect to some holy and saving matter, but that he did not receive his birth from the Virgin Mary and the Holy Spirit, but from Joseph and Mary, he would, even in this, be deficient in beliefs that are indispensable for possessing all faith.[174]

(192) And again, if someone should accept his divinity, but take offence at his humanity and believe that nothing human occurred concerning him, or that he did not receive substantive existence, he would, even in this, be deficient in beliefs that are not trivial for all faith.[175]

(193) Or, on the contrary, if he should accept the human things about him, but reject the substantive existence of the Only-Begotten and Firstborn of all creation,[176] this person too would not be able to say that he has all faith.

---

172. Cf. Hermas, *Shepherd, Mand.* 1.1; Wis 1.14; Origen, *Jo.* 1.103 (FOTC 80.55); *princ.* Praef. 4; 1.3.3.
173. Cf. Ps 18.2.
174. Origen's reference is probably to heretical sects of Jewish Christians, such as the Ebionites. Cf. a similar statement above at 20.269.
175. The reference is to the views of the docetic Gnostics.
176. Cf. Col 1.15.

(194) And so consider with me next, in order that we may perceive what a great thing it is to possess all faith without deficiency and with certainty, which, when all faith is in a man's soul, can be so great that he can remove whatever mountains there are,[177] that while all people are capable of removing the mountain pointed out by Jesus[178] and those pointed out to him, if one is deficient in anything in all faith, he is deficient in the power to remove mountains.

(195) We will also use the following example for these matters. Just as a set number of men have sufficient strength to drag a ship into the sea for the first time, but if they should lack even one of their co-workers, or the strength of one of them, the ship would not be launched, so all faith is like having many people removing mountains. One who is still imperfect in faith is deficient in the power to remove mountains to the extent that he is deficient in possessing all faith.

(196) Consider if it has not been advantageous to examine all these matters on account of Jesus' statement to the disciples whose feet he washed, "I tell you this now before it comes to pass, that when it comes to pass you may believe that I am he," since one who has not examined them might think he said this because they had not yet believed. At the same time, when the word is pondered, it shows how great the virtue related to all faith is, and that it is rarely found, and it shows how much each of us falls short of possessing all faith so as to remove mountains.[179]

(197) In any case, believing is not negligible in relation to action; according to the words now before us, the prophets prophesied the things about Jesus, and in accordance with their word the things prophesied happened to the Savior.

---

177. Cf. 1 Cor 13.2.
178. Cf. Mt 21.21; Mk 11.23.
179. Cf. 1 Cor 13.2.

Truly, truly I say to you, he who receives whomever I shall send receives me, and he who receives me receives him who sent me. (John 13.20)

### Apostles of Christ

(198) Jesus sends not only saints, but also saints and angels; and he sends those who are called apostles because they are sent by him.

(199) In addition, some of these are men, and others are higher powers. For we shall not err if we apply the name "apostle" also to these of whom it has been written, "They are all ministering spirits, sent to minister for them who will inherit salvation."[180]

(200) For if they are apostles because they are sent, and they are all sent to minister by the one who makes "his angels spirit,"[181] and his ministers a flame of fire,"[182] because they are ministering spirits, these too would be apostles of the one who sent them. And each one indeed who is sent by someone is an apostle of the one who sent him.

(201) Wherefore it has also been said in the words above, after the statement, "A servant is not greater than his lord," "nor an apostle greater than the one who sent him."[183]

(202) In accordance with this, he will not err who says that John was an apostle of God because of the statement, "There was a man sent from God, whose name was John";[184] as was also Isaias, because of the question, "Whom shall I send, and who will go to this people?" when he answered saying, "Here am I, send me."[185]

(203) And why do I speak of these when in the Epistle to the Hebrews our Savior, too, who is so great, is said to be an apostle of the Father? For it is written, "Having, therefore, a great high priest and apostle Jesus Christ."[186]

(204) And now, therefore, whomever the Savior sends to

---

180. Heb 1.14.
181. Preuschen prints the singular in his text and notes that the plural in M is a corrected reading.
182. Heb 1.7; cf. Ps 103.4.
183. Jn 13.16.
184. Jn 1.6.
185. Cf. Is 6.8.
186. Cf. Heb 4.14; 3.1.

COMMENTARY ON JOHN, BOOK 32

minister to the salvation of anyone, that person who is sent is an apostle of Jesus Christ.

(205) But just as the apostle is an apostle of the one who sent him, so is he an apostle only to those to whom he is sent.

(206) Paul, having this in mind, said, "Even if I am not an apostle to others, but at least I am to you, for you are the seal of my apostleship in the Lord."[187]

(207) It is possible, therefore, for someone to be an apostle of Jesus Christ although he has been sent to one person only if, in the foreknowledge of God, he has ministered the word to one person only.

(208) We say these things that we may see again the abundance of those called apostles of Jesus Christ. For Paul says, "They gave the right hand of fellowship to me and Barnabas, that we should go to the Gentiles, and they to the circumcision."[188] Paul, therefore, was an apostle to the Gentiles only, and Peter to all the circumcision.

(209) Now, if someone of us should be considered worthy to become an apostle to one person perhaps, or to a few more, he becomes an apostle as the Apostle has presented it.

(210) But if this should occur, let him not exalt himself, remembering the saying, "But for the rest, what is sought in stewards is that one be found faithful."[189] For what is sought is not necessarily found if it is sought.

(211) We have made these remarks because of the saying, "He who receives whomever I shall send."[190] It is possible that as many as are sent by Jesus, even if they are not those whom we have been accustomed[191] to call apostles, are such, and[192] it is also possible that a being higher than human nature be sent by Jesus.

---

187. Cf. 1 Cor 9.2.
188. Gal 2.9.
189. Cf. 1 Cor 4.2.
190. I have followed Brooke's punctuation in breaking the sentence here. Preuschen has only a comma.
191. The text is tenuous in this section. Preuschen and Brooke have corrected the MS reading in different ways. I have followed Preuschen.
192. I have omitted the conjunction "that" (ὅτι).

(212) He, therefore, who receives whom[ever] Jesus may send, receives Jesus in the one sent, and he who receives Jesus receives the Father. Therefore, he who receives whomever Jesus may send receives the Father who sent Jesus.

(213) The explanation, however, can also be as follows. "He who receives whomever I shall send, receives me," and attains the point of having received me. He, however, who does not receive me through some apostle of mine, but contains me, since I am not served by men nor through men,[193] but sojourn in the souls of those who have prepared themselves to receive me, receives the Father who sent me, since it is not I, the Christ, alone who am in him, but also the Father.

(214) It is also possible, on the basis of these words, to consider their opposites. For he who receives whomever the son of the wicked one sends, receives the antichrist. And he who receives the son of the wicked one, since he has also received the antichrist as a word which pretends to be true and which falsely proclaims that it is justice, receives the wicked one himself.

(215) Let us take heed, therefore, that as good money changers[194] we may approve the ministry of the true [apostles] and reject the ministry of those who are false.

(216) At this point, therefore, Jesus says, "He who receives whomever I shall send, receives me; and he who receives me receives him who sent me," and, "He who sees me, sees him who sent me."[195] He has not said, however, 'He who believes in you, believes in me,' nor, 'He who sees you, sees me.' For he wishes us to receive his apostles, but not also to believe in them.

(217) Let us, therefore, receive those who are sent to us by the Word, and let us receive the Word of God himself. But let us never receive an apostle of the antichrist and a false word.

193. Cf. Gal 1.1.
194. See above, Book 19.44.
195. Jn 12.45.

> When Jesus had said these things he was troubled in spirit, and he testified and said, Truly, truly I say to you, one of you shall betray me. (John 13.21)

### A Distinction Between "Soul" and "Spirit"

(218) Earlier he had said, "Now is my soul troubled,"[196] but now it is said, "When Jesus had said these things he was troubled in spirit." I raise the following questions in relation to the passage. Why was it not said, 'The spirit of Jesus is troubled,' parallel to, "Now is my soul troubled," or, 'Now is my soul troubled,' parallel to, "He was troubled in spirit"? I have dared modestly to raise these questions since I have noticed a distinction between soul and spirit in all Scripture. I observe that the soul is something intermediate and capable of both virtue and evil,[197] but the spirit of man that is in him is incapable of receiving things that are inferior, for the best things are said to be fruits of the spirit,[198] and not, as one might think, of the Holy Spirit, but of the human spirit.

(219) For in contradistinction to this, the works of the flesh are said to be manifest,[199] all being blameworthy, since no work of the flesh is praiseworthy.

(220) Only once hitherto have I found the spirit of an evil man said to be hardened by the Lord God.

(221) For thus it has been written in Deuteronomy, "And Sehon the king of Hesebon did not wish us to pass through it, because the Lord God hardened his spirit, and he strengthened his heart to deliver him into your hands as in this day."[200]

(222) The matters related to this, however, would more properly be examined in the books on Deuteronomy.

### Jesus Was Troubled in Spirit

(223) It is proposed now, however, that we explain how, in respect to the previously mentioned words, "when Jesus

---

196. Jn 12.27.
197. Cf. *princ.* 2.6.5; 1.8.3; 2.8.4; 3.4.2.
198. Cf. Gal 5.22–23.    199. Cf. Gal 5.19.
200. Cf. Dt 2.30.

had said these things he was troubled," not his soul, nor in his soul, nor even of the spirit, but "in spirit." That our observation concerning the spirit, then, may not be useless, we must say that in the statement, "Now is my soul troubled,"[201] the experience of trouble belonged to the soul, but in the statement, "Jesus was troubled in spirit," which is the human spirit, the experience had come to the realm of the spirit.

(224) For just as the saint lives in the spirit, which is the origin, while he lives, of every act and prayer and hymn to God, so everything he does, whatever it may be, he does in the spirit, even to the extent that if he suffers, he suffers in the spirit.

(225) And if the saint does this, by how much more must we say these things of Jesus, the leader of the saints, whose human spirit in him, in that he has taken up the whole man, stirred up the other human elements in him?

(226) And so "he was troubled in spirit" that he might testify and say with a divine oath, as it were, the "truly" in respect to the statement, "I say to you that one of you will betray me."

(227) For I think, when the spirit beheld that the devil had already put into the heart of Judas Iscariot, son of Simon, to betray the teacher, Jesus, having been enlightened on what was to be, was troubled, and since the trouble had come from knowledge in the spirit, which was also in a state of disturbance, "Jesus," it is said, "was troubled in spirit."

(228) But perhaps the flesh was troubled too according to one interpretation of the saying, "The flesh is weak."[202] Now, Jesus was these things, of whom Gabriel had said to Mary, "And behold, you shall conceive in your womb, and you shall call his name Jesus. He will be great, and will be called Son of the Most High."[203]

---

201. Jn 12.27.
202. Cf. Mt 26.41; Mk 14.38.
203. Cf. Lk 1.31–32.

### "One of You Will Betray Me"

(229) Now, you should note how, in the words being examined, the verb "he testified," has reference to the statement, "One of you will betray me."

(230) For this too, which is said and prophesied to the disciples about Judas, the "one" of them, was an equivocal testimony,[204] I think, in relation to what is meant by testifying and dying on behalf of religion.

(231) For I do not think the verb "he testified" means the same thing when the verb from which the witness [martyr] of God and of his Christ is derived is meant, and now when it is referred to the statement, "One of you will betray me."[205]

(232) Further, as I am able, I also give attention to the phrase "one of you" which is referred to Judas. Does it mean that he has fallen from the apostolic order in which he too, being once in a condition similar to the other disciples, was exalted?

(233) For this is how I understand the statement, "Behold Adam has become as one of us,"[206] since it is said there, neither 'as we,' nor 'as I,' but because of the one who had fallen from blessedness, "as one of us." [And the phrase], "as one" seems to me to agree also with the statement, "But you indeed die as men,[207] and fall like one of the princes."[208] For of the many who are princes, one has fallen, with whom sinners fall in close imitation of his fall.

(234) For just as that one who partook of deity has fallen, so too have those to whom the Word says, "I have said, you are gods and all sons of the Most High,"[209] fallen from blessedness and, although they were not originally men, they die as men, and fall as one of the princes.

(235) I also think that what is said is said marvelously with the following meaning. He who betrays me is not alien

---

204. Cf. Aristotle, *Cat.* 1.
205. For the construction of this sentence, cf. *Jo.* 1.215 (FOTC 80.76).
206. Gn 3.22.
207. I have followed Brooke in omitting the dative article between the two halves of this verse.
208. Cf. Ps 81.7.  209. Ps 81.6.

from my disciples, and he is not even one of the many disciples, but he is one of the apostles honored by my choice.

(236) There are many, therefore, who condemn Jesus and say, "Crucify him, crucify him,"[210] and, "Away with such a one from the earth."[211]

(237) But to betray him was the work of one who had seen and observed him; for because he was acquainted with him as a teacher of such great and numerous teachings, which he had heard in private with the apostles, and because he knew him as Lord, when he betrayed him he betrayed his greatness, which he had known, something that one who had not beheld his greatness could not have done.

(238) For he betrayed the great one, not insofar as he is great, since he did not see him insofar as he is great; but when he had learned how great he was and had become a hearer of the greatness of the wisdom and reason and grace in him, and then betrayed him, he betrayed all his greatness insofar as he perceived it.

(239) For this reason it would have been better for him if he had not been born,[212] whether birth be understood of regeneration, as one might understand it at a deeper level, or even in the more common way. He who wishes to free himself from the problems associated with this subject, and has learned by investigation that for whom it is better, it is better when he exists, and having assumed that it would not be better for him if he did not exist, will return rather to the second interpretation and accept it as correct.

The disciples looked at one another, doubting of whom he spoke. (John 13.22)

### Judas Did Not Belong Totally to Evil

(240) If Judas' evil had been obvious to Jesus' disciples it would have been known who was to betray the teacher, since Jesus had said, "One of you will betray me."[213] But now the

210. Lk 23.21.
211. Acts 22.22.
212. Cf. Mt 26.24; Mk 14.21.
213. Jn 13.21.

disciples look "at one another, doubting of whom he spoke."

(241) Perhaps indeed the apostles were ashamed to suspect anything wicked of Judas because of his previous worthy deeds. It may have been, too, that Judas did not belong totally to evil, even though the devil had already put it in his heart that Judas Iscariot, son of Simon, should betray him.[214] It was because there was still a remnant of good choice in him that, when he saw that Jesus was condemned when "they bound him and lead him away and delivered him to Pilate the governor,"[215] he repented and returned the thirty pieces of silver to the chief priests and elders, saying, "I have sinned in betraying innocent blood."[216] When they replied, "What is that to us? You see to it,"[217] Judas, who loved money, threw the money down and "went and hanged himself."[218] He did not even wait to see the end of Jesus' judgment before Pilate.

(242) In Judas' case neither was his repentance without error, nor his evil unmixed with something better. For had his repentance been pure, even as that of the thief when he said, "Remember me, Jesus, when you come in your kingdom,"[219] he would have approached the Savior and would have done what was in his power to make atonement for the treason that had already taken place.

(243) On the other hand, if he had cast the thought of good from his soul completely, he would not have repented when he saw that Jesus was condemned, but in addition would have accused him and added words proper to his treason.

(244) And furthermore, as a lover of money, he would have enjoyed the thirty pieces of silver that he received, "the price of him who had been priced,"[220] and would not have been willing to reject the money. He would not have returned it to the chief priests and elders, nor would he have confessed before those very men, on the one hand accusing

---

214. Cf. Jn 13.2.
216. Mt 27.3–4.
218. Mt 27.5.
220. Mt 27.9.

215. Mt 27.2.
217. Mt 27.4.
219. Cf. Lk 23.42.

himself, [but on the other], praising the teacher in the statement, "I have sinned in betraying just blood."[221]

(245) But also, it was none other who made Judas hang himself than the one who had put it into his heart to betray the Savior. He gave place indeed to the devil on both counts.

(246) I have investigated these subjects as fully as I was able, partly to show those who think that Judas was incapable by nature of receiving salvation that he was not such, and partly to explain that the disciples had good reason when, at the Lord's word, they "looked at one another, doubting of whom he spoke."[222]

(247) But it is enough to quote also a prophetic text from the fortieth Psalm which proves that Judas was holy and changed for the worse, since it is written, "For even the man of my peace, in whom I hoped, who eats my bread, has kicked powerfully against me."[223]

(248) In addition, the following statement, which has reference to him, makes it clear that he was not originally an enemy. "If an enemy had reviled me, I would have borne it."[224]

(249) Furthermore the words, "If he who hated me had boasted, I would have been hidden from him,"[225] show that he once loved Jesus; and he also anticipated being of equal spirit with him, since it is written, "But you, a man of equal spirit, my guide and companion."[226]

(250) And you would also find numerous other statements that will show that the disciples, with good reason, "looked at one another, doubting of whom he spoke."

### The Disciples Doubt Themselves

(251) Luke has recorded that when the Savior said, "But behold the hand of him who betrays me is with me on the table; the Son of Man goes according to that which is determined for him, but woe to that man by whom he is be-

---

221. Cf. Mt 27.4.
223. Ps 40.10.
225. Cf. Ps 54.13.
222. Cf. Jn 13.22.
224. Ps 54.13.
226. Cf. Ps 54.14.

trayed,"[227] the disciples "began to discuss among themselves which of them, then, it might be who was to do this."[228] For they discussed it, "doubting of whom he spoke."

(252) Now, according to Luke it does not appear that each one also suspected himself; but according to Matthew and Mark even this is presented.

(253) For Matthew says, "And being exceedingly troubled, they began to say, Is it I, Lord?"[229]

(254) And Mark says, "They began to be troubled, and to say to him one by one, Is it I? And another, Is it I?"[230]

(255) For they remembered, I think, being men, that the choice of those still advancing is changeable and susceptible to willing the opposite to what it formerly preferred.

(256) But perhaps, too, since they had learned with what powers we wrestle,[231] they were cautious because of the uncertainty in men, lest perhaps they be overcome and take upon themselves even the betrayal of their teacher.

(257) For even Peter did not intend to deny Jesus when he strongly affirmed, "Although all shall be scandalized in you, I will not be scandalized."[232] But he was overcome by the spirit of deceit and denied him three times before the cock crow.

(258) Such words teach us, "Let him who stands take heed lest he fall,"[233] and "Boast not for tomorrow for you do not know what the coming day will bring forth."[234] It may be too that the statement, "The disciples looked at one another," makes something like what follows clear to one who has a more simple understanding. Each one, so far as human nature is able, looked into the choice of the other, raising the question if the soul that had done such things and was so disposed in respect to the unerring teacher, seeing that he had testified truly when he said, "Truly, truly I say to you that one of you will betray me,"[235] can be turned aside so far,

227. Cf. Lk 22.21–22.
228. Cf. Lk 22.23.
229. Cf. Mt 26.22.
230. Cf. Mk 14.19.
231. Cf. Eph 6.12.
232. Cf. Mt 26.33; Mk 14.29.
233. Cf. 1 Cor 10.12.
234. Cf. Prv 27.1.
235. Jn 13.21.

and forget the teachings of the teacher, even to the point of betraying him.

(259) For the phrase about the disciples, "doubting of whom he spoke," is vivid. For they were unable to conceive of whom this had been said, and were in doubt about it, and found nothing clear either to think or say.

> There was leaning on Jesus' breast one of his disciples, whom Jesus loved. Simon Peter, therefore, beckons to this man and says to him, Tell me who it is of whom he speaks. He leaned on Jesus' breast and said to him, Lord, who is it? Jesus, therefore answered, It is he with whom I shall dip the morsel. Therefore, when he dipped the morsel, he took it and gave to Judas Iscariot, son of Simon, and after the morsel then Satan entered him. Therefore, Jesus says to him, What you do, do quickly. But no one of those reclining knew why he said this to him. For some thought, since Judas had the money box, that Jesus was saying to him, Buy what we need for the feast, or that he should give something to the poor. (John 13.23–29)

### The Disciple Whom Jesus Loved

(260) It is likely that the one reclining on Jesus' breast, one of the disciples whom Jesus loved, was John, who wrote the Gospel. For at the end of the Gospel it is written, "Peter turned and saw the disciple whom Jesus loved following, who also leaned on Jesus' breast at the supper, and said, Lord, who is it who betrays you? Therefore when Peter saw, he said to Jesus, Lord, and what about this man? Jesus says to him, If I wish him to remain until I come, what is that to you? You follow me. Therefore the word went out to the brethren that that disciple was not going to die. But Jesus did not say to him that he was not going to die, but, If I wish him to remain until I come, what is that to you?"[236]

(261) Now, that this disciple was John who wrote the

---

236. Jn 21.20–23.

Gospel is clear from the words which are added, which go as follows, "This is the disciple who also testifies of these things, who wrote these things."[237]

(262) But observe in both passages in the Gospel how Peter, since he is bolder and inclined towards him, in the one passage, "beckons to him and says, Tell me who it is of whom Jesus says he will betray him," and in the other passage, when he saw him following,[238] because he thought him superior to the rest, asks Jesus about him, "Lord, and what about this man?"[239] He wants to learn John's end along with knowing the things about himself, namely that when he grows old he will stretch out his hands and another will gird him and carry him where he does not wish.[240]

(263) But if the words that Jesus spoke were spirit and not letter, there is life in their entirety, and no death at all, and if, in imitation of him, the disciple whom he loved records spirit and life, we must hear the statement, "There was leaning on Jesus' breast one of his disciples" in a manner worthy of the honor which it is fitting to give the Son of God, and of the one loved by him to receive.

### The Bosom of Jesus

(264) I think that if indeed John was at that time reclining symbolically on the bosom of Jesus, having been considered worthy of this privilege because he was judged worthy of remarkable love from the teacher, this symbolism shows that John, by reclining on the Word and resting on more mystical things, was reclining in the bosom of the Word, analogous also to the Word being in the bosom of the Father, according to the statement, "The only-begotten God, who is in the bosom of the Father, he has declared him."[241]

(265) And unless we take the following statement in a more lowly manner, "And it came to pass that the poor man died and was carried by the angels into the bosom of Abraham,"[242] we shall understand some such thing also about the

237. Cf. Jn 21.24.
239. Jn 21.21.
241. Cf. Jn 1.18.
238. Cf. Jn 21.20.
240. Cf. Jn 21.18.
242. Cf. Lk 16.22.

bosom of Abraham. If we interpret[243] it in this way, we will have to make a defense against the difficulty that arises from ignorance of the Scripture, which has been mentioned by the one who wanted to reject our interpretation of the rich man and poor man. For if Lazarus were reclining in the bosom of Abraham, he says, then before he died another would have been in the bosom of Abraham, and before that one, another.

(266) But he also says the poor man will get up to make room when another just man expires. For he who raises difficulties concerning these matters has not beheld the bosom of Abraham, and the fact that it is possible for tens of thousands to rest in the bosom of Abraham at the same time, sharing in the things that have been revealed to him.

(267) But if you shall demand that we cite another passage from Scripture which contains the word "bosom," come, let us examine how the Lord said to Moses, "Again put your hand into your bosom. And he put his hand into his bosom and brought it out of his bosom, and his hand was leprous as snow. And he said, Put your hand into your bosom. And he put his hand into his bosom, and brought it out of his bosom, and it was again restored to the color of his flesh."[244]

(268) It is difficult to see what this sign can symbolize for us. But since we must not stop seeking, and must deliver to the reader what occurs to us as an interpretation, we will say that in many passages the hand is a symbol of deeds. Now the bosom of Moses has two meanings. The first, in accordance with the sense of the letter, makes the deed of the doer like snow, as it says in the Hebrew, and leprous. The second, however, in accordance with the spiritual law, shows that the conduct is pure, and that it is restored to the will of the nature of the Word.

(269) Observe that it is added to these words, "If they should not believe you, nor hear the voice of the first sign, they will believe the voice of your second sign."[245] For he

243. I have followed Brooke's text here.
244. Cf. Ex 4.6–7.   245. Cf. Ex 4.8.

who did not believe in the interpretation of the letter because of the loftiness of his mind, believes in the spiritual interpretation of the law.

(270) But if someone should not believe in these two signs, in the first, that makes the deed leprous, and in the second that restores it to the natural state, the water becomes blood for him.

(271) For it is written, "And it shall be, if they should not believe in these two signs, nor hear your voice, you shall take from the water of the river and pour it out upon the dry ground, and the water which you took from the river will be blood on the dry ground."[246]

(272) Now, notice also that in the case of this sign it is no longer said, "they will believe you," or, "they will not believe."

(273) For it is made clear that the water taken from the river becomes blood for the one who did not believe in these two signs and who cannot enjoy the fresh water of the Word because of his unbelief.

(274) But indeed, since we have ascertained in the passage more than what is necessary concerning the bosom of Jesus, let us return to the task at hand and, since we have learned that he whom Jesus loved was reclining in the bosom of Jesus, let us do all things that we may be reckoned in his choice love; for in this way shall we too recline in the bosom of Jesus. But Simon Peter beckons to the beloved disciple, and not being satisfied with beckoning, says to him, "Tell me who it is of whom he speaks."

(275) Now, beckoning is taken as slander in Proverbs, for the wicked man "beckons with his eyes," it says, "and makes signs with his foot, and teaches with signs of his fingers, and devises evil with his perverse heart,"[247] and, "He who beckons with his eyes deceitfully gathers griefs for men."[248] For this reason, therefore, we must say that it is not beckoning that is wicked, but beckoning with the eye, which means to turn the eye aside and not to look straight; to beckon deceit-

---

246. Ex 4.9.
248. Prv 10.10.
247. Cf. Prv 6.13–14.

fully is also blameworthy. Peter's act, however, was to beckon out of his eagerness for knowledge, and subsequent to such beckoning, to say to his fellow-disciple, since he was more intimate with the teacher, "Tell me who it is of whom he speaks."

(276) For he wished, perhaps, to perceive the mystery concerning Judas' betrayal of Jesus. That Peter might learn this, John, although he formerly reclined on Jesus' bosom, moved up and leaned on his breast.

(277) Perhaps he would not have delivered the word that John or Peter wished to learn to one who did not lean on his breast, but continued to recline on his bosom.

(278) Therefore, although he formerly reclined in Jesus' bosom, but later leaned on Jesus' breast, the genuine disciple of Jesus is characterized in the final words of the Gospel by the second act, since it is greater and superior.

(279) For it is written, "Peter turned and saw the disciple whom Jesus loved following, who also leaned on his breast at the supper, and said, Lord, who is it who betrays you?"[249] For it is not written, 'Who was reclining on Jesus' bosom.'

*"It Is He with Whom I Shall Dip the Morsel"*

(280) But let us also see what the Lord said when he answered. "He it is," he says, "with whom I shall dip the morsel and give it to him." Jesus said this, then, and "when he had dipped the morsel, he took it and gave it to Judas, son of Simon Iscariot."

(281) And after the morsel, then Satan entered him. He had not been able to enter earlier, not even at the moment he put it into his heart that Judas Iscariot, son of Simon, should betray him.

(282) For I think it was necessary, by the gift of the morsel to take back that better gift from the unworthy man, which he seemed to have, for even what he seems to have will be taken from him who does not have.[250]

(283) Judas, therefore, when he had been removed, be-

249. Jn 21.20.
250. Cf. Mt 25.29; Lk 8.18.

cause he was unworthy, from the greater gift of the one who addressed him, admitted the entrance of Satan into himself.

(284) Now, as an example, to understand how the Lord gave a morsel to Judas, and Judas then laid aside something better that was in him, perhaps even peace, which returns to the speaker from the one who hears it and does not accept it, according to the words, "If there be a son of peace there, your peace shall rest upon him, but if there is not a son of peace there, your peace shall return to you,"[251] we shall quote the following words from the Second Epistle to the Corinthians, "Let your abundance supply their want, that also their abundance may supply your want."[252]

(285) For when you have perceived the exchange of earthly things for spiritual in these words, you will be able to see how he gave a morsel to the one unworthy of bread, that by means of the morsel he might take peace away from him since he was unworthy of continuing to hear the words, "For even the man of my peace"[253] ("for let him that is filthy be filthy still"[254]). Once his peace was removed, the one who was watching for opportunities to enter his soul [entered] Judas, who also gave him a place to enter.[255]

(286) Now observe at the same time that Satan did not enter Judas earlier, but only put it into his heart "that Judas Iscariot, son of Simon, should betray the teacher."[256] According to what is now being examined, he entered him after the morsel.

(287) Wherefore, let us also be on guard that the devil may not put it into our heart by one of his fiery darts,[257] for if he does this, he afterwards watches to enter himself.

(288) But someone may ask why it is not written, 'It is he to whom I shall give the morsel,' but is instead written with the addition, "I shall dip." For he says, "I shall dip the morsel and give it."

(289) And "when he had dipped the morsel he took it

251. Cf. Lk 10.6.
253. Ps 40.10.
255. Cf. Eph 4.27.
257. Cf. Eph 6.16.

252. 2 Cor 8.14.
254. Cf. Rv 22.11.
256. Cf. Jn 13.2.

and gave it to Judas Iscariot, son of Simon." As in such passages, note if you can say that the pure bread is undipped and is nourishing in itself, but the morsel that was given to Judas was neither bread nor an undipped morsel, but one that had been dipped by him who could withdraw from his soul the tincture of the Word that was in it for a while, so that after the morsel Satan might enter him.

(290) Now I would investigate, as related to this, that statement from the Gospel according to Matthew, "He who dips his hand with me in the dish, he will betray me,"[258] and that from the Gospel according to Mark, "He who dips with me in the dish,"[259] and that also from the Gospel according to Luke, although he does not mention the word "dipped," but insofar as he says, at least, "But behold, the hand of my betrayer is with me on the table."[260]

(291) Those much wiser than me may discover the true explanation of this, but I offer a conjecture. Perhaps Judas' shamelessness is manifest even in this, since he neither honors the teacher by eating with him, nor does he give place to him in respect of dipping into the dish, as the others gave place.

(292) Wherefore, none of those dipped a hand into the dish with him, but this man, who was not worthy to dip with them, dipped with him, because he wished to have equality with him, although he should have given place to him in respect of pre-eminence.

(293) Perhaps, then, this statement too pertains to the same man, "But behold the hand of my betrayer is with me on the table."[261] But also, to be polite at certain times and to encourage young men concerning the honor of elders at a banquet, one will use this saying to mean that they not reach their hand with the elders. For this also has been written, "Reach not with him in the dish."[262]

(294) Although we are not unaware of the [possible] opinion, by those who hear these words, that this is a curi-

258. Cf. Mt 26.23.
260. Lk 22.21.
262. Cf. Sir 31.14.

259. Mk 14.20.
261. Lk 22.21.

ous investigation and a defense incapable of convincing the hearer to appropriate it, we have ventured these remarks because we think it is better to test all things than to pass anything by untested that has been written.

*"What You Do, Do Quickly"*

(295) When Satan had entered Judas, however, it says, "Jesus says to him, What you do, do quickly." Now it is ambiguous to whom the expression "to him" refers, since the Lord could have said either to Judas himself, or to Satan, "What you do, do quickly," thus summoning the opponent to the battle, or summoning the betrayer to render his service to the economy [of suffering] that was to bring salvation to the world. He no longer wished this economy to be imminent, nor to tarry, but as much as possible, to hasten. He was not afraid, as some think, who have not understood in what way he says, "Father, if it is possible, let this cup pass,"[263] but, if I may put it this way, he stripped down for the contest most confidently.

(296) Now, I also think the twenty-sixth Psalm prophesies of the person of the Savior precisely at the time of his Passion, and also of the evil one, with all his forces, when he struggles against him. He sees these forces equipped and prepared for combat against him, when "the kings of the earth were present, and the princes were gathered together, against the Lord, and against his Christ,"[264] and he says, "The Lord is my light, and the Lord is my Savior, whom shall I fear? The Lord is the protector of my life, of whom shall I be afraid? When the wicked draw near against me to devour my flesh, those who afflict me and my enemies themselves have grown weak and fallen. If a company of soldiers be drawn up against me, my heart will not fear. If war arise against me, in this I hope."[265]

(297) But none of those reclining knew why the statement, "What you do, do quickly," which was said either to Satan or to Judas, was made.

263. Cf. Mt 26.39, and *Cels.* 2.24.  264. Ps 2.2.
265. Cf. Ps 26.1–3.

398                    ORIGEN

(298) For some, because the feast of the Pasch was imminent, thought he said to the one who had the money-box for expenses and gifts for the needs of the poor, that he should buy what was needed for the feast, or give some of what had been collected to the poor.[266]

(299) For Jesus did not say this, but when he beheld the one who entered and the one who received him, and the whole plot against him, he stripped down for the fight, and in order to prevail against the wicked one for the salvation of men, he said, "What you do, do quickly."

Therefore when he had received the morsel, he went out immediately; and it was night. (John 13.30)

*It Is Not Said That Judas Ate the Morsel*

(300) The Savior said to Judas, "What you do, do quickly,"[267] and now in this alone the betrayer obeys the teacher. For when he had received the morsel, he neither hesitated nor tarried, but as it is written, "He went out immediately" to do quickly the work of betrayal in accordance with Jesus' command.

(301) And "he went out" truly, for he not only went out of the house in which the supper was held, according to the simpler meaning, but he also went out from Jesus in a final sense, analogous to the statement, "They went out from us."[268]

(302) I think that Satan, who entered Judas after the morsel, could not bear to be in the same place with Jesus, for there is no "concord between Christ and Belial."[269]

(303) But unless I am conducting a useless investigation, you yourself also will give attention to why the words, "and ate," are not added to the phrase, "when he had received the morsel."

(304) For where the Word wishes, he adds also "to eat" to the phrase to "receive," as it is written in the case of the

266. Cf. Jn 13.29.
268. Cf. 1 Jn 2.19.
267. Jn 13.27.
269. 2 Cor 6.15.

bread of blessing that Jesus said to his disciples, "Take, eat."[270]

(305) Did Judas, then, not eat when he had received the morsel? Come then, although there will appear to be no agreement between what will be said and what was said previously, let us examine the matters according to the passage, while what is read determines what we must accept of the things that are said.

(306) Jesus, it says, "dipped the morsel."[271] It is clear that he took it after he had left it in the dish, for this is the way you will understand the words, "therefore when he had dipped the morsel," in order that the verb "to take" not be superfluous.

(307) Then it is said that "he gave it to Judas, son of Simon Iscariot. And after the morsel, then Satan entered him."[272] "After the morsel," therefore, which perhaps was not eaten by Judas, Satan entered Judas because he anticipated the usefulness of the morsel, lest Judas be benefitted by Jesus' gift of the morsel.

(308) For it had beneficial power for the one who used it; but he who once put it into his heart to betray the teacher, fearing lest what was put in fall out of the recipient through the use of the morsel, anticipated this and entered Judas at the same time as he received the morsel, when also the statement was made, "What you do, do quickly." Judas, therefore, when he had received the morsel, "went out immediately."

(309) Consequently, it might be said in relation to this passage, and not without persuasion, that just as he who eats the bread of the Lord or drinks his cup unworthily eats and drinks to judgment,[273] the one supernatural[274] power in the bread and in the cup producing what is better when the underlying disposition is better, but producing judgment when

---

270. Mt 26.26. The Greek verb is the same here ("to take") as that rendered "to receive" earlier in the paragraph.
271. Cf. Jn 13.26.   272. Jn 13.26–27.
273. Cf. 1 Cor 11.27–29.
274. This is Gögler's understanding of κρείττων here.

it is worse, so the morsel from Jesus was of the same kind with that which was also given to the rest of the apostles with the statement, "Take, eat."[275] To the others it was for salvation, but to Judas it was for judgment, because Satan entered him after the morsel.

(310) Let the simple understand the bread and the cup according to the more common interpretation concerning the Eucharist, but let those who have learned to hear in a deeper way understand them in accordance with the promise that is more excellent and concerns the nourishing word of truth. It is as if I had said, as an example, that the bread that is most nourishing in the physical sense will increase the underlying fever, but on the other hand, it restores one to health and vigor.

(311) Wherefore, frequently, when the true word is given to a soul that is sick and is not in need of such food, it afflicts that soul, and causes its condition to worsen. Consequently, it is dangerous to speak even the truth.[276]

(312) Now I have said these things [because of] the morsel that Jesus dipped and "gave to Judas Iscariot, son of Simon."[277] We have discussed the subject from each side. Must we say that he ate the morsel after he received it? Or, was he prevented by Satan who entered Judas?

### *"And It Was Night"*

(313) But if we must also examine the statement, "And it was night," so that it has not been interjected in vain by the Evangelist, we must say that the perceptible night at that time was symbolical, being an image of the night that was in Judas' soul when Satan, the darkness that lies over the abyss,[278] entered him. "For God called the darkness night,"[279] of which night, indeed, Paul says we are not children, nor of darkness, when he says, "Therefore, brothers we are not of

---

275. Mt 26.26.
276. See our note above, Book 20, fn. 7.
277. Cf. Jn 13.26.
278. Cf. Gn 1.2.
279. Cf. Gn 1.5.

the night, nor of darkness,"²⁸⁰ and, "But let us who are of the day be sober."²⁸¹

(314) There was no night, therefore, but brightest day, for those who allowed their feet to be washed by Jesus, who were cleansed and allowed the filth on the feet of their soul to be cast aside. And there was no night par excellence in the one who reclined on Jesus' breast, for Jesus loved him,²⁸² and destroyed all darkness with his love.

(315) Nor was there night in Peter when he confessed, "You are the Christ, the Son of the living God,"²⁸³ when the heavenly Father revealed it to him, but there was night in him too at the moment of his denial.²⁸⁴

(316) And in the present instance, moreover, when Judas received the morsel [and] went out immediately, night was present in him at the time he went out, for the man whose name is "Sunrise"²⁸⁵ was not present with him because he left "the sun of justice"²⁸⁶ behind when he went out. And Judas, who was filled with darkness, pursued Jesus; but the darkness and the one who had taken it up did not apprehend the light that was pursued.²⁸⁷

(317) Wherefore, also, when he said as a word of justification, "I have sinned because I betrayed just blood,"²⁸⁸ and "went and hanged himself,"²⁸⁹ Satan, who was in him, led him to the noose and hung him, at which time the devil also touched his soul. For Judas was not such that the Lord could say to the devil on his behalf what he said on Job's behalf, "But touch not his soul."²⁹⁰

---

280. Cf. 1 Thes 5.4, 5.
281. 1 Thes 5.8.
282. Cf. Jn 13.23.
283. Mt 16.16.
284. Cf. Mt 26.69–74.
285. Cf. Zec 6.12. The word is Ἀνατολή, and can also mean the east, i.e. the place where the sun rises.
286. Mal 3.20 (LXX; 4.2 Douay).
287. Cf. Jn 1.5.
288. Cf. Mt 27.4.
289. Mt 27.5.
290. Cf. Job 1.12; 2.6.

> When, therefore, he went out Jesus said, Now is the
> Son of Man glorified, and God is glorified in him. If
> God be glorified in him, God will also glorify him in
> himself, and he will glorify him immediately.
> (John 13.31–32)

### *"Now Is the Son of Man Glorified"*

(318) Judas' departure, along with Satan who had entered him, from the place where Jesus was marked the beginning of the glorification of the Son of Man after the glories in his signs and wonders and that in the transfiguration.

(319) This is why the Lord said, "Now is the Son of Man glorified." In addition the Savior also said, "If I be lifted up from the earth, I will draw all men to myself,"[291] showing "by what death he would glorify God,"[292] for he also glorified God in dying.

(320) This is why he says, "Now is the Son of Man glorified," at the time the beginning of the economy [of suffering] wherein Jesus was to die was actualized, when Judas had gone out after the morsel to transact his business against Jesus.

(321) Then, because it is not possible that the Christ be glorified if the Father is not glorified in him, the statement, "And God is glorified in him," is added to the words, "Now is the Son of Man glorified."

(322) But the glory that resulted from his death for men did not belong to the only-begotten Word, which by nature does not die, nor to wisdom and truth, nor any of the other titles that are said to belong to the divine aspects in Jesus, but belonged to the man who was also the Son of Man born of the seed of David according to the flesh.[293]

(323) For this reason he said earlier, "Now you seek to kill me, a man who has spoken the truth to you."[294] In the words we are examining, however, he says, "Now is the Son of Man glorified."

(324) Now I think God also highly exalted this man when

---

291. Jn 12.32.
293. Cf. Rom 1.3.
292. Jn 21.19.
294. Cf. Jn 8.40.

he became obedient "unto death, and the death of a cross."²⁹⁵ For the Word in the beginning with God, God the Word,²⁹⁶ was not capable of being highly exalted.

(325) But the high exaltation of the Son of Man which occurred when he glorified God in his own death consisted in the fact that he was no longer different from the Word, but was the same with him.

(326) For if "he who is joined to the Lord is one spirit,"²⁹⁷ so that it is no longer said that "they are two" even in the case of this man and the spirit, might we not much more say that the humanity of Jesus became one with the Word when he who did not consider "equality with God"²⁹⁸ something to be grasped was highly exalted? The Word, however, remained in his own grandeur, or was even restored to it, when he was again with God, God the Word being man.

(327) But if Jesus glorified God in death, and "when he had despoiled the principalities and powers, he exposed them confidently, having triumphed in the cross,"²⁹⁹ and, "having made peace through the blood of his cross, whether in respect to the things on earth or the things in heaven,"³⁰⁰ ...³⁰¹ for in all these the Son of Man was glorified, and God was glorified in him.

(328) Now, since he who is glorified is glorified by someone, you will ask who this is in the statement, "The Son of Man is glorified." You will ask the same thing also in the statement, "God is glorified in him."

(329) Now, for the sake of clarity, let us give careful attention to what is said in the first proposition, "Now is the Son of Man glorified"; and in the second, "And God is glorified in him"; and in the third, which is a conditional proposition³⁰² as follows, "If God be glorified in him, God

---

295. Phil 2.8.  
296. Cf. Jn 1.1.  
297. Cf. 1 Cor 6.17.  
298. Phil 2.6.  
299. Cf. Col 2.15.  
300. Col 1.20.  
301. The main verb is lacking in the sentence.  
302. Origen here employs a technical term from Stoic logic, συνημ-μένον, which Mates, *Stoic Logic*, 135, defines as "a molecular proposition compounded by means of the connective 'if.'" The same word occurs twice in the following sentence in paragraph 330.

will also glorify him in himself"; and in the fourth, "And he will glorify him immediately."

(330) One might perhaps construe this latter proposition as a conjunctive proposition[303] which is the consequent[304] of the conditional proposition, so that the conditional begins after[305] the proposition, "God is glorified in him," and concludes with the conjunctive proposition, "And God will glorify him in himself, and he will glorify him immediately."[306]

### The Meaning of "Glory"

Now we must turn our attention to the noun "glory," which is not used with reference to an indifferent entity, in the way some of the Greeks take it,[307] wherefore they define glory to be approval by the multitude. It is clear that the noun is used of something over and above this from the following words in Exodus.

(331) "And the tabernacle was filled with the glory of the Lord. And Moses was not able to enter the tabernacle of testimony because the cloud overshadowed it and the tabernacle was filled with the glory of the Lord."[308]

(332) The following has also been recorded in the Third Book of Kings. "And it came to pass when the priests came out of the sanctuary, and the cloud filled the house of the Lord.

---

303. συμπλοκήν is another technical term of Stoic logic which, according to Mates, *Stoic Logic,* 135, refers to "a molecular proposition compounded by means of the connective 'and.'" On Origen's argument in this section, see my discussion in R. E. Heine, "Stoic Logic as Handmaid," JTS n.s. 44 (1993): 110–17.

304. λήγοντι, another term from Stoic logic. See Mates, *Stoic Logic,* 134.

305. ἀπό, lit.: "from," i.e. the conditional begins from *the end of* this proposition.

306. I have followed Brooke in putting a full stop here. Preuschen has only a comma. There is, however, a rather abrupt change of subject at this point.

307. The Stoics classed δόξα ("glory," "reputation") among indifferent things (see D. L. 7.104 and SVF I.190). See B. Neuschäfer, *Origenes als Philologe.* SBA 1 and 2. (Basel: Friedrich Reinhardt, 1987), 150–51, 406–7.

308. Ex 40.34–35.

(333) "And the priests could not stand ministering[309] before the cloud, because the glory of the Lord filled the house."[310]

(334) The following things have also been said of Moses' glory in Exodus. "And when Moses descended from the mountain, and the two tablets of the covenant were in Moses' hands; and when he descended from the mountain Moses also did not know that the appearance of his facial skin had been glorified while he spoke with him. And Aaron and all the sons of Israel saw Moses, and the appearance of his facial skin had been glorified. And they were afraid to come near him."[311]

(335) This meaning of glory is also revealed in the Gospel according to Luke in the words, "And while he prayed the appearance of his face became different, and his garment was changed and became gleaming white. And behold two men were speaking with him, who were Moses and Elijah, who appeared in glory and spoke of his departure, which he was to accomplish in Jerusalem."[312]

(336) And notice also the things to which Paul refers with the noun "glory." In this passage he says, "Now if the ministration of death, engraved with letters on stone was glorious, so that the sons of Israel did not look at Moses' face because of the glory of his face, which glory is made void, how shall not the ministration of the Spirit be rather in glory? For if there is glory in the ministration of condemnation, much more the ministration of justice abounds in glory. For even that which was glorious in this part has not been glorified because of the exceeding glory. For if that which is made void came to be through glory, by how much more is that which abides in glory?"[313] In another passage he says, "But we all, beholding the glory of the Lord with un-

---

309. λειτουργίαν. The LXX has an infinitive, "to minister," where Origen has the noun, "ministry."
310. Cf. 3 Kgs (1 Kgs) 8.10–11.
311. Cf. Ex 34.29–30.
312. Cf. Lk 9.29–31.
313. Cf. 2 Cor 3.7–11.

veiled face are transformed into the same image from glory to glory, just as by the Lord who is the Spirit."[314]

(337) And again, a few words later, "And if our gospel has been veiled, it has been veiled among those who are perishing, in whom the god of this world has blinded the minds of the unbelievers, that the light of the gospel of the glory of Christ, who is the image of God, might not illuminate them."[315]

(338) And again, after a few more words, "For it is the God who said, Let light shine out of darkness, who has shone in our hearts for a light of the knowledge of the glory of God in the face of Jesus Christ."[316] The interpretation of the text of the Gospel that is proposed does not demand that we explain each of these statements carefully now. But we must make the following remarks in as few words as possible. So far as the literal sense is concerned, there was a divine epiphany in the tabernacle and in the temple, which were destroyed, and in the face of Moses when he had conversed with the Divine Nature. But so far as the anagogical sense is concerned, the things that are accurately known of God might also be referred to as the visible glory of God that is contemplated by that mind which has the aptitude for such contemplation because of its pre-eminent purification, since the mind that has been purified and has ascended above all material things, that it may scrupulously contemplate God, is made divine by what it contemplates.

(339) We must say that this is what is meant when it is said that the face of the one who contemplated God, conversed with him, and spent time with such a vision, was glorified. Consequently, the figurative meaning of the glorification of Moses' face is that his mind was made godlike.

(340) It is in this same sense that the Apostle said, "But we all, beholding the glory of the Lord with unveiled face are transformed into the same image."[317]

(341) And just as the brightness of the nocturnal light is

---

314. 2 Cor 3.18.
316. 2 Cor 4.6.
315. Cf. 2 Cor 4.3–4.
317. 2 Cor 3.18.

obscured when the sun has risen, so the glory of Moses is obscured by that which is in Christ.

(342) For the superiority in Christ, knowing which he glorified the Father concerning himself, admitted of no comparison with what was known by Moses, and which glorified the face of his soul.

(343) This is why the glory of Moses is said to be made void by the surpassing glory in Christ.

(344) But since we have made these remarks in as few words as we were able in reference to the words that we quoted, let us return to the statement, "Now is the Son of Man glorified, and God is glorified in him."

### "And God Is Glorified in Him"

(345) In that the Son, therefore, knows the Father, he is glorified by him because he knows him, since such perfect knowledge as the Son has of the Father is the greatest good.[318]

(346) [But] I think that also because he knew himself, which itself does not fall far short of the former, he was glorified as a result of having known himself.

(347) And if knowledge of the universe completes the greatness of his glory who knows all things that are hidden and manifest, you will ask also whether this may be what it means to be absolute wisdom, or for the so-called very Son of Man to be glorified by being made one with wisdom. But he is glorified when the Father has bestowed all this glory with which the Son of Man is glorified.

(348) And while there are many things that constitute the complete glory of man, God is the most outstanding of all these, who is glorified not simply by being known by the Son, but is glorified in the Son.

(349) Concerning this, it is presumptuous and beyond our ability to devote ourselves to the examination of such a great teaching. Nevertheless, we must presume to suggest what[319] can be investigated in the passage.

---

318. Conjectural translation. The text is corrupt at this point.
319. I have accepted Brooke's emendation of τὸν to τὸ Concerning God's contemplation of himself, see above, Introduction, par. 42.

(350) Now, I ask if it is possible that God is glorified, in addition to being glorified in the Son as we have explained, in a greater manner in himself, when he engages in self-contemplation on the basis of that knowledge and contemplation of himself, which surpasses the contemplation in the Son. Because we must think such things in the case of God, we must say that he is gladdened with a certain ineffable satisfaction, gladness, and joy, and that he is pleased with himself and rejoices.

(351) Now, I use these terms, which would not properly be applied to God, because I am at a loss, if I may put it this way, for those unutterable words which he alone, and after him his Only-Begotten, can speak or think in their proper sense about himself.

(352) Now, since we have been on the subject of God being glorified in Christ, we might investigate next how he might be glorified also in the Holy Spirit, and in all those to whom the glory of the Lord has appeared or will appear.

(353) In my opinion, the Son is the reflection of the total glory of God himself, according to Paul who said, "Who, being the reflection of his glory,"[320] anticipating, however, a partial reflection on the rest of the rational creation from this reflection of the total glory. For I do not think that anyone except his Son can contain the whole reflection of the full glory of God.

(354) Now, therefore, when the economy of the suffering of the Son of Man for all men occurs, it is not without God,[321] "wherefore God has highly exalted him."[322] It does not say "the Son of Man is glorified," alone, for indeed "God is glorified in him."[323] One might interpret the matters in this passage as follows.

(355) It has been written, "No one has known the Son, except the Father,"[324] and it is said, "And blessed are you,

---

320. Heb 1.3.
321. Cf. Heb 2.9, where some New Testament MSS. have "without God" instead of "by the grace of God." See above, Introduction, pars. 55–61.
322. Cf. Phil 2.9.     323. Cf. Jn 13.31.
324. Cf. Mt 11.27.

Simon Bar-Jona, because flesh and blood did not reveal it to you, but my heavenly Father."[325]

(356) Insofar, then, as the Son has not been known by the world ("For he was in the world and the world was made by him, and the world knew him not"[326]), he has not yet been glorified in the world. And the loss from the fact that he was not glorified in the world did not fall on him who was not glorified, but on the world which did not glorify him.

(357) But when the heavenly Father revealed the knowledge of Jesus to those who were from the world, then the Son of Man was glorified in those who knew him, and by means of the glory with which he was glorified in those who knew him, he brought about a glory for those who knew him. For those who behold the glory of the Lord with unveiled face are transformed into the same image.[327]

(358) And observe that it mentions from where, namely "from glory," and to where, namely "to glory." "From glory" is said of the glory of the one who is glorified; "to glory" means the glory of those who glorify.

(359) When, then, he came to the economy [of suffering], beginning with which he was to rise up for the world, and because he was aware that he would be glorified over and above the glory of those glorifying him, he said, "Now is the Son of Man glorified," and further, "No one has known the Father except the Son, and he to whom the Son may reveal him."[328] But the Son was about to reveal the Father by means of the economy [of suffering], wherefore he said, "And God is glorified in him." Or, you shall compare the words, "And God is glorified in him" with the statement, "He who has seen me has seen the Father who sent me."[329] For the Father who begot him is contemplated in the Word, since the Word is God and the image of the invisible God,[330] and he who beholds the image of the invisible God is able to behold the Father directly, too, for he is the prototype of the image.

325. Cf. Mt 16.17.
327. Cf. 2 Cor 3.18.
329. Cf. Jn 14.9; 12.45.
326. Cf. Jn 1.10.
328. Cf. Mt 11.27.
330. Cf. Jn 1.1; Col 1.15.

(360) But the matters in this passage might be understood even more clearly as follows. Just as the name of God is blasphemed among the Gentiles because of some,[331] so, because of the saints whose good works are seen very distinctly before men,[332] the name of the Father who is in heaven is glorified.

(361) In whom, then, was it glorified to the extent that it was in Jesus, since he committed no sin nor was deceit found in his mouth, nor did he know sin?[333]

(362) And since he is such as this, therefore, the Son is glorified, and God is glorified in him.

(363) But if God is glorified in him, the Father presents something to him in return that is greater than what the Son of Man has done. For the fact that the Son of Man is glorified in God, the lesser in the greater, is greater for the one who glorifies God, who is superior to the lesser, according to the statement, "The Father who sent me is greater than me."[334]

(364) Indeed, the glory is much more excessive in the Son when the Father glorifies him than it is in the Father when the Father is glorified in the Son.

(365) And it is fitting indeed that the one who is greater, in repaying the glory with which the Son glorified him, grants to the Son what he said, namely, to "glorify him in himself,"[335] that the Son might be glorified in God. Since, then, these things were not yet to take place (I mean for the Son to be glorified in God), he adds, "And he will glorify him immediately."

(366) Now, we are not unaware that these words fall far short of what the passage being examined contains, since it is God who reveals, and the Word himself who appears that he may present the glory of God, and the Father grants that the whole glory of God be known to whomever he can grant it.

---

331. Cf. Rom 2.24.
332. Cf. Mt 5.16.
333. Cf. 1 Pt 2.22; 2 Cor 5.21.
334. Cf. Jn 14.28.
335. Jn 13.32b.

(367) Wherefore, as briefly as possible, and much more humbly than the worth of the words, we give thanks to God for the things that have been expounded, things that are much greater than we deserve.

> Little children, yet a little while I am with you; you will seek me, [and] as I said to the Jews, where I am you cannot come, I also say to you now. (John 13.33)

*First a Disciple, Then a Little Child, Then a Brother of Christ*

(368) Having gathered from the Gospels the words of our Savior spoken to children as by a father, fear not to say that the Savior is a father of certain ones. For to the paralytic he says, "Fear not, child, your sins are forgiven";[336] and to the hemorrhaging woman, "Daughter, your faith has saved you";[337] and now he says to the disciples, "Little children." The diminutive is significant, I think, and teaches the smallness of the apostles' soul even at that time.

(369) Now someone may ask, "Since, then, the paralytic is called 'child,' was he more mature than those to whom the Word says, 'Little children'?" You will understand in this case that if someone is a little child, he is certainly a child.

(370) For this reason the paralytic, who is called a child, is not excluded from being a little child too, so that the paralytic, who is designated a child does not have to be more mature than those whom the Word addressed as little children.

(371) But you must understand that it is not impossible to change from being a child of Jesus to become his brother, as, on the human level, it would not be possible for a child later to become a brother of him of whom he was first a child.

(372) After the Savior's Resurrection, these, at any rate, who were addressed as "little children" become brothers of him who earlier called them little children, as if they were changed by Jesus' Resurrection.

---

336. Cf. Mt 9.2.   337. Cf. Mt 9.22.

(373) This is why it is written, "Go to my brothers, and say to them, I am ascending to my Father and to your Father, and to my God and your God."[338]

(374) Perhaps it is also possible in the same way[339] to change from being a servant of Jesus. Now, the disciples were servants before they were little children, as is clear from the words, "You call me Teacher and Lord, and you speak correctly, for so I am,"[340] and the words, "A servant is not greater than his lord,"[341] which precede the words, "Little children, yet a little while I am with you." But you will notice if the servant first becomes a disciple, then a little child, then a brother of Christ and son of God.

(375) Now we must say that the disciple referred to in these words is the one who will receive an understanding of the Word because he has submitted himself, thereby coming to know the wisdom of God from so great a teacher.

### "Yet a Little While I Am with You"

(376) The statement, "Yet a little while I am with you," is clear in the simple sense, so far as the literal sense is concerned, since he would soon no longer be with the disciples. First, he was arrested by the cohort and the tribune and the servants of the Jews who bound him and led him off to Annas first,[342] and after this he was delivered to Pilate. Next, he was condemned to the cross, and then he spent three days and three nights in the heart of the earth.[343]

(377) But in relation to the deeper sense, you will ask whether he was no longer with them after the "little while," not insofar as he was not present with them according to the flesh and his soul had descended into Hades (for he who said, "Where two or three are gathered in my name, I too am in their midst,"[344] and, "Behold I am with you all the days, until the end of the world,"[345] was [not], for this rea-

---

338. Cf. Jn 20.17.
339. Preuschen thinks the text is corrupt here.
340. Jn 13.13.     341. Jn 13.16.
342. Cf. Jn 18.12–13.     343. Cf. Mt 12.40.
344. Cf. Mt 18.20.     345. Mt 28.20.

son, prevented from being also with his disciples), but insofar as, when the saying was fulfilled, "You will all be scandalized in me in this night, for it is written, I will strike the shepherd and the sheep of the flock will be scattered,"[346] he who is with the worthy alone is no longer with them.

(378) Now, someone may respond with the statement, "In your midst stands one whom you do not know,"[347] and say that he is even with those who do not know him.

(379) But consider whether for him to be with someone, which is promised to those who are worthy, is the same with him to have stood unknown in the midst of those who do not know him.

(380) For the saying, "Where two or three are gathered in my name, I too am in their midst,"[348] and the saying, "Behold I am with you all the days, until the end of the world"[349] are promises, but the saying, "In your midst stands one whom you do not know,"[350] is not such.

(381) In the statement before us, therefore, he who said, "Behold I am with you,"[351] says, "Yet a little while I am with you." But he who says, "Yet a little while I am with you," would not have said this to Judas even if he were literally present, since the devil had already put in into his heart to betray the Savior;[352] he would not have said to him, "I am with you" (for he was no longer with him), not even when he dipped the morsel and gave it to him.[353]

(382) But to an even greater extent Christ was not with Judas when Satan had entered him after the morsel, since he had removed himself far from the Savior, "for what concord is there between Christ and Belial?"[354]

(383) Now, although their father, Jesus, was to be with the little children yet a little while, they had to know about that period after the "little while"; although he would not be with them, they were destined to seek Jesus none the less,

346. Mt 26.31.
347. Cf. Jn 1.26.
348. Cf. Mt 18.20.
349. Mt 28.20.
350. Cf. Jn 1.26.
351. Mt 28.20.
352. Cf. Jn 13.2.
353. Cf. Jn 13.26.
354. Cf. 2 Cor 6.15.

just as Peter, I think, wept bitterly seeking Jesus after he denied him.

(384) At this time, therefore, the statement was made, "Yet a little while I am with you," [but] a little later he says, "A little while and you will no longer see me, and again a little while [and] you will see me,"[355] when the disciples say, "What is this that he says, A little while? We do not know what he is saying. Because Jesus knew also that they wished to ask him, he said to them, Are you inquiring about this with one another, that I said, A little while and you will not see me, and again a little while and you will see me? Truly, truly I say to you that you will weep and lament; the world will rejoice, but you will be grieved, but your grief will become joy."[356]

(385) For in that "little while" in which they would not see him, they would seek Jesus, and for this reason they would weep and lament, although their grief would change to joy when the saying was fulfilled, "And again a little while and you will see me."[357]

(386) You will ask on these matters if he who will not see him after a little while, will see him after this, and if he will see him after not much time at all, as we perceive the statement, "And again a little while and you will see me."[358]

### "Where I Am Going You Cannot Come"

(387) But to seek Jesus is to seek the Word, and wisdom, and justice, and truth, and the power of God, all of which Christ is.[359]

(388) Now some of those who saw signs seek him, and along with seeing signs, they received bread from him and ate. Their reason for seeking was to be nourished by the Word, for he says, "You seek me not because you saw signs, but because you ate of the loaves and were filled."[360]

---

355. Jn 16.16.
356. Cf. Jn 16.18–20.
357. Jn 16.19.
358. Jn 16.19.
359. Cf. 32.322–26, where Origen asserts that the Son of Man, i.e. the human Jesus, becomes identical with the Word in the exaltation consequent to his suffering.
360. Cf. Jn 6.26.

(389) Then, since he had earlier said to the Jews, "I am going away, and you will seek me, and you will die in your sin. Where I am going you cannot come,"[361] he now says, with reference to that statement, "And as I said to the Jews, Where I am going you cannot come, I also say to you now."

(390) For as I said this to them, he says, so also I say it to you, but I also say this to you not about a later time.

(391) For this is how I understand the phrase, "I also say to you now," which is not the same with, "And I say to you," without the addition of "now." For the Jews, whom he foresaw dying in their own sin, were not able to come where Jesus was going after a brief time. The disciples, however, after the little time for which he was no longer to be with them, because of what has been said previously, could not follow the Word when he departed to the economy [of suffering] that was his own.[362]

(392) If the words, "As I said to the Jews," had not been placed before the words, "Where I go you cannot come," we would have supposed that these remarks were made literally, and referred to the departure of Jesus' soul from life. But as it is, both the Jews in dying, and Jesus, when he died, were to descend into Hades.

(393) How is it that they could not go where Jesus went? But someone will reply that since he was also to be in the paradise of God, and those who die in their sins were not to be there, nor could Jesus' disciples be there at that time, but only later, that this is why it was said to those Jews dying in their sins, "Where I am going you cannot come,"[363] but to the disciples, "Where I am going you cannot come now."

(394) For the sequence of the text is as follows, "As I said to the Jews, I also say to you, Where I am going you cannot come now."[364] And so there is no small discussion on the sub-

---

361. Jn 8.21.
362. οἰκονομία. See above, Introduction, par. 59.
363. Jn 8.21.
364. Origen has rearranged the text so that the adverb "now" does not have reference to the time when Jesus makes the statement, but to the time when the disciples will come to where he is going. Cf. Book 19.86.

ject because of the statement, "The Son of Man will spend three days and three nights in the heart of the earth."[365]

(395) For how will he spend three days and three nights in the heart of the earth, [who] at the time of his departure was to be in the paradise of God, according to the statement, "Today you will be with me in the paradise of God"?[366] This contradiction has troubled some so much that they have dared to assume that the statement itself, "Today you will be with me in the paradise of God," has been added to the Gospel by forgers.

(396) We say, however, at the literal level, that perhaps before he departed into the so-called heart of the earth, he restored the one who said to him, "Remember me when you come in your kingdom,"[367] to the paradise of God. But at the profound level, we note that everywhere in Scripture the term "today" also applies to the entire present age, as it does in the words, "This word was spread among the Jews until today,"[368] and, "He is the father of the Moabites until today,"[369] and, "Today if you hear his voice,[370] and stand not aloof from the Lord."[371]

(397) In the expression, "today," Jesus promises him who thought it important that he be remembered in the kingdom of God, that he has effected it for him to be with him in the kingdom of God in the present age, before the age to come.

(398) But let this be said as an intervening digression on our previous comments. The Lord now says to the disciples who wish to follow Jesus, not literally as the simple would assume, but in the sense revealed in the statement, "Whoever does not take up his cross and follow me is not worthy to be my disciple,"[372] "Where I am going you cannot come now."

(399) Would that they had wanted to follow the Word

---

365. Mt 12.40.
366. Cf. Lk 23.43.
367. Cf. Lk 23.42.
368. Cf. Mt 28.15.
369. Cf. Gn 19.37.
370. Ps 94.7.
371. Cf. Jos 22.16. Preuschen indicates that the text is corrupt where the two clauses join.
372. Cf. Mt 10.38.

and confess him, without being scandalized in him. But they could not yet do this, "for as yet the Spirit was not, because Jesus was not yet glorified,"[373] and "no one is able to say Jesus is Lord except in the Holy Spirit."[374]

(400) The Word, however, departs on his own courses, and he who follows the Word follows him; but he who is not prepared to walk in his steps persistently cannot follow, since the Word leads those to his Father who do all things that they might be able to follow him, and that they may follow him until they may say to the Christ, "My soul has clung to you."[375]

(401) But since the thirty-second book of the commentaries on the Gospel of John has reached a suitable stopping point, we shall, I suppose, conclude its explanation.

---

373. Cf. Jn 7.39.
375. Cf. Ps 62.9.

374. 1 Cor 12.3.

# INDICES

# INDEX OF PROPER NAMES

*Numbers in the indices refer to Book and Paragraph numbers of the Commentary.*

Aaron, 13.9; 32.334
Abel, 20.12
Abraham, 13.106, 177–78, 212, 214, 275–76, 295, 309, 346, 392, 399, 400–402, 404, 407, 439; 19.18, 30, 64, 72; 20.2, 4–5, 8–16, 24, 30, 31–33, 37–42, 45, 52–53, 58–63, 66–72, 74–77, 79, 87–88, 93, 95, 123, 125–26, 128, 132, 168, 222–23, 380–81, 383, 388, 393–98, 400, 418–19; 28.217; 32.47, 265–66
Achab, 20.258–59, 261, 264; 28.139
Adam, 13.332–33; 19.23; 20.11–12, 25, 221, 224–25, 234, 364–65, 388; 32.27, 265
Amalikites, 28.37
Ambrose, 13.1; 20.1; 28.6; 32.2
Andrew, 13.435
Annas, 32.376
Anoth Ramatha, 28.142, 144–45
Aquila, 13.161
Aran, 20.11, 13
Armathaim, 28.144
Aser, 13.77
Assyrians, 20.321

Balaam, 13.155, 157; 28.99, 132–33, 135–36, 138, 177
Balac, 28.135, 138
Barabbas, 28.111, 233
Barnabas, 32.208
Beelzebub, 19.93–96; 20.314
Belial, 32.302, 382
Beliar, 19.139
Benjamin, 13.77
Bethabara, 13.455
Bethel, 20.71
Bethlehem, 13.290; 19.10, 104–5

Caesar, 13.395; 28.234–35
Cain, 19.117; 20.25–26, 78
Caiphas, 28.98, 106–8, 116, 119–20, 127–29, 140–41, 150, 152–54, 172, 175, 186–91
Cana, 13.253, 258, 347, 367, 391, 393, 437, 442–43, 455
Capharnaum, 13.253, 258, 395, 402, 409, 411, 416, 442–43, 445–46, 455; 28.202
Cedron, 28.202
Cenchria, 13.111
Cham, 20.14, 78
Chanaan, 20.33, 37, 69, 78
Charan, 19.30
Christ, 13.19, 35, 39, 47–48, 83, 101, 118, 154, 158–65, 169, 172–73, 176, 179–80, 187, 189–90, 215, 219, 236, 305–6, 314–15, 319, 321, 333, 351, 405–6, 409, 413, 447; 19.1, 7, 12, 28, 30–34, 57, 68, 76, 79, 104–5, 113, 139–41, 151–53, 156, 158, 160; 20.6, 50, 55, 76, 92–93, 224, 226, 228, 231–33, 240, 245, 248, 255, 271, 279, 285, 341, 344–45, 347–48, 350, 363–66, 390, 392, 413, 415–16, 418; 28.6, 18–19, 25, 54–55, 60, 97, 109, 117, 166, 241–42; 32.1, 28–29, 33, 133, 162, 170, 188, 203–4, 207–8, 213, 231, 296, 302, 315, 321, 337–38, 341–43, 352, 374, 382, 387, 400
Corinthians, 13.208, 217
Creator, 13.12, 103, 105, 109, 117–18; 19.12–15, 17, 32; 20.182, 271

Dan, 13.77
Daniel, 20.33; 28.34
David, 13.330; 19.31, 105; 20.220;

David (*continued*)
28.122, 141, 142, 144, 176; 32.26, 322
Demiurge, 13.416, 422–25, 432; 20.362
Diaspora, 28.92
Dositheos, 13.162
Dosithians, 13.162

Edom, 13.157
Egypt, 13.9, 156, 454; 20.73; 28.226
Egyptians, 20.29, 73; 28.4
Elect, 13.341
Elias, 13.145, 310; 19.160
Elijah, 32.335
Elimmen, 13.161
Eliseus, 13.210
Enos, 20.12, 14
Ephrem, 28.200, 212–13, 221–23
Esau, 13.157
Evangelist, 13.86, 173–74, 183, 317, 367, 436; 19.40; 28.78; 11, 313
Eve, 19.23; 20.221
Ezechiel, 19.84; 20.174

Father, 13.5, 19, 78, 83, 88–89, 97–100, 109–10, 112, 117, 119–20, 146, 148, 151–53, 165, 219, 220, 228–30, 232–33, 237–38, 247–49, 298, 310, 382, 385, 389, 393, 398; 19.1–9, 11–12, 15, 18, 21, 24–28, 30–36, 39, 54, 72, 74, 86, 109–10; 20.1, 46–56, 58–59, 61, 63–65, 106–7, 130, 131, 135, 137–40, 142–44, 147, 149–51, 153, 155–62, 181, 191–92, 271–72, 289–90, 292, 309, 313, 335–42, 351, 353–58, 362, 419–21; 28.41–42, 44, 47–49, 52, 68–69, 71, 73–74, 84–85, 94, 166; 32.25–29, 32, 34–35, 37, 40, 81, 121, 203, 212–13, 264, 295, 315, 321, 342, 345, 347, 355, 357, 359–60, 363–64, 366, 373, 400

Gabriel, 32.228
Gad, 13.77
Galilean, 13.387, 256–57, 369, 381, 384, 388

Galilee, 13.253, 255–58, 347, 364, 366–70, 381, 384, 390, 410, 417, 434, 435–36, 455; 19.105, 107; 28.202
Garizim, 13.77, 80–82
Gehenna, 13.417; 20.83
Gentiles, 13.5, 95–96, 102–4, 107, 315, 333, 342–43, 374, 392; 19.115; 28.55–56, 93–94, 170, 214, 218, 220; 32.63, 208, 360
God, 13.22, 27, 35, 47, 48, 78, 79, 83–85, 92–94, 100, 104, 106–7, 109–10, 113, 117, 123–25, 127–32, 134–40, 143–50, 153, 156, 168, 210, 219–20, 223, 225, 228, 230–37, 240–43, 245, 249, 279–82, 297, 304, 307, 310, 319, 321, 328–33, 343, 346, 354, 356, 359–60, 369, 374, 386–87, 388, 393, 400, 402, 413, 415, 439, 451, 455; 19.6, 11–14, 16–18, 21, 23–33, 35–38, 41, 43–44, 49–50, 52–53, 56–58, 64, 69, 74, 77, 86, 103, 118–20, 124, 139, 144, 146–47, 153, 155–56, 160; 20.1, 6–8, 12, 25, 28–29, 31, 38, 45, 47, 48, 50, 53, 58–59, 61, 62, 64–66, 68–71, 76, 80, 81, 83–85, 89–90, 93–94, 99–101, 105–8, 110–22, 126, 130–40, 146, 148, 151–57, 161–62, 168, 176, 181, 183–84, 186, 188, 190, 192–93, 195–96, 213, 220, 222–23, 226, 229–31, 236, 242, 257–58, 272, 284–98, 302–6, 308–9, 313, 332–33, 335, 337, 339–40, 342, 344, 346, 350–51, 357, 363, 369–70, 384, 390, 393, 398, 403, 410, 415, 422; 28.5, 6, 12–13, 15, 17, 19, 25–27, 29–30, 33, 35, 39, 42, 49, 50, 55, 73, 88, 91, 98–99, 109, 126, 129, 130, 132, 133, 135–39, 145, 147, 150, 154–55, 159, 161, 163, 167, 178–79, 182–85, 195, 211, 214, 218, 223, 230, 232, 234–38, 242, 246, 249; 32.1, 3, 4, 19, 25, 28–29, 33, 35, 40, 74, 97, 102, 107, 111, 122, 149, 165, 184, 187, 190, 202, 207, 217, 220–21, 224, 231, 263, 264, 313, 315, 319, 321,

## INDEX OF PROPER NAMES

324–30, 337–39, 344, 348,
350–54, 359–60, 362–63, 365–67,
373–75, 393, 395–97
Gog, 13.155
Goliath, 20.220
Gomorrah, 20.28
Greeks, 13.132; 20.184; 28.162;
32.330

Hades, 13.244; 19.83, 140; 28.55;
32.377, 392
Hai, 20.71
Hebel, 13.77
Hebrews, 13.251; 20.321
Heli, 19.13–15
Henoch, 20.12, 14
Heracleon, 13.57, 65, 67, 69, 70–71,
91–92, 95, 97, 102, 104, 114,
117–18, 120, 147–49, 164, 172,
187, 191–92, 200, 225–26,
247–48, 271, 294, 299, 322,
336–37, 341, 349, 363, 416, 418,
427; 19.89, 124; 54, 168, 169,
198, 211, 213, 252, 254, 358, 360
Herod, 13.395
Hesebon, 32.221

Iar, 13.252
Isaac, 13.106, 309; 20.77, 93,
222–23, 393, 398
Isaias, 13.212, 222, 274, 401, 426;
20.398; 28.164, 227; 32.202
Israel, 13.9, 133, 157, 332, 343, 374;
19.15; 20.39, 220, 258–59, 261,
320, 321; 28.94, 177, 185, 188,
214, 226; 32.334, 336
Issachar, 13.77

Jacob, 13.2, 23, 26, 31, 35, 37–42,
56–57, 66, 90, 106, 154, 157, 159,
163, 185–86, 255, 257, 309, 332,
340, 344, 368, 392, 455; 20.24,
77, 93, 222–23, 386, 393, 398;
28.7, 8, 9; 32.123
James, 13.310; 19.10, 152
Japheth, 20.14
Jeremias, 13.330, 403; 20.160, 398;
28.105
Jericho, 20.317
Jeroboam, 13.81–82

Jerusalem, 13.80, 83–85, 88–89,
95–96, 98–100, 111, 253, 256–58,
367, 370, 381, 384, 386–90, 397,
455; 19.1–4, 7, 10, 115–16;
20.317; 28.202, 231, 236, 242;
32.335
Jesus, 13.3, 6, 18, 20, 24–27, 31, 37,
39, 49, 52, 54, 91–92, 101, 162,
175, 181–82, 194, 215–16,
220–21, 242, 245–46, 248,
251–53, 255–56, 258, 260–61,
275, 277, 306, 308, 310, 319–21,
325–26, 344, 346–47, 351,
364–67, 371, 381, 384, 387,
389–91, 393, 410, 434–35, 438,
442–49, 452–53, 455; 19.8, 12,
18–19, 30–31, 33, 40–42, 44, 48,
51, 53, 55, 59, 60, 62, 64, 68, 71,
73–74, 81, 83, 86–87, 93, 97–98,
101, 103, 105, 108, 115, 121–23,
139, 141, 144, 148, 150–53; 20.1,
32, 41, 58–59, 83, 87, 89, 93–94,
99, 103, 131–32, 135, 137–39,
162–66, 168, 172, 218, 228, 268,
270–72, 275, 285, 315, 322–24,
329–30, 335, 341–42, 349, 364,
366, 373, 379, 384, 389–90, 392,
394, 397, 402, 410, 420, 422;
28.6–9, 14–17, 22–23, 32, 34, 38,
44–45, 47, 50–51, 53–54, 56–57,
59–60, 66–68, 72–73, 76–77,
81–87, 94, 95, 98, 108–9, 111,
113, 115–20, 123, 127–29,
150–53, 156–57, 163, 166, 175,
178, 184–85, 187–90, 193,
195–96, 198, 200, 202, 206–8,
210–12, 221–222, 230, 232,
237–41, 243, 245, 247–48;
32.1–2, 8–9, 10–11, 14–16, 18,
24–27, 35, 40, 44, 50, 52, 57,
60–62, 65–68, 71–81, 83, 85,
89–93, 95–97, 100, 102–4,
110–11, 115, 117, 123, 125,
128–30, 135, 139, 142–43, 150,
155, 159, 162–63, 166, 168, 171,
188, 190, 194, 196–98, 203–4,
207–8, 211–12, 216, 218, 223,
225, 227–28, 236, 240–43, 249,
257, 260, 262–64, 274, 276,
278–80, 295, 299, 300–302, 304,

424  INDEX OF PROPER NAMES

Jesus (*continued*)
  306–7, 309, 312, 314, 316, 318, 320, 322, 326, 327, 338, 357, 361, 371–72, 374, 383, 384–85, 387, 391–93, 397–99
Jesus of Bethsames, 28.147
Jew, 13.395
Jews, 13.53, 77–78, 80–81, 95–96, 99, 101–7, 115, 160, 162, 253, 258, 370, 372–73, 394, 455; 19.12, 18–19, 91–92, 104, 111, 122–26; 20.49–50, 52–53, 85, 96, 98, 103, 128, 131, 268, 273, 310, 312, 316, 319–20, 379, 381, 387–88, 400–401, 413; 28.66, 75, 77, 80, 86, 95, 199–200, 208, 211–12, 217, 221, 224, 229, 231–32, 234, 238, 242, 247; 32.63, 376, 389, 391–94, 396
Job, 13.330; 32.317
John, 13.28, 33, 124, 131, 188, 255, 310, 345, 367, 405; 19.3, 10, 43, 84, 97, 139; 20.24, 99, 108, 110, 113, 115; 28.119; 32.108, 202, 260–62, 264, 276–77
Jordan, 13.77, 455
Josaphat, 20.261
Joseph, 13.77, 159, 368; 32.48, 191
Josue, 32.82
Juda, 13.77, 154, 158; 19.15, 104; 20.33
Judah, 20.321
Judaism, 28.97
Judas, 19.10, 63; 28.107, 113, 115, 204, 303; 32.19, 23–25, 34, 68, 84, 109–10, 145, 148, 151–52, 154–55, 158–59, 165–68, 227, 230, 232, 240–42, 245–47, 276, 280–81, 283–86, 289–91, 295, 297, 300, 305, 307–9, 312–13, 316–18, 320, 381–82
Judea, 13.115, 251, 254–57, 368–69, 372, 395, 410, 417, 434–36, 455; 20.270

Laban, 28.7–8
Lazarus, 13.276; 19.82; 20.414; 28.42–44, 47–48, 51–52, 54, 62, 67–71, 74–75, 77, 79; 32.23, 265
Lazaruses, 28.54

Levi, 13.77
Levite, 20.317
Levites, 28.86
Lord, 13.5, 9–10, 40, 52, 75, 83, 101, 107, 137–38, 140, 145, 211, 224, 249, 253, 263, 286–87, 298–99, 306, 308, 332, 338, 357, 358, 360–61, 368, 374, 376, 380, 397, 406, 432, 435, 436, 444; 19.13–14, 23–25, 27–28, 31, 56, 83, 99, 118, 139, 157, 159; 20.1, 7–8, 12, 22, 36, 49, 50, 57, 68, 69–72, 83, 134, 152–53, 182, 187, 220, 222, 228, 231, 233, 235, 240, 259–61, 277, 320, 385, 387, 401, 406–7, 414; 28.21, 34, 39, 61, 71, 91, 123, 133, 139, 143, 150, 166, 186, 211, 215–16, 219–20, 223–27, 229; 32.4, 11, 17, 19, 26–27, 33, 47, 57, 65, 76, 106, 114–15, 120–28, 130, 137, 154, 174, 185, 188, 206, 220–21, 237, 246, 253, 261–62, 267, 279–80, 284, 295–96, 309, 317, 319, 326, 331–33, 336, 340, 352, 357, 374, 398, 399
Lot, 20.13, 69
Luke, 19.41, 46, 51; 20.46, 404; 28.113; 32.251, 252

Manasses, 28.213
Mark, 19.41, 46, 51–52; 20.403; 28.115; 32.252, 254
Martha, 28.13, 15, 22, 71; 32.23
Mary, 13.377; 19.10, 27; 20.162, 269; 28.66, 75, 80, 83–85, 112; 32.191, 228
Mary Magdalene, 28.112
Mathusala, 20.12
Matthew, 13.446; 20.106, 402; 28.107, 108; 32.252–53
Melchisedech, 13.146; 19.120
Mesopotamia, 19.30; 28.99, 177
Messias, 13.161
Micheas, 20.258, 261
Moab, 13.157
Moabites, 32.396
Moses, 13.9–11, 77, 81, 154, 158–60, 165, 295, 305, 308, 310, 314, 316, 319–20, 325, 374, 452; 19.27,

# INDEX OF PROPER NAMES 425

101; 20.50, 92, 222–23, 240–41,
358–59, 364–66; 28.4, 37, 62;
32.82, 267–68, 331, 334–36,
338–39, 341–43

Nabuchodonosor, 20.78
Nachor, 20.11, 13
Nazareth, 28.202, 206–7
Nephtali, 13.77
Nephthalim, 28.202
Nicodemus, 13.254, 386; 19.107
Nisan, 13.251
Noah, 20.11–13; 20.14, 37
Nun, 32.82

Osee, 20.398

Paraclete, 13.316; 20.263
Pasch, 13.251, 253–54, 256, 258,
386; 28.224–26, 228–32, 235–37,
240, 242; 32.85, 298
Paul, 13.12, 28, 34, 111, 113, 153,
208–9, 217, 355, 359, 431; 19.31,
44, 68, 119, 128; 20.135, 137–39,
196, 217, 233, 285, 290–91, 319,
363, 374; 28.25, 29, 130, 161,
173; 32.31, 63, 106, 177, 206,
208, 313, 336, 353
Peter, 13.104, 153, 208, 310, 435,
445–46; 19.86, 118; 32.16, 36, 53,
56–57, 61, 65, 68–69, 71, 76,
89–92, 96, 98, 102, 137, 208, 257,
260, 262, 274–77, 279, 315, 383
Pharao, 20.78
Pharisee, 28.248
Pharisees, 13.255, 380; 19.1–2, 8,
10–12, 15, 21, 24, 33, 63, 106,
108, 116; 20.298; 28.76–77, 79,
81–82, 86, 89, 94–96, 115, 151,
156, 186, 188–90, 198, 203–4,
244, 247
Philip, 13.435
Philistines, 28.147
Phinees, 20.220
Pilate, 19.61; 20.269, 272; 28.118,
232–34; 32.191, 241, 376
Place, 13.324

Rachel, 28.7
Ramoth Galaad, 20.258–59, 261
Raphidim, 13.11
Rebecca, 13.177–78, 212
Romans, 28.86, 90–91, 93
Rome, 19.31
Ruben, 13.77

Sabbaths, 28.227–28
Sadducees, 20.222
Samaria, 13.82, 171–72, 248, 255,
340, 345, 348, 365, 368, 447, 455
Samaritan, 20.311, 316–20, 343
Samaritans, 13.53–54, 77, 80–81, 83,
101, 154, 158–59, 162, 179–80,
182, 184–86, 195, 200, 256,
342–45, 362, 364, 368, 369;
20.310, 311–12, 319, 321
Samuel, 20.393; 28.142, 144–45, 148
Sara, 13.401
Satan, 19.95, 118; 28.26, 113;
32.110, 167, 281, 283, 286, 289,
295, 297, 302, 307, 309, 312–13,
317–18, 382
Saul, 20.136; 28.139, 141–45, 148,
176
Savior, 13.5, 23, 40, 59–60, 67–68,
75, 106–7, 151–52, 160, 168,
179–80, 187–89, 191, 238, 241,
247–50, 265, 275, 287, 295,
299–300, 316, 320, 324, 333,
338–39, 342, 352, 362–63,
375–76, 381, 384, 391, 396, 400,
404, 413, 420–23, 432, 437; 19.6,
12, 17, 25, 27, 34, 38, 40, 77, 93,
95–97, 102, 118, 124–26, 128,
136, 159; 20.1, 23, 30, 46–47, 49,
52–53, 56, 60–61, 64, 67–68, 85,
89, 91, 93, 106, 128, 130, 188,
191, 222, 277, 280, 310, 311, 318,
319, 322, 335, 338, 343–44, 351,
353–54, 356–57, 362, 371,
381–82, 395–96, 401, 414;
28.39–40, 42, 86, 96, 106–7, 112,
129, 151, 155, 184, 186, 190, 195,
229, 232, 235; 32.57, 107, 120,
130, 148, 150–51, 153, 158, 160,
197, 203–4, 242, 245, 251, 296,
300, 319, 368, 372, 381, 382
Sehon, 32.221
Sem, 20.12–14
Seth, 13.157; 20.12, 14

## INDEX OF PROPER NAMES

Sichem, 20.69
Simeon, 13.77; 32.48
Simon, 19.10; 32.23–25, 34, 84, 109, 166, 227, 241, 280–81, 286, 289, 307, 312
Simon Bar-Jona, 32.355
Sodomites, 20.27–28
Solomon, 13.17, 78, 284, 315; 20.405; 28.174; 32.18
Son, 13.5, 119, 146, 151, 220, 225, 228–31, 233–34, 307, 310, 324, 388; 19.3–5, 17–18, 24, 27, 31, 35, 68, 103, 115–16; 20.1, 46–48, 53, 65, 89–90, 100, 105, 108–10, 153–59, 236, 270, 350–51, 356–57, 398, 402, 404, 410, 420; 28.19, 68–69, 71, 109, 117, 126, 150, 234; 32.37, 97, 121, 165, 228, 251, 263, 315, 318–23, 325, 327–29, 344–45, 347–48, 350, 353–57, 359, 362–65, 394
Sophein, 28.144
Spirit, 13.35–36, 47, 61, 85, 112, 140, 141, 145, 151, 187, 221, 231, 321, 354, 356, 359, 361, 379, 405; 19.20, 31, 57, 88; 20.89, 263, 285, 338; 28.55, 121–29, 140, 146, 151, 153, 187–89, 191; 32.26, 75, 79, 86, 128–29, 189, 191, 218, 336, 352, 399

Stephen, 19.29
Stromateis, 13.298
Susanna, 28.34

Tanis, 13.454
Thare, 20.11, 12
Thomas, 13.180
Timothy, 13.111

Urias, 28.122

Wisdom, 13.41; 19.36, 71, 87, 147, 156; 20.33, 370
Word, 13.21, 41–42, 48, 52, 76, 115, 152, 169–71, 198–99, 237, 262, 265, 268, 274, 279, 284, 294–95, 297, 307, 326, 348, 352, 389, 392; 19.35, 45, 46–47, 56, 61, 69, 71, 74, 78, 80, 86–88, 147, 153, 155; 20.7, 39, 40, 42–46, 68, 81–86, 134, 164, 275–76, 295, 342, 367, 370, 380, 398; 28.50, 72, 159, 192, 211; 32.14–15, 33, 36, 44, 46, 50, 127, 130, 142, 149, 217, 234, 264, 268, 273, 289, 304, 322, 324–26, 359, 366, 369–70, 375, 387–88, 391, 399–400

Zabulon, 13.77; 28.202
Zion, 13.78, 81, 83, 171, 397

# INDEX OF HOLY SCRIPTURE

### Books of the Old Testament

Genesis
  1.2: 32.313
  1.5: 13.134; 32.313
  1.10: 13.280, 281
  1.20: 13.281
  1.21: 13.281
  1.24: 13.282
  1.25: 13.282
  1.26: 13.167, 331; 20.183, 224
  1.31: 20.196
  2.7: 13.140, 142; 20.182
  2.8: 13.223
  2.9: 13.240
  2.15: 13.240
  2.16–17: 13.223
  2.23: 19.23
  3.1–6: 20.221
  3.13: 13.169
  3.17: 20.234
  3.22: 32.233
  3.23: 20.234
  4.1: 19.23
  4.14: 19.117
  4.15: 19.117
  4.25: 20.12
  4.26: 20.12
  5: 20.11
  5.22: 20.12
  6.1: 13.243
  6.2: 13.425
  6.9: 20.12
  6.13: 20.25
  9.26: 20.12
  11.7: 13.331
  11.11–26: 20.11
  11.26: 20.11
  12.1: 13.346; 20.67, 68, 124
  12.4: 20.69
  12.6: 20.69
  12.7: 20.70
  12.8: 20.71, 72
  12.9 (LXX): 20.72
  12.10: 20.72
  12.11–13: 20.72
  12.16: 20.72
  14.14: 13.407
  15.6: 19.18; 20.66; 28.12
  15.15: 20.79
  16.1–4: 20.67
  17.10–11: 13.451
  17.12: 13.407
  18.2–3: 32.47
  18.4: 32.47
  18.6: 13.214
  19.37: 32.396
  24.12–16: 13.177
  24.17: 13.177
  24.18–19: 13.178
  25.1: 20.67
  27.29: 32.123
  27.40: 32.123
  29.2–3: 28.7
  29.8: 28.7
  29.10: 28.7
  30.42: 28.8
  41.51–52: 28.213
  41.52: 28.222
  43.23–24: 32.48
  47.12: 28.222
  49.8: 13.154
  49.10: 13.154

Exodus
  3.5: 32.82
  4.6–7: 32.267
  4.8: 32.269
  4.9: 32.271
  4.22: 28.185
  10.23: 13.133
  12.11: 28.226
  12.26–27: 28.226
  14.19–20: 32.2
  15.24: 13.10
  15.25: 13.10
  16.1–4: 13.9
  17.3: 13.11
  17.11: 28.37
  20.12: 20.339
  26.2: 28.5
  33.21: 20.240, 241
  34.29–30: 32.334
  34.33–35: 28.62
  40.34–35: 32.331

Leviticus
  26.12: 13.143

Numbers
  16.5: 19.24; 32.154
  22.22–24: 28.132
  22.27: 28.133
  22.32–35: 28.133
  22.35: 28.136
  22.38: 28.99
  23.4–5: 28.135
  23.5: 28.136
  23.7: 28.99, 137, 177
  23.16: 28.138
  24.2: 28.177

# INDEX OF HOLY SCRIPTURE

**Numbers** (*continued*)
24.7–9: 13.156
24.17–19: 13.157
25.6–12: 20.220

**Deuteronomy**
2.30: 32.221
4.24: 13.124
6.5: 19.139
16.20: 28.100, 103
18.15: 13.374
27.11–13: 13.77
30.12–14: 19.77
32.8–9: 13.332
32.32–33: 20.28
33.7: 13.158

**Joshua**
5.15: 32.82
13.22: 28.99
22.16: 32.396

**Ruth**
1.22: 13.290

**1 Kings**
2.12: 19.13
6.2–9: 28.147
16.7: 19.52
16.14: 28.139
17.45: 20.220
19.19–24: 28.145
19.20–24: 28.176
28.7–13: 20.393
28.7–19: 28.148

**3 Kings**
2.46e(LXX): 32.18
8.10–11: 32.333
19.11–12: 13.145
19.5–8: 13.220
22.15: 20.258
22.19–22: 20.260
22.20: 28.139
22.21: 28.139

**4 Kings**
4.40: 13.210
17: 20.321

**2 Chronicles**

18.18–21: 20.261

**Ezra**
18.4: 13.429
18.20: 19.84
28.19: 20.174
34.16: 13.119
37.27: 13.143

**Job**
1.12: 32.317
2.6: 32.317
12.10: 13.330
14.4: 20.328, 335
15.25: 32.33
40.19(LXX): 20.182
40.19: 20.235

**Psalms**
1.3: 20.322
2.2: 32.296
2.6–7: 13.397
2.7–8: 13.5
2.8: 13.333
6.6: 19.140
7.10: 13.432
7.13–15: 32.21
8.7: 13.48
11.7: 19.56
12.4: 13.135
18.2: 32.190
18.10–11: 20.187
21.15: 20.45
21.16: 20.225, 374
21.23: 19.28
21.30: 13.224
22.1–3: 13.212
26.1: 13.137
26.1–3: 32.296
32.9: 28.9
32.10: 28.91
32.15: 13.168
33.9: 20.406
35.7: 28.216
36.4: 32.106
37.6: 20.414
38.8: 19.157
40.10: 32.157, 162, 164, 165, 247, 285

41.2–3: 13.22
43.20: 20.225
45.11: 19.16
47.3: 19.44
48.6: 32.168
50.13: 28.122
54.13: 32.248, 249
54.14: 32.249
62.9: 32.400
71.11: 28.91
72.2: 20.239
77.25: 13.214
77.43: 13.454
77.47: 20.29
81.6: 20.242, 266; 32.234
81.7: 20.242; 32.59, 233
87.5 (LXX): 19.102
87.7: 19.140
88.49: 20.371
93.11: 13.432
94.7: 32.396
103.4: 32.200
103.15: 13.213
103.24: 19.147
103.29: 13.141
103.30: 13.141
104.6: 20.24
106.33–38: 28.214
106.35–36: 28.215
106.37–38: 28.215
106.38: 28.216
106.39–40: 28.217
106.41–42: 28.218
106.43: 28.219
109.1: 13.48; 32.26
109.4: 13.146
113.25–26(LXX): 19.83
114.6: 20.320
115.2: 20.241, 265; 32.94
117.14: 19.157
117.17: 20.222
118.57: 13.330
118.73: 13.328, 330
119.7: 20.346
120.4: 20.320
122.1–2: 28.33

## INDEX OF HOLY SCRIPTURE

125.5-6: 13.289
125.6: 20.18, 20, 21
127.2: 13.448
128.6-8: 20.22
140.2: 28.37

Proverbs
1.5: 32.172
3.16: 32.106
3.18: 20.322
3.28: 28.21
4.6: 20.406
4.23: 32.20
6.13-14: 32.275
8.9: 13.284
8.22 (LXX): 19.36
8.22: 19.56; 20.134, 370
9.8: 32.180
9.9: 32.181
10.3: 13.224
10.10: 32.275
14.30: 20.285
15.17: 13.210
16.23: 13.316; 28.174
16.31: 20.79
27.1: 32.258

Ecclesiastes
7.20: 20.328, 335

Song of Songs
2.8: 13.17
5.3: 32.135

Isaiah
1.2: 13.426
1.4: 13.426
1.13-14: 28.227, 228
1.16: 32.12
2.1: 20.398
5.2: 13.426
6.8: 32.202

9.1 (LXX): 13.134
11.4: 20.83
11.7: 13.212
29.11-12: 13.315
35.10: 13.309
40.8: 13.48
40.26: 13.274; 28.33
51.2: 13.401
52.5: 20.350
52.7: 32.77, 78, 86, 87
53.3: 28.164
53.4: 28.160; 32.83
53.4-5: 28.165
53.5: 28.166
53.7: 28.166
53.8: 28.167
54.1: 28.211
58.9: 28.39, 40
65.13: 13.222

Jeremiah
1.5: 13.168, 328, 330
3.25: 20.285
5.8: 20.332
14.1: 20.398
23.21: 20.160
23.24: 13.432
51.31 (LXX): 28.105

Daniel
8.27: 13.315

Hosea
1.1: 20.398
1.9: 28.94
10.12: 13.133
10.12 (LXX): 13.314

Amos
5.21: 28.228, 230
8.11: 13.224

Micah
1.2-4: 20.152

Zechariah
6.12: 32.316
13.7: 32.61

Malachai
3.20: 32.316

Judith
9.11: 13.168

Wisdom
1.5: 28.122
1.14: 20.235
2.24: 20.236; 32.22
4.9: 20.79
7.9: 19.54, 56
7.22-23: 20.405
7.25-26: 13.153
7.26: 13.234
8.2: 20.406
10.3-4: 20.26
10.7: 20.27
11.24,26: 20.148
12.11: 20.33
17.1: 20.6

Sirach
3.21: 13.32
4.28: 28.192
5.7: 28.21
21.15: 13.319
31.14: 32.293

Susanne
9: 28.34
35: 28.34
35a: 13.433
56: 20.33

2 Maccabees
15.14: 13.403

## Books of the New Testament

Matthew
2.1: 19.10
3.9: 13.400; 20.38
3.11: 32.79
4.11: 28.66
4.12–13: 28.202
4.16: 13.134
4.23: 20.176
5.6: 13.21
5.8: 19.17
5.16: 32.360
5.17: 13.107
5.27–28: 20.149
5.28: 20.189
5.29–30: 20.149
5.33–34: 20.150
5.35: 13.83, 397
5.43–45: 20.106, 142
5.44: 20.147
5.44–45: 20.290, 292, 309
5.45: 20.147, 149, 151
6.2: 28.100
6.4: 13.298
6.20: 19.138
6.21: 19.138
6.30: 32.183
7.1: 32.185
7.7: 13.5; 20.324
7.8: 13.5; 19.73
7.16: 20.105
7.18: 13.73
7.21: 20.361; 32.126
7.22: 32.123, 124, 153
7.23: 32.125, 153, 154
8.5–13: 13.444
8.8: 13.444
8.11: 13.309
8.12: 13.425
8.13: 13.444
8.14–15: 13.445
8.16: 13.446
8.17: 28.160; 32.83

8.26: 32.183
9.2: 32.368
9.12: 20.285; 28.183; 32.119
9.22: 32.184, 368
9.29: 32.184
9.37: 13.294
9.37–38: 13.287
10.5: 13.342, 343
10.10: 32.83
10.23: 28.198
10.24–25: 32.144
10.25: 32.107, 119, 122
10.28: 13.417; 20.82
10.38: 32.398
11.11: 20.419
11.27: 13.146; 19.17, 18; 20.46; 32.355, 359
11.29: 13.166; 32.49
12.24: 19.93
12.27: 19.95
12.31: 28.124
12.32: 19.88
12.40: 32.376, 394
12.42: 13.315; 32.18
12.44: 28.240
13.17: 13.315, 316
13.30: 13.271, 294, 325
13.36: 13.286
13.39: 13.286
13.55: 19.10
13.55–56: 13.377
13.57: 13.375
15.2: 32.102
15.9: 28.246
15.24: 20.39
16.16: 32.315
16.17: 32.355
16.21: 19.116
16.22: 19.118
16.23: 19.118
16.26: 19.85
16.28: 20.402, 408, 410, 411

17.1–3: 13.310
17.22–23: 19.116
18.20: 32.377, 380
19.17: 28.42
20.17–19: 19.115
21.21: 32.194
21.28–31: 28.20
21.44: 20.239
22.11: 28.61
22.13: 28.61, 63
22.31–32: 20.222
22.32: 20.93, 229, 393, 398
22.37: 19.139
23.9: 20.340
23.15: 20.215, 298
23.29: 13.378, 380; 20.393
23.33: 20.215
25.1–13: 13.200
25.15: 19.45
25.29: 32.72, 108, 282
26.14–15: 28.107
26.22: 32.253
26.23: 32.290
26.24: 32.239
26.26: 32.304, 309
26.31: 32.53, 61, 377
26.33: 32.61, 257
26.34: 32.62
26.39: 13.249; 32.295
26.40–44: 13.201
26.41: 32.228
26.47: 28.107
26.57: 28.108
26.59–66: 28.109
26.69–74: 32.315
26.75: 32.62
27.2: 32.241
27.3–4: 32.241
27.4: 32.241, 244, 317
27.5: 32.241, 317
27.9: 32.244

## INDEX OF HOLY SCRIPTURE

27.12: 28.110
27.20: 28.111
27.50: 19.103, 116
27.51–53: 19.103
27.54: 19.103
28.11–14: 28.112
28.15: 32.396
28.18: 13.437
28.19: 13.334
28.20: 13.350;
    32.377, 380, 381

Mark
1.24: 28.129
3.29: 19.88; 28.124
7.34: 20.164
8.34: 19.150
9.1: 20.403, 410
10.18: 13.151, 234
11.23: 32.194
12.26–27: 20.223
12.41: 19.51
12.41–44: 19.42
12.43: 19.52
14.10–11: 28.115
14.15: 28.240
14.19: 32.254
14.20: 32.290
14.21: 32.239
14.29: 32.61, 257
14.36: 13.249
14.37–41: 13.201
14.38: 32.228
14.43: 28.115
14.53: 28.116
14.60–63: 28.117
15.1: 28.118
15.3: 28.118
15.5: 28.118
15.37: 19.116

Luke
1.2: 20.46
1.31–32: 32.228
2.34: 28.188
3.8: 13.400
4.24: 13.375
5.32: 28.183
6.20: 13.275; 28.23
6.21: 20.23
6.25: 20.23

6.38: 32.184
6.40: 32.144
7.9: 20.39
7.12: 28.46
7.19: 28.241
7.28: 20.24
8.8: 28.215
8.13: 20.295
8.18: 32.282
8.31: 28.129
8.55: 28.45
9.16: 13.220
9.25: 19.85
9.27: 20.404, 410
9.29–31: 32.335
9.48: 13.389
10.5–6: 32.159
10.6: 32.284
10.22: 20.46
10.30–34: 20.317
11.15: 19.93; 20.314
11.19: 19.95
12.4: 20.82
12.10: 19.88
12.20: 19.78, 98
12.28: 32.183
12.42: 20.8
13.11: 13.274, 277
13.26: 32.124, 153
13.27: 32.125, 153, 154
14.16–17: 13.221
16.22: 32.265
16.23: 13.276
17.5: 32.174
17.21: 19.77
18.13: 28.26, 28, 32, 35
18.19: 13.234
19.10: 13.119, 136
19.12: 13.397
20.36: 13.99
20.37–38: 20.222
21.1–2: 19.48, 51, 58
21.1–4: 19.41
21.3: 19.48
21.4: 19.50
22.3–4: 28.113
22.15: 20.188; 28.240

22.21: 32.290, 293
22.21–22: 32.251
22.23: 32.251
22.27: 32.49, 100
22.45: 13.201
22.52: 28.113
22.54: 28.113
22.66: 28.114
23.10: 28.113
23.21: 19.116;
    32.236
23.42: 32.242, 396
23.43: 32.395

John
1.1: 19.56, 74, 155;
    20.85, 134, 398;
    28.159; 32.324,
    359
1.1,4: 20.369
1.3: 13.118
1.4–5: 20.370
1.5: 32.316
1.6: 32.202
1.9: 20.288
1.10: 32.356
1.12: 20.288, 291, 308, 309
1.14: 13.237, 268, 305; 20.85; 32.44
1.16: 20.324
1.18: 32.264
1.19–21: 19.160
1.26: 32.378, 380
1.27: 13.172
1.28: 13.455
1.29: 19.39, 120;
    28.155, 237
1.33–34: 13.405
1.38–40: 13.435
1.43: 13.435
2.1: 13.347
2.1–2; 4.46: 13.391
2.1–11: 13.253, 435, 442, 455
2.12: 13.253, 455
2.12–13: 13.253
2.13: 13.455
2.14: 13.253
2.14–16: 13.382
2.15: 13.253, 387

John (*continued*)
2.16: 13.385, 389
2.23: 13.386
3.1–21: 13.254
3.2: 13.386
3.3: 19.138
3.20: 20.348
3.22: 13.254, 455
3.31–32: 19.127
3.31: 19.130
4.1: 13.255
4.3: 13.255
4.4: 13.255, 368
4.4–42: 13.455
4.7: 13.24; 20.384
4.8: 13.195
4.9: 13.53; 20.310
4.10: 13.3, 41, 50
4.10–11: 20.385
4.11: 13.40, 55, 226
4.12: 13.2, 38, 56, 57, 90
4.13: 13.8
4.14: 13.14, 17, 40, 41, 50, 60, 62, 175
4.15: 13.4, 6, 50, 65, 66; 20.385
4.16: 13.25, 67, 68, 69
4.17: 13.52
4.18: 13.447
4.19: 13.447
4.20: 13.77
4.21: 13.83, 89
4.21,23: 13.86
4.22: 13.81, 114, 115
4.23: 13.86, 88, 89, 97
4.24: 13.129, 130
4.26: 13.163
4.28: 13.340
4.28–29: 13.338
4.29: 13.169, 447
4.29,39: 13.339
4.30: 13.169, 184, 191, 344
4.31: 13.338
4.34: 13.216, 227
4.35: 13.295, 296, 307, 319, 320, 326; 28.32
4.36: 13.311, 321, 322, 335
4.37: 13.272, 292, 293
4.38: 13.272, 312
4.39: 13.348
4.39–40: 13.184
4.40: 13.182, 185, 342, 388
4.42: 13.180
4.43: 13.186
4.45: 13.256, 367
4.45–50: 13.369
4.46: 13.258, 367, 402, 442, 455
4.46–47: 13.391
4.46–50: 13.258
4.48: 13.449, 453
4.50: 13.258, 443
4.51: 20.397
4.52: 13.443
4.54: 13.410, 417, 449
5.1: 13.258, 370
5.5–9: 13.258
5.18: 20.130, 313
5.19–20: 13.233
5.21: 28.71
5.22: 20.360, 362
5.22–23: 20.351
5.26: 20.420
5.27: 20.357, 362
5.30: 20.352, 354, 420
5.38: 19.21
5.44: 20.337
5.45: 20.358
5.46: 13.160, 165
6.15: 28.210
6.26: 32.388
6.32–35: 20.313
6.38: 20.313
6.45: 20.53
6.45–46: 20.51
6.51: 20.387, 406
6.52: 20.387
6.55: 19.39
6.68: 19.53, 57; 20.409
7.2: 13.258
7.25–27: 19.7
7.26–27: 19.1
7.27: 19.10
7.28: 19.1, 3, 5, 7, 10, 12
7.28–29: 19.2
7.30: 19.72; 28.196
7.39: 28.127; 32.129, 399
7.40–42: 19.105
7.43: 19.105
7.46: 19.106
7.47–49: 19.157
7.51–52: 19.107
8.12: 19.54, 108, 125; 20.348
8.13: 19.1, 108
8.13–16: 19.9
8.14: 19.10
8.14–18: 19.109
8.18: 13.165; 19.11
8.19: 19.11, 39, 54, 110
8.20: 19.40
8.21: 19.91, 111, 114, 151; 32.389, 393
8.23: 19.148
8.24: 19.158, 159
8.28: 19.68
8.29: 20.155
8.30: 19.65, 70
8.31: 20.103, 128, 131
8.31–32: 19.18, 19, 66; 20.268
8.32: 19.67; 20.274
8.33: 13.399; 20.132
8.34: 32.148
8.37: 19.72; 20.54
8.38: 20.58, 59, 61, 63, 65
8.39: 20.2, 9, 30, 32, 53, 60, 125, 132, 168
8.40: 19.6, 72; 20.88, 94; 28.158, 238; 32.323
8.41: 20.176, 194

# INDEX OF HOLY SCRIPTURE

8.42: 20.64, 137, 155
8.44: 20.97, 98, 103, 168, 172, 175, 211, 256
8.46: 20.279
8.48: 20.314, 343
8.49: 20.315, 316
8.51: 20.379, 382, 401, 408, 413
8.52: 20.383, 400
8.53: 13.399
8.54: 20.421, 422
8.56: 13.398; 20.88, 394, 395
8.58: 19.64
8.59: 19.64
9.1: 19.64
9.32: 20.376
9.39: 28.188, 190
10.1: 20.55
10.11: 19.39
10.16: 28.184
10.18: 19.99, 101
10.26: 13.39; 20.55, 413
10.27: 20.294, 413
10.30: 13.228; 19.6
10.33: 28.88
10.34–35: 28.88
11.4: 19.80, 82
11.11: 28.67, 68, 69, 70
11.14: 28.70
11.25: 13.19; 19.6; 20.363; 28.71; 32.106
11.39: 20.414; 28.14, 15, 16, 22
11.40: 28.13, 15, 17
11.41: 28.22, 39, 41, 47, 48, 74
11.41–42: 28.73, 84
11.42: 28.48, 83, 85
11.43: 28.44, 54, 68, 69
11.44: 28.59, 60
11.45: 28.79
11.45–46: 28.81
11.46: 28.79
11.47: 28.79, 88
11.48: 28.90
11.49: 28.108, 156
11.49–51: 28.152
11.50: 28.156, 169
11.51–52: 28.178
11.52: 28.184
11.54: 28.211
11.55: 28.231, 235
11.56: 28.239
12.2: 28.60; 32.23
12.6: 32.109, 160
12.27: 32.218, 223
12.32: 32.319
12.45: 13.153, 228; 32.216
13.2: 32.24, 84, 109, 148, 152, 155, 160, 241, 286, 381
13.2–3: 32.34
13.3–4: 32.40
13.4: 32.83
13.5: 32.104
13.7: 32.16
13.8: 32.16, 19, 49, 134, 136, 137
13.12: 32.112
13.13: 32.123, 126, 374
13.14: 32.140
13.14–15: 32.10
13.16: 32.201, 374
13.17: 32.4
13.18: 32.169, 175
13.21: 32.240, 258
13.22: 32.246
13.23: 32.314
13.26: 32.166, 306, 312, 381
13.26–27: 32.307
13.27: 32.110, 167, 300
13.31: 32.354
13.32b: 32.365
13.36: 19.86; 32.36
13.38: 32.53
14.6: 13.19; 19.6; 20.173, 240, 245; 28.95, 156; 32.1, 80
14.9: 13.153; 19.35; 20.47; 32.39
14.10: 20.155
14.28: 13.19, 151, 237; 32.363
14.30: 20.281, 330
15.5: 28.215
15.19: 19.136, 150
16.2: 28.235
16.14: 20.263
16.16: 32.384
16.18–20: 32.384
16.19: 32.385, 386
17.1: 20.354
17.21: 28.184
17.24: 19.149
18.1: 19.62; 28.202
18.3: 19.63; 28.204
18.4–5: 28.206
18.6: 28.206, 208
18.7: 28.207
18.12: 28.208
18.12–13: 32.376
18.28: 28.119
18.31: 28.232
18.35: 28.232
18.40: 28.233
19.7: 28.234
19.9: 19.61
19.12: 28.234
19.15: 13.373; 28.234, 235
19.32: 19.102
19.32–33: 19.116
20.17: 13.180; 19.27; 20.340; 32.373
20.18: 13.179
20.22: 28.129
20.27: 13.180
21.18: 32.262
21.19: 32.319
21.20: 32.262, 279
21.20–23: 32.260
21.21: 32.262
21.24: 32.261
21.25: 13.27, 33; 19.59; 20.304

# INDEX OF HOLY SCRIPTURE

Acts
3.22: 13.374
7.2–3: 19.30
7.22: 28.4
7.42: 13.106
7.52: 13.373
9.3–18: 13.431
9.4: 20.136
16.3: 13.111
16.16–17: 28.130
18.18–22: 13.111
22.22: 32.236

Romans
1.1–7: 19.31
1.3: 32.322
1.25: 13.96
2.24: 32.360
2.29: 13.103; 32.111
3.19: 19.16
3.23: 20.335
3.30: 13.108
4.3: 19.18; 20.66
5.12: 20.388
5.12–14: 20.364
5.14: 20.388
5.15: 20.389, 390
5.16: 20.391
5.17: 20.364, 392
6.4: 20.93, 226, 230
6.9–10: 13.48
7.1: 13.43
7.2: 13.44, 45
7.3: 13.46
7.4: 13.47
7.13: 13.420
7.14: 13.84
7.22: 32.111
7.24: 20.225, 374
8.7: 20.176
8.8: 13.359, 360
8.9: 13.359
8.15: 19.28; 20.289, 293, 303, 304, 308, 336; 32.116, 121
8.28: 20.196
9.1: 20.338
9.6–8: 28.94
10.6–8: 19.77
10.15: 32.77, 78, 86, 87, 101
11.11: 13.374; 28.93
11.25: 13.392
12.1: 13.148
13.4: 20.358
13.7: 20.338, 342
14.2: 13.207, 209
14.9: 20.228, 394

1 Corinthians
1.24: 19.156; 20.76, 344, 345
1.30: 28.156
2.2: 19.68
2.3: 19.68
2.6: 13.241; 19.56
2.8: 13.411
2.9: 13.34, 35
2.10: 20.74
2.12–13: 13.35
2.12–15: 20.74
2.13: 13.361
2.15: 13.361; 28.179
2.16: 13.35
2.16, 12: 20.6
3.2: 13.208, 217; 19.68
3.12: 13.137
3.15: 19.85
4.1: 20.7
4.2: 32.210
4.5: 32.185
4.6: 13.31, 32, 34
4.11: 13.12
4.13: 28.161
5.7–8: 28.242
6.12: 13.28
6.16: 20.134
6.16–17: 19.23; 20.134
6.17: 20.134; 32.326
7.40: 13.359
9.1: 13.355
9.2: 32.206
9.20: 13.99; 20.319
9.22: 20.319
10.4: 20.240
10.11: 13.305
10.12: 20.411; 32.258

10.24: 28.194
11.1: 20.279; 28.18, 25
11.7: 32.102
11.27–29: 32.309
11.28: 28.27
11.31: 28.27
12.3: 28.123; 32.128, 399
12.8: 13.354
12.8: 28.189
12.8–9: 19.20
12.9: 13.354; 20.285
12.28: 32.122
12.31: 32.101
13.2: 20.305; 32.177, 183, 194, 196
13.9: 13.58, 91; 20.306
13.10: 20.306
13.12: 13.58, 113
15.22: 20.224; 32.27, 28
15.23: 32.28
15.23–24: 32.29
15.24: 32.29, 31, 39
15.25: 32.31
15.25–26: 20.236; 32.39
15.26: 19.79, 142; 20.363; 32.31
15.27: 32.32
15.28: 20.48
15.41–42: 32.107
15.47: 19.128
15.47–49: 13.141; 20.181
15.49: 19.138; 20.229
15.52: 20.231
15.53: 13.429, 430
15.53–54: 13.418

2 Corinthians
2.7: 28.26
2.15–16: 20.415
3.6: 13.110, 140, 146, 361, 379
3.7–11: 32.336
3.14–15: 28.60

# INDEX OF HOLY SCRIPTURE

3.17: 13.361
3.18: 13.280; 32.64, 336, 340, 357
4.2: 28.95
4.3–4: 32.337
4.4: 13.231
4.6: 32.338
5.5: 13.112
5.5–7: 13.357
5.6: 13.360
5.6–7: 13.360
5.6,8: 32.4
5.7: 13.353, 355, 356
5.8: 13.357, 361
5.21: 28.160, 161; 32.361
6.14–16: 19.139
6.15: 32.302, 382
6.16: 13.143
8.14: 32.284
9.6: 13.295
9.10: 13.308
10.3: 13.109, 361; 28.39
10.5: 13.333
11.3: 13.169
11.13–15: 20.413
12.4: 13.28, 29, 34, 316; 20.304
13.3: 28.54
13.4: 19.61

Galatians
1.1: 32.213
1.4: 19.87
1.13: 20.136
2.9: 32.208
2.14: 32.63
2.19: 20.92
2.20: 13.351; 20.93
3.19: 13.329, 336; 20.47
4.4: 13.85, 319; 20.339
4.9: 19.24
4.24: 20.74
4.27: 28.211
5.15: 20.347
5.17: 20.232; 28.95
5.19: 19.139; 32.219

5.22: 19.139
5.22–23: 32.218
6.7–8: 13.288
6.8: 13.291
6.14: 19.139; 28.166
6.16: 13.343

Ephesians
1.4: 19.149
1.5: 19.28
1.21: 13.151
1.22: 13.48
2.3: 20.217, 290, 291
2.7: 13.351; 19.88
2.14: 19.156; 20.347; 28.156
3.5: 13.305
3.5–6: 13.315
3.9: 13.305
3.10: 19.147
4.9–10: 19.137, 140
4.10: 19.144
4.11: 13.333
4.14: 32.60
4.27: 32.285
5.2: 19.119
5.32: 19.23
6.2: 20.339
6.12: 32.30, 256
6.13–16: 32.19
6.16: 13.402, 441; 32.24, 287

Philippians
1.29: 20.285
2.6: 32.326
2.6–7: 13.319; 20.153
2.7: 20.155; 32.45
2.8: 28.167, 205, 222; 32.324
2.9: 32.354
2.10: 19.141
2.13: 20.196
3.20: 19.134
3.21: 20.225
4.7: 20.346
4.13: 20.341
4.22: 13.395

Colossians
1.15: 19.10, 128, 147, 154; 20.303, 367; 28.159; 32.33, 193, 359
1.19: 20.1
1.20: 32.327
2.12: 20.93
2.15: 20.330; 32.327
2.21: 32.59
3.3: 20.363
3.10: 20.182

1 Thessalonians
4.15–17: 20.231
4.16–17: 20.233
5.4–5: 32.313
5.8: 32.313

2 Thessalonians
2.3: 20.192
2.8,4: 20.83
2.15: 13.316

1 Timothy
1.7: 28.173
2.8: 28.36
2.14: 13.169
3.15: 28.29; 32.2
4.10: 28.155
5.10: 32.131, 132
6.8: 32.106
6.11: 32.2
6.15: 20.7
6.20: 13.343

2 Timothy
1.10: 13.101
2.2: 13.316
2.19: 19.24; 32.154
4.7–8: 13.242

Titus
2.3: 32.132
3.5: 20.340

Hebrews
1.3: 13.153; 32.353
1.7: 32.200
1.14: 32.199
2.2: 13.329

Hebrews *(continued)*
2.9: 28.154, 163; 32.354
2.12: 19.28
2.17: 28.6
3.1: 32.203
4.14: 32.203
4.15: 20.277
5.6: 13.146
5.12: 13.207, 217; 19.68
5.14: 13.144, 210, 241; 20.286
6.4–6: 20.89; 28.55, 126
6.20: 19.120
8.5: 13.146
10.12: 13.48
10.29: 32.165
11.37: 13.372
12.9: 13.129, 130
12.29: 13.124, 138

James
2.10: 20.296
2.17: 19.152
2.23: 20.66
2.26: 20.66

1 Peter
1.20: 13.305
1.21: 19.28
1.25: 13.48
2.2: 13.208
2.5: 13.84
2.10: 28.94
2.22: 20.277; 28.160; 32.361

2 Peter
1.4: 20.176

1 John
1.1: 20.413
1.5: 13.124, 129, 130, 131, 135
2.3: 20.296
2.15: 19.139
2.19: 32.301
2.2: 19.4
2.22–23: 19.3
2.23: 19.4, 5, 21
3.6: 20.108
3.8: 20.78, 102, 104, 105, 107, 114, 115, 176, 255
3.8–10: 20.101
3.9: 20.107, 113, 115
3.10: 20.107
3.14: 20.363
5.1: 19.151, 153; 20.285
5.16: 19.79, 84, 153; 28.50
5.18: 19.153; 20.121, 337

Jude
6: 13.243

Revelation
2.7: 32.4
3.20: 13.199; 32.18
10.4: 13.28, 33
19.16: 13.397
22.11: 32.108, 110, 285
22.12: 13.298

www.ingramcontent.com/pod-product-compliance
Lightning Source LLC
Chambersburg PA
CBHW032022290426
44110CB00012B/635